BUSINESS AND SOCIETY

BUSINESS AND SOCIETY

A Reader in the History, Sociology, and Ethics of Business

Edited by

BARRY CASTRO

New York   Oxford
OXFORD UNIVERSITY PRESS
1996

Oxford University Press

Oxford   New York
Athens   Auckland   Bangkok   Bombay
Calcutta   Cape Town   Dar es Salaam   Delhi
Florence   Hong Kong   Istanbul   Karachi
Kuala Lumpur   Madras   Madrid   Melbourne
Mexico City   Nairobi   Paris   Singapore
Taipei   Tokyo   Toronto

and associated companies in
Berlin   Ibadan

Published by Oxford University Press, Inc.
198 Madison Avenue New York, New York 10016

Oxford is a registered trademark of Oxford University Press

Library of Congress Cataloging-in-Publication Data
Business and society : a reader in the history, sociology, and
ethics of business / Barry Castro, editor.
p. cm.
Includes bibliographical references and index.
ISBN 0-19-509566-9
1. Social responsibility of business.   2. Industries—Social
aspects.   3. Business ethics.   4. Industrial sociology.
5. Industrial relations   I. Castro, Barry.
HD60.B878 1996   658.4'08—dc20
95-6663

1 3 5 7 9 8 6 4 2

Printed in the United States of America
on acid-free paper

Preface

I like to begin my Business and Society classes with the ancient tale of six blind men and an elephant. You may know the story. Each blind man feels a particular part of a passing elephant. Each one comes away with his own particular impression. One touches the trunk and pronounces an elephant like a snake; one the leg and finds an elephant to be like a tree. For the man who feels a tusk, an elephant is as hard and sharp as a spear. For another, who chances on the ear, the elephant is soft and floppy like a leaf. The man who leans on the body reports the elephant to be a kind of house. The man gripping the tail reports that an elephant resembles a whip. The story suggests that if each blind man regards his own perceptions as the whole truth, they are collectively likely to produce little more than a loud argument. If, on the other hand, they hear each other out and try to put their perceptions together, some useful synthesis is possible. They are still unlikely to conjure up an elephant, but they will get closer than they could have alone and they will have engaged each other in some interesting problem-solving in the process.

The study of business and society is like that. The subject matter is larger than our sensory apparatus can handle. Neither we nor anyone we read can see the whole elephant. My premise is that in that circumstance we are well advised to consider the reports of a variety of sophisticated blind men, scholars able to perceive one part of the elephant or another well, able to explain the critical standards that can be used to resolve differences and build synthesis, and able to evoke the relevant experiences of their readers. This anthology is intended to be an invitation to join a conversation with them. None of their perspectives is meant to be definitive. The student has to figure out what he or she thinks and why—has to work toward an understanding of the critical standards that would enable blind men (or women) to engage in a constructive conversation about elephants. To approach the course in this way suggests doing without the comforting assurances of a textbook. It raises anxiety but it also promotes intellectual engagement.

It seems to me that the business and society course ought to provide historical and sociological perspective on the study of business; that it ought to sharpen critical sensibility; that it ought to stimulate moral imagination; that it ought to be a means of enriching the dialogue we can have with ourselves and with others. In teaching the course, I have asked many students to read these selections and to write about them. I have participated in a substantial number of seminars and tutorials based on what they have written. I have solicited formal student assessments of what they have read for years. I am confident that these readings have been an integral part of my ability to realize the goals I have brought to the course. I hope they will do that for you too.

Allendale, Michigan   B. C.
August 1995

Contents

BUSINESS AND SOCIETY

Introduction

We study the historical evolution of business, government, and society in order to understand the present character of each more deeply. We study them together because we know they have evolved in relation to each other. We study the way they have been, and attend to the way they are now, so that we can act on them with greater power, and so that we can speculate more intelligently about their continuing evolution.

We look at the past critically. We attend to the ways in which the historical data to which we have access are distorted. What was recorded? Which records survive? Which of these enter into our perception of the past? How does that perception affect the values we maintain, the decisions we make, the sense of membership we feel in some groups and not in others? History is invoked as a means of more clearly seeing ourselves, our work, and the institutions in which we work.

Business ethics too, like ethics generally, can be centered on a conscious effort to know ourselves—an effort to struggle against settling for views of reality that are merely convenient or comfortable. The ethicist's approach, in contrast to the historian's empiricism, is likely to emphasize reasoning; to draw on the implications of example and counterexample. Ethical reasoning, however, cannot be altogether divorced from information about what has actually happened in the world and what is happening there now.

We cannot respond to the ethicist's injunction to know ourselves, as we cannot know history, without knowing something of the institutions that shape what we know. A sociological perspective helps us to stand back from the organizations, interrelationships, and ideas that inform our daily lives so as to see them from the outside. The ability to do that—to deconstruct our situation sociologically as well as historically—is a prerequisite to the ability to reconstruct it ethically. In that sense, history, sociology, and ethics are all relevant to the critical scrutiny of our subject matter. They are especially relevant if the course in business and society is the major source of critical perspective in the business curriculum.

Taken together, the readings in this volume suggest that the modern world can be seen as part of a momentous and irreversible journey to an unknown destination. They establish that this journey began centuries ago; that it is moving us along more and more quickly; that almost everyone on earth has now embarked, or wants to, or fears that he or she must. Daniel Lerner, Oscar Handlin, Stephen Meyer III, Anthony Giddens, Clifford Geertz, Alfred D. Chandler, Jr., John

3

Maynard Keynes, Stephen F. Cohen, Wendell Berry, and the immigrant poets Morris Rosenfeld and Pedro Pietri—the authors of the first group of readings in this anthology—can be seen as reporters from way stations on that journey. Their perspectives differ. Geertz's view implicitly challenges Lerner's in one way and Handlin's in another. Rosenfeld, Pietri, and Meyer all emphasize the social and cultural costs associated with the process as, without intending to, does the unnamed 1893 *New York Times* correspondent reporting on New York's Lower East Side. When he hears immigrants speak their own language, he notes only that they do not speak in English; when he describes the diseases from which they suffer, he seems concerned only with how contagious they may be; when he sees the terribly crowded and difficult conditions under which they live, he judges them to be filthy, indecent, immoral—really less than fully human—for living there. He concludes that they "cannot be lifted up to a higher plane because they do not want to be." In so doing, he tells us a great deal about the way respectable societies received poor outsiders like these and perhaps something important about the ways in which we still receive them.

My intention here is to help the reader to become aware of how profound and ongoing the process of social dislocation that accompanies economic progress has been, aware of the connections between the historical and contemporary variants of that process, and aware of the role it has had in shaping who we are. The selections note that at some not terribly distant point most of our ancestors were regarded as greenhorns or hillbillies or hayseeds or worse—and that many of them learned to regard themselves that way too; that the skills they brought with them often no longer mattered and, like their language and culture, could not be passed on to their children; that, while their journey was a good deal more dramatic than any we are likely to have to undertake, it is one many of our contemporaries are just beginning.

Chandler returns us to the positive side of the ledger, supporting Lerner's emphasis on the enormous benefits—and not just material benefits—associated with modernization. He, however, adds to Lerner an appreciation of the considerable differences between the entrepreneur and the corporate manager and explores the reasons the latter evolved from the former. Geertz tells us something about why that evolution may not take place—about why commerce may not lead to capital accumulation and technological advance. His thick description of a microcosm is a sharp contrast to Chandler's sweeping macrocosm. He does not assume that economic development is a good thing. The implicit dialogue between these authors is rich but clearly does not cover all the bases. It certainly does not offer right answers. The intention is to invite the reader into the dialogue—to invite her to introduce new questions and new cases in point, to urge him to see how multifaceted, interesting, and relevant this historical and cross-cultural material can be.

The short selections from John Maynard Keynes and Stephen Cohen give us an opportunity to consider the underlying economic forces that made modernization inevitable. It is clear that the forces that initially moved us out of village-based agricultural societies are closely related to the market processes we respond to today; that we still go to where the work is; that capital continues to find its way to where the profits are; that an increase in capital most often requires temporarily reducing consumption now as it did then. John Maynard Keynes's comments on the capital–consumption trade–offs that made possible nineteenth-century European economic growth and Stephen Cohen's analysis of those same trade-offs in the Soviet Five-Year Plans of the 1930s suggest just how dramatic economic forces of this sort can be—and how much influence they can have on the shape of government and society.

Wendell Berry's essay suggests that this process can be seen as a very powerful historical subversion of community. He suggests that, while even the worst enemies of community praise it, of the powerful institutions of modernization, "neither our economy, nor our government, nor our educational system runs on the assumption that community has a value" and he goes on to suggest that this is a deeply flawed assumption for which we have already paid a great deal and are likely to pay still more. My "Socrates in Dallas" can be seen as an extrapolation of Berry's themes to the corporation, to the universities, and to the physical structure of our lives. It should serve to connect the themes of this first set of historically oriented readings to both our immediate surroundings in a university classroom and the sociological and ethical themes that follow.

The second section of the anthology focuses on the relationship between work and power. Robert Frost, Simone Weil, George Orwell, and Robert Jackall all explore that relationship as it is shaped by the marketplace, by industrial technology, and by perhaps compelling bureaucratic forces. These writers all speak to the ways in which our efforts to comfort ourselves, natural efforts in all of their views, may compound our disempowerment. They all suggest that a willingness to accept the discomforts of seeking truth is critical to attaining a degree of freedom from the power relations under which we must live. They all suggest that this is likely to be very hard to sustain. Frost is a poet and a New Englander writing in the tradition of New England individualism. Weil is a French moral philosopher writing in an older Catholic tradition. Weil, like Orwell, puts herself in the belly of the beast. Jackall, like Frost, keeps some distance. Jackall and Orwell are both concerned with ethical issues but Orwell's mode is confessional. His own perspective, for better or worse, is always part of the equation. Jackall writes only about others. The implications of the differences between these authors seem to me as important as what they have in common.

The dangers associated with otherness are central to William Langer's treatment of the "Black Masses" of mid-nineteenth-century Europe, and relevant to all of the readings on marginalization. Herbert Gutman, Cornel West, and John Tierney, in different ways, remind us of how easy it may be for us to fall prey to those dangers ourselves. None of these reminders seems more dramatic than one I found in a little travel column that appeared in the *Sunday New York Times* travel section almost twenty years ago. The author warns travelers against the smaller motorized schooners that ply the Grenadines and, being cheaper, "attract poorer passengers willing to put up with the crowding and occasional sinkings." The stress on their "willingness" makes those occasional sinkings almost a matter of taste—certainly a matter of individual choice. The reader, planning his or her vacation, is warned about a danger and relieved of an unwanted burden of responsibility. The vacation planner's mood is not muddied by inconvenient considerations. It is a familiar mechanism that is worth some attention.

The political perspectives central to the modern world, implicit in all of these pieces, have developed in reaction to each other and it is useful to see them in counterpoint. Conservatives, like the Chief in Lerner's "Grocer and the Chief," see the need for cohesion and continuity with great clarity. They stress loyalty and honor as values, and values as a bottom line. They mistrust change based on either market pressure or government policy. Liberals, like Lerner's Grocer, are driven by a vision of open inquiry, individual liberty, and economic enterprise. Progress is a key word and tradition is taken to be a constraint—something they must struggle against in order to be free. They are especially respectful of the rule of law because of the protection it offers from both overweening traditional authorities and governmental high-handedness. Radicals, like Lerner's Tosun B., see injustice most clearly. They are apt to regard traditional values and institutions as ways of perpetuating these old injustices—to regard market-based economies as a means of creating new injustices. They will often favor strong government intervention in the short run so as to build the basis for a more just and inclusive community in the long run. Each position is likely to be taken as the basis for a principled defense of a beleaguered faith in an uncaring world.

The selection from T. S. Eliot's *Notes toward the Definition of Culture* is a powerful statement of the conservative case. A selection from Karl Marx and Friedrich Engels' *The German Ideology* provides a classic radical counterpoint. Both together present a sharp contrast to Lerner's democratic pluralism—a politics that most students are likely to identify with. Ben Bagdikian's analysis of a marketing crisis at the *New Yorker* and Gloria Steinem's parallel account of her difficulties at *Ms.* may be taken as cases in which democratic pluralism is tested by market-generated pressures. Both cases can be seen as vindications of Eliot's point of view. Both also can be seen as vindications of Marx and Engels' position. Each case has what its authors regard as an exemplary outcome though in neither case is the outcome based on actions that are likely to make much sense to a business student. That may be the most important reason for considering them.

The final essay in this section, my "Learning about Education at the Workplace," is an account of my own industrial work and managerial experience, as it informed my understanding of what was taking place in the university. This section, like the one that precedes it and the one that follows, will end with an attempt to apply the abstract reasoning and perhaps remote referents of some of the selections to a shared immediate environment.

The selections I have grouped together under an ethics heading begin with an effort to establish a generalizable paradigm. I believe Douglas Hofstadter's analysis of conflict and cooperation in the context of Prisoner's Dilemma games gives us a valuable way of doing that. Hofstadter introduces students to the idea of the prisoner's dilemma, gives us some important experimental findings to support the logic of the model, and leads us to the pivotal next questions, which can be drawn from Aristotelean notions of virtue and community. Robert Solomon sees the corporate decision maker as "part of a complex interwoven metaphysical social fabric." He sees the corporation as a pattern of interrelated

social roles. He argues powerfully that neither the individual nor the corporation can be well understood through a single postulated goal like profit
maximization—or through the negotiated balance of power settlements that char-
acterize prisoner's dilemma models. For Solomon, "Corporations, like individuals, are part and parcel of the communities that created them and the responsibilities they bear are not products of argument or implicit contract but intrinsic
to their very existence as social entities."

Solomon's corporate communities are quite different from the communities
Wendell Berry speaks to earlier in this anthology. Solomon does not argue that
shared cultures, customs, and mores are organic to the corporation. For him, they
are functional necessities—required to mediate the critical interrelationships that
make the corporation viable. The differences between Hofstadter's perspectives
and Solomon's can provide the framework for a useful discussion of both the
power and the limits of the individual profit-maximizing assumptions historically
associated with economics.

Roger Rosenblatt's treatment of Philip Morris suggests the power of the marketplace to corrupt both of Solomon's Aristotelean virtues: conscience and community. A short selection from Montesquieu's *Spirit of the Laws* has quite the
opposite thrust. For Montesquieu, "it is almost a general rule that wherever
manners are gentle there is commerce; and wherever there is commerce, manners
are gentle." The selection from Albert Hirschman that follows, considers the
roots of both views over the past several centuries and, in so doing, helps the
reader to see what has been, and what continues to be, ethically ambiguous about
the marketplace. I have chosen these pieces because I want to stress that issues
that have been around for a long time are likely to be more fundamental and more
important than ones that have just emerged; that their long history should not
suggest that they have either been solved or that they have become irrelevant.

Environmental issues are not new either, but they are arguably taking on a new
force. Garret Hardin's "Tragedy of the Commons" provides us with an excep-
tionally powerful metaphor with which to dramatize the importance of the environmental implications of the road we have taken—of the ethical dilemmas to
which these environmental issues may lead us. The underlying historical forces
that set us on that road are explored in quite different terms by Max Oelschlaeger
and Lynn White, Jr. The dialogue between them is in a way a dialogue between
natural history and theology. Oelschlaeger invokes Darwin. White invokes Saint
Francis. The reader should feel invited into the conversation—one close to the
heart of ethics. Alan Ryan's review of Dasgupta's *Inquiry into Well-Being and
Destitution* develops the role of economics in all of this. Ryan and Dasgupta
particularly challenge the "emancipation" of economics from history, sociology, and ethics. In doing this they bring into question Hardin's assumptions
about the commons, Keynes' assumptions about capital/consumption trade-offs,
and Cohen's assumptions on the trade-offs between economic development and
liberty. They suggest that political economy, as it was understood by Smith, Mill,
and Marshall, continues to have a great deal to offer us.

Many of these readings emphasize the power of a self-conscious examination
of our own perceptions to enhance our ability to act on the world in an informed

and effective way. Some of them also note that practical accommodation to the world can require taking many things for granted—that it can require that we not ask the wrong kind of questions—and that we not acknowledge, even to ourselves, that we are doing that. Because the tension between the injunction to know ourselves and the need to protect ourselves is arguably at the heart of business ethics, and because that is a tension we have been advised to do our best to acknowledge for a long time, I have ended this anthology with an essay of my own on that theme. I have argued that a continuing effort to avoid self-deception is at the heart of any ethical analysis; that this effort cannot be altogether successful; and that it is likely to even be dysfunctional in a variety of organizational contexts, perhaps particularly in the context of corporate middle management, but that it ought not therefore be ignored. This concluding selection is an invitation to examine ourselves and our contexts as we examine business ethics—an invitation to both students and faculty to consider their own business curricula and their responsibilities toward them as they would have corporate managers consider their own roles in their own firms.

The anthology as a whole is based on the premise that a good business education, like a good liberal education, needs to stimulate both personal involvement and theoretical abstraction; on the premise that business schools, like the universities in which they are housed, should be helping students to foster a taste for the joys associated with both open-ended dialogue and critical power; on the premise that business education ought to be worldly without using worldliness as an excuse for narrowness or ethical irresponsibility. It seems to me that business education can and should embrace the traditional goals of the university—that it is important that both business students and business faculty affirm that we are not money changers who have found our way into some arts and humanities–based temple. I hope that this anthology will make some small contribution toward that affirmation.

I
HISTORY

1

A Parable to Begin With

The Grocer and the Chief: A Parable

DANIEL LERNER

The village of Balgat lies about eight kilometers out of Ankara, in the southerly direction. It does not show on the standard maps and it does not figure in the standard histories. I first heard of it in the autumn of 1950 and most Turks have not heard of it today. Yet the story of the Middle East today is encapsulated in the recent career of Balgat. Indeed the personal meaning of modernization in under-developed lands can be traced, in miniature, through the lives of two Balgati—The Grocer and The Chief.

My first exposure to Balgat came while leafing through several hundred interviews that had been recorded in Turkey during the spring of 1950. One group caught my eye because of the underlying tone of bitterness in the interviewer's summary of the village, his earnest sense of the hopelessness of place and people. These five interviews in Balgat were moving; even so, something in the perspective seemed awry. For one thing, the interviewer was more highly sensitized to what he saw than what he heard. The import of what had been said to him, and duly recorded in his reports, had somehow escaped his attention. I, having only the words to go by, was struck by the disjunction between the reported face and the recorded voice of Balgat. For another thing, the interviews had been made in the early spring and I was reading them in the late fall of 1950. Between these dates there had been a national election in which, as a stunning surprise to everybody including themselves, practically all qualified Turks had voted and the party in power—Atatürk's own *Halk* Party—been turned out of office.

Nothing like this had ever happened before in Turkey, possibly because neither universal suffrage nor an opposition party had ever been tried before. The dazed experts could only say of this epochal deed that the Anatolian villagers had done it. Since it would be hard to imagine Anatolian villagers of more standard pattern than the Balgati whose collected opinions were spread before me, I had it on top authority that during the summer they had entered History. But it was not immediately obvious by what route.

What clues existed were in a few words spoken by the villagers. These words we collated with the words that had been spoken to the interviewers by hundreds of villagers and townspeople throughout the Middle East. As we tabulated and cross-tabulated, a hunch emerged of what in Balgat spoke for many men, many deeds. Comparing cases by class and country we gradually enlarged our miniature into a panorama. Our hypothesis, heavy now with vivid details and many meanings, took shape. Four years later an oversize manuscript on the modernizing Middle East was in hand. To see how close a fit to Middle East reality was given by our picture of it, I went out for a self-guided tour and final round of interviews in the spring of 1954. My odyssey terminated where my ideas originated: in Balgat, on the eve of a second national election. With Balgat, then, our account begins.

BALGAT PERCEIVED: 1950

The interviewer who recorded Balgat on the verge—his name was Tosun B.—had detected no gleam of the future during his sojourn there. ''The village is a barren one,'' he wrote. ''The Main color is gray, so is the dust on the divan on which I am writing now.'' Tosun was a serious young scholar from Ankara and he loved the poor in his own fashion. He had sought out Balgat to find the deadening past rather than the brave new world. He found it:

> I have seen quite a lot of villages in the barren mountainous East, but never such a colorless, shapeless dump. This was the reason I chose the village. It could have been half an hour to Ankara by car if it had a road, yet it is about two hours to the capital by car without almost any road and is just forgotten, forsaken, right under our noses.

Tosun also sought and found persons to match the place. Of the five villagers he interviewed, his heart went straight out to the village shepherd. What Tosun was looking for in this interview is clear from his obiter dicta:

> It was hard to explain to the village Chief that I wanted to interview the poorest soul in the village. He, after long discussions, consented me to interview the shepherd, but did not permit him to step into the guestroom. He said it would be an insult to me, so we did the interview in someone else's room, I did not quite understand whose. The Chief did not want to leave me alone with the respondent, but I succeeded at the end. This opened the respondent's sealed mouth, for he probably felt that I, the superior even to his chief, would rather be alone with him.

When the shepherd's sealed mouth had been opened, little came out. But Tosun was deeply stirred:

> The respondent was literally in rags and in this cold weather he had no shoe, but the mud and dirt on his feet were as thick as any boot. He was small, but looked rugged and sad, very sad. He was proud of being chosen by me and though limited tried his best to answer the questions. Was so bashful that his blush was often evident under

the thick layer of dirt on his face. He at times threw loud screams of laughter when there was nothing to laugh about. These he expected to be accepted as answers, for when I said ''Well?'' he was shocked, as if he had already answered the question.

His frustration over the shepherd was not the only deprivation Tosun attributed to the Chief, who ''imposed himself on me all the time I was in the village, even tried to dictate to me, which I refused in a polite way. I couldn't have followed his directions as I would have ended up only interviewing his family.'' Tosun did succeed in talking privately with two Balgat farmers, but throughout these interviews he was still haunted by the shepherd and bedeviled by the Chief. Not until he came to interview the village Grocer did Tosun find another Balgati who aroused in him a comparable antipathy. Tosun's equal hostility to these very different men made me curious. It was trying to explain this that got me obsessed, sleeping and waking over the next four years, with the notion that the parable of modern Turkey was the story of The Grocer and The Chief.

Aside from resenting the containment strategy which the Chief was operating against him, Tosun gave few details about the man. He reported only the impression that ''the *Muhtar* is an unpleasant old man. Looks mean and clever. He is the absolute dictator of this little village.'' Nor did Tosun elaborate his disapproval of the *Muhtar*'s opinions beyond the comment that ''years have left him some sort of useless, mystic wisdom.'' As a young man of empirical temper, Tosun might be expected to respond with some diffidence to the wisdom of the ancients. But the main source of Tosun's hostility, it appeared, was that the Chief made him nervous. His notes concluded: ''He found what I do curious, even probably suspected it. I am sure he will report it to the first official who comes to the village.''

Against the Grocer, however, Tosun reversed his neural field. He quickly perceived that he made the Grocer nervous; and for this Tosun disliked *him*. His notes read:

> The respondent is comparatively the most city-like dressed man in the village. He even wore some sort of a necktie. He is the village's only grocer, but he is not really a grocer, but so he is called, originally the food-stuffs in his shop are much less than the things to be worn, like the cheapest of materials and shoes and slippers, etc. His greatest stock is drinks and cigarettes which he sells most. He is a very unimpressive type, although physically he covers quite a space. He gives the impression of a fat shadow. Although he is on the same level with the other villagers, when there are a few of the villagers around, he seems to want to distinguish himself by keeping quiet, and as soon as they depart he starts to talk too much. This happened when we were about to start the interview. He most evidently wished to feel that he is closer to me than he is to them and was curiously careful with his accent all during the interview. In spite of his unique position, for he is the only unfarming person and the only merchant in the village, he does not seem to possess an important part of the village community. In spite of all his efforts, he is considered by the villagers even less than the least farmer. Although he presented to take the interview naturally, he was nervous and also was proud to be interviewed although he tried to hide it.

All of this pushed up a weighty question: Why did the Chief make Tosun nervous and why did Tosun make the Grocer nervous? These three men, repre-

senting such different thoughtways and lifeways, were a test for each other.
Looking for answers, I turned to the responses each had made to the fifty-seven
varieties of opinions called for by the standard questionnaire used in Tosun's
interviews.

The Chief was a man of few words on many subjects. He dismissed most of
the items on Tosun's schedule with a shrug or its audible equivalent. But he was
also a man of many words on a few subjects—those having to do with the primary
modes of human deportment. Only when the issues involved first principles of
conduct did he consider the occasion appropriate for pronouncing judgment. Of
the Chief it might be said, as Henry James said of George Eliot's salon style,
"Elle n'aborde que les grandes thèmes."

The Chief has so little trouble with first principles because he desires to be, and
usually is, a vibrant soundbox through which echo the traditional Turkish virtues.
His themes are obedience, courage, loyalty—the classic values of the Ottoman
Imperium reincarnate in the Atatürk Republic. For the daily round of village life
these are adequate doctrine; and as the Chief has been outside of his village only
to fight in two wars he has never found his austere code wanting. This congruence
of biography with ideology explains the Chief's confidence in his own moral
judgment and his short definition of a man. When asked what he wished for his
two grown sons, for example, the Chief replied promptly: "I hope they will fight
as bravely as we fought and know how to die as my generation did."

From this parochial fund of traditional virtues, the Chief drew equally his
opinions of great men, nations, issues. The larger dramas of international *politique* he judged solely in terms of the courage and loyalty of the actors, invoking,
to acknowledge their magnitude, the traditional rhetoric of aphorism. Generations of Anatolian *Muhtars* resonated as he pronounced his opinion of the British:

> I hear that they have turned friends with us. But always stick to the old wisdom: "A
> good enemy is better than a bad friend." You cannot *rely* on them. Who has heard of
> a son being friends with his father's murderers?

With his life in Balgat, as with the Orphic wisdom that supplies its rationale,
the Chief is contented. At sixty-three his desires have been quieted and his
ambitions achieved. To Tosun's question on contentment he replied with another
question:

> What could be asked more? God has brought me to this mature age without much
> pain, has given me sons and daughters, has put me at the head of my village, and has
> given me strength of brain and body at this age. Thanks be to Him.

The Grocer is a very different style of man. Though born and bred in Balgat,
he lives in a different world, an expansive world, populated more actively with
imaginings and fantasies—hungering for whatever is different and unfamiliar.
Where the Chief is contented, the Grocer is restless. To Tosun's probe, the
Grocer replied staccato: "I have told you I want better things. I would have liked
to have a bigger grocery shop in the city, have a nice house there, dress nice
civilian clothes."

Where the Chief audits his life placidly, makes no comparisons, thanks God, the Grocer evaluates his history in a more complicated and other-involved fashion. He perceives his story as a drama of Self *versus* Village. He compares his virtue with others and finds them lacking: "I am not like the others here. They don't know any better. And when I tell them, they are angry and they say that I am ungrateful for what Allah has given me." The Grocer's struggle with Balgat was, in his script, no mere conflict of personalities. His was the lonely struggle of a single man to open the village mind. Clearly, from the readiness and consistency of his responses to most questions, he had brooded much over his role. He had a keen sense of the limits imposed by reality: "I am born a grocer and probably die that way. I have not the possibility in myself to get the things I want. They only bother me." But desire, once stirred, is not easily stilled.

Late in the interview, after each respondent had named the greatest problem facing the Turkish people, Tosun asked what he would do about this problem if he were the president of Turkey. Most responded by stolid silence—the traditional way of handling "projective questions" which require people to imagine themselves or things to be different from what they "really are." Some were shocked by the impropriety of the very question. "My God! How can you say such a thing?" gasped the shepherd. "How can I . . . I cannot . . . a poor villager . . . master of the whole world."

The Chief, Balgat's virtuoso of the traditional style, made laconic reply to this question with another question: "I am hardly able to manage a village, how shall I manage Turkey?" When Tosun probed further ("What would you suggest for *your village* that you cannot handle yourself?"), the Chief said he would seek "help of money and seed for some of our farmers." When the Grocer's turn came, he did not wait for the question to be circumscribed in terms of local reference. As president of Turkey, he said: "I would make roads for the villagers to come to towns to see the world and would not let them stay in their holes all their life."

To get out of his hole the Grocer even declared himself ready—and in this he was quite alone in Balgat—to live outside of Turkey. This came out when Tosun asked another of his projective questions: "If you could not live in Turkey, where would you want to live?" The standard reply of the villagers was that they would not live, could not imagine living, anywhere else. The forced choice simply was ignored.

When Tosun persisted ("Suppose you *had* to leave Turkey?"), he teased an extreme reaction out of some Balgati. The shepherd, like several other wholly routinized personalities, finally replied that he would rather kill himself. The constricted peasant can more easily imagine destroying the self than relocating it in an unknown, that is, frightful, setting.

The Chief again responded with the clear and confident voice of traditional man. "Nowhere," he said. "I was born here, grew old here, and hope God will permit me to die here." To Tosun's probe, the Chief replied firmly: "I wouldn't move a foot from here." Only the Grocer found no trouble in imagining himself outside of Turkey, living in a strange land. Indeed he seemed fully prepared, as a man does when he has already posed a question to himself many times. "America," said the Grocer, and, without waiting for Tosun to ask him why, stated his reason: "because I have heard that it is a nice country, and with possibilities to be rich even for the simplest persons."

Such opinions clearly marked off the Grocer, in the eyes of the villagers around him, as heterodox and probably infidel. The vivid sense of cash displayed by the Grocer was a grievous offense against Balgat ideas of tabu talk. In the code regulating the flow of symbols among Anatolian villagers, blood and sex are permissible objects of passion but money is not. To talk much of money is an impropriety. To reveal excessive *desire* for money is—Allah defend us!—an impiety.

Balgati might forgive the Grocer his propensity to seek the strange rather than reverse the familiar, even his readiness to forsake Turkey for unknown places, had he decently clothed these impious desires in pious terms. But to abandon Balgat for the world's fleshpots, to forsake the ways of God to seek the ways of cash, this was insanity. The demented person who spoke thus was surely accursed and unclean.

The Grocer, with his "city-dressed" ways, his "eye at the higher places" and his visits to Ankara, provoked the Balgati to wrathful and indignant restatements of the old code. But occasional, and apparently trivial, items in the survey suggested that some Balgati were talking loud about the Grocer to keep their own inner voices from being overheard by the Chief—or even by themselves.

As we were interested in knowing who says what to whom in such a village as Balgat, Tosun had been instructed to ask each person whether others ever came to him for advice, and if so what they wanted advice about. Naturally, the Balgati whose advice was most sought was the Chief, who reported: "Yes, that is my main duty, to give advice. (Tosun: *What about?*) About all that I or you could imagine, even about their wives and how to handle them, and how to cure their sick cow." This conjunction of wives and cows, to illustrate all the Chief could imagine, runs the gamut only from A to B. These are the species that the villager has most to do with in his daily round of life, the recurrent source of his pains and pleasures and puzzlements. The oral literature abounds in examples of *Muhtar* (or this theological counterpart, the *Hoca*) as wise man dispensing judgment equally about women and cows.

Rather more surprising was Tosun's discovery that some Balgati went for advice also to the disreputable Grocer. What did they ask *his* advice about? "What to do when they go to Ankara, where to go and what to buy, how much to sell their things." The cash nexus, this suggested, was somehow coming to Balgat and with it, possibly, a new role for the Grocer as cosmopolitan specialist in how to avoid wooden nickels in the big city. Also, how to spend the real nickels one got. For the Grocer was a man of clear convictions on which coffee-houses played the best radio programs and which were the best movies to see in Ankara. While his opinions on these matters were heterodox as compared, say, to the Chief's, they had an open field to work in. Most Balgati had never heard a radio or seen a movie and were not aware of what constituted orthodoxy with respect to them. Extremists had nonetheless decided that these things, being new, were obviously evil. Some of them considered the radio to be "the voice of The

Devil coming from his deep hiding-place'' and said they would smash any such ''Devil's-box'' on sight.

At the time of Tosun's visit, there was only one radio in Balgat, owned by no less a personage than the Chief. In the absence of any explicit orthodox prohibition on radio, the Chief, former soldier and great admirer of Atatürk, had followed his lead. Prosperous by village standards, being the large landowner of Balgat, he had bought a radio to please and instruct his sons. He had also devised an appropriate ceremonial for its use. Each evening a select group of Balgati foregathered in the Chief's guest room as he turned on the newscast from Ankara. They heard the newscast through in silence and, at its conclusion, the Chief turned the radio off and made his commentary. ''We all listen very carefully,'' he told Tosun, ''and I talk about it afterwards.'' Tosun, suspecting in this procedure a variant of the Chief's containment tactics, wanted to know whether there was any disagreement over his explanations. ''No, no arguments,'' replied the Chief, ''as I tell you I only talk and our opinions are the same more or less.'' Here was a new twist in the ancient role of knowledge as power. Sensing the potential challenge from radio, the Chief restricted the dangers of innovation by partial incorporation, thus retaining and strengthening his role as Balgat's official opinion leader.

Tosun inquired of the Grocer, an occasional attendant at the Chief's salon, how he liked this style of radio session. The grocer, a heretic perhaps but not a foolhardy one, made on this point the shortest statement in his entire interview: ''The Chief is clever and he explains the news.'' Only obliquely, by asking what the Grocer liked best about radio, did Tosun get an answer that had the true resonance. Without challenging the Chief's preference for news of ''wars and the dangers of wars''—in fact an exclusive interest in the Korean War, to which a Turkish brigade had just been committed—the Grocer indicated that after all *he* had opportunities to listen in the coffeehouses of Ankara, where the audiences exhibited a more cosmopolitan range of interests. ''It is nice to know what is happening in the other capitals of the world,'' said the Grocer. ''We are stuck in this hole, we have to know what is going on outside our village.''

The Grocer had his own aesthetic of the movies as well. Whereas the Chief had been to the movies several times, he viewed them mainly as a moral prophylactic: ''There are fights, shooting. The people are brave. My sons are always impressed. Each time they see such a film they wish more and more their time for military service would come so that they would become soldiers too.'' For the Grocer, movies were more than a homily on familiar themes. They were his avenue to the wider world of his dreams. It was in a movie that he had first glimpsed what a *real* grocery store could be like—''with walls made of iron sheets, top to floor and side to side, and on them standing myriads of round boxes, clean and all the same dressed, like soldiers in a great parade.'' This fleeting glimpse of what sounds like the Campbell Soup section of an A & P supermarket had provided the Grocer with an abiding image of how his fantasy world might look. It was here, quite likely, that he had shaped the ambition earlier confided to Tosun, ''to have a bigger grocery shop in the city.'' No pedantries intervened in the Grocer's full sensory relationship to the movies. No eye had he, like the Chief, for their value as filial moral rearmament and call to duty. The Grocer's judgments were formed in unabashedly hedonist categories. "The Turkish ones," he said, "are gloomy, ordinary. I can guess at the start of the film how it will end. . . . The American ones are exciting. You know it makes people ask what will happen next?"

Here, precisely, arose the local variant of a classic question. In Balgat, the Chief carried the sword, but did the Grocer steer the pen? When Balgati sought his advice on how to get around Ankara, would they then go to movies that taught virtue or those that taught excitement? True, few villagers had ever been to Ankara. But things were changing in Turkey and many more Balgati were sure to have a turn or two around the big city before they died. What would happen next in Balgat if more people discovered the tingle of wondering what will happen next? Would things continue along the way of the Chief or would they take the way of the Grocer?

BALGAT REVISITED: 1954

I reached Ankara in April after a circuitous route through the Middle East. The glories of Greece, Egypt, Lebanon, Syria, Persia touched me only lightly, for some part of me was already in Balgat. Even the Blue Mosque and Saint Sophia seemed pallid, and I left Istanbul three days ahead of schedule for Ankara. I had saved this for last, and now here I was. I was half afraid to look.

I called a transportation service and explained that I wanted to go out the following day, a Sunday, to a village some eight kilometers south that might be hard to reach. As I wanted to spend the day, would the driver meet me at 8 A.M. and bring along his lunch?

While waiting for the car, next morning, my reverie wandered back through the several years since my first reading of the Balgat interviews. Was I chasing a phantom? Tahir S. appeared. With solitude vanished anxiety; confidently we began to plan the day. Tahir had been a member of the original interview team, working in the Izmir area. As Tosun had joined the Turkish foreign service and was stationed in North Africa, where he was conducting an inquiry among the Berbers, I had arranged in advance for Tahir to revisit Balgat with me in his place. Over a cup of syrupy coffee, we reviewed the questions that had been asked in 1950, noted the various responses and silences, decided the order in which we would repeat the old questions and interpolate the new ones.

As the plan took shape, Zilla K. arrived. She had no connection with the original survey, but I wanted a female interviewer who could add some Balgat women to our gallery. I had "ordered" her, through a colleague at Ankara University, "by the numbers": thirtyish, semitrained, alert, compliant with instructions, not sexy enough to impede our relations with the men of Balgat but chic enough to provoke the women. A glance and a word showed that Zilla filled the requisition. We brought her into the plan of operations. The hall porter came in to say our car was waiting. We got in and settled back for a rough haul. Twenty minutes later, as we were still debating the niceties of question-wording and reporting procedure, the driver said briskly: "There's Balgat."

We looked puzzled at each other until Tosun's words of 1950 recurred to us: "It could have been half an hour to Ankara if it had a road." Now it did have a road. What was more, a *bus* was coming down the road, heading toward us from the place our driver had called Balgat. As it passed, jammed full, none of the passengers waved or even so much as stuck out a tongue at us. Without these unfailing signs of villagers out on a rare chartered bus, to celebrate a great occasion of some sort, we could only make the wild guess that Balgat had acquired a regular bus service. And indeed, as we entered the village, there it was—a "bus station," freshly painted benches under a handsome new canopy. We got out and looked at the printed schedule of trips. "The bus leaves every hour, on the hour, to Ulus Station. Fare: 20 Kurus." For about four cents, Balgati could now go, whenever they felt the whim, to Ulus in the heart of Ankara. The villagers were getting out of their holes at last. The Grocer, I thought, must be grinning over the fat canary he had swallowed.

We took a quick turn around the village, on our way back to check in with the Chief. Things looked different from what Tosun's report had led us to expect. Overhead wires were stretched along the road, with branch lines extended over the houses of Balgat. The village had been electrified. Alongside the road deep ditches had been dug, in which the graceful curve of new water pipe was visible. Purified water was coming to Balgat. There were many more buildings than the fifty-odd Tosun had counted, and most of them looked new. Two larger ones announced themselves as a school and a police station. An inscription on the latter revealed that Balgat was now under the jurisdiction of the Ankara district police. They had finally got rid of the *gendarmerie*, scavengers of the Anatolian village and historic blight on the peasant's existence. "These fellows are lucky," said Tahir drily. Feeling strange, we made our way along the erratic path through the old village, led and followed by a small horde of children, to the house of the Chief. Tahir knocked, an old woman with her head covered by a dark shawl appeared, the children scattered. We were led into the guest room.

The Chief looked as I had imagined. His cheeks a bit more sunken, perhaps, but the whole *présence* quite familiar. Tall, lean, hard, he walked erect and looked me straight in the eye. His own eyes were Anatolian black and did not waver as he stretched out a handful of long, bony fingers. *"Gün aydin, Bey Efendim,"* he said. "Good day, sir, you are welcome to my house." I noted in turn the kindness which opens a door to strangers and the Chief responded that we honored his house by our presence. This completed the preliminary round of *formules de politesse* and steaming little cups of Turkish coffee were brought in by the Chief's elder son. The son was rather a surprise—short, pudgy, gentle-eyed, and soft spoken. He bowed his head, reddening slightly as he stammered, *"Lütfen"* (Please!) and offered the tray of demitasses to me. I wondered whether he had learned to fight bravely and die properly.

, As the Chief set down his second cup of coffee, signifying that we could now turn to the business of our visit, I explained that I had come from America, where I taught in a university, with the hope of meeting him. There, in my own country,

I had read about Balgat in some writing by a young man from Ankara who, four years ago, had talked at length with the Chief and other persons in his village. This writing had interested me very much and I had often wondered, as the years passed by, how things were going in the village of Balgat and among its people. When I had the opportunity to come to Turkey I immediately decided that I would visit Balgat and see the Chief if I could.

The Chief heard me through gravely, and when he spoke I knew I was in. He bypassed the set of formulas available to him—for rejecting or evading my implied request—and responded directly to the point. I was right to have come to see Balgat for myself. He remembered well the young man from Ankara (his description of Tosun in 1950 was concise and neutrally toned). Much had changed in Balgat since that time. Indeed, Balgat was no longer a village. It had, only last month, been incorporated as a district of Greater Ankara. This was why they now had a new headquarters of metropolitan police, and a bus service, and electricity, and a supply of pure water that would soon be in operation. Where there had been fifty houses there were now over five hundred, and even he, the Muhtar, did not know any more all the people living here.

Yes he had lived in Balgat all his life and never in all that time seen so much happen as had come to pass in these four years:

> It all began with the election that year. The *Demokrat* men came to Balgat and asked us what was needed here and told us they would do it when they were elected. They were brave to go against the government party. We all voted for them, as the *Halk* men knew no more what to do about the prices then, and the new men did what they said. They brought us this road and moved out the *gendarmerie*. Times have been good with us here. We are all *Demokrat* party here in Balgat now.

The Chief spoke in a high, strong, calm voice, and the manner of his utterance was matter-of-fact. His black eyes remained clear as he gazed steadily at the airspace adjoining my left ear, and his features retained their shape. Only his hands were animated, though he invoked only the thumbs and the index fingers for punctuation. When he had completed his statement, he picked his nose thoughtfully for a moment and then laid the finger alongside the bridge. The tip of the long, bony finger reached into his eyesocket.

I explained then that the young lady had come with us to learn how such changes as the Chief mentioned were altering the daily round for village women. Might she talk with some of them while Tahir Bey and I were meeting the men? The Chief promptly suggested that Zilla could speak with the females of his household. (Tosun's resentful remark that, had he followed the Chief's suggestions, "I would have ended up only interviewing his family" came back to me later that evening, when Zilla reported on her interviews with the Chief's wife and daughters-in-law. All three had identified Balgat's biggest problem as the new fashion of young men to approach girls shamelessly on the village outskirts—precisely what the Chief had told me in answer to the same question. Tosun had been wise.) But if the Chief still used his containment tactics with the women, in other directions he had taken a decidedly permissive turn. Tahir and I, he said, could walk about Balgat entirely as we wished and speak with whomsoever it pleased us to honor—even, he added with a smile in response to my jest, some non-*Demokrat* Party men, if we could find any. We chatted a bit longer and then, having agreed to return to the Chief's house, we set out for a stroll around Balgat. Our next goal was to find the Grocer.

After a couple of bends and turns, we came to a coffeehouse. Here was something new and worth a detour. We stopped at the door and bade the proprietor *"Gün aydin!"* He promptly rushed forward with two chairs, suggested that we sit outdoors to benefit of the pleasant sunshine, and asked us how we would like our coffee. (There are five ways of specifying the degree of sweetening one likes in Turkish coffee.) Obviously, this was to be on the house, following the paradoxical Turkish custom of giving gratis to those who can best afford to pay. In a matter of minutes, the male population of Balgat was assembled around our two chairs, squatting, sitting on the ground, looking us over with open and friendly curiosity, peppering Tahir with questions about me.

When our turn came, the hierarchy of respondents was already clear from the axis along which their questions to us had been aligned. Top man was one of the two farmers Tosun had interviewed in 1950. He too was tall, lean, hard. He wore store-clothes with no patches and a sturdy pair of store-shoes. His eyes were Anatolian black and his facial set was much like the Chief's. But his body was more relaxed and his manner more cocky. He sat with his chair tilted back and kept his hands calmly dangling alongside. This seemed to excise punctuation from his discourse and he ambled along, in response to any question, with no apparent terminus in view. Interrupting him, even long enough to steer his flow of words in another direction, was—the obvious deference of the whole group toward him constrained us—not easy. His voice was deep and harsh, with the curious suggestion of strangling in the throat that Anatolian talk sometimes has. The content was elusive and little of his discourse made concrete contact with my notebook.

As I review my notes on that tour of monologue-with-choral-murmurs, he appears to have certified the general impression that many changes had occurred in Balgat. His inventory included, at unwholesome length, all the by-now familiar items: road, bus, electricity, water. In his recital these great events did not acquire a negative charge, but they lost some of their luster. The tough old farmer did not look shining at new styles of architecture, nor did he look scowling, but simply looked. Under his gaze the new roofs in Balgat were simply new roofs. The wonder that these new roofs were *in Balgat* shone in other eyes and cadenced other voices.

These other voices were finally raised. Either the orator had exhausted the prerogative of his position (he had certainly exhausted Tahir S., whose eyes were glazed and vacant) or the issue was grave enough to sanction discourtesy toward a village elder. The outburst came when the quondam farmer undertook to explain why he was no longer a farmer. He had retired, over a year ago, because there was none left in Balgat to do an honest day's work for an honest day's lira. Or rather two lira (about thirty-six cents)—the absurd rate, he said, to which the daily wage of farm laborers had been driven by the competition of the voracious Ankara labor market. Now, all the so-called able-bodied men of Balgat had forsaken the natural work praised by Allah and swarmed off to the Ankara factories where, for eight hours of so-called work, they could get five lira a day. As for himself, he would have none of this. Rather than pay men over two lira a day to do the work of men, he had rented out his land to others and retired. He was rich, his family would eat, and others might do as they wished.

The protests that rose did not aim to deny these facts, but simply to justify them. Surprised, we asked whether it was indeed true that there were no farm laborers left in Balgat any more. "How many of you," we quickly rephrased the question, "work on farms now?" Four hands were raised among the twenty-nine present, and all of these turned out to be smallholders working their own land. (These four were sitting together and, it later turned out, were the only four members of the *Halk* Party among the group, the rest being vigorous *Demokrat* men.

Galvanized by the intelligence now suddenly put before us (even Tahir S. had reawakened promptly upon discovering that there were hardly any farmers left in Balgat), we started to fire a battery of questions on our own. As this created a din of responding voices, Tahir S.—once again the American-trained interviewer— restored order by asking each man around the circle to tell us, in turn, what he was now working at and how long he had been at it. This impromptu occupational census, begun on a leisurely Sunday, was never quite completed. As it became clear that most of the male population of Balgat was now in fact working in the factories and construction gangs of Ankara—*for cash*—our own impatience to move on to our next questions got the better of us.

How did they spend the cash they earned? Well, there were now over a hundred radio receivers in Balgat as compared to the lone receiver Tosun had found four years earlier. There were also seven refrigerators, four tractors, three trucks, and one Dodge sedan. Most houses now had electric lights and that had to be paid for. Also, since there was so little farming in Balgat now, much of the food came from the outside (even milk!) and had to be bought in the grocery stores, of which there were now seven in Balgat. Why milk? Well, most of the animals had been sold off during the last few years. What about the shepherd? Well, he had moved to a village in the east a year or so ago, as there were no longer any flocks for him to tend. How was the Grocer doing? *"Which one?"* The original one, the great fat one that was here four years ago? "O, that one, he's dead!"

Tahir S. later told me that my expression did not change when the news came (always the American-trained interviewer!). I asked a few more questions in a normal way—"What did he die of? . . . How long ago?"—and then let the questioning pass to Tahir. I don't recall what answers came to my questions or to his. I do recall suddenly feeling very weary and, as the talk went on, slightly sick. The feeling got over to Tahir S. and soon we were saying goodbye to the group, feeling relieved that the ritual for leavetaking is less elaborate than for arriving. We promised to return and said our thanks. *"Güle, güle,"* answered those who remained. ("Smile, smile," signifying farewell.)

"What a lousy break," growled Tahir in a tone of reasonable indignation as we started back toward the house of the Chief. He was speaking of the Grocer. I didn't know what to say by way of assent. I felt only a sense of large and diffuse regret, of which indignation was not a distinct component. "Tough," I agreed. As we came up to the Chief's house, I told Tahir we might as well return to Ankara. We had gathered quite a lot of information already and might better spend the afternoon putting it together. We could come back the next day to interview the Chief. The Chief agreed to this plan and invited me to be his guest for lunch next day. We collected Zilla K. and our driver and drove back to the city. Zilla did most of the talking, while Tahir and I listened passively. The driver said only, as I paid him, "I didn't need to bring along my lunch after all."

THE PASSING OF BALGAT

While dressing slowly, the next morning, I planned my strategy for lunch with the Chief. Had he learned anything from the Grocer? Clearly his larger clues to the shape of the future had come from Atatürk, whose use of strong measures for humane new goals had impressed him deeply as a young man. But surely he had also responded to the constant stimuli supplied by the Grocer, whose psychic antennae were endlessly *seeking* the new future here and now. The Chief, rather consciously reshaping his ways in the Atatürk image, had to be reckoned a major figure in the Anatolian transformation. But the restless sensibility of the Grocer also had its large, inadequately defined, place. Whereas the masterful Chief had been able to incorporate change mainly by rearranging the environment, the nervous Grocer had been obliged to operate through the more painful process of rearranging himself. Most villagers were closer to his situation than to the Chief's. The Grocer then was my problem and, as symbol of the characterological shift, my man. It was he who dramatized most poignantly the personal meaning of the big change now under way throughout the Middle East.

I recalled Tosun's unflattering sketch of him as an anxiety-ridden pusher, an "unfarming person" who "even wore some sort of necktie." What had located these details, what had made the Grocer a man I recognized, was Tosun's acid remark: "He most evidently wished to feel that he is closer to me than he is to [other villagers] and was curiously careful with his accent all during the interview." Tosun had seen this as vulgar social climbing, but there was something in this sentence that sounded to me like History. Maybe it was the eighteenth-century field hand of England who had left the manor to find a better life in London or Manchester. Maybe it was the nineteenth-century French farm lad, wearied by his father's burdens of *taille* and *tithe,* who had gone off to San Francisco to hunt gold and, finding none, had then tried his hand as mason, mechanic, printer's devil; though none of these brought him fortune, he wrote home cheerfully (in a letter noted by the perspicacious Karl Marx) about this exciting new city where the chance to try his hand at anything made him feel "less of a mollusk and more of a man." Maybe it was the twentieth-century Polish peasant crossing continent and ocean to Detroit, looking for a "better 'ole" in the new land.

The Grocer of Balgat stood for some part of all these figures as he nervously edged his psyche toward Tosun, the young man from the big city. I'm like you, the Grocer might have been feeling, or I'd like to be like you and wish I could get the chance. It was harsh of Tosun, or perhaps only the antibourgeois impatience of an austere young scholar looking for the suffering poor in a dreary village, to cold-shoulder this fat and middle-aged man yearning to be comfortably rich in an interesting city. But the Grocer had his own sort of toughness. He had, after all, stood up to the other villagers and had insisted, even when they labeled him infidel, that they ought to get out of their holes. Though dead, he had won an important victory. For the others, despite their outraged virtues, *had* started to come around, once they began to get the feel of Ankara cash, for advice on *how* to get out of their holes. Had they also acquired, along with their new sense of cash, some feel for the style of life the Grocer had desired? That was what I wanted to find out in Balgat today.

I walked out of the hotel toward Ulus station, just around the corner. This time I was going to Balgat by bus, to see how the villagers traveled. We crowded into a shiny big bus from Germany that held three times as many passengers as there were seats. The bus was so new that the signs warning the passengers not to smoke or spit or talk to the driver (while the bus is moving) in German, French, and English had not yet been converted into Turkish. There was, in fact, a great deal of smoking and several animated conversations between the driver and various passengers occurred, in the intervals between which the driver chatted with a crony whom he had brought along for just this purpose.

In Balgat I reported directly to the Chief. He appeared, after a few minutes, steaming and mopping his large forehead. He had been pruning some trees and, in this warm weather, such work brought the sweat to his brow. This was about the only work he did any more, he explained, as he had sold or rented most of his land in the last few years, keeping for himself only the ground in which he had planted a small grove of trees that would be his memorial on earth. Islamic peoples regard a growing and "eternal" thing of nature, preferably a tree, as a fitting monument, and a comfortable Muslim of even diffident piety will usually be scrupulous in observing this tradition—a sensible one for a religion of the desert, where vegetation is rare and any that casts a shade is especially prized. The Chief agreed to show me his trees and as we strolled away from the house he resumed his discourse of yesterday.

Things had changed, he repeated, and a sign of the gravity of these changes was that he—of a lineage that had always been *Muhtars* and landowners—was no longer a farmer. Nor was he long to be *Muhtar*. After the coming election, next month, the incorporation of Balgat into Greater Ankara was to be completed and thereafter it would be administered under the general municipal system. "I am the last *Muhtar* of Balgat, and I am happy that I have seen Balgat end its history in this way that we are going." The new ways, then, were not bringing evil with them?

No, people will have to get used to different ways and then some of the excesses, particularly among the young, will disappear. The young people are in some ways a serious disappointment; they think more of clothes and good times than they do of duty and family and country. But it is to be hoped that as the *Demokrat* men complete the work they have begun, the good Turkish ways will again come forward to steady the people. Meanwhile, it is well that people can have to eat and to buy shoes they always needed but could not have.

And as his two sons were no longer to be farmers, what of them? The Chief's voice did not change, nor did his eyes cloud over, as he replied:

They are as the others. They think first to serve themselves and not the nation. They had no wish to go to the battle in Korea, where Turkey fights before the eyes of all the world. They are my sons and I speak no ill of them, but I say only that they are as all the others.

I felt at this moment a warmth toward the Chief which I had not supposed he would permit himself to evoke. His sons had not, after all, learned to fight bravely and die properly. His aspiration—which had led him, four years earlier, to buy a radio so his sons would hear the Korean war news and to see movies that would make them "wish more and more their time for military service would come"—had not been fulfilled. Yet the old Chief bore stoically what must have been a crushing disappointment. These two sons through whom he had hoped to relive his own bright dreams of glory had instead become *shopkeepers*. The elder son owned a grocery store and the younger one owned Balgat's first clothing store. With this news, curiosity overcame sympathy. I rattled off questions on this subject which, clearly, the Chief would rather have changed. As we turned back to the house, he said we would visit the shops after lunch and his sons would answer all my questions.

Lunch consisted of a huge bowl of yogurt, alongside of which was stacked a foot-high pile of village-style bread, freshly baked by the Chief's wife and served by his younger daughter-in-law. Village bread fresh from the oven is one of the superior tastes that greets a visitor. As I went to work with obvious relish, the Chief suggested that I eat only the "corner" of each sheet. Village bread is baked in huge round double sheets, each about the diameter of a manhole cover and the thickness of a dime. A large glob of shortening is spread loosely around the center between the sheets, which are baked together around the circumference. These sheets are then folded over four times, making the soft buttery center into a "corner." The corner is the prerogative of the male head of the household, who may choose to share it with a favored child. To invite a guest to eat *only* the corners is, in the frugal Anatolian village, a sign of special cordiality that cannot be ignored.

As I chewed my way happily through a half-dozen corners, I wondered who was going to be stuck with my stack of cornerless circumferences. Mama and the daughters-in-law? I asked about the children and learned that, as befits the traditional extended family, the Chief now had nine descendants living under his roof. Moreover, while some were taking to new ways, *his* grandchildren had been and were being swaddled in the traditional Anatolian fashion—for three months a solid mudpack on the body under the swaddling cloths, thereafter for three months a mudless swaddle. (Geoffrey Gorer's association of Russian swaddling with *ochi chornya* seemed due for an Anatolian confirmation, since Turkish eyes are every bit as lustrous black as Slavic eyes.) I glanced up at the large clock on the wall, which had stood firmly at 11:09 since I first entered the room at 9:16 the preceding day. It was clearly intended only as an emblem of social standing. In the very household where swaddling continued, possibly the first clock in Balgat (as once the first radio) had won a place. And though the clock was only decorative rather than useful, yet the hourglass was no longer visible. Times had changed. The Chief noticed my glance and suggested that we could now go out to see the shops of his sons.

We went first to the elder son's grocery store, just across the road and alongside the village "fountain," where Balgat women did the family wash as in ages past (though this would pass when the new municipal water supply became available at reasonable rates). The central floor space was set out with merchandise in the immemorial manner—heavy, rough, anonymous hemp sacks each laden with a commodity requiring no identity card, groats in one and barley in another, here lentils and there chicory. But beyond the sacks was a distinct innovation, a counter. What is more, the counter turned a corner and ran parallel to two sides of the square hut. Built into it was a cash drawer and above each surface a hygienic white porcelain fixture for fluorescent lighting. Along the walls was the crowning glory—rows of shelves running from "top to floor and side to side, and on them standing myriads of round boxes, clean and all the same, dressed like soldiers in a great parade." The Grocer's words of aspiration came leaping back as I looked admiringly around the store. His dream-house had been built in Balgat—in less time than even he might have forecast—and by none other than the Chief!

The irony of the route by which Balgat had entered history accompanied us as we walked in quartet, the Chief and I ahead, the sons behind, to the clothing store of the younger son. This was in the newer part of the village, just across the new road from the "bus station." The entrance to the store was freshly painted dark blue, a color imbued by Muslim lore with power to ward off the evil eye. The stock inside consisted mainly of dungarees, levis, coveralls (looking rather like U.S. Army surplus stocks). There was a continuous and growing demand for these goods, the Chief stated solemnly, as more and more Balgati went into the labor market of Ankara, first discarding their *sholvars* (the billowing knickers of traditional garb in which Western cartoons always still portray the "sultan" in a harem scene). In a corner of the store there was also a small stock of "gentleman's haberdashery"—ready-made suits, shirts, even a rack of neckties.

The younger son, who maintained under his smile of proprietary pleasure a steady silence in the presence of the Chief, replied to a direct question from me that he had as yet sold very few items from this department of the store. One suit had gone to a prospective bridegroom, but the Balgat males by and large were still reticent about wearing store-bought clothes. A few, indeed, had purchased in a *sub rosa* sort of way neckties which remained to be exhibited in public. But wearing them would come, now that several owned them, as soon as an older man was bold enough to wear his first. The owners of the neckties had only to get used to them in private, looking at them now and then, showing them to their wives and older sons, and some one of them had to show the way. I remembered

Tosun's rather nasty comment about the Grocer: *"He even wore some sort of a necktie."* As one saw it now, the Grocer *had* shown the way, and it was now only a hop, skip, and jump through history to the point where most men of Balgat would be wearing neckties.

The Grocer's memory stayed with me all that afternoon, after I had expressed intense satisfaction with the shops, wished the sons good fortune, thanked the Chief again, and, with his permission, started out to walk among the alleys and houses of Balgat. On the way, I absently counted sixty-nine radio antennas on the roofs and decided that yesterday's estimate of "over a hundred" was probably reliable. And only four years ago, I counterpointed to myself, there was but a single battery set in this village. The same theme ran through my recollection of the numbers of tractors, refrigerators, and "unfarming persons." Several of these newly unfarming persons, recognizing their interlocutor of yesterday's coffee-house session, greeted me as I strolled along. One stopped me long enough to deliver his opinion of the Turkish-Pakistani pact (strong affirmation) and to solicit mine of the proposed law to give Americans prospecting rights on Turkish oil (qualified affirmative).

Weary of walking, I turned back to the coffeehouse. The ceremony of welcome was warm and the coffee was again on the house. But the conversational group was smaller, this being a workday. Only eleven Balgati appeared to praise the weather and hear my questions. The group got off on politics, with some attention to the general theory of power but more intense interest in hearing each other's predictions of the margin by which the *Demokrat* party would win the elections next month. There was also general agreement, at least among the older men, that it would be better to have a small margin between the major parties. When the parties are competing and need our votes, then they heed our voices— thus ran the underlying proposition of the colloquy. "The villagers have learned the basic lesson of democratic politics," I wrote in my notebook.

The afternoon was about over before I got an appropriate occasion to ask about the Grocer. It came when the talk returned to the villagers' favorite topic of how much better life had become during the past four years of *Demokrat* rule. Again they illustrated the matter by enumerating the new shops in Balgat and the things they had to sell that many people could buy. There was even a new barber shop, opened last month by the son of the late Altemur after going for some time to Ankara as apprentice. "How are these new grocery shops better than the old grocery shop of years ago owned by the fat grocer who is now dead?" I asked. The line of response was obvious in advance, but the question served to lead to another. What sort of man had the Grocer been?

The answers were perfunctory, consisting mainly of pro forma expressions of goodwill toward the departed. I tried to get back of these ritual references by indirection. How had the Grocer dressed? Why had he been so interested in the life of Ankara? The light finally shone in one of the wiser heads and he spoke the words I was seeking:

Ah, he was the cleverest of us all. We did not know it then, but he saw better than all what lay in the path ahead. We have none like this among us now. He was a prophet.

As I look back on it now, my revisit to Balgat ended then. I went back several times, once with gifts for the Chief's grandchildren, another time with my camera (as he had coyly suggested) to take his picture. On these visits I felt less tense, asked fewer questions, than during the earlier visits. The last time I went out with the publisher of a prominent Istanbul newspaper ("The New York Times of Turkey"), a dedicated *Demokrat* man, who was eager to see the transformed village I had described to him. He was enchanted with the Chief, the stores, the bus service, and electricity and other symbols of the history into which his party had ushered Balgat. He decided to write a feature story about it and asked permission to call it "Professor Lerner's Village." I declined, less from modesty than a sense of anachronism. The Balgat his party needed was the suburb inhabited by the sons of the Chief, with their swaddled children and their proud new clock, their male "corners" and their retail stores, their filiopietistic silence and their movies that teach excitement. The ancient village I had known for what now seemed only four short years was passing, had passed. The Grocer was dead. The Chief—"the last *Muhtar* of Balgat"—had reincarnated the Grocer in the flesh of his sons. Tosun was in North Africa studying the Berbers.

2

Opportunity and Dislocation

Peasant Origins

OSCAR HANDLIN

The immigrant movement started in the peasant heart of Europe. Ponderously balanced in a solid equilibrium for centuries, the old structure of an old society began to crumble at the opening of the modern era. One by one, rude shocks weakened the aged foundations until some climactic blow suddenly tumbled the whole into ruins. The mightly collapse left without homes millions of helpless, bewildered people. These were the army of emigrants.

The impact was so much the greater because there had earlier been an enormous stability in peasant society. A granite-like quality in the ancient ways of life had yielded only slowly to the forces of time. From the westernmost reaches of Europe, in Ireland, to Russia in the east, the peasant masses had maintained an imperturbable sameness; for fifteen centuries they were the backbone of a continent, unchanging while all about them radical changes again and again recast the civilization in which they lived.

Stability, the deep, cushiony ability to take blows, and yet to keep things as they were, came from the special place of these people on the land. The peasants were agriculturists; their livelihood sprang from the earth. Americans they met later would have called them "farmers," but that word had a different meaning in Europe. The bonds that held these men to their acres were not simply the personal ones of the husbandman who temporarily mixes his sweat with the soil. The ties were deeper, more intimate. For the peasant was part of a community and the community was held to the land as a whole.

Always, the start was the village. "I was born in such a village in such a parish"—so the peasant invariably began the account of himself. Thereby he indicated the importance of the village in his being; this was the fixed point by which he knew his position in the world and his relationship with all humanity.

The village was a place. It could be seen, it could be marked out in boundaries, pinned down on a map, described in all its physical attributes. Here was a road along which men and beasts would pass, reverence the saint's figure at the crossing. There was a church, larger or smaller, but larger than the other structures about it. The burial ground was not far away, and the smithy, the mill, perhaps an inn. There were so many houses of wood or thatch, and so built, scattered among the fields as in Ireland and Norway, or, as almost everywhere else, huddled together with their backs to the road. The fields were round about, located in terms of river, brook, rocks, or trees, All these could be perceived; the eye could grasp, the senses apprehend the feel, the sound, the smell, of them. These objects, real, authentic, true, could come back in memories, be summoned up to rouse the curiosity and stir the wonder of children born in distant lands.

Yet the village was still more. The aggregate of huts housed a community. Later, much later, and very far away, the Old Countrymen also had this in mind when they thought of the village. They spoke of relationships, of ties, of family, of kinship, of many rights and obligations. And these duties, privileges, connections, links, had each their special flavor, somehow a unique value, a meaning in terms of the life of the whole.

They would say then, if they considered it in looking backward, that the village was so much of their lives because the village *was* a whole. There were no loose, disorderly ends; everything was knotted into a firm relationship with every other thing. And all things had meaning in terms of their relatedness to the whole community.

Their all-embracing quality gave peasant ways a persistent quality, forced each generation to retrace the steps of its predecessors. Family and land in the village were locked in an unyielding knot. And the heart of the bond was the marriage system.

Marriage affected not only the two individuals most directly involved; it affected deeply the lives and the lands of all those related to them. Marriage destroyed the integrity of two old productive units and created a new one. The consummation of the union could be successful only with provisions for the prosperity of both the new and the old families, and that involved allocation of the land among the contracting parties in a proper and fitting manner.

Long-standing custom that had the respect and usually the effect of law regulated these arrangements, and also determined the modes of inheritance. Almost everywhere the land descended within the family through the male line, with the holding passing as a whole to a single son. But provision was also made for the other children. The brothers had portions in money or goods, while substantial amounts were set aside as dowries for the sisters.

The marriage of the oldest son was the critical point in the history of the family. The bride came to live in her father-in-law's home in anticipation of the time when the old man would retire and her husband become the head of the household. In a proper marriage, she brought with her a dowry profitable enough to set up the younger brothers in the style to which they were accustomed and to add to the dowries of the daughters of the family.

No marriage was therefore isolated; the property and the future welfare of the whole family hung in the balance each time an alliance was negotiated. And not only the family's; the whole community was directly concerned. Naturally matters of such importance could not be left to the whim of individuals; they rested instead in the hands of experienced, often of professional, matchmakers who could conduct negotiations with decorum and ceremony, who could guarantee the fitness of the contracting families and the compatibility in rank of the individuals involved.

The whole family structure rested on the premise of stability, on the assumption that there would be no radical change in the amount of available land, in the size of the population, or in the net of relationships that held the village together. Were there daughters without dowries or sons without portions, were no lands made vacant to be bought with dowry and portion, then a part of the community would face the prospect of economic degradation and perhaps, even more important, of serious loss in status.

For the peasant loss of the land was a total calamity. The land was not an isolated thing in his life. It was a part of the family and of the village, pivot of a complex circle of relationships, the primary index of his own, his family's status. What was a man without land? He was like a man without legs who crawls about and cannot get anywhere. Land was the only natural, productive good in this society.

Within the village economy there was little the landless could do. Paid labor was degrading. The demand for any kind of work for others was slight. Those who sought such labor had to enter service—in a measure, they surrendered their freedom, their individuality, the hope of establishing families of their own. They lost thereby the quality and rank of peasants. That was why the peasant feared to encumber his land with mortgages, preferred to pay high interest for personal loans. That was why he hesitated to divide his holding, felt threatened by every new charge against it.

Yet time in its changes had made it difficult for some men to assume the position and maintain the station of peasants. Son after son found that modifications in the pattern of land ownership prevented him from taking the place his father had held.

By the beginning of the nineteenth century the effects were noticeable in almost every part of Europe. As landlords, eager to consolidate holdings, combined the old strips into contiguous plots, the peasant suffered. Whether he emerged with the same or lesser acreage, the creation of larger productive units put him at a competitive disadvantage in the marketplace. He could thrive only if he managed to become a farmer, that is, managed to rent a large plot under a long-term lease, perhaps for life, or for several lifetimes, or without limit of term. (Some indeed were fortunate enough to become proprietors.)

Consolidation widened the differences among peasants. A few grew wealthy as they rose to the status of farmers (*gospodarze*, the Poles called them; *bøndar*, the Norwegians). Many more became poor, were completely edged off the land, and sank helplessly into the growing class of landless peasants, ironic contradiction in terms. Cottiers they were named where English was spoken, *husmaend* in Norweigian, *Häusler* in German, *komorniki* in Polish. The designation described their condition. Their only right was to rent the cottage in which they lived. By sufferance they used the common fields. But their livelihood they earned by day labor for others or by renting small plots under short-term leases or from year to year.

Their livelihood! Such huts they lived in as they themselves in a few days could build. Such clothes they wore as their wives alone could make. Food was what the paid rent left. In Ireland the annual expenditures of a family of cottiers ran not above thirty-two shillings a year. Calculate a shilling how you will, that is still a grim standard of living.

Could anything be worse? Indeed it could—the times disaster struck, broke in upon the even tenor of these plowmen's ways. Within the rigid, improvident system of production, no reserve absorbed the shock of crop failures. No savings tided him over whose roots rotted in the hostile ground. The very idea was a mockery; if he had had those coins, to what market would he turn? Trade took food from the village, never brought it back. When the parched earth yielded only the withered leaves of famine, then, alas, conditions were somewhat equalized. Farmer and cottier looked to their larders, already depleted since the last year's harvest, and, reconciled, delayed the day the last measured morsel would disappear. Many then reached in vain, found starvation in the empty barrels. No power could help them.

So the peasants learned that poverty was a dog whose teeth sank deep. The struggle for existence grew fiercer; yet there was no halt to the steady recession in standard of living. The mark of that deterioration was the uninterrupted advance across Europe of the cultivation of the potato, the cheapest of foods, the slimmest sustenance to keep bodies alive. In place after place, the tillers of the soil came to rely for their own nourishment upon this one crop, while their more valuable products went to markets to pay rents, to maintain the hold upon the soil. The peasant diet became monotonously the same—potatoes, and milk. Meat was a rare luxury, and even tea. The housewife found there was never enough for the mouths to be fed; and those whom the constricted acreage condemned to idleness were not likely to be left a share. Often the old folk were sent out in winter to beg for the bread of God's giving, only to come home like the birds to their nests in the spring.

To hold to the land, those strong in arm would also sometimes venture away, roam the countryside in search of a hirer, move in ever-wider circles away from the home, for which they still labored and to which they seasonally returned. In time these migratory workers became familiar to every part of Europe.

The Irish spalpeen made somehow his way to the sea, crossed to Liverpool, to toil for a spell in the fertile English Midlands. On the same errand, Italian peasants drifted across the border to Austria, France, and Switzerland, then moved still deeper into Germany. Polish peasants became known in the wheat fields of Prussia, in the beet fields of the Ukraine, or as drivers on the barges that moved down the river to Danzig. Thus they bent their backs over alien soil, tended the crops of strangers, to the end that enough would be paid them, while the family got on at home, to hold their own dear land which alone could no longer sustain them and meet as well the other charges against it.

Of these migrants, some sought refuge in the growing cities, perhaps like the others, with the intention of making the stay temporary. For to accept permanent residence there was truly the last resort; only those thought of it who gave up entirely the struggle for the land, who surrendered ancestral ways and the hope of maintaining status. Every instinct spoke against that course; the peasant knew well that he ''who rides away from his lands on a stallion will come back on foot a tatterdemalion.''

You cannot make the land to stretch, the peasants said; and that was true enough in their own experience. But others witnessed with impatience the multitude of buyers, calculated the advance in prices and the prospect of profit, and disagreed. What if the land could be made to stretch under a more efficient organization of production? In the Netherlands and in England experiments tested the utility of new crops. Perhaps there were ways of eliminating the fallow year that had kept one third of the land annually out of production. Perhaps it was possible to bring more meat to the butcher not only by increasing the number of beasts, but also by increasing the weight of each through scientific breeding.

Landlords everywhere were quick to sense the potentialities. In region after region, England, Ireland, France, the Rhineland, Italy, Prussia, Hungary, Poland, Russia, there were excited speculations, eager efforts to apply the new developments.

But everywhere the old wasteful peasant village stood in the way. In these minuscule plots too many men followed stubbornly their traditional communal ways. As long as they remained, there could be no innovations. Sometimes the landlords tried to introduce the changes on their own lands, using outsiders as intermediaries, English farmers in Ireland, for instance, or Germans in Poland. But such compromises left untouched the great common meadows and forests, to say nothing of the arable lands on the grip of the peasants themselves. The ultimate solution, from the viewpoint of efficient exploitation, was consolidation of all the tiny plots into unified holdings and the liquidation of the common fields.

Only the power of government could effect the transition, for the dissolution of vested rights, centuries old, called for the sanctions of law. From England to Russia, in the century or so after 1750, a series of enactments destroyed the old agricultural order. The forms were varied; there were statutes by parliament, decrees from the Crown. The terms varied—enclosure, reform, liberation. But the effect did not vary.

Men drove into the village. They had the appearance of officers and the support of law. They were heavy with documents and quick in reckoning. They asked questions, wished to see papers, tried to learn what had been in time beyond the memory of man. There came with them also surveyors to measure the land. Then the peasants were told: they were now to be landowners, each to have his own farm proportionate to his former share and in one piece. The communal holdings were to disappear; every plot would be individual property, could be fenced around and dealt with by each as he liked.

The change, which weakened all, desolated those whose situation was already marginal. The cottiers, the cropsharers, the tenants on short-term leases of any kind could be edged out at any time. They had left only the slimmest hopes of remaining where they were.

Some early gave up and joined the drift to the towns, where, as in England, they supplied the proletariat that manned the factories of the Industrial Revolution. Others swelled the ranks of the agricultural labor force that wandered seasonally to the great estates in search of hire. Still others remained, working the land on less and less favorable terms, slaving to hold on.

A few emigrated. Those who still had some resources but feared a loss of status learned with hope of the New World where land, so scarce in the Old, was abundantly available. Younger sons learned with hope that the portions which at home would not buy them the space for a garden, in America would make them owners of hundreds of acres. Tempted by the prospect of princely rewards for their efforts, they ventured to tear themselves away from the ancestral village, to undertake the unknown risks of transplantation. The movement of such men was the first phase of what would be a cataclysmic transfer of population.

But this phase was limited, involved few peasants. A far greater number were still determined to hold on; mounting adversities only deepened that determination. In addition, the costs of emigration were high, the difficulties ominous; few had the energy and power of will to surmount such obstacles. And though the landlords were anxious to evict as many as possible, there was no point in doing so without the assurance that the evicted would depart. Otherwise the destitute would simply remain, supported by parish charity, in one way or another continue to be a drain upon the landlords' incomes.

Soon enough disaster resolved the dilemma. There was no slack to the peasant situation. Without reserves of any kind these people were helpless in the face of the first crisis. The year the crops failed there was famine. Then the alternative to flight was death by starvation. In awe the peasant saw his fields barren, yielding nothing to sell, nothing to eat. He looked up and saw the emptiness of his neighbors' lands, of the whole village. In all the country round his startled eyes fell upon the same desolation. Who would now help? The empty weeks went by, marked by the burial of the first victims; at the workhouse door the gentry began to ladle out the thin soup of charity; and a heartsick weariness settled down over the stricken cottages. So much striving had come to no end.

Now the count was mounting. The endless tolling of the sexton's bell, the narrowing family circle, were shaping an edge of resolution. The tumbled huts, no longer home to anyone, were urging it. The empty road was pointing out its form. It was time.

He would leave now, escape; give up this abusive land his fathers had never really mastered. He would take up what remained and never see the sight of home again. He would become a stranger on the way, pack on back, lead wife and children toward some other destiny. For all about was evidence of the consequences of staying. Any alternative was better.

East Side Street Vendors

THE NEW YORK TIMES

"We take everything in sight," said a Russian fish vendor to a reporter for the New York *Times* yesterday, at Essex and Hester Streets. "What difference does it make if we take up the street with our carts? There is nobody in this neighborhood but Russians, and I am sure none of them complain." This vendor was one of the many who obstruct the streets in the old Seventh Ward, making Ludlow, Suffolk, Hester, and Canal Streets almost impassible for pedestrians. The claim of the vendor that Russians and Polanders in the neighborhood did not complain was evidently true. The streets thereabout swarm with people with pushcarts and stands. Early in the morning the people start out to buy food for the day. The street stands are piled high with food, but it is food that would make the average citizen turn his nose high in the air.

A bread stand first attracted the reporter's attention. "The bread," said the woman attendant, "is called Polish bread." It is made up of huge loaves as black as tar. Next to the bread stand was a fish stand, attended by two stalwart Rumanians. Every time the Rumanians handled a fish they made movements which threw fish scales and slime on the loaves of bread on the next stand. This they did not seem to mind; neither did they notice the horrible stench that came from the putrid fish. A little way from the fish stand was another pushcart, on which were pieces of fresh meat and dead fowl. A huge swarm of great blue flies buzzed about and laid their eggs on the meat, which was already alive with the larvae of insects. Another stand had cheese for sale. A slatternly young woman, who had a scarcity of clothing and who was tending the stand, called it *käse*. It did not require a microscope to detect the mites, for they were large and lively. The reporter got to the windward of the stand and received such a shock from the powerful odor thrown out that he almost had a spasm. Phew, how that cheese did smell! Yet, in spite of the fact that the cheese was a reeking mass of rottenness and alive with worms, the long whiskered descendants of Abraham, Isaac, Jacob, and Judah on the East Side would put their fingers in it and then suck them with great and evident relish.

Nearby was a soda fountain, from which a dirty boy, about fifteen years of age, was drawing a turbid liquor which he called "Jewish beer." This was drunk by the vendors with great gusto and smacking of lips. After the vendors had swallowed their beer the attendant would give the tumblers a hurried rinse in a pail of water which looked as if it had been used to mop out a cow stable. Then the glass, dirty and foul, would be ready for the next customer for "Jewish beer."

A writer might go on for a week reciting the abominations of these people and still have much to tell. One of their greatest faults is that they have an utter disregard for law. There is a certain hour when they are required to set out their garbage and ash cans, but they pay no attention to that. The ash cart comes along and takes what is in sight, and perhaps five minutes later some of these people will empty pail after pail of household ashes and garbage into the middle of the street. If they are arrested for this or any other offense, hundreds of their compatriots and coreligionists follow them to the courts and stand ready to swear in their favor. Filthy persons and clothing reeking with vermin are seen on every side. Many of these people are afflicted with diseases of the skin. Children are covered with sores, and hundreds of them are nearly blind with sore eyes. There is hardly a person among the whole crowd of street vendors who has not sores underneath the finger nails and between the fingers. Some time ago the city government decided to help these people to keep clean. Asphalt pavements were laid in the district with the hope that the streets would be kept cleaner, but they are now a sight to behold, being filthier than the old block pavement ever was.

The neighborhood where these people live is absolutely impassable for wheeled vehicles other than their pushcarts. If a truck driver tries to get through where their pushcarts are standing, they apply to him all kinds of vile and indecent epithets. The driver is fortunate if he gets out of the street without being hit with a stone or having a putrid fish or piece of meat thrown in his face. This neighborhood, peopled almost entirely by the people who claim to have been driven from Poland and Russia, is the eyesore of New York and perhaps the filthiest place on the western continent. It is impossible for a Christian to live there because he will be driven out, either by blows or the dirt and stench. Cleanliness is an unknown quantity to these people. They cannot be lifted up to a higher plane because they do not want to be. If the cholera should ever get among these people, they would scatter its germs as a sower does grain.

Sweat Shop

MORRIS ROSENFELD

The machines rush through the shop as if they were wild
   so that often, I forget, caught in the rush, that I am—
My soul is lost in the shrieking tumult,
   my spirit is deadened, I become a machine.
I work and work, I work without pause
   It drains me, It drains me, It drains me endlessly:
For what? and for whom? I don't know, I don't ask—
   It doesn't do for a machine to stop and think.

There is no feeling, no thought, no understanding—
   the bitter bloody work beats them down.
The noblest, the most beautiful and the best; the richest,
   the deepest, the highest that life can attain.
Seconds, minutes, and hours pass as if in a dream.
   like clock work, the nights fly by with the days
I drive the machines as if I wanted to kill them,
   I rush and I dry up, rush and break apart.

. . .

From *The Works of Morris Rosenfeld* (New York City, Evalenko: 1908). Translated from the Yiddish by the editor.

Puerto Rican Obituary

PEDRO PIETRI

They worked
They were always on time
They were never late
They never spoke back
When they were insulted
They worked
They never went on strike
Without permission
They never took days off
That were on the calendar
They worked
Ten days a week
And were only paid for five
They worked
They worked
They worked
And they died
They died broke
They died owing
They died never knowing
What the front entrance
Of the first national bank looks like

Juan
Miguel
Milagros
Olga
Manuel
All died yesterday today
And will die tomorrow
Passing their bill collectors
On to the next of kin
All died
Waiting for the Garden of Eden
To open up again

Excerpt from poem by Pedro Pietri from M. Abramson, *Palante: Young Lords Party,* 1971, McGraw-Hill. Reprinted by permission of McGraw-Hill.

Under a new management
All died
Dreaming about america
Waking them up in the middle of the night
Screaming: Mira! Mira!
Your name is on the winning lottery ticket
For one hundred thousand dollars
All died
Hating the grocery stores
That sold them make-believe steak
And bullet-proof rice and beans
All died waiting dreaming and hating
Dead Puerto Ricans
Who never knew they were Puerto Ricans
Who never took a coffee break
From the ten commandments
TO KILL KILL KILL
The landlords of their cracked skulls
And communicate with their Latin Souls

Juan
Miguel
Milagros
Olga
Manuel
From the nervous breakdown streets
Where the mice live like millionaires
And the people do not live at all
Are dead and were never alive

Juan
Died waiting for his number to hit
Miguel
Died waiting for the welfare check
To come and go and come again
Milagros
Died waiting for her ten children
To grow up and work
So she could quit working
Olga
Died waiting for a five dollar raise
Manuel
Died waiting for his supervisor to drop dead
So that he could get a promotion

Is a long ride
From Spanish Harlem
To long island cemetery
Where they were buried
First the train
And then the bus
And the cold cuts for lunch

And the flowers
That will be stolen
When visiting hours are over
Is very expensive
Is very expensive
But they understand
Their parents understood
Is a long nonprofit ride
From Spanish Harlem
To long island cemetery

Juan
Miguel
Milagros
Olga
Manuel
All died yesterday today
And will die again tomorrow
Dreaming
Dreaming about Queens
Clean cut lily white neighborhood
Puerto Ricanless scene
Thirty thousand dollar home

The first spics on the block
Proud to belong to a community
Of gringos who want them lynched
Proud to be a long distance away
From the sacred phrase: Qué Pasa?

. . .

Juan
Died dreaming about a new car
Miguel
Died dreaming about new antipoverty programs
Milagros
Died dreaming about a trip to Puerto Rico
Olga
Died dreaming about real jewelry
Manuel
Died dreaming about the irish sweepstakes

. . .

They are dead
They are dead
And will not return from the dead
Until they stop neglecting
The art of their dialogue
For broken english lessons
To impress the mister bosses
Who keep them employed
As dishwashers porters messenger boys

Factory workers maids stock clerks
Shipping clerks assistant mailroom
Assistant, assistant, assistant, assistant
To the assistant, assistant dishwasher
And automatic smiling doorman
For the lowest wages of the ages
And rages when you demand a raise
Because it's against the company policy
To promote SPICS SPICS SPICS

Juan
Died hating Miguel because Miguel's
Used car was in better condition
Than his used car
Miguel
Died hating Milagros because Milagros
Had a color television set
And he could not afford one yet
Milagros
Died hating Olga because Olga
Made five dollars more on the same job

Olga
Died hating Manuel because Manuel
Had hit the numbers more times
Than she had hit the numbers
Manuel
Died hating all of them
Juan
Miguel
Milagros
Olga
Because they all spoke broken english
More fluently than he did

And now they are together
In the main lobby of the void
Addicted to silence
Under the grass of oblivion

Off limits to the wind
Confined to worm supremacy
In long island cemetery
This is the groovy hereafter
The protestant collection box
Was talking so loud and proud about

Here lies Juan
Here lies Miguel
Here lies Milagros
Here lies Olga
Here lies Manuel
Who died yesterday today

And will die again tomorrow
Always broke
Always owing
Never knowing
That they are beautiful people
Never knowing
The geography of their complexion

. . .

Assembly-Line Americanization

STEPHEN MEYER III

From the very beginning, the Ford profit-sharing plan (the Five Dollar Day of 1914) attempted to fit the immigrant worker into its preconceived mold of the ideal American. An early memorandum clarified the objectives of the Ford plan to a branch manager. "It is our aim and object," the home office noted, "to make better men and better American citizens and to bring about a larger degree of comforts, habits, and a higher plane of living among our employees. . . ." Henry Ford expressed his concern about non-American workers to an interviewer: "These men of many nations must be taught American ways, the English language, and the right way to live." He then elaborated on the "right" life for the foreign-born worker. Married men "should not sacrifice family rights, pleasure, and comfort by filling their homes with roomers and boarders." Single men should live "comfortably and under conditions that make for good manhood and good citizenship." A company report on progress among immigrant workers noted that the Ford ideal was to create "a comfortable and cozy domesticity."

In its literature for workers, the Ford Motor Company repeatedly advised them where and how to live. A pamphlet pointed toward "right" living conditions:

> Employees should live in clean, well conducted homes, in rooms that are well lighted and ventilated. Avoid congested parts of the city. The company will not approve, as profit sharers, men who herd themselves into overcrowded boarding houses which are menaces to their health. . . .
>
> Do not occupy a room in which one other person sleeps, as the company is anxious to have its employees live comfortably, and under conditions that make for cleanliness, good manhood, and good citizenship.

Ford and his managers deeply believed that tenement life in the immigrant neighborhoods of the city polluted body and soul. They also considered physical and moral cleanliness important attributes for work in modern industrial society. A clean home reduced the chances for illness and absenteeism. A clean mind provided the sound foundation for the construction of good work habits.

The Ford Sociological Department even extended its interest and attention to the children of immigrant workers. It prescribed a strong dose of Victorian morality for them in order to promote and develop good bodies and souls. "Choose a home," a pamphlet advised,

From *The Five Dollar Day: Labor Management and Social Control in the Ford Motor Company, 1908–1921* by Stephen Meyer © State University of New York Press. Reprinted by permission.

> where ample room, good wholesome surroundings, will enable the children to get the greatest benefit possible from play, under conditions that will tend to clean helpful ideas, rather than those likely to be formed in the streets and alleys of the city.

Particularly in adolescence, young men and women "should be guarded well, and not allowed to contract habits and vices injurious to their welfare and health."

S. S. Marquis, who headed the Ford Sociological Department, recalled Ford's own reason for this concern about the morality of children. "By underpaying men," Ford told the Episcopalian minister:

> we are bringing up a generation of children undernourished and underdeveloped morally as well as physically; we are breeding a generation of workingmen weak in body and mind, and for that reason bound to prove inefficient when they come to take their places in industry.

The good worker was both physically fit to perform his tasks in the factory, and morally fit to perform these tasks diligently.

Often, Ford's paternalistic advice on the care of the home and family contained overt manifestations of middle-class arrogance toward the new immigrant workers. In one instance, a Ford pamphlet advised:

> Employees should use plenty of soap and water in the home, and upon their children, bathing frequently. Nothing makes for right living and health so much as cleanliness. Notice that the most advanced people are the cleanest.

Again, the advice cut in two directions. On the one hand, health and cleanliness were important for immigrant workers. On the other hand, the assumption was that lower classes were generally unclean. Indeed, these sentiments typified upper- and middle-class American attitudes toward Southern and Eastern European immigrants.

Boris Emmett examined the Ford Profit-sharing Plan for the U.S. Bureau of Labor Statistics. He discovered a class and ethnic bias in the administration of the Ford program. Although the rules and standards of the plan were "strictly applied," he reported that the "rigidity of application" depended on "the specific character of the group of employees concerned." Overall, the Sociological Department and its investigators tended to favor the life-style and the culture of American workers and office employees. "The company," Emmett wrote, "pays very little attention to the manner of life, etc., of their office employees." It believed that "the employees of the commercial and clerical occupations, who mostly are native Americans with some education, need not be told how to live decently and respectably." Consequently, the Ford welfare program concerned "chiefly the manual and mechanical workers, many of whom are of foreign birth and unable to speak the English language."

Additionally, the instructions to the Ford investigators indicated that even American factory workers received preferential treatment. For example, as part of the sociological investigation, the worker who lived with a woman had to furnish proof of marriage. Yet, "especially in American homes," the company left "the question to the discretion of the investigator." If the worker lived in an exemplary American home environment, he need not embarrass the worker with this question. He simply assumed marriage. "If it is the opinion of the investigator," the instructions noted, "that the surroundings and the atmosphere of the home are such as to be above reflecting suspicion on the marriage relation, it is not necessary to obtain documentary proof."

Furthermore, two Ford "Human Interest" stories illustrated how Southern and Eastern European immigrant workers met their good fortune in the form of the Five Dollar Day. One story involved a Russian immigrant and his family; the other a Turkish workman.

F. W. Andrews, a Ford investigator, wrote his story on Joe, a former peasant, his wife, and their six children. Three years earlier, they left Russia for the United States. "Life was an uphill struggle for Joe since landing in America," Andrews reported. Nevertheless, he had a positive trait—his willingness to work hard. "He was a willing worker and not particular about the kind of employment he secured." In the recent past, he dug sewers and worked as an agricultural laborer. When work ran out, he moved to Detroit with his family. "And here," Andrews noted, "for five long months he tramped with the 'Army of the Unemployed'— always handicapped by his meager knowledge of the English language, and was unable to find anything to do." Consequently, his wife bore the "burden of supporting the family." She "worked at the washtub or with the scrubbing brush when such work could be found."

Fortunately, the tale continued, Joe applied for and received a job at the Ford factory. After the company hired him, Andrews went to Joe's home to determine his eligibility for the Ford Five Dollar Day. The scene could have been from a Dickens novel. He discovered "an old, tumbled down, one and a half story frame house." The family's apartment, Andrews related, "Was one half of the attic consisting of three rooms, which were so low that a person of medium height could not stand erect—a filthy, foul-smelling hole." It had virtually no furniture, only "two dirty beds . . . a ragged filthy rug, a rickety table, and two bottomless chairs (the five children standing up at the table to eat)." The family led a precarious hand-to-mouth existence and ate only when the wife earned enough to purchase food for the evening meal. They owed money to the landlord, the grocer, and the butcher. The oldest daughter went to a charity hospital a few days earlier. The wife and the other five children "were half clad, pale, and hungry looking."

This scene of poverty and misery set the Sociological Department's paternalistic programs into motion. Through special arrangements, the pay office issued Joe's wages each day instead of every two weeks. The company provided him with an immediate loan from its charity fund for "the family's immediate start toward right living." However, the investigator, and not Joe, took the fifty-dollar loan and paid the bills and rented a cottage. He also purchased inexpensive furniture and kitchen utensils, provisions, and cheap clothes for the wife and children. (Andrews reported that he bought "a liberal amount of soap" and gave the family "instructions to use freely.")

After Andrews arranged for this initial assistance for Joe and his family, a remarkable ritual followed. The Ford investigator

had their dirty, old, junk furniture loaded on a dray and under the cover of night
moved them to their new home. This load of rubbish was heaped in a pile in the back
yard, and a torch was applied and it went up in smoke.

There upon the ashes of what had been their earthly possessions, this Russian
peasant and his wife, with tears streaming down their faces, expressed their gratitude
to Henry Ford, the FORD MOTOR COMPANY, and all those who had been instrumental
in bringing about this marvelous change in their lives.

In this ritual of fire, an old life went up in smoke as Joe and his family expressed
their gratitude and loyalty to Henry Ford.

In time, the children were well dressed and clean. They attended public
school. The wife wore "a smile that 'won't come off.'" Joe soon repaid his loan
and expected "to soon have a saving for the inevitable 'rainy day.'"

Another investigator, M. G. Torossian, reported on the case of Mustafa, a
young Turkish worker. He also was a former peasant. In his homeland, Mustafa
"was the sole help of his father in the field." Nevertheless, he had positive
virtues and the potential for right living even in an industrial job. "Young
Mustafa," Torossian related, "unlike his race, who mostly wander in the mountains and make money quickly robbing others, had a natural intuition for an
honest living." He learned about "this land of wealth and happiness" from
friends, left his young wife and child with his parents, and went to Canada.
Again, through friends, he learned about work with the Ford Motor Company. He
came to Detroit and obtained work in the Ford factory before the announcement
of the Five Dollar Day.

As in the case of so many other Southern and Eastern European workers,
Mustafa lived in an immigrant boarding house. Torossian noted that he lived
"with his countrymen in the downtown slums in a squalid house. . . ." However, even in this atmosphere, Mustafa demonstrated his abilities and his potential to change and to live in accordance with American standards. The Ford
investigator pointed out that "he used to wash his hands and feet five times a day,
as part of their religion before praying." But even in his native religion, the
Turkish worker learned and accepted American social and cultural norms. In
America, he only prayed three times a day. "This," said Torossian, "was
modified from five times a day washing on account of time being too valuable."

With the announcement of the Five Dollar Day, Mustafa's "almost unimagin-
able dream came true." At first, he did not receive the "big money," because he
did not speak English and did not comprehend "his trouble." Among other
things, the investigator "advised [him] to move to a better locality." The Turkish
worker even demonstrated his initiative and "voluntarily took out his first natu-
ralization papers." In the end, he too received the Ford Five Dollar Day.

With the prospect of doubling his income, Mustafa readily abandoned his
traditional customs and values for American ones. Torossian concluded:

> Today he has put aside his national red fez and praying, no baggy trousers anymore.
> He dresses like an American gentleman, attends the Ford English school and has
> banked in the past year over $1,000.00 Now he is anxious to send for his young wife
> and child to bring her and to live happily through the grace of Mr. Henry Ford.

Moreover, the Turkish worker also dutifully expressed his gratitude for Ford's paternalism. Torossian related Mustafa's words: "Let my only son be sacrificed for my boss (Mr. Ford) as a sign of my appreciation of what he has done for me. May Allah send my boss Kismet."

Against these uplifting cases a single and revealing incident demonstrated the nature of the company's concern for the ways in which immigrant traditions affected industrial efficiency. In January 1914, a few days after its impressive gesture—the announcement of the Five Dollar Day—the Ford Motor Company dismissed "between eight and nine hundred Greeks and Russians, who remained away from work on a holiday celebration." The holiday happened to be Christmas. Using the Julian calendar, the Greek and Russian Orthodox Christian workers celebrated Christmas thirteen days later than the rest of the Ford work force. As justification for this large-scale dismissal, which amounted to about 6 percent of the Ford work force, a Ford official stated that "if these men are to make their home in America they should observe American holidays." The absence of this many workers disrupted production in the mechanized Highland Park plant. "It causes too much confusion in the plant," the official concluded, ". . . when nearly a thousand men fail to appear for work."

The Ford English School extended the Ford Americanization program into the classroom. Its exclusive concern was the Americanization of the immigrant worker and his adaptation to the Ford factory and to urban and industrial society. In the English School, as adult immigrant workmen struggled to learn and to comprehend the strange sounds of a new language, they also received the rudiments of American culture. In particular, they learned those habits of life which resulted in good habits of work. In 1916, S. S. Marquis defended the objectives of the Ford educational program before an audience of American educators. The Ford English School, he noted, "was established especially for the immigrants in our employ." It was one part of a total program to adapt men to the new factory system. "The Ford School," he reported, "provides five compulsory courses. There is a course in industry and efficiency, a course in thrift and economy, a course in domestic relations, one in community relations, and one in industrial relations." Later, using the Ford factory as a metaphor for the entire educational program, he added:

> This is the human product we seek to turn out, and as we adapt the machinery in the shop to turning out the kind of automobile we have in mind, so we have constructed our educational system with a view to producing the human product in mind.

The Ford managers and engineers devised a system wherein men were the raw materials which were molded, hammered, and shaped into products which had the proper attitudes and habits for work in the factory.

In April 1914, the Ford Motor Company called upon Peter Roberts, a Young Men's Christian Association educator, to develop a program of English-language instruction for imigrant workers in the Highland Park factory. In 1909, as the result of his activities among immigrant coal miners in Pennsylvania, Roberts published a preparatory course of English-language instruction, *English for Coming Americans*. This course provided a complete package of materials to teach the basic elements of the English language. The core of the program centered around a domestic, a commercial, and an industrial series of lessons. Each series applied the English language to a different aspect of the immigrant worker's life. This Roberts package formed the basis of language instruction in the Ford English School.

The domestic series provided specific English lessons for the immigrant worker in his role as the head of an "American" family unit. This series, Roberts explained, identified "the experiences common to all peoples reared in the customs of western civilization." The ten lessons included such topics as "Getting Up in the Morning," "Table Utensils," "The Man Washing," and "Welcoming a Visitor."

The commercial series supplied the immigrant worker with the vocabulary to serve in his role as consumer. In particular, it attempted to break the economic power of immigrant bosses, who sold goods and services, who served as employment, travel, and shipping agents, and who functioned as bankers in the immigrant neighborhoods. Moreover, the lessons emphasized and encouraged the virtues of thrift and property ownership, which created stable and reliable citizens. "These lessons," Roberts noted, "describe the acts which foreigners in a strange land daily perform. When they are mastered the pupils will be able to transact their business outside the narrow circle of places controlled by men conversant with their language." The lessons intended to make the immigrant worker a consumer of American goods and services from American merchants. In this series, the subject matter included "Buying and Using Stamps," "Pay Day," "Going to the Bank," "Buying a Lot," "Building a House."

Finally, the industrial series provided flexible lessons to meet the immigrant worker's needs as a producer in the factory. The aim of this series was "to meet the need of thousands who have common experience in industrial life." Here, the lessons included "Beginning the Day's Work," "Shining Shoes," "A Man Looking for Work," and "Finishing the Day's Work."

The lessons in each series had characteristically prosaic titles. And, indeed, the lessons provided helpful and useful information for the immigrant worker. Nevertheless, each lesson contained specific social and cultural norms for life in urban and industrial America. Ford workers learned the value of time in their personal and working lives. They learned the importance of cleanliness and health. They learned self-discipline through regular habits of saving and work. They learned to invest in and to purchase property and to become responsible citizens. These positive virtues—timeliness, cleanliness, thrift, self-discipline, regularity, and citizenship—represented the Ford, and generally the American middle-class, ideal for remaking former European peasants into reliable and efficient factory workers. The English language was an important means for the adaptation of immigrant workers to the regimen and the discipline of the mechanized factory.

As part of its instructional program, the Ford English School also taught immigrant workers not to offend their social betters in their manner and their behavior. For this reason, table manners and etiquette were important parts of the curriculum. "Last, but not least," S. S. Marquis reported, "must be mentioned our professor of table manners who with great dramatic art teaches the use of napkins, knife and fork and spoon.'' The Ford instructor taught the immigrant worker "the art of eating a meal in a manner that will not interfere with the appetite of the other fellow." In addition, Marquis continued, "We also have a professor of etiquette, such as is required for the ordinary station in life." Moreover, Ford English instructors expected their students to dress properly for the classes. "A by-product of the classes," a report noted, "was a rise in the 'standard of living' by making men conscious of their personal appearance." Instead of going directly from work to school, the instructors required that "class members first go home, wash, and change clothes."

In 1919, Clinton C. DeWitt, the director of the Ford English School, defended the Ford system of industrial Americanization with its practical teachers from the shop floor before an unfriendly audience of American educators. He argued that "a real live American-born man, who is a leader among the fellows of his department" would make "in a short time out of Europe's downtrodden and outcasts, good Americans." He also catalogued the advantages of the industrial teacher:

> Both teacher and student have so many things in common. He works for the same employer, he works the same hours, he has the same pay day, he has the same environment, he has the same legal holidays, he refers to the same head office, the same pay office, the same superintendent's office, the same safety department, the same Americanization school. The main doorway, the different buildings, and all the printed signs are thoroughly common to teacher and student.

From DeWitt's perspective, the factory hierarchy facilitated instruction. The foreman, the natural leader in his shop, instructed his subordinates in the English language, American values and customs, and Ford shop practices.

In 1915, Oliver J. Abell, an industrial journalist, praised Ford's "benevolent paternalism" in industry. He maintained that the "greater must care for the less." Furthermore, he continued, "we provide schools for the child. Instruction and discipline are compulsory, and it is well. But we forget that measured in the great scale of knowledge, there are always children and grownups, pupils and teachers, and age is nothing." Here, Abell captured the essence of Ford paternalism and of the relationship between dominant and subordinate groups in American society. Superiors considered their inferiors—blacks, servants, women, and even workers—as no more than children. Indeed, the Ford immigrant worker was no more than a child to be socialized, in this case, Americanized, to the reigning social and cultural norms of American society.

S. S. Marquis, the liberal clergyman, explained how the company coerced workers into attending their English lessons. "Attendance," he reported:

> is virtually compulsory. If a man declines to go, the advantages of the training are carefully explained to him. If he still hesitates, he is laid off and given uninterrupted meditation and reconsideration. When it comes to promotion, naturally preference is given to the men who have cooperated with us in our work. This, also, has its effect.

In the early twentieth century, Ford officials duplicated the disciplinary patterns which early industrialists utilized in eighteenth-century England. The carrot and the stick rewarded or punished the worker as though he were an errant child.

Gregory Mason, a strong advocate of Americanization programs, questioned "the grotesquely exaggerated patriotism in the Ford plant." In the course of the English lessons, "the pupils are told to 'walk to an American blackboard, take a piece of American chalk, and explain how the American workman walks to his American home and sits down with his American family to their good American dinner.'" "The first thing we teach them to say," Marquis related, "is 'I am a good American,' and then we try to get them to live up to that statement." "It is a very common thing," DeWitt noted, "to have a fellow born in Austria yell to a teacher passing by, 'We are all good Americans!'" In this period, Ford and other employers began to give good citizenship and Americanism their own definition. A Ford pamphlet noted:

> Automatically, upon graduation, the English School alumni become members of the American Club. At weekly meetings they practice speaking, reading, debating, and discuss points of history, civil government, and national problems of current interest.

By the end of the First World War, Americanism countered those social and economic philosophies which threatened managerial prerogatives of production, namely Bolshevism, socialism, and even trade unionism.

The mass ritual of graduation was the most spectacular aspect of Americanization in the Ford factory. Ford English School graduates underwent a symbolic ritual which marked the transformation from immigrant to American. DeWitt described the ceremony as

> a pageant in the form of a melting pot, where all the men descend from a boat scene representing the vessel on which they came over; down the gangway . . . into a pot 15 feet in diameter and $7^1/_2$ feet high, which represents the Ford English School. Six teachers, three on either side, stir the pot with ten foot ladles representing nine months of teaching in the school. Into the pot 52 nationalities with their foreign clothes and baggage go and out of the pot after vigorous stirring by the teachers comes one nationality, viz., American.

Marquis enriched this image and emphasized the conformity of the one nationality: "Presently the pot began to boil over and out came the men dressed in their best American clothes and waving American flags."

3

Business: Culture and Technology

The Themes of The Protestant Ethic

ANTHONEY GIDDENS

In seeking to specify the distinctive characteristics of modern capitalism in *The Protestant Ethic,* Weber first of all separates off capitalistic enterprise from the pursuit of gain as such. The desire for wealth has existed in most times and places, and has in itself nothing to do with capitalistic action, which involves a regular orientation to the achievement of profit through (nominally peaceful) economic exchange. "Capitalism," thus defined, in the shape of mercantile operations, for instance, has existed in various forms of society: in Babylon and Ancient Egypt, China, India, and medieval Europe. But only in the West, and in relatively recent times, has capitalistic activity become associated with the *rational organization of formally free labor.* By "rational organization" of labor here Weber means its routinized, calculated administration within continuously functioning enterprises.

A rationalized capitalistic enterprise implies two things: a disciplined labor force, and the regularized investment of capital. Each contrasts profoundly with traditional types of economic activity. The significance of the former is readily illustrated by the experience of those who have set up modern productive organizations in communities where they have not previously been known. Let us suppose such employers, in order to raise productivity, introduce piece-rates, whereby workers can improve their wages, in the expectation that this will provide the members of their labor force with an incentive to work harder. The result may be that the latter actually work less than before: because they are interested, not in maximizing their daily wage, but only in earning enough to satisfy their traditionally established needs. A parallel phenomenon exists among the wealthy in traditional forms of society, where those who profit from capitalist enterprise do so only in order to acquire money for the uses to which it can be put, in buying material comfort, pleasure, or power. The regular reproduction of

From *The Protestant Ethic and the Spirit of Capitalism* by Max Weber, Translator T. Parsons, contribution by A. Gidden. Reprinted by permission.

capital, involving its continual investment and reinvestment for the end of economic efficiency, is foreign to traditional types of enterprise. It is associated with an outlook of a very specific kind: the continual accumulation of wealth for its own sake, rather than for the material rewards that it can serve to bring. "Man is dominated by the making of money, by acquisition as the ultimate purpose of his life. Economic acquisition is no longer subordinated to man as the means for the satisfaction of his material needs." This, according to Weber, is the essence of the spirit of modern capitalism.

What explains this historically peculiar circumstance of a drive to the accumulation of wealth conjoined to an absence of interest in the worldly pleasures which it can purchase? It would certainly be mistaken, Weber argues, to suppose that it derives from the relaxation of traditional moralities: this novel outlook is a distinctively *moral* one, demanding in fact unusual self-discipline. The entrepreneurs associated with the development of rational capitalism combine the impulse to accumulation with a positively frugal life-style. Weber finds the answer in the "this-worldly asceticism" of Puritanism, as focused through the concept of the "calling." The notion of the calling, according to Weber, did not exist either in antiquity or in Catholic theology; it was introduced by the Reformation. It refers basically to the idea that the highest form of moral obligation of the individual is to fulfill his duty in worldly affairs. This projects religious behavior into the day-to-day world, and stands in contrast to the Catholic ideal of the monastic life, whose object is to transcend the demands of mundane existence. Moreover, the moral responsibility of the Protestant is cumulative: the cycle of sin, repentance, and forgiveness, renewed throughout the life of the Catholic, is absent in Protestantism.

Although the idea of the calling was already present in Luther's doctrines, Weber argues, it became more rigorously developed in the various Puritan sects: Calvinism, Methodism, Pietism, and Baptism. Much of Weber's discussion is in fact concentrated upon the first of these, although he is interested not just in Calvin's doctrines as such but in their later evolution within the Calvinist movement. Of the elements in Calvinism that Weber singles out for special attention, perhaps the most important, for his thesis, is the doctrine of predestination: that only some human beings are chosen to be saved from damnation, the choice being predetermined by God. Calvin himself may have been sure of his own salvation, as the instrument of Divine prophecy; but none of his followers could be. "In its extreme inhumanity," Weber comments, "this doctrine must above all have had one consequence for the life of a generation which surrendered to its magnificent consistency . . . a feeling of unprecedented inner loneliness." From this torment, Weber holds, the capitalist spirit was born. On the pastoral level, two developments occurred: it became obligatory to regard oneself as chosen, lack of certainty being indicative of insufficient faith; and the performance of "good works" in worldly activity became accepted as the medium whereby such surety could be demonstrated. Hence success in a calling eventually came to be regarded as a "sign"—never a means—of being one of the elect. The accumulation of wealth was morally sanctioned insofar as it was combined with a sober, industrious career; wealth was condemned only if employed to support a life of idle luxury or self-indulgence.

Calvinism, according to Weber's argument, supplies the moral energy and drive of the capitalist entrepreneur; Weber speaks of its doctrines as having an "iron consistency" in the bleak discipline which it demands of its adherents. The element of ascetic self-control in worldly affairs is certainly there in the other Puritan sects also: but they lack the dynamism of Calvinism. Their impact, Weber suggests, is mainly upon the formation of a moral outlook enhancing labor discipline within the lower and middle levels of capitalist economic organization. "The virtues favored by Pietism," for example, were those "of the faithful official, clerk, laborer, or domestic worker."

Economic Development in Modjokuto

CLIFFORD GEERTZ

In Modjokuto, the problem of economic development presents itself primarily as an organizational one. What the entrepreneurial group of Islamic small business-men most lacks is not capital, for in terms of the realistic opportunities for innovation which they actually have, their resources are not inadequate; not drive, for they display the typically "Protestant" virtues of industry, frugality, independence, and determination in almost excessive abundance; certainly not a sufficient market, for the possibilities for significant expansion of both trade and industry stand apparent in Modjokuto on all sides. What they lack is the power to mobilize their capital and channel their drive in such a way as to exploit the existing market possibilities. They lack the capacity to form efficient economic institutions; they are entrepreneurs without enterprises.

As noted, Modjokuto from its beginning has had a bazaar economy, that is, one in which the total flow of commerce is fragmented into a very great number of unrelated person-to-person transactions. In contrast to the firm-centered economy of the West, where trade and industry occur through a set of impersonally defined social institutions which organize a variety of specialized occupations with re-spect to some particular productive or distributive end, this sort of economy is based on the independent activities of a set of highly competitive commodity traders who relate to one another mainly by means of an incredible volume of ad hoc acts of exchange. Although such an economy has the advantage that it can employ vast numbers of people on a marginal or near-marginal level of living, it has the disadvantage that it turns even the established businessman away from an interest in reducing costs and developing markets and toward petty speculation and short-run opportunism. In the absence of developed organizational forms in terms of which to make sustained collective economic activity possible, the bazaar-trader is unable actively to search out and create new sources of profit; he can only grasp occasions for gain as they fitfully and, from his point of view, spontaneously arise.

Progress toward more effective patterns of economic activity in Modjokuto consequently takes the form of a movement, hesitant and circumscribed, away from a bazaar-type economy toward a firm-type economy. It is the creation, or attempted creation, of firm or firm-like distributive or productive institutions, of small stores, service shops, and factories, which represents the process of devel-

From *Peddlers and Princes* by Clifford Geertz. Reprinted by permission of University of Chicago Press and Clifford Geertz.

opment in the present state of Modjokuto's economy. Out of the diffuse, individualistic, confused tumult of the marketplace, a few of the more ambitious members of the town's established trading class are attempting, as did their fathers before them, to organize their activities in a more systematic manner and conduct them on a larger scale. Without the stimulus of an expanding, locally based export trade, even of an enclave sort, and hampered by the tremendous overcrowding of the market network by marginal operators, these men face an even more difficult task than did their fathers. But they have the advantages of political freedom and, particularly if significant expansion of trade and industry takes place in the country as a whole, they may yet enjoy a happier fate than befell the victims of the Great Depression. In any case, in the means they use and the obstacles they face in their endeavor to move out of the world of the marketplace and into the world of the buisness establishment, they display most clearly the characteristic texture of the problem of economic growth as it appears in Modjokuto today.

THE BAZAAR TYPE ECONOMY:
THE TRADITIONAL PASAR[1]

The *pasar* (probably from the Persian "bāzār" by the way of Arabic), or traditional market, is at once an economic institution and a way of life, a general mode of commercial activity reaching into all aspects of Modjokuto society, and a sociocultural world nearly complete in itself. As agriculture for the peasant, so petty commerce provides for the trader the permanent backdrop against which almost all his activities occur. It is his environment—as much, from his perspective, a natural phenomenon as a cultural one—and the whole of his life is shaped by it. Thus by the *pasar* we mean not simply that particular square eighth of a mile or so of sheds and platforms, set apart in the center of the town, where (as someone has said of the classical emporium) men are permitted each day to deceive one another, but the whole pattern of small-scale peddling and processing activity characteristic of the Modjokuto area generally. The marketplace is the climax of this pattern, its focus and center, but it is not the whole of it; for the *pasar* style of trading permeates the whole region, thinning out somewhat only in the most rural of the villages.

To understand the *pasar* in this broad sense, one needs to look at it from three points of view: first, as a patterned flow of economic goods and services; second, as a set of economic mechanisms to sustain and regulate that flow of goods and services, and third as a social and cultural system in which those mechanisms are imbedded.

The Flow of Goods and Services

From the point of view of the flow of goods and services, the most salient characteristic of the *pasar* is the sort of material with which it mainly deals: unbulky, easily portable, easily storable foodstuffs, textiles, small hardware, and the like, whose inventories can be increased or decreased gradually and by degrees; goods which permit marginal alterations in the scale of trading operations rather than demanding discontinuous "jumps." In cases where a discontinuous jump is involved between small- and large-scale operations (furniture is an example), the *pasar* traders always remain small. It is only in those goods whose investment curve is continuous along its entire length (for example, textiles) where you sometimes find rather large-scale market-type traders. For the others—dry-season crops, household furnishings, prepared foods—market traders tend to control the trade up to the point where marginal increases in inventory can no longer be profitably made. On the other side of the "jump" from peddling to merchandising, the Chinese storekeepers, truckers, and warehouse owners have—with a few striking exceptions—complete control.

In any case, whatever the wares, turnover is very high, and volume in any one sale very small. Goods flow through the market channels at a dizzying rate, not as broad torrents but as hundreds of little trickles, funneled through an enormous number of transactions. And this flow of goods is anything but direct: the proportion of retail sales (in the sense of sale to a consumer) to wholesale sales (in the sense of sale to another seller) within the *pasar* is rather small. Commodities, at least nonperishable ones, once injected into the market network tend to move in circles, passing from trader to trader for a fairly extended period before they come within the reach of a genuine consumer. One piece of cloth often has ten or a dozen owners between the time it leaves the Chinese-owned factory in a nearby city and the time it is finally sold to someone in a Modjokuto village who seems likely to use it. A basket of maize may be sold by a peasant to a local village trader, who carries it to market and sells it to a second trader, who in turn sells it to a larger market-trader, who gathers it together with similar baskets from other petty traders and sells it to a local Chinese, who ships it to Surabaja to another Chinese, after which it may begin the whole process in reverse in some other area.[2] Like Javanese agriculture, Javanese trading is highly labor intensive; and perhaps the best, if slightly caricatured image for it is that of a long line of men passing bricks from hand to hand over some greatly extended distance to build, slowly and brick by brick, a large wall.

The other aspect of the flow of goods and services which needs to be emphasized is that most of the processing and manufacturing activities which take place in Modjokuto are also included within it. Simple processing (mostly drying) of crops is perhaps the most elementary example. But bamboo weaving, garment making, food preparing (there are hundreds of small restaurants and coffee shops), house building, and various sorts of repair work—bicycle, shoe, watch, blacksmith—are also integrated into the general system. So are the more purely service trades, such as haircutting, and horse-cart or pedi-cab transport. The *pasar* must not be seen simply as a distributive apparatus which adds no real value to the goods which flow through it. It is a manufacturing, productive apparatus as well, and the two elements, the movement of goods and their processing—insofar as this is accomplished in Modjokuto—are wholly intertwined. Production, distribution, and sales are fused into one comprehensive economic institution.[3]

Regulatory Mechanisms

As for the set of economic mechanisms which sustain and regulate this flow of goods and services, three are of central importance: (1) a sliding price system, (2) a complex balance of carefully managed credit relationships, (3) an extensive fractionation of risks and, as a corollary, of profit margins.

The sliding price system, accompanied by the colorful and often aggressive bargaining which seems to mark such systems everywhere, is in part simply a means of communicating economic information in an indeterminate pricing situation. The continual haggling over terms is to a degree a mere reflex of the fact that the absence of complex bookkeeping and long-run cost or budgetary accounting makes it difficult for either the buyer or the seller to calculate very exactly what, in any particular case, a "reasonable" price is. Pricing is much more a matter of estimates in a situation where highly specific comparative and historical data are simply not available; instead of exactly calculated prices, one finds the setting of broad limits within which buyer and seller explore together the finer details of the matter through a system of offer and counteroffer. The ability to operate effectively in the gap of ignorance between a price obviously too high and one obviously too low is what makes a good market-trader: skill in bargaining— which includes as its elements a quick wit, a tireless persistence, and an instinctive shrewdness in evaluating men and material on the basis of very little evidence—is his primary professional qualification.

Even more important, however, the sliding price system tends to create a situation in which the primary competitive stress is not between seller and seller, as it is for the most part in a firm economy, but between buyer and seller.[4] The fixed-price system, along with brand names, advertising, and the other economic customs which accompany it, relieves the buyer-seller relation of competitive pressure and places it on the relations between sellers. Lacking fixed prices, *pasar* competition takes a rather different form from that to which, except to a degree in the automobile and real-estate markets, we are accustomed: the buyer pits his knowledge of the contemporary state of the market, as well as his stubbornness and persistence, against a similar knowledge on the part of a seller, as well as the latter's nerve and *his* stubbornness. The characteristics of a "good" buyer and a "good" seller are thus identical. In fact, there is little if any differentiation between the buying role and the selling role as long as one remains within the *pasar;* the trader is either or both indifferently. The relatively high percentage of wholesale transactions (i.e., transactions in which goods are bought with the express intention to resell them) means that in most cases both buyer and seller are professional traders and the contest is one between experts. When the sale is "retail" and the buyer is not a professional trader, then the seller clearly has a marked advantage, and Javanese commercial folklore is replete with stories of sharp traders deceiving gullible peasants.

In fact, the general reputation of the bazaar-type trader for "unscrupulousness," "lack of ethics," and the like, arises mainly from this role asymmetry in the retail market in a bazaar economy, rather than from an uninhibited, normatively unregulated expression of the "acquisitive impulse" as Max Weber and others seem to think.[5] Within the *pasar* context "let the buyer beware" is a challenge rather than a ruthless or amoral attitude, a reasonable and legitimate expectation for a seller to have, and is accepted as such by a buyer; in any case, it is balanced by an equally strong "let the seller beware." If everyone in the society were a trader, there would be little problem. It is when the villager, manual laborer, or civil servant comes up against this sort of pure and unmixed trader, and the warning "let the seller beware" is unheeded due to the buyer's lack of commercial skills, that the complaints begin to arise, as witness the nearly worldwide fear, hatred, and suspicion which peasants have for traders.

This tendency for competition to be stressed between buyer and seller rather than between sellers has yet other effects on the general style of commercial life. In a fully developed firm economy, price, less subject to bargaining pressure from the individual buyer, is, so far as any single transaction is concerned, generally not problematical. What is problematical is somehow getting someone to buy at a particular price. Consequently, a merchant tends to regard his primary task as one of creating or stimulating buyers, through advertising, aggressive salesmanship, choosing a strategic location, building a reputation, providing better service, or offering "greater" value in the sense of a lower overall price level. In the *pasar,* conditions are reversed. Traders often say quite explicitly that finding prospective customers is not a problem in their minds: they either come or they do not, the market is either crowded or it is not; and whatever the causes may be for the flurries and dead spots which so mark *pasar* trading, they are not within the control of the trader. True, people will choose a normally busy market over a normally dull one. One naturally goes where the buyers and sellers are likely to be and where deals are being made. But the idea is not so much to create or stimulate a market for whatever you have to sell; rather it is to be present when a chance to sell appears, and most especially, to be capable of making the most of it. If you ask Modjokuto traders whether they feel envious if a customer goes to the booth next to them (all the people selling a given ware are lined up next to one another in one section of the marketplace), they say no, that it is wholly a matter of chance, and if the customer does not buy from a neighbor he will in all probability come to them next, or another customer will come along in a few minutes. But they do feel depressed when a customer who has come to them does not buy (especially after a protracted bargaining session with him), for that is their failure; they have had their chance and have failed to capitalize on it.

The bargaining, sliding price pattern thus tends to focus all the trader's attention on the individual two-person transaction: the aim is always to get as much as possible out of the deal immediately at hand. The *pasar* trader is perpetually looking for a chance to make a smaller or larger killing, not attempting to build up a stable clientele or a steadily growing business. He sees his activities as a set of essentially unrelated exchanges with a very wide variety of trading partners and customers, which taken together form no overall pattern and build toward no cumulative end. Similarly, traders tend to think of the average business career not as a Horatio Alger rags-to-riches pattern of linear progress, but as a series of cycles in which one oscillates, more or less rapidly, between being ahead of the game, and being behind it, between being well-off and being bankrupt. The sliding price provides the flexibility needed in a system where economic conditions are unstable, market information poor, and trading hyperindividuated; but it does so at the cost of stimulating an essentially speculative, carpe diem attitude toward commerce.

NOTES

1. For a general empirical description of the Modjokuto market, see A. Dewey, *Peasant Marketing in Java* (New York: Free Press, 1962).

2. See ibid. for detailed descriptions of such processes.

3. Of course, the processing value added locally to the goods which flow through the market is a very small percentage of such value as a whole. Most of the manufactured goods sold in the market are produced outside the Modjokuto area, often outside Indonesia. The argument here is simply that, with the partial exception of the more differentiated manufacturing enterprises we shall discuss below, what processing and manufacturing activities do take place in the local area are structurally part and parcel of the *pasar* pattern.

4. See T. Parsons and N. Smelzer, *Economy and Society* (Glencoe, Ill.: Free Press, 1956).

5. "The *auri sacri fames* of a Neapolitan cabdriver . . . and certainly of Asiatic representatives of similar trades as well as of the craftsmen of southern Europe or Asiatic countries, is, as anyone can find out for himself, very much more intense, and especially more unscrupulous than that of, say an Englishman in similar circumstances. The universal reign of absolute unscrupulousness in the pursuit of selfish interests by the making of money has been a specific characteristic of precisely those countries whose bourgeois-capitalistic development, measured according to Occidental standards, has remained backward." M. Weber, *The Protestant Ethic and the Spirit of Capitalism,* trans. T. Parsons (New York and London: Scribner, 1930), pp. 56–57. Similarly, Weber's view was that market relationships in traditional China stood, in Parsons's paraphrase "outside [the category of moral valuation] in a realm of ethical indifference, with a general unwillingness to assume ethical obligations," T. Parsons, *The Structure of Social Action* (Glencoe, Ill.: Free Press, 1949), p. 551. This view, curious for a scholar who elsewhere consistently insisted on the central role of norms in structuring social behavior, seems to derive from an assumption that because the ethical code of the trading classes is not that of the wider society in which they are imbedded, they lack a code altogether.

The Role of Business in the United States: A Historical Survey

ALFRED D. CHANDLER, Jr.

For a paper on the historical role of business in America to provide a solid foundation for discussions of the present and future, it must examine a number of questions: Who were the American businessmen? How did they come to go into business? How were they trained? How broad was their outlook? And, of even more importance, what did they do? How did they carry out the basic economic functions of production, distribution, transportation, and finance? How was the work of these businessmen coordinated so that the American economic system operated as an integrated whole? Finally, how did these men and the system within which they worked adapt to fundamental changes in population, to the opening of new lands, resources, and markets, and to technological developments that transformed markets, sources of supply, and means of production and distribution? The answers to these questions, as limited as they may be, should help to make more understandable the present activities and future capabilities of American business.

THE COLONIAL MERCHANT

The merchant dominated the simple rural economy of the colonial period. By the eighteenth century he considered himself and was considered by others to be a businessman. His economic functions differentiated him from the farmers who produced crops and the artisans who made goods. Although the farmers and artisans occasionally carried on business transactions, they spent most of their time working on the land or in the shop. The merchant, on the other hand, spent nearly all his time in handling transactions involved in carrying goods through the process of production and distribution, including their transportation and finance.

The colonial merchant was an all-purpose, nonspecialized man of business. He was a wholesaler and a retailer, an importer and an exporter. In association with other merchants he built and owned the ships that carried goods to and from his town. He financed and insured the transportation and distribution of these goods. At the same time, he provided the funds needed by the planter and the

"The Role of Business in the United States: A Historical Survey," *Daedalus, Journal of the American Academy of Arts and Sciences,* from the issue entitled "Perspectives on Business," Winter 1969, vol. 98, no. 1. Reprinted by permission.

artisan to finance the production of crops and goods. The merchant, operating on local, interregional, and international levels, adapted the economy to the relatively small population and technological changes of the day and to shifts in supply and demand resulting from international tensions.

These men of business tended to recruit their successors from their own family and kinship group. Family loyalties were important, indeed essential, in carrying on business in distant areas during a period when communication between ports was so slow and uncertain. Able young clerks or sea captains might be brought into the family firm, but sons and sons-in-law were preferred. Trading internationally as well as locally, the merchants acquired broader horizons than the farmer, artisan, and day laborer. Only a few of the great landowners and leading lawyers knew the larger world. It was the colonial merchants who, allied with lawyers from the seaport towns and with the Virginia planters, encouraged the Revolution, brought about the ratification of the Constitution, and then set up the new government in the last decade of the eighteenth century.

THE RISE OF THE WHOLESALER, 1800–1850

During the first half of the nineteenth century, although the American economy remained primarily agrarian and commercial, it grew vigorously. The scope of the economy expanded as the nation moved westward into the rich Mississippi Valley, and as increasing migration from Europe still further enlarged its population. Even more important to American economic expansion were the techological innovations that occurred in manufacturing in Great Britain. Without the new machines of the Industrial Revolution, the westward movement in the United States and the migration to its shores would have been slower. These innovations reshaped the British textile industry, creating a new demand for cotton from the United States. Before the invention of the water frame, the spinning jenny, the mule, and then the power loom, cotton had never been grown commercially in the United States, but by 1800 it had become the country's major export. The new plantations in turn provided markets for food grown on the smaller farms in both the Northwest and Southwest. The growth of eastern commercial cities and the development of the textile industry in New England and the middle states enlarged that market still further. The titanic struggle between Great Britain and Napoleon obscured the significance of these economic developments, but shortly after 1815 the economy's new orientation became clear.

The merchants who continued to act as economic integrators had the largest hand in building this new high-volume, regionally specialized, agrarian-commercial system. The merchants of Philadelphia, Baltimore, and New York took over the task of exporting cotton, lumber, and foodstuffs and of importing textiles, hardware, drugs, and other goods from Great Britain and the Continent. Those in the southern coastal and river ports played the same role in exporting cotton and importing finished goods to and from the eastern entrepôts; those in the growing western towns sent out local crops and brought in manufactured goods in a similar way. At first the western trade went via rivers of the Mississippi Valley and New

Orleans. Later it began to be transported east and west through the Erie Canal and along the Great Lakes. To meet the needs of the expanding trade, the merchants, particularly those of the larger eastern cities, developed new forms of commercial banking to finance the movement of crops, set up packet lines on "the Atlantic Shuttle" between New York and Liverpool to speed the movement of news and imports, founded specialized insurance companies, and helped to organize and finance the new canals and turnpikes that improved transportation between them and their customers.

These innovations enabled the merchants to handle still more business, and the high-volume trade in turn forced the merchants to alter their functions and, indeed, their whole way of life. They began to specialize, becoming primarily wholesalers or retailers, importers or exporters. They came to concentrate on a single line of goods—dry goods, wet goods, hardware, iron, drugs, groceries or cotton, wheat or produce. Some became specialists in banking and insurance and spent their time acting as managers for these new financial corporations.

Of the new specialists, the wholesalers played the most influential role, taking the place of the colonial merchants as the primary integrators and adaptors of the economy. More than the farmers or the retailers, the wholesalers were responsible for directing the flow of cotton, corn, wheat, and lumber from the West to the East and to Europe. More than the manufacturers, they handled the marketing of finished goods that went from eastern and European industrial centers to the southern and western states.

Moreover, the wholesalers financed the long-term growth of the economy. Enthusiastic promoters of canals, turnpikes, and then railroads, they provided most of the local capital for these undertakings. They pressured the state and municipal legislatures and councils (on which they or their legally trained associates often sat) to issue bonds or to guarantee bonds of private corporations building transportation enterprises. At times they even persuaded the state to build and operate transport facilities.

The wholesalers also encouraged the adoption of the new technology in manufacturing. In Boston, the Appletons, the Jacksons, and the Cabots financed the new textile mills of Lowell and Lawrence. In New York, the Phelps and the Dodges started the brass industry in the Connecticut Valley, while in Philadelphia and Baltimore wholesalers like Nathan Trotter and Enoch Pratt financed the growing Pennsylvania iron industry. They not only raised the funds for plants and machinery, but also supplied a large amount of the cash and credit that the new manufacturers needed as working capital to pay for supplies and labor.

Although the wholesalers made important contributions to early nineteenth-century economic life, they played a less dominant role in the economy than had the colonial merchant of the eighteenth century. The economic system had become too complex—involving too many units of production, distribution, transportation, and finance—for one group to supervise local, interregional, and international flows. nonetheless, the wholesalers had more influence in setting prices, managing the flow of goods, and determining the amount and direction of investment than had other groups—the farmers, manufacturers, retailers, and bankers.

As the economy expanded, the recruitment of businessmen became more open than it had been in the colonial period. At the same time, the outlook of even the most broad-gauged businessmen grew narrower. Family and family ties became less essential, although they could still be a useful source of capital. Businessmen began to place more value on personal qualities, such as aggressiveness, drive, and self-reliance. Nor did one need any lengthy training or education to set up a shop as a wholesaler. Because of their increasing functional specialization, this new breed of wholesalers rarely had the international outlook of the colonial merchants. Not surprisingly, they and the lawyers and politicians who represented them saw their needs in sectional rather than national terms—as did so many Americans in the years immediately prior to the Civil War.

THE RISE OF THE MANUFACTURER BEFORE 1900

By midcentury the American agrarian and commercial economy had begun to be transformed, into the most productive industrial system in the world. The migration of Americans into cities became more significant in this transformation than the final settling of the western frontier. Immigration from Europe reached new heights, with most of the new arrivals staying in the cities of the East and the old Northwest. By 1900, therefore, the rate of growth of the rural areas had leveled off. From then on, the nation's population growth would come almost wholly in its cities.

The second half of the nineteenth century was a time of great technological change—the age of steam and iron, the factory and the railroad. The steam railroad and the steamship came quickly to dominate transportation. In 1849 the United States had only six thousand miles of railroad and even fewer miles of canals, but by 1884 its railroad corporations operated 202,000 miles of track, or 43 percent of the total mileage in the world. In 1850 the factory—with its power-driven machinery and its permanent working force—was a rarity outside the textile and iron industries, but by 1880 the Bureau of the Census reported that 80 percent of the three million workers in mechanized industry labored in factories. And nearly all these new plants were powered by steam rather than by water.

America's factories made a vital contribution to the nation's economic growth. By 1894 the value of the output of American industry equaled that of the combined output of the United Kingdom, France, and Germany. In the next twenty years American production tripled, and by the outbreak of World War I the United States was producing more than a third of the world's industrial goods.

As manufacturing expanded, the wholesaler continued for many years to play a significant role in the economy. The period up to 1873 was one of increasing demand and rising prices. The manufacturers, concentrating on building or expanding their new factories, were more than happy to have the wholesalers supply them with their raw and semifinished materials and to market their finished goods. In addition, wholesalers continued to provide manufacturers with capital for building plants, purchasing equipment and supplies, and paying wages.

After the recession of 1873, however, the manufacturer began to replace the wholesaler as the man who had the most to say about coordinating the flow of goods through the economy and about adapting the economy to population and technological changes. The shift came for three reasons. First, the existing wholesale network of hundreds of thousands of small firms had difficulty in handling efficiently the growing output of the factories. Second, the manufacturer no longer needed the wholesaler as a source of capital. After a generation of production, he was able to finance plant and equipment out of retained profits. Moreover, until 1850 the commercial banking system had been almost wholly involved in financing the movement of agricultural products, but about midcentury it began to provide working capital for the industrialist. Commercial banks also began to provide funds for plant and equipment, particularly to new manufacturing enterprises.

The third and most pervasive reason why the manufacturer came to a position of dominance resulted from the nature of factory production itself. This much more efficient form of manufacturing so swiftly increased the output of goods that supply soon outran demand. From the mid-1870s to the mid-1890s, prices fell sharply. Moreover, the large investment required to build a factory made it costly to shut down and even more expensive to move into other forms of business activity. As prices fell, the manufacturers organized to control prices and the flow of goods within their industries. If the wholesalers would and could help them in achieving such control, the manufacturers welcomed their cooperation. If not, they did it themselves. In most cases, the industrialist came to play a larger role than the wholesalers in integrating the economy.

The wholesaler was pushed aside in transportation before he was in manufacturing. Railroad construction costs were high, and after 1849 when railroad expansion began on a large scale, the local merchants simply could not supply the necessary capital. Modern Wall Street came into being during the 1850s to meet the need for funds. By 1860 the investment banker had replaced the wholesaler as the primary supplier of funds to American railroads.

In the 1850s and 1860s the railroads also captured many of the merchant's functions. They took over freight forwarding in large towns and eliminated the merchant by handling through traffic in many commercial centers along the main routes west and south. Indeed, during the 1860s the railroads had absorbed most of the fast freight and express companies developed earlier by the wholesalers in order to use the new rail transportation. By the 1870s the coordination of the flow of most interregional transportation in the United States had come under the direction of the traffic departments of a few large railroads.

The first manufacturers to move into the wholesalers' domain were those who found that the wholesaler could not meet their special needs. These were of two types. The makers of new technologically complex and relatively expensive durable products quickly realized that wholesalers were unable to handle the initial demonstration to the consumer, provide consumer credit, or ensure the repair and servicing of the products sold. Thus manufacturers of agricultural implements, sewing machines, typewriters, cash registers, carriages, bicycles, or, most important of all, electrical machinery and equipment created national and even international marketing organizations well before the turn of the century. So did the second type, the processors of perishable goods requiring refrigeration, quick transportation, and careful storage for their distribution—fresh meat, beer, bananas, and cigarettes.

Once the pioneers of both types of enterprises—the McCormicks, the Remingtons, George Westinghouse and Charles Coffin, the Swifts and Armours, the Pabsts and Schlitzes, Andrew Preston and James B. Duke—had created their widespread distribution networks, they began again to eliminate the wholesaler by doing their own purchasing. They could not run the risk of stopping complex fabricating or assembling processes because they lacked critical parts or materials. Some integrated backwards even further, doing their own purchasing by building or buying factories to manufacture parts, controlling their own iron, steel, or lumber, or obtaining their own refrigerated cars and ships.

The manufacturers who produced standard commodities that might be distributed easily through the existing wholesaler network were slower to move into wholesaling. Even though the pioneering firms were demonstrating the economies resulting from a combination of mass production and mass distribution, most manufacturers had to be pushed rather than enticed into a strategy of vertical integration. They did so only after they failed to meet the oppressive pressure of falling prices by the more obvious methods of price control through trade associations, cartels, and other loose combinations.

The railroads pioneered in developing ways to control prices in the face of excess capacity and heavy fixed costs. During the 1870s, the railroads formed regional associations, of which the Eastern Trunk Line Association was the most powerful. By the 1880s, however, the railroad presidents and traffic managers admitted defeat. The associations could only be effective if their rulings were enforced in courts of law, but their pleas for legalized pooling went unheard. Indeed, the Interstate Commerce Act of 1887 specifically declared pooling illegal. As a result, the American railroad network became consolidated into large "self-sustaining," centrally managed regional systems. By 1900 most of American land transportation was handled by about twenty-five great systems informally allied in six groupings.

Where the railroads had hoped for legalized pooling, the manufacturers sought other ways of obtaining firmer legal control over the factories in their industries. They began personally to purchase stock in one another's companies. After 1882 when the Standard Oil Company devised the trust as a way of acquiring legal control of an industry, companies began to adopt that device. The holding company quickly superseded the trust as a more effective and inexpensive way of controlling price and production after 1889, when New Jersey passed a general incorporation law that permitted one company to hold stock in many others. The Supreme Court's interpretations of the Sherman Antitrust Act (1890) encouraged further consolidation in manufacturing. Court decisions discouraged loose combinations of manufacturers (or railroads) in any form, but (at least until 1911) appeared to permit consolidation of competing firms through a holding company if that company came to administer its activities under a single centralized management.

In many cases these new consolidations embarked on a strategy of vertical integration. Where the railroads formed "self-sustaining" systems to assure control of traffic over primary commercial routes, the manufacturers attempted to assure the uninterrupted flow of goods into and out of their production and processing plants. John D. Rockefeller and his associates at Standard Oil were the first of the combinations to adopt this strategy. The Standard Oil Trust had been formed after associations in the petroleum industry had proven to be, in Rockefeller's words, "ropes of sand." Legal control of the industry was followed by administrative consolidation of its refineries under a single centralized management. In the mid-1880s, the trust began to build its own distribution network of tank farms and wholesaling offices. Finally, after enlarging its buying organization, it moved in the late-1880s into the taking of crude oil out of the ground.

The examples of Standard Oil, the Swifts, the McCormicks, and others who had bypassed the wholesaler, the rulings of the Supreme Court, the memories of twenty years of declining prices resulted between 1898 and 1902 in the greatest merger movement in American history. Combinations, usually in the form of holding companies, occurred in nearly all major American industries. Holding companies then were often transformed into operating companies. After manufacturing facilities were centralized under a single management, the new consolidated enterprise integrated forwards and backwards.

At the same time, retailers who began to appreciate the potential of mass markets and economies of scale also moved to eliminate the wholesalers—although they did so in a more restricted way than the manufacturers. The mail-order houses (Sears, Roebuck and Montgomery Ward), which turned to the rural markets, and the department and chain stores, which looked to the growing cities, began to buy directly from the manufacturers. By the turn of the century, some large retailers had even bought into manufacturing firms. As a result, wholesalers' decisions were of less significance to the operation of the economy than they had been fifty years earlier. Far more important were the decisions of the manufacturers who had combined, consolidated, and integrated their operations and the few giant retailers who had adopted somewhat the same strategy.

As manufacturers replaced wholesalers as key coordinators in the national economy, they became the popular symbol of American business enterprise. The industrialists and the railroad leaders were indeed the reality as well as the symbol of business power in the Gilded Age. The recruitment of this new dominant business group remained open, at least for a generation. As had been true earlier for the wholesaler, aggressiveness, drive, and access to capital or credit were prerequisites for success. Lineage or specialized training were less important, but some technological know-how was an advantage. Although the manufacturers' horizons were more national and less regional than the wholesalers', they came to view the national scene from the perspective of their particular industry. They and their representatives in Washington tended to take positions on the major issues of the day—tariff, currency, immigration, and the regulation of business—from an industrial rather than a sectional or regional viewpoint.

It was not long, however, before the needs of the manufacturers and their response to these needs altered the recruitment and training of the nation's most powerful businessmen. The increasingly high investment required for large-scale production made the entry of new men and firms more difficult. The emergence of the vertically integrated enterprise limited opportunities still further. By 1900 it was becoming easier to rise to positions of business influence by moving through the new centralized managements than by starting a business enterprise of one's own. This pattern was already clear in the railroads, the nation's first modern business bureaucracies.

THE DOMINANCE OF THE MANAGER SINCE 1900

Although the twentieth century was to become the age of the manager, the growing significance of the manager's role in the operation of the American economy was not immediately apparent. Until the 1920s manufacturers and their assistants concentrated on rounding out their integrated enterprises, creating the internal structures and methods necessary to operate these business empires, and employing the managers necessary to staff them.

At first, external conditions did not seriously challenge the new enterprises. Population trends continued, and heavy migration from abroad sustained urban growth until the outbreak of World War I. During the war, migration from the rural areas to the cities increased. At the same time, impressive technological innovations, particularly those involved with the generating of power by electricity and the internal combustion engine, created new industries and helped transform older ones. The continuing growth of the city, the expansion of the whole electrical sector, and the coming of the automobile and auxiliary industries made the first decades of the twentieth century ones of increasing demand and rapid economic growth.

The initial task of the men who fashioned the first integrated giants at the beginning of this century was to build internal organizational structures that would assure the efficient coordination of the flow of goods through their enterprises and permit the rational allocation of the financial, human, and technological resources at their command. First came the formation of functional departments—sales, production, purchasing, finance, engineering, and research and development. At the same time, central offices were organized, usually in the form of an executive committee consisting of the heads of the functional departments. These offices supervised, appraised, and coordinated the work of the departments and planned long-term expenditures.

By the late-1920s the pioneer organization-builders at du Pont, General Motors, General Electric, Standard Oil of New Jersey, and Sears, Roebuck had developed new and sophisticated techniques to perform the vital coordinating and adaptive activities. They based both long- and short-term coordination and planning on a forecast of market conditions. On the basis of annual forecasts, revised monthly and adjusted every ten days, the companies set production schedules, purchases of supplies and semifinished products, employment and wage rolls, working capital requirements, and prices. Prices were determined by costs, which in turn closely reflected estimated volume of output. The annual forecasts took into consideration estimates of national income, the business cycle, seasonal fluctuations, and the company's normal share of the market. Long-term allocations were based on still broader estimates of demand. After 1920, the managers of many large corporations began to include in these allocations the funds and personnel needed to develop new products and processes through technological innovation. From that time on, the integrated firm began to diversify. The Depression and World War II helped to spread these methods, so that by midcentury most of the key industries in the United States were dominated by a few giant firms administered in much the same way.

Their managers considered themselves leaders in the business community and were so considered by others. Yet they differed greatly from the older types of dominant businessmen—the merchants, the wholesalers, and the manufacturers: they were not owners; they held only a tiny portion of their company's stock; they neither founded the enterprise nor were born into it; and most of them had worked their way up the new bureaucratic ladders.

Even to get on a ladder they were expected to have attended college. Studies of business executives in large corporations show that by 1950 the large majority had been to college—an advantage that was shared by few Americans of their age group. Like most of those who did receive higher education, these managers came primarily from white Anglo-Saxon Protestant stock. Once the college man with his WASP background started up the managerial ladder, he usually remained in one industry and more often than not in a single company. That company became his career, his way of life.

As he rose up the ranks, his horizon broadened to national and international levels. Where his firm diversified, his interests and concerns spread over several industries. Indeed, in some ways his perspectives were wider in the 1950s than those of most Americans; nevertheless, because of his specialized training, he had little opportunity to become aware of the values, ideas, ambitions, and goals of other groups of Americans. He had even fewer direct contacts with farmers, workers, and other types of businessmen than had the wholesaler and the manufacturer.

The dominance of the large integrated, enterprise did not, of course, mean the disappearance of the older types of businessmen. Small business remained a basic and essential part of the American economy. The small nonintegrated, manufacturer, the wholesaler, and retailer have all continued to be active throughout the twentieth century. The number of small businesses has continued to grow with the rapid expansion of the service industries (such as laundries and dry cleaners, service and repair shops not directly tied to the large firm); with the spread of real-estate dealers, insurance agencies, and stock brokerage firms; and with the continuing expansion of the building and construction industries. Throughout the century small businessmen have greatly outnumbered the managers of big business. The former were, therefore, often more politically powerful, particularly in the local politics, than the latter. Economically, however, the managers of the large integrated and often diversified enterprises remained the dominant decision makers in the urban, industrial, and technologically sophisticated economy of the twentieth century. Their critically significant position has been repeatedly and properly pointed out by economists ever since Adolph A. Berle and Gardner C. Means wrote the first analysis of the role and functions of the modern corporation in 1932.

4

Capital Accumulation

On European Economic Development

JOHN MAYNARD KEYNES

Europe was so organized socially and economically as to secure the maximum accumulation of capital. While there was some continuous improvement in the daily conditions of life of the mass of the population, society was so framed as to throw a great part of the increased income into the control of the class least likely to consume it. The new rich of the nineteenth century were not brought up to large expenditures, and preferred the power which investment gave them to the pleasures of immediate consumption. In fact, it was precisely the *inequality* of the distribution of wealth which made possible those vast accumulations of fixed wealth and of capital improvements which distinguished that age from all others. Herein lay, in fact, the main justification of the capitalist system. If the rich had spent their new wealth on their own enjoyments, the world would long ago have found such a regime intolerable. But like bees they saved and accumulated, not less to the advantage of the whole community because they themselves held narrower ends in prospect.

The immense accumulations of fixed capital, which to the great benefit of mankind, were built up during the half century before the [First World] war, could never have come about in a society where wealth was divided equitably. The railways of the world, which that age built as a monument to posterity, were, not less than the pyramids of Egypt, the work of labor which was not free to consume in immediate enjoyment the full equivalent of its efforts.

Thus this remarkable system depended for its growth on a double bluff or deception. On the one hand the laboring classes accepted from ignorance or powerlessness, or were compelled, persuaded, or cajoled by custom, convention, authority, and the well-established order of society into accepting, a situation in which they could call their own very little of the cake that they and nature and the capitalists were cooperating to produce. And on the other hand the capitalist classes were allowed to call the best part of the cake theirs and were theoretically free to consume it, on the tacit underlying conditions that they consumed very little of it in practice. . . .

On Soviet Economic Development

STEPHEN F. COHEN

It was during this process of the 1930s that the Soviet Union, with its great military-industrial power, took shape, and that Stalinism, a new political phenomenon, was established.

From 1929 to 1936, the period of the first and second five-year plans, Stalin's "great change" was primarily an economic revolution, a farrago of brutal coercion, memorable heroism, catastrophic folly, and spectacular achievement. Few of the targets of the first plan were attained on schedule; but its actual accomplishments, consolidated and expanded at an annual rate of 13–14 percent during the more pragmatic and modest second plan, nonetheless created the foundations of an urban, industrial society.

By 1937, heavy industrial production was three to six (depending on the indexes used) times greater than in 1928: steel production had quadrupled, coal and cement production more than tripled, oil production more than doubled; electrical output had grown sevenfold, that of machine tools twentyfold. While old plants were expanded and retooled, new cities, industries, power stations, iron and steel complexes, and technologies came into being, many in formerly undeveloped areas. The industrial labor force and urban population doubled. The total number of students grew from 12 million to over 31 million; by 1939, illiteracy among citizens under fifty had been eliminated (Nove, 1969).

The costs of this leap into economic modernity were no less spectacular. For a zealous minority—mostly party members but also ordinary men and women—it was a time of genuine enthusiasm, feverish exertion, and willing sacrifice (Lyons, 1937). For the majority, including several millions whose fate was deportation, forced labor camps, and death, it was one of repression and misery. The concentration of resources in heavy industry, the suppression of private manufacturing and trade, the virtual collapse of agriculture during the years of collectivization, and the epidemic of waste generated by mismanagement, chronic breakdowns, overstrained and abused equipment, and unskilled labor had a devastating and lasting impact on Soviet life. In the cities, which suffered less, housing space declined sharply and per capita consumption of meat, lard, and poultry in 1932 was only a third of what it had been in 1928. Factory workers lost the right to change jobs without official permission and incurred severe penalties for absenteeism, while real wages dropped by perhaps as much as 50 percent in the early thirties (Nove, 1969). Rationing and queues became the norm; consumer goods and services all but disappeared.

Far heavier blows fell on the countryside during the four-year civil war known as collectivization. Great revolutions almost always victimize a social class; in this case, it was 25 million peasant families. Most did not want to relinquish their meager plots, tools, and animals and become collective farmers. They were forced to do so by the party-state which, in addition to fiscal and administrative compulsion, resorted to prolonged confiscations, mass arrests, deportations, and military assaults by rural cadres, urban brigades, police, and even army detachments. The peasants fought back, often in sporadic pitched battles, occasionally in mass uprisings, but mainly in traditional rural fashion by destroying their crops and livestock. (For the story of collectivization, see Lewin, 1968; Nove, 1969; and Fainsod, 1958.)

The nature of the struggle was determined in January–February 1930. Driven by Stalin's menacing directives and purge of "rightists," local authorities unleashed a reign of terror against recalcitrant kulaks, middle and poor peasants alike. Half of all the households—more than 10 million families—were collectivized by March. The holocaust, however, compelled Stalin to call a temporary halt in a remarkable article blaming local officials for the "excesses" and for having grown "dizzy with success." A mass exodus from the collective farms followed, plummeting the percentage of enrolled households from 57.6 in March to 23.6 in June (Lewin, 1968). But the retreat had come too late to stave off disaster. Figures published in 1934 revealed that more than half of the country's 33 million horses, 70 million cattle, 26 million pigs, and two-thirds of its 146 million sheep and goats had perished, most during what one official history now disparages as the "cavalry march" of January–February 1930 (Nove, 1969). A greater catastrophe could hardly befall an agrarian society. Twenty-five years later, livestock herds were still smaller than in 1928.

Later in 1930, with more deliberation but hardly less coercion, the state resumed its offensive. Repression "on an extraordinary scale" still swept the countryside in 1933 (Fainsod, 1958). By 1931, 50 percent of the households had again been collectivized, and by 1934, 70 percent; the remainder followed shortly. What finally broke the peasant resistance, ending the unequal war, was the deliberately created famine of 1932–33, one of the worst in Russian history. Having procured the meager harvest of 1932, the state withheld grain from the countryside. Firsthand accounts tell of deserted villages, burned-out houses, cattle cars still carrying deportees northward, roaming hordes of begging, starving peasants, incidents of cannibalism, and the uncollected bodies of men, women, and children; in short, a ravaged totally defeated countryside (see, for example, Chamberlain, 1935; Koestler, 1965; Reswick, 1952; Medvedev, 1971). At least 10 million peasants, possibly many more, died as a direct result of collectivization, about half during the imposed famine of 1932–33 (Churchill [1950] reports Stalin having confided the figure 10 million to him).

REFERENCES

Readers interested in reference to Cohen's Russian sources should consult his book. Only the citations available in English are referred to here.

Chamberlain, William Henry. (1935). *Russia's Iron Age*. London: Duckworth.

Churchill, Winston. (1950). *The Hinge of Fate*. Boston: Houghton-Mifflin.

Fainsod, Merle. (1958). *Smolensk under Soviet Rule*. Cambridge, Mass.: Harvard University Press.

Koestler, Arthur. (1965). *The Yogi and the Commissar*. New York: Collier Books.

Lewin, Moshe. (1968). *Russian Peasants and Soviet Power: A Study of Collectivization*. Evanston, Ill.: Northwestern University Press.

Lyons, Eugene. (1937). *Assignment in Utopia*. New York: Harcourt-Brace.

Medvedev, Roy A. (1971). *Let History Judge: The Origins and Consequences of Stalinism*. New York: Alfred A. Knopf.

Nove, Alec. (1969). *An Economic History of the USSR*. London: Allen Lane.

Reswick, William. (1952). *I Dreamt Revolution*. Chicago: H. Regnery.

5

Community

Does Community Have a Value?

WENDELL BERRY

Community is a concept, like humanity or peace, that virtually no one has taken the trouble to quarrel with; even its worst enemies praise it. There is almost no product or project that is not being advocated in the name of community improvement. We are told that we, as a community, are better off for the power industry, the defense industry, the communications industry, the transportation industry, the agriculture industry, the food industry, the health industry, the medical industry, the insurance industry, the sports industry, the beauty industry, the entertainment industry, the mining industry, the education industry, the law industry, the government industry, and the religion industry. You could look into any one of these industries and find many people, some of them in influential positions, who are certifiably "community spirited."

In fact, however, neither our economy, nor our government, nor our educational system runs on the assumption that community has a value—a value, that is, that *counts* in any practical or powerful way. The values that are assigned to community are emotional and spiritual—"cultural"—which makes it the subject of pieties that are merely vocal. But does community have a value that is practical or economic? Is community necessary? If it does not have a value that is practical and economic, if it is not necessary, then can it have a value that is emotional and spiritual? Can "community values" be preserved simply for their own sake? Can people be neighbors, for example, if they do not need each other or help each other? Can there be a harvest festival where there is no harvest? Does economy have spiritual value?

Such questions are being forced upon us now by the loss of community. We are discouraged from dealing with them by their difficulty in such a time as this, and yet these questions and others like them are indispensable to us, for they describe the work that we must do. We can only be encouraged to see that this work, though difficult, is fascinating and hopeful. It is homework, doable in some part by everybody, useful to everybody—as far as possible unlike the massive, expensive, elitist projects that now engross virtually every government of the world.

But, before I go any farther, let me make clear what I mean by community. I will give as particular an example as I know.

My friends, Loyce and Owen Flood married in October 1938, and moved to a farm in hilly country near Port Royal, Kentucky. She was seventeen; Owen was eighteen.

Loyce had graduated from high school and had been to college for a short while. Although she had been raised on a farm she did not know a great deal about being a farmer's wife on a small, poor, hillside place. She and Owen had little money, and she had to learn quickly the arts of subsistence.

Fortunately, they were living in a neighborhood of households closely bound together by family ties or friendships and by well-established patterns of work and pleasure. This neighborhood included, in varying degrees of intimacy and interdependence, nine households, all more or less within walking distance. The women kept house individually, but all the big jobs they did together: housecleaning, wallpapering, quilting, canning, cooking for field crews. Though Loyce looked up to these women and called them "Miss Suzy," "Miss Berthy," and so on, most of them were still fairly young, in their late thirties or early forties. They were a set of hearty, humorous, industrious women, who saw whatever was funny and loved to make up funny names for things.

They became Loyce's teachers, and now, nearly fifty years later, she remembers with warmth and pleasure their kindness to her and their care for her. They helped her to learn to cook and can, to work in the hog killing and in the field (for, at planting and harvest times, the women went to the field with the men); they looked after her when she was sick; they taught her practical things, and things having to do with their mutual womanhood and community life. Although she had more formal schooling than any of them, she says now, "Everything I know I learned from those people." And the men were as kind and useful to Owen as the women were to Loyce. "They took us under their wing," she says.

The men farmed their own farms, but, like the women, they did the big jobs together. And when they worked together, they ate together. They always had a big dinner. "They never shirked dinner," Loyce says, "that was one thing sure." In hot weather, chicken would be the only fresh meat available, and they ate a lot of chicken. The women were perfectionists at making noodles.

By our standards now, these people were poor. The farms ranged in size from thirty-seven to perhaps a hundred acres. But only the thirty-seven-acre farm was entirely tillable. The others included a lot of "hill and holler." Then, as now, most of the money made on the produce of that place was made by manufacturers and merchants in other places; probably no household grossed more than $1,000 a year. The subsistence economy was necessarily elaborate and strong. The people raised and slaughtered their own meat, raised vegetable gardens, produced their own milk, butter, and eggs. They gathered the wild fruit as it ripened. They canned and dried and cured and preserved. They spent little money. The cash for the household came mainly from the sale of cream, and each farm kept three or four milk cows for that purpose. Loyce remembers that her weekly cream check was three dollars; they budgeted half of that for groceries and gasoline for the car and half for payment on a debt.

These people worked hard, and without any modern conveniences or labor savers. They had no tractors, no electricity, no refrigerators, no washing machines, no vacuum cleaners. Their one luxury was the telephone party line, which cost fifty cents a month. But their work was in limited quantities; they did not work at night or away from home; they knew their work, they knew how to work, and they knew each other. Loyce says, "They didn't have to do a lot of explaining."

Their work was mingled with their amusement; sometimes it *was* their amusement. Talk was very important: They worked together and talked; they saw each other in Port Royal on Saturday night and talked; on Sunday morning they went to church early and stood around outside and talked; when church was over, they talked and were in no hurry to go home.

In the summer they would get fifty pounds of ice and make ice cream, and eat the whole freezer full, and sometimes make another, and eat that. In the winter they would all go to somebody's house at night and pop corn, and the men would play cards and the women would talk. They played cards a lot. One of the households had books that could be borrowed. Loyce's private amusements were reading and embroidery. She does not remember ever getting lonesome or bored.

There are, as I see it, two salient facts about this neighborhood of 1938:

1. It was effective and successful as a community. It did what we know that a good community does: It supported itself, amused itself, consoled itself, and passed its knowledge on to the young. It was something to build on.
2. It no longer exists. By the end of World War II, it was both reduced and altered, and the remnants of its old life are now mainly memories.

The reasons why it no longer exists are numerous and complexly interrelated. Some of them are: increased farm income during and after the war; improved roads and vehicles; the influence of radio and then of television; rising economic expectations; changing social fashions; school consolidation; and the rapid introduction of industrial technology into agriculture after the war. And so the disappearance of this community into the modern world and the industrial economy is both a fact and, to a considerable extent, an understandable fact.

But we must take care not to stop with the mere recognition and understanding of facts. We must go ahead to ask if the fact exists for our good, if it can be understood to our good, and if its existence is necessary or inescapable. After establishing that a community has died, for example, we must ask who has been served by its death.

Such a community as I have described has often been caricatured and ridiculed and often sentimentalized. But, looked at in its facts, as my friend recalls them, it escapes both extremes. The people were manifestly equal to their lot; they were not oafish or stupid. On the other hand, they were not perfect; they were not living an idyll. The community was not immune either to change or to the need to change. Anyone familiar with the history of farming on Kentucky hillsides knows its practices could always have been improved.

But another fact that we must now reckon with is that this community did not change by improving itself. It changed by turning away from itself, from its place, from its own possibility. Somehow the periphery exhausted and broke the center. This community, like thousands of similar ones, was not changed by anything that *it* thought of, or by anything thought of by anybody who believed that community had a practical or an economic value. It was changed, partly to its own blame, by forces, originating outside itself, that did not consider, much less desire, the welfare or the existence of such communities. This community, like any other, had to change and needed to change, but what if its own life, its own good, had been the standard by which it changed, rather than the profit of distant entrepreneurs and corporations?

We are left with questions—that one and others.

Is such a community desirable? My answer, unhesitatingly, is yes. But that is an answer notoriously subject to the charge of sentimentality or nostalgia. People will ask if I "want to turn back the clock." And so I am pushed along to another question, a more interesting one: Is such a community necessary? Again, I think, the answer must be yes, and here we have access to some manner of proof.

For one thing, the place once occupied by that community is now occupied by people who are not, in the same close, effective sense, a community. The place is no longer central to its own interest and its own economy. The people do not support themselves so much from the place or so much by mutual work and help as their predecessors did; they furnish much less of their own amusement and consolation; purchasing has more and more replaced growing and making; and less and less of local knowledge and practical skill is passed on to the young. In 1938, the community and its economy were almost identical. Today, the community is defined mostly by the mere proximity of its people to one another. The people belong, often to their own detriment, to a *national* economy whose centers are far from home.

For another thing, we now have before us the failure of the industrial system of agriculture that supplanted the community and the ways of 1938. There is, so far as I am aware, no way of denying the failure of an agricultural system that destroys both land and people, as the industrial system is now doing. Obviously, we need a way of farming that attaches people to the land much more intimately, carefully, and democratically than the industrial system has been able to do, and we can neither establish good farming nor preserve it without successful communities.

It is easy to suppose, as many powerful people apparently have done, that the principle of subsistence on family farms and in rural communities will be bad for the larger economy, but this supposition has proved to be a dangerous and destructive error. Subsistence is bad for the industrial economy and for the paper economy of the financiers; it is good for the actual, real-world economy by which people live and are fed, clothed, and housed. For example, in 1938, in the time of subsistence, there were three thriving grocery stores that were patronized by the neighborhood I have been talking about—one at Drennon's Lick and two at Port Royal. Now there is only one, at Port Royal. The "standard of living" (determined, evidently, by how much money is spent) has increased, but community life has declined, economically and every other way. In the neighborhoods around Port Royal, we now have many modern conveniences, but we buy and pay for them farther and farther from home. And we have fewer and fewer people at home who know how to maintain these conveniences and keep them running. Port Royal, in other words, now exists for "the economy"—that abstract accumulation of monetary power that aggrandizes corporations and governments and that does not concern itself at all for the existence of Port Royal.

For many years, I think, the people of rural America have been struggling with the realization that we are living in a colony. It is an irony especially bitter for Americans that, having cast off the colonialism of England, we have proceeded to impose a domestic colonialism on our own land and people, and yet we cannot deny that most of the money made on the products that we produce in rural America—food and fiber, timber, mineable fuels and minerals of all kinds—is made by other people in other places. We cannot deny that all of these fundamental enterprises, as now conducted, involve the destruction of the land and the people. We cannot deny that there is no provision being made and no thought being taken in any segment of the rural economy for the long-term welfare of the people who are doing the work. Indeed, we cannot deny that our leaders appear to take for granted that the eventual destruction of lives, livelihoods, homes, and communities is an acceptable, though not a chargeable, cost of production. The washed-out farm and bankrupt farmer, the strip-mined mountain and the unemployed or diseased miner, the clear-cut forest and the depressed logging town— all are seen as the mere natural results of so-called free enterprise. The pattern of industrial "development" on the farm and in the forest, as in the coal fields, is that of combustion and exhaustion—not "growth," a biological metaphor that is invariably contradicted by industrial practice.

The fault of a colonial economy is that it is dishonest; it misrepresents reality. In practice, it is simply a way of keeping costs off the books of an exploitive interest. The exploitive interest is absent from the countryside exactly as if the countryside were a foreign colony. The result of this separation is that the true costs of production are not paid by the exploitive interest but only suffered by the exploited land and people. The colony, whether foreign or domestic, becomes unstable, both as an ecosystem and as a community because colonialism does not permit the development of strong local economies. The economy of a colony exports only "raw material" and imports only finished goods. It buys and sells on markets over which it has no control; thus, both markets drain value from the colony. The economy of a colony is thus as far as possible from E. F. Schumacher's just (and safe) ideal of "local production from local resources for local use."

The way that a national economy preys on its internal colonies is by the destruction of community—that is, by the destruction of the principle of local self-sufficiency not only in the local economy but also in the local culture. Thus, local life becomes the dependent—indeed, the victim—not just of the food industry, the transportation industry, the power industries, the various agribusiness industries, and so on, but also of the entertainment, the education, and the religion industries—all involving change from goods once cheap or free to expensive goods having to be bought.

That the economy of most of rural America is a colonial economy became plain as soon as the local economies of subsistence lapsed and were replaced by the so-called consumer economy. The old local economies of subsistence, which in America were often incomplete and imperfect, were nevertheless sources of local strength and independence, and, as I have suggested, they were a beginning on which we could have built. Their replacement by the consumer economy has brought a helpless dependence on distant markets, on transported manufactured goods, on cash, and on credit.

Even so cursory a description of one of the old local subsistence economies as I gave at the beginning of this essay reveals that its economic assets were to a considerable extent intangible: culture-borne knowledge, attitudes, and skills; family and community coherence; family and community labor; and cultural or religious principles such as respect for gifts (natural or divine), humility, fidelity, charity, and neighborliness. Such economies, furthermore, were mainly sun-powered, using plants and the bodies of animals and humans as "solar converters." By means of neighborhood, knowledge, and skill, they were turning free supplies to economic advantage. Theirs was an economy that took place, largely, off the books. The wonderful fact, then, is that those emotional and spiritual values that are now so inconsequentially associated with the idea of community were economic assets in the old communities, and they produced economic results.

REFERENCE

E. F. Schumacher (1973). *Small Is Beautiful: Economics as if People Mattered.* New York: Harper & Row.

6

Bringing It Back Home

Socrates in Dallas: Managing the Facilities
BARRY CASTRO

Some years ago I was asked to prepare a paper on the ethical questions that might be associated with the evolution of the field of facilities management. I was to deliver it at the 1987 Meetings of the International Facilities Management Association (IFMA) in Dallas. Facilities management, like the young men searching for meaning in their lives who gathered around Socrates, came with very little history. Like them, it was in the midst of some turmoil about how it ought to be defined. I thought it might be fun to extend the Socratic injunction, "know thyself," to knowing oneself in the context of the working environment of a new field—. . . to bring Socrates to Dallas.

I planned to begin my presentation by disclaiming the otherworldly quality business people often ascribe to ethical inquiry. My intention was to emphasize, as Socrates did, that working hard to see what was true and then going on to try to help others to see it was likely to be of considerable practical value. I wanted to underscore Socrates' insistence on the difference between seeking to be of practical value in this way and seeking to be consistent with the perceived interests of a sponsor. My paper suggested that Socrates, despite the circumstances of his death, did not seek confrontation with those in power. Neither, I noted, did he defer to the sensibilities of those who were paying for his dinner or those whose favors he sought. Socrates knew that if he was to have value for those who heard him, that must be because he sought truth and was happy to share whatever he discovered—about his own self-deceptions as well as the self-deceptions of those with whom he talked.

I acknowledged that corporate norms do not necessarily make this easy—that a serious inquiry into our own propensity for self-deception requires that we purge ourselves of puffery, of scientific pretension, and of whatever similar devices many of us use to promote a desired new contract as consultants or a sought-after promotion as employees. I tried to make it clear that none of us, not even

---

An earlier version of this article appeared in *Bridges* (Fall–Winter 1990).

Socrates, is able to achieve this level of purity altogether, even when we, like him, seem to desire to achieve it very much. However, knowing that we cannot altogether achieve something, I suggested, is not justification for passivity. I planned to stress the Socratic teaching that it was the failure to maintain the ideal—to work toward it—that destroys moral legitimacy and, in so doing, undermines the basis of shared enterprise altogether.

Serious self-scrutiny would require that the underlying issues associated with the practice of facilities management be brought to the surface. What are the constraints associated with the time frames or budgets within which the practitioner must operate? How often does he yield to the demand for rigorous-looking presentations designed to impress clients and discourage questioning? Under what circumstances is she willing to give those to whom she reports answers they do not welcome? How carefully have the systematic errors that are likely to be associated with even the most rigorous scientific instruments and techniques been sought out and acknowledged? To what degree have evolving notions of truth or rigor or professionalism been adaptations to a failure to address such questions? My point in all of this was to provoke what I hoped would be a discussion that would continue after the meetings had adjourned.

I intended to stress the importance of seeing the values implicit in any facility in terms of the opportunity costs with which they were associated. The senses in which one person's display function was perceived as another's lost wages and, perhaps, a third's reminder of his own powerlessness had to be understood. I also knew it was important to talk about the ethical premises with which facilities managers inquire into these costs: the implications of one facilities manager discovering what his client wanted to hear and saying it to her, of another saying only what he believed to be true but not saying whatever he expected his client would find unacceptable, and a third insisting, as a psychotherapist normally would, that a client's resistence to deep internal conflicts become part of their work together. Finally I thought it critical to recognize that the organization for which the facilities manager was working should not be regarded as synonymous with a particular decision maker inside that organization. I wanted to particularly emphasize that there are always intraorganizational pressures to constrain public exploration of opportunity costs—and that, at the very least, we ought not deceive ourselves about the extent to which these pressures are deferred to.

Interestingly, I had applied very little of that good advice to an inquiry into the context in which I was to present my paper. I did not consider that IFMA, like the Facilities Management Program at my own university, could not exist without the support of the office systems industry. I did not consider that such a host would have interests of its own and that, in the case of a meeting like the one I was about to attend, they were not likely to center on the sort of issues I had come to discuss. I did not consider that, even on campus, a host of competing constituencies constrains the nature of the dialogue and renders our curricula subject to funding contingencies, market forces, bureaucratic delivery systems, intraorganizational politics, and the like. I had assumed, perhaps as Socrates sometimes did, that the world was a kind of seminar where we could happily pursue truth and motivate others to do so. Luckily, I was to be disabused of that assumption in a much gentler way than he was.

There were early indications that the IFMA meetings were not to be the sort of event I had envisioned. The program featured some eminent (and very expensive) speakers-qua-entertainers, a black-tie dinner, and a costly postmeeting junket to Puerto Vallarta. The convention hotel was sumptuous, much more so than the site of any academic meeting I could remember having attended, but it was not rich in the printed word. There were no publisher's exhibits and what little literature there was, was overwhelmingly hardware oriented. The registration fee, which I did not have to pay, was four or five times the kind of fee to which I had been accustomed. The exhibition hall, where the latest in facilities-related equipment was being shown, was beautifully appointed and many of the individual exhibits had clearly required an enormous amount of advance preparation. The display function of the facilities was unmistakable and the implicit message it gave was that, without question, we were entitled to nothing but the finest.

The substantive end of the meetings seemed to have a very different priority. There were no small workshops where the sharing of problems and a joint consideration of solutions might be undertaken by practitioners. Actually, there were no meetings planned for an audience of fewer than 150 and half were planned for 600. There were 600 people at mine—a few too many for a dialogue—and a sound system that made it difficult for most of them to even hear me, much less raise questions of their own. The spoken word seemed to matter little more than the written one. My initial interest in using a Socratic form to develop my questions and relate them to the agendas those in the audience brought with them could hardly have been more dissonant from the circumstances in which I was presenting. It was as if the audience was being driven back down to the exhibition hall where they might be tempted to buy one or another of the many items on display there. That, it occurred to me quickly, was the primary purpose of the meeting—at least as far as its sponsors were concerned.

The big vendors seemed to have had the money and the staff to take control of the meetings and make them responsive to their own priorities. I can't document that but I have no doubt that it was true. Neither did many of the frustrated facilities managers I spoke to about it later. Some of their frustrations were of course allayed by all of the glitz. Finding that you are entitled to nothing but the best—even if it is only for a brief time—is not unpleasant and it puts you in the mood for spending your firm's money if you can pull it off. You need, one heard again and again though never quite in so many words, to think of yourself as an independent professional, entitled to state of the art equipment, rather than merely an employee of the company. The implication was that if you could talk about that equipment knowledgably everyone would know that you were a professional and entitled to all of the appropriate perquisites. There wasn't much interest in what else professionalism might mean, certainly not on the part of the organizers of the convention. People like me provided academic respectability and evidence of proper high-mindedness. Our travel expenses and hotel rooms were paid for, as were our registration fees, and we were given handsome little gifts after our presentations. We were treated well but the conveners seemed to think that any success we might have in promoting substantive involvement could become a competing priority—an opportunity cost if you will—and one that should not be allowed to take too prominent a place in the proceedings.

My first reaction to all of that was a mixture of frustration and a resort to the sense of moral superiority that we academics can cultivate when confronted by the taint of the marketplace. In retrospect, there was nothing I found at IFMA that I had not seen on campus: the UC-Berkeley calculus class I attended twenty-five years ago with 900 other students; the introductory economics I taught at Brooklyn College, limited to 250 only by the size of the largest room available to the department; the field house enrollments I remember as both a student and a faculty member in many schools, places where a substantive conversation would be more difficult than it was in Dallas. I have seen academic junkets with precious little substance to them go further afield than Puerto Vallarta. I have written about the relationship between the sources of academic funding and the nature of academic research (Castro, 1968) and about the relationship between public relations concerns, organizational dynamics, and curriculum (Castro, 1974 and 1984). I know that the long-range plans of my own university have a great deal to do with the projected economic future of western Michigan—that my academic career, along with that of many of my most idealistic colleagues, was facilitated by a national response to Sputnik that had little to do with anything substantive in the curriculum. I had ample reason to believe that what I saw at IFMA was a fairly general phenomenon.

That recognition was underscored for me by looking at Dallas, a city I had never visited before. The dominance of the city's corporate skyscrapers was impressive. Each of them was conceived on a massive scale and none of them was ordinary. They had been built at great cost by the most eminent of contemporary architects. Yet each seemed to have almost no relationship to each of the others but to be on an island of its own. Perhaps insularity does not quite get at what I mean. Nothing continuous seemed to flow between these buildings. Collectively, they seemed altogether dissonant from whatever city was left in their wake. Nevertheless, there was a sense that the only life worth living, Socrates to the contrary, was the one inside those buildings—the corporate one heralded by an architecture of high-tech display and by a scale overwhelming its occupants. The buildings were altogether alien to life on the streets: breathtaking from a distance, humbling up close, and deserted after five. Whatever else was visible seemed well past its time—permitted to remain until the next building boom brought a more profitable use for the space. The past was honored as if it were an exhibit in a corporate gallery: an old church, a turn of the century governor's house, a stretch of antique roadway. Our meetings were held in one such exhibit, an impressive replica of the Crystal Palace—again a building with no visible relationship to anything around it. When on the last day of the meetings I tried briefly to reconnect to my surroundings by walking the mile and a half back to my hotel, I was told there was no way to do that. The freeways and building construction made it impossible.

Again, as I had earlier to remember that nothing that was troubling me at

IFMA was especially confined to IFMA, I had also to remember that none of it had anything special to do with Dallas. I had recently walked through luxurious new housing developments on the dunes of Lake Michigan, near my own home, and noted that each seemed to have been built at a different level, to overlook the lake from a slightly different angle, to announce its intention to have as little as possible to do with any of the others. They had splendid views but did not seem otherwise concerned with the outside. There were no sidewalks. Nothing connected them but roadway and that hilly, curving, and altogether uninviting to the pedestrian. It was hard to imagine what was there that might become a public place—impossible to imagine anyone borrowing a cup of sugar—you would have to do it with the car. They were all private houses but they were clearly analogous to the corporate buildings that had disturbed me in Dallas. Like them, these lakefront homes were unrelated to each other and still more profoundly unrelated to the rest of the world. They were impressive but there was nothing organic about their development, nothing that seemed to have evolved from what had been there before. Like their counterparts in Dallas, their opulence was part of what separated them from ordianry life. One has to suspect that the private buildings in western Michigan were built on the same foundations as the corporate ones in Dallas, and that these foundations support a great deal more of the way we live.

I was being treated very well at the IFMA meetings but I was not altogether comfortable with that treatment. I knew that the man who drove me in from the airport and the woman who sold me a newspaper at my hotel did not have access to anything like the level of luxury I was then enjoying. They and I shared the knowledge that their work had far fewer intrinsic rewards than my own and that my hotel room cost several times their daily earnings. Neither of us had any decent way to deal with that information and neither of us could do anything about it. The tension implicit in our need to keep silent about what we could neither justify nor change was hard to escape.

I was also aware, as perhaps the cabdriver and newspaper seller were not, that this was a level of living I could not approach without sponsorship. Would I, having written this, ever be invited back to Dallas? Did I really not care or was that only an attempt to not need what I knew I could not have? Are the contrasts between what I found in Dallas and the simpler pleasures of my ordinary life calibrated to get people like me to lust after return invitations? Do they function so as to elicit our deference toward those who do get them? Is that any different now than it has been in the past? And not least, am I attracted to such questions only because my father drove a taxi and my mother sold newspapers?

The questions were not new. Matthew Arnold saw Dallas across the Channel ". . . like a land of dreams—so various, so beautiful, so new (which) hath really neither joy, nor love, nor light, nor certitude, nor peace, nor help for pain." Henry Adams saw it in the power of the dynamo. George Orwell saw it as that force which ultimately required one to believe that two plus two equaled five. Arguably, the concern goes back to Socrates, and will be with us for a long time yet. There are no crisp little answers. We need to be purposeful and efficient but we also need to question the progressive compartmentalization of our lives, which serves that purposefulness and efficiency. The second is as practical a need as the first. We need to allow ourselves to become part of larger organized wholes or face chaos, but we need also to find alternatives to merely instrumental inter-connectedness, and that too is a practical need. We need a global marketplace, and to some degree we even need the rootlessness that goes with it, but we need also to be aware of the ways in which those needs can lead us to be increasing our reliance on hardware and media hype to make our value judgments. Despite all the talk of a corporation's responsibility to its stakeholders, we need to consider that we may be losing our abilities to imagine those who lack the power to make their stakes known. It seems to me that we need to think about whether we are allowing our corporations, our professions, and perhaps our consciousnesses, to develop along the lines of those sparkling new Dallas skyscrapers, and that that too is very much a practical need.

Let me end by stressing Socrates again. Knowing ourselves is critical. Being concerned with knowing ourselves implies neither passivity nor powerlessness. Socrates has proven to be a good deal more powerful than the Athenian state that killed him. He was as relevant to an action agenda as he was to a contemplative one in Dallas. That, I would argue, is important to remember. He is relevant to practitioners who need to take themselves, their work, and their place in the larger scheme of things, seriously. He is also relevant to office systems manufacturers who want to see facilities managers armed with powerful research findings, exert-ing pressure on their firms to buy state of the art equipment, and demonstrating the wisdom of those purchases through their abilities to use that equipment well.

Nevertheless, Socrates has always kept his listeners from going on about their business on the schedules they had in mind when they encountered him. He has always asked questions that were troublesome. He has not often been sought out by those in positions of power and responsibility—least sought out when they were embarking on ventures in which they were unsure of themselves, and for which they thought they needed affirmation rather than critical questioning. If our society specializes in the brand-new, in both characterlogical and institutional versions of the Dallas skyscrapers and Michigan residences I have described, it is not likely to provide a milieu congenial to ethical dialogue. Neither is it likely to find it useful to acknowledge what cannot be discussed. To acknowledge it is to talk about it. Ethics in general and business ethics in particular must go on to pursue that conversation anyway—not bury it in esoteric philosophic references or hypothetical case studies—but keep hammering away at the self-knowledge relevant to the particular individuals and groups who are part of the dialogue. The greater the urgency with which the new field, or the facilities manager, or the student of business avoids probing questions and calls for us to get on with the business at hand, the greater the need for the ethicist not to yield to that urgency. Could Socrates' message have been received had the IFMA meetings been structured differently? What I got from those in the front few rows who could hear me suggested that perhaps it could have been. That we have no alternative but to try should be, perhaps, my bottom line.

REFERENCES

Barry Castro. (July 1968). "The Scientific Opportunities Foregone Because of More Readily Available Support for Research in Experimental Than Theoretical Physics." *Journal of Political Economy* 76: 601–14.

————. (May 1974). "Hostos: Report from a Ghetto College." *Harvard Educational Review* 44: 270–94.

————. (May 1984). "Outside the Ivory Tower: Learning about Education at the Workplace." *Change* 16: 34–41.

II
SOCIOLOGY

7

A Poem to Begin With

Two Tramps in Mudtime

ROBERT FROST

Out of the mud two strangers came
And caught me splitting wood in the yard.
And one of them put me off my aim
By hailing cheerily "Hit them hard!"
I knew pretty well why he dropped behind
And let the other go on a way.
I knew pretty well what he had in mind:
He wanted to take my job for pay.

Good blocks of beech it was I split,
As large around as the chopping block;
And every piece I squarely hit
Fell splinterless as a cloven rock.
The blows that a life of self-control
Spared to strike for the common good
That day, giving a loose to my soul,
I spent on the unimportant wood.

The sun was warm but the wind was chill.
You know how it is with an April day
When the sun is out and the wind is still,
You're one month on in the middle of May.
But if you so much as dare to speak,
A cloud comes over the sunlit arch,
A wind comes off a frozen peak,
And you're two months back in the middle of March.

A bluebird comes tenderly up at alight
And fronts the wind to unruffle a plume

His song so pitched as not to excite
A single flower as yet to bloom.
It is snowing a flake: and he half knew
Winter was only playing possum.
Except in color he isn't blue,
But he wouldn't advise a thing to blossom.

The water for which we may have to look
In summertime with a witching-wand,
In every wheelrut's now a brook,
In every print of a hoof a pond.
Be glad of water, but don't forget
The lurking frost in the earth beneath
That will steal forth after the sun is set
And show on the water its crystal teeth.

The time when most I loved my task
These two must make me love it more
By coming with what they came to ask.
You'd think I never had felt before
The weight of an ax-head poised aloft,
The grip on earth of outspread feet.
The life of muscles rocking soft
And smooth and moist in vernal heat.

Out of the woods two hulking tramps
(From sleeping God knows where last night,
But not long since in the lumber camps).
They thought all chopping was theirs of right.
Men of the woods and lumberjacks
They judged me by their appropriate tool.
Except as a fellow handled an ax,
They had no way of knowing a fool.

Nothing on either side was said.
They knew they had but to stay their stay
And all their logic would fill my head:
As that I had no right to play
With what was another man's work for gain.
My right might be love but theirs was need.
And where the two exist in twain
Theirs was the better right—agreed.

But yield who will to their separation,
My object in living is to unite
My avocation and my vocation
As my two eyes make one in sight.
Only where love and need are one,
And the work is play for mortal stakes,
Is the deed ever really done
For Heaven and the future's sakes.

8

Workers and Managers

Factory Time

SIMONE WEIL

It is possible to conceive of factories filling the soul of those who work in them, providing a sense of cohesion, a sense of collective life, that is almost overwhelming. All the noises have their meaning, all are rhythmic. They can come together like a shared breath of common work, which is intoxicating to take in. An awareness of solitude remains and enhances the intoxication. There is no sound that can override the metallic noises, the turning wheels, the metal biting into metal—noises which do not speak of nature or of life but of the uninterrupted action of men upon things. The worker is lost in this great clamor, but at the same time he dominates it, because over the permanent and ever-changing din, what stands out is the particular noise of the machine that he himself is using. He does not feel lost in a mob, but necessary—even indispensable. The belts of the assembly line can help him to become part of this rhythm—to absorb it through his entire body, through both the noise and the light vibrating all around him. In the dark hours of the morning and in the winter evenings, when nothing shines but the electric light, all the senses can participate in a universe where nothing recalls nature, where nothing is free, where everything is a collision, the hard and forceful impact of man on matter. The lamps, the belts, the noise, the hard cold metal—all contribute to the transformation of man into worker.

If factory life were only this, it would be a joy. But the joys of work are the joys of free men and the factory worker can feel them only in those rare moments when he is able to forget that he is not free. The evils of his loss of freedom—of subservience—are felt through all of his senses. They come to him through the thousand little details of which his life is constructed.

Each day the first detail to awaken the worker to his servitude is the time clock. The journey from his home to the factory is dictated by the need to arrive before a minutely specified time. It does not help him to be five or ten minutes early. Time

"Experience de la Vie d'Usine" de *Oeuvres Complètes Il Ecrits historiques et politique. L'experience ouvriere et l'adieu a la revolution (juillet 1934–juin 1937*) by Simone Weil. Copyright © 1991 Editions Gallimard. Translated by Zoe Newman Castro and Barry Castro.

is a pitiless taskmaster, leaving nothing to chance. Chance has no rights in the factory. It exists there, indeed, as everywhere else, but it is not recognized. That which is recognized, often at great detriment to production, is the principle of the barracks: "Don't ask why." There are rules that are never observed but are perpetually enforced. Contradictory orders are not contradictory to the logic of the factory. Nonetheless, the work must be done. The worker must manage to do it, under the threat of dismissal, and he does it.

The annoyances, large and small, to which the human organism is continually exposed, or, as Jules Romains says, "That assortment of physical irritations that the task does not demand and which may be altogether at odds with advancing it," contribute to an awareness of servitude. It is not the many physical demands of the work itself which wound the spirit. It is those which are useless. The worker does not dream of complaining about them. He knows that in a factory one does not complain. He knows that if he complained, he would be rebuked, and would not be able to respond—not be able to say a word. To speak would be to seek humiliation. Often, if there is something that a worker cannot tolerate, he prefers to keep quiet and simply ask for his time. His problems may not by themselves amount to much; if they leave him bitter, it is because they again and again remind him of how difficult it is for him to do anything about them. It is because he would like so much to forget that he is not at home in the factory, that he has no rights there, that he is a stranger, admitted as a simple intermediary between machines and the things they produce, and he is not allowed to forget. It is as if someone were repeating into his ear from minute to minute, without the possibility of a response: "You are nothing here. You do not count. You are here to bend, to submit entirely, and to keep quiet." Such repetition is almost irresistible. As a result of it, the worker is likely to admit in the deepest part of his soul that he counts for nothing. All the workers in the factory, or nearly all of them, even those seemingly most self-reliant, have something nearly imperceptible in their movements, in their gaze, and, most of all, in the fold of their lips, which expresses that someone has condemned them to count for nothing.

What hurts most is the way the factory worker has to submit to orders. Workers are often said to not suffer from the monotony of their work, because it is noted that they are likely to be annoyed by changes in its routines. Change can be annoying because, as in the case of piecework, a reduction in earnings is likely to follow, and because it is a habit and nearly a convention to attach more importance to money, a clear and measurable thing, than to the obscure, untouchable, inexpressible feelings which take hold of the spirit during work. But even if work is paid for by the hour, the way the changes are prescribed can feel humiliating. The new work is imposed without preparation, in the form of an order that one must obey immediately and without reply. He who obeys in this manner is brutally reminded that his time is at the disposal of other people.

The small artisan who owns a machine shop, and who knows that in the next few weeks he will produce so many braces, so many faucets, so many connecting rods, is not free to use his time as he wishes either, but at least, once the order has been given, it is he who determines when he will do what. If only the foreman said to the worker, a week or two in advance: for two days you will make me connecting rods, then braces, and so on, one after the other, he would have to obey, but it would be possible to embrace what was coming, to plan it in advance, to own what one was going to do. Nothing like that happens in a factory. From the moment the worker enters until he leaves, he must continuously submit to orders like an inert object that anyone can move at will. If the worker is making a piece which takes two hours, he cannot think about what he will be doing in three hours without being aware that he is powerless, that he will have to do whatever the foreman requires; if he makes ten pieces in ten minutes, his sense of impotence will be the same for the five minutes that follow. If he supposes that perhaps no order will be given, he is condemned to imagine an uninterrupted repetition of a process that is always the same, a dismal and desertlike future through which thought cannot penetrate.

A thousand minor incidents may populate this desert, but, however interesting they may be at the moment, they will be little remembered. By their nature they cannot be reflected on. Falling back on the present produces a sort of stupor. The only future that can come to mind is the point at which the work in progress is completed, if the worker is lucky enough to have the time to think. At certain moments, work is absorbing enough for thought to maintain itself within these limits. Then one does not suffer. But at night, when it is time for the worker to leave, or in the morning, when he is about to begin, it is hard to think of the day's work before him. And Sunday evenings, when the prospect is not merely a day, but a whole week, the future is something too dismal, too overwhelming, to allow into consciousness.

The monotony of factory time, even if it is unbroken by a change in the task at hand, is punctuated by a thousand little incidents which fill each day and make it a new story. But directed changes in the work routine wound more often than they comfort. For pieceworkers they seem always to lead to lost salary, and no one wishes for them. Beyond that, they are often intrinsically wounding. The pervasive anxiety, the sense of never going quickly enough, that is present through every working moment becomes concentrated at the point at which the routine is broken, and when, as is often the case, one needs others to be able to continue—a supervisor, a shopkeeper, a regulator—the feeling of dependence, of powerlessness, and of counting for nothing in the eyes of those on whom one depends can become painful to the point of wringing tears from men as well as women. The continual possibility of such incidents, a stalled machine, a misplaced toolbox, and the like, far from diminishing the weight of the monotony, deprives it of the one remedy that is generally inherent to it, the power to lull consciousness so that the worker becomes insensitive to pain. Anxiety restores that sensitivity and obliges the worker to remain aware of his condition, although the awareness of it is unbearable.

Nothing is worse than a mixture of monotony and accident. They feed on each other, at least when accident is an occasion for anxiety, which in a factory it always is. Accident has no status there. The crates in which the finished parts are to be boxed are never missing, the foreman never keeps the worker waiting, and every slowdown in production is the fault of the worker. The worker has to be in a state of constant readiness, following the monotonous progress of movements rather than being lulled by them, so that he can find within himself the resources to cope with the unexpected. His obligations are contradictory, impossible, and dehabilitating. The body may be exhausted at night, when it is time to leave the factory, but the mind is more so and invariably so. Whoever has experienced this exhaustion can read it in the eyes of the workers who emerge from the factory after their day is done. How one would like to be able to set aside his spirit upon entering, like a punch card, and take it back intact upon leaving! But the opposite occurs. One brings it with him into the factory, where it is abused; by evening, there is little of it left, and leisure hours must be spent spiritlessly.

Workers can find joy in their work, sometimes at the expense of their pay: a precious moment of cameraderie, a problem to be solved, an obstacle overcome, opportunities acted on through their own initiative. But such joys are likely to remain incomplete because rarely are there people, whether fellow laborers or supervisors, who appreciate the worth of what the worker has accomplished. Supervisors, like workers, busy themselves with what has been produced rather than with what has had to be done to produce it. Their indifference is the opposite of human warmth. It is not a climate in which human beings can thrive. Anyone would feel lonely in a place where it is understood that one is only what one is doing; where the manner in which one does it is irrelevant. Because of this, the joys of work are relegated to unformulated impressions, fugitive, disappearing as soon as they are born. The workers' cameraderie, not successful in sustaining itself, remains an imperfect passing fancy, and the supervisors are not men who guide and lead other men, but organs of impersonal subordination, as brutal and cold as iron. The supervisor may intervene, but only sometimes, and this reprieve through his whim, mixing impersonal brutality and caprice, far from improving things, aggravates them.

Shops, markets, and stock exchanges are not the only places in which products of work are all that is taken into account; not the only places where the labor which has created them is altogether ignored. Coorperation, comprehension, and a shared appreciation of other people's work are not possible in the factory. Their joys are monopolized by those in loftier positions. At the worker's level, the relationships established between various jobs and functions are relationships between things, not relationships between people. The parts circulate with their slips of paper, an indication of name, of form, of primary material; one could almost believe that the parts were the citizens of the place, and that the workers were the interchangeable parts. It is as if the parts were there by right. When it is necessary, as it is in many large factories, for the worker to show an identity card upon entering, he will find himself photographed with a number on his chest, like a convict. The contrast is a poignant and painful one.

Objects play the role of men, men play the role of objects; this is the root of evil. There are many different jobs in a factory: the fitter in a machine shop, for example, who makes molds for printing presses, marvels of ingenuity, difficult to fashion, always different—he does not lose anything by entering the factory, but his case is rare. Much more numerous are those in large factories, and even in many small ones, who carry out at full speed, in a specified order, five or six indefinitely repeated simple actions, about one per second, with no respite but a few anxious races to look for a tool box, a regulator, other papers, until their supervisor comes to take them away like objects and put them in front of another machine; they will stay there until someone moves them elsewhere. They are as much things as a human being can bear to be, but things that are not allowed to put their consciousness altogether aside, since it is always necessary for them to be able to face the unexpected. The succession of their actions is not denoted, in the factory's language, by the word "rhythm," but by "cadence," and this is fair because what they do is the opposite of a rhythm. Any series of movements that can be called beautiful and can be carried out without a loss of dignity requires instants of pause, perhaps as brief as a flash of lightning. It is those pauses which are the secret of rhythm and give the spectator, even when he sees movements as quick as any in the factory, the impression of slowness. The sprinter, at the moment when he breaks a world record, seems to glide slowly, while one sees mediocre runners hurrying far behind him; the more quickly a harvester swings his scythe, the more those who watch him have the impression that he is taking his time. On the contrary, machine-paced work nearly always gives the impression of miserable hurriedness from which all grace and dignity are absent. It is natural for a human being to stop when he has made something, even if only for a moment, in order to take note of it, as God did in Genesis. It is these flashes of immobility, of contemplation, and of equilibrium that it is necessary to eliminate if one is to survive in the factory.

The factory worker's cadence requires that the actions of one moment are followed by a second, uninterruptedly, like the ticking of a clock, with nothing to notice when something is finished and something else is begun. This ticking, a monotonous moan, intolerable to listen to for very long, suggests a kind of sleep, but one must tolerate it without sleeping. It is not merely painful. If its only consequence were suffering, it would be less evil than it is. Every human action requires a motive which provides the energy necessary to accomplish it, and it is good or bad depending on whether the motive is heroic or base. To yield to the exhausting passivity that is necessary in the factory, one must motivate oneself. There are no whips, no chains. Whips and chains might make the transformation easier. The organization of the work excludes all motivations except the fear of reprimand and dismissal, the urgently felt need to make more money, and, sometimes, a diversionary interest in speed records. Everything is done to make these workers stop thinking; to transform their thoughts into obsessions. The worker is never called to anything higher. He must become obsessed if he is to be efficient enough to do his job. When he is reduced to such motives, his thought is retracted to a fixed point in time so as to avoid unnecessary pain, and his consciousness fades as much as the demands of the work will permit. An almost irresistible force, comparable to gravity, then blocks an awareness of other human beings, like him in pain, like him at work, and nearby. It is almost impossible not to become indifferent and brutal, mirroring the system in which one is trapped; and reciprocally, the brutality of the system is reflected and made sensible by the gestures, the looks, and the words of those who people it. After a day passed in this manner, a worker has nothing but a sigh, a sigh which does not reach the ears of those who are strangers to the factory floor, and does not tell them anything even if it does reach them. He has had a long day.

Time drags on. He lives in unending exile. He has spent his day in a place where he cannot feel at home. The machines and the parts to be machined are very much at home. To repeat, he is allowed into this place only in order to bring these machines and these parts together. They are what he is there to care about, not himself. Perversely, it is not rare to see a workshop where the supervisors are busy hurrying the workers, watching that they do not lift their heads even to exchange a glance, while piles of scrap iron rust in the courtyard. Nothing is more bitter.

Whether the factory is productively efficient or not, the worker will feel himself to be an alien there. A man will find it compelling to appropriate, not materially or juridically, but in thought, the places and objects with which he spends his life. A cook says ''my kitchen,'' a gardener says ''my lawn,'' and this is as it should be. Legal property is one of the ways to create this feeling, and the perfect social organization would be one which, by the use of this and other methods, would give a proprietary feeling to all human beings. A worker, except in rare cases, cannot regard anything in the factory as belonging to him in this way. The machines are not his. He uses one or the other depending on which order he receives. He serves them. He does not make them serve him. They are not for him a means of creating something. He is there to make sure that they are fed the materials they require. The relationship between what he is doing and what else is being done at that place remains a mystery to him.

The Social Structure
of Managerial Work

ROBERT JACKALL

I

The hierarchical authority structure that is the linchpin of bureaucracy dominates the way managers think about their world and about themselves. Managers do not see or experience authority in any abstract way; instead, authority is embodied in their personal relationships with their immeidate bosses and in their perceptions of similar links between other managers up and down the hierarchy. When managers describe their work to an outsider, they almost always first say: "I work for [Bill James]" or "I report to [Harry Mills]" or "I'm in [Joe Bell's] group,"[1] and only then proceed to describe their actual work functions. Such a personalized statement of authority relationships seems to contradict classical notions of how bureaucracies function but it exactly reflects the way authority is structured, exercised, and experienced in corporate hierarchies.

American businesses typically both centralize and decentralize authority. Power is concentrated at the top in the person of the chief executive officer (CEO) and is simultaneously decentralized; that is, responsibility for decisions and profits is pushed as far down the organizational line as possible. For example, Alchemy Inc. is one of several operating companies of Covenant Corporation. When I began my research, Alchemy employed 11,000 people; Covenant had over 50,000 employees and now has over 100,000. Like the other operating companies, Alchemy has its own president, executive vice-presidents, vice-presidents, other executive officers, business area managers, staff divisions, and more than eighty manufacturing plants scattered throughout the country and indeed the world producing a wide range of specialty and commodity chemicals. Each operating company is, at least theoretically, an autonomous, self-sufficient organization, though they are all monitored and coordinated by a central corporate staff, and each president reports directly to the corporate CEO. Weft Corporation has its corporate headquarters and manufacturing facilities in the South; its marketing and sales offices, along with some key executive personnel, are in New York City. Weft employs 20,000 people, concentrated in the firm's three textile divisions that have always been and remain its core business. The Apparel Division produces seven million yards a week of raw, unfinished cloth in several greige (colloquially gray) mills, mostly for sale to garment manufacturers; the Consumer Division produces some cloth of its own in several greige mills and also finishes—that is, bleaches, dyes, prints, and sews—twelve million yards of raw cloth a month into purchasable items like sheets, pillowcases, and tablecloths for department stores and chain stores; and the Retail Division operates an import-export business, specializing in the quick turnaround of the fast-moving cloths desired by Seventh Avenue designers. Each division has a president who reports to one of several executive vice-presidents, who in turn report to the corporate CEO. The divisional structure is typically less elaborate in its hierarchical ladder than the framework of independent operating companies; it is also somewhat more dependent on corporate staff for essential services. However, the basic principle of simultaneous centralization and decentralization prevails and both Covenant and Weft consider their companies or divisions, as the case may be, "profit centers." Even Images Inc., while much smaller than the industrial concerns and organized like most service businesses according to shifting groupings of client accounts supervised by senior vice-presidents, uses the notion of profit centers.

The key interlocking mechanism of this structure is its reporting system. Each manager gathers up the profit targets or other objectives of his or her subordinates and, with these, formulates his commitments to his boss; this boss takes these commitments and those of his other subordinates, and in turn makes a commitment to his boss.[2] At the top of the line, the president of each company or division, or, at Images Inc., the senior vice-president for a group of accounts, makes his commitment to the CEO. This may be done directly, or sometimes, as at Weft Corporation, through a corporate executive vice-president. In any event, the commitments made to top management depend on the pyramid of stated objectives given to superiors up the line. At each level of the structure, there is typically "topside" pressure to achieve higher goals and, of course, the CEO frames and paces the whole process by applying pressure for attainment of his own objectives. Meanwhile, bosses and subordinates down the line engage in a series of intricate negotiations—managers often call these "conspiracies"—to keep their commitments respectable but achievable.

This "management-by-objective" system, as it is usually called, creates a chain of commitments from the CEO down to the lowliest product manager or account executive. In practice, it also shapes a patrimonial authority arrangement that is crucial to defining both the immediate experiences and the long-run career chances of individual managers. In this world, a subordinate owes fealty principally to his immediate boss. This means that a subordinate must not overcommit his boss, lest his boss "get on the hook" for promises that cannot be kept. He must keep his boss from making mistakes, particularly public ones; he must keep his boss informed, lest his boss get "blindsided." If one has a mistake-prone boss, there is, of course, always the temptation to let him make a fool of himself, but the wise subordinate knows that this carries two dangers—he himself may get done in by his boss's errors, and, perhaps more important, other managers will view with the gravest suspicion a subordinate who withholds crucial information from his boss even if they think the boss is a nincompoop. A subordinate must also not circumvent his boss nor ever give the appearance of doing so. He must never contradict his boss's judgment in public. To violate the last admonition is thought to constitute a kind of death wish in business, and one who does so should practice what one executive calls "flexibility drills," an exercise "where you put your head between your legs and kiss your ass goodbye." On a social level, even though an easy, breezy, first-name informality is the prevalent style of American business, a concession perhaps to our democratic heritage and egalitarian rhetoric, the subordinate must extend to the boss a certain ritual deference. For instance, he must follow the boss's lead in conversation, must not speak out of turn at meetings, must laugh at his boss's jokes while not making jokes of his own that upstage his boss, must not rib the boss for his foibles. The shrewd subordinate learns to efface himself, so that his boss's face might shine more clearly.

In short, the subordinate must symbolically reinforce at every turn his own subordination and his willing acceptance of the obligations of fealty. In return, he can hope for those perquisites that are in his boss's gift—the better, more attractive secretaries, or the nudging of a movable panel to enlarge his office, and perhaps a couch to fill the added space, one of the real distinctions in corporate bureaucracies. He can hope to be elevated when and if the boss is elevated, though other important criteria intervene here. He can also expect protection for mistakes made, up to a point. However, that point is never exactly defined and depends on the complicated politics of each situation. The general rule is that bosses are expected to protect those in their bailiwicks. Not to do so, or to be unable to do so, is taken as a sign of untrustworthiness or weakness. If, however, subordinates make mistakes that are thought to be dumb, or especially if they violate fealty obligations—for example, going around their boss—then abandonment of them to the vagaries of organizational forces is quite acceptable.

Overlaying and intertwined with this formal monocratic system of authority, with its patrimonial resonance, are patron-client relationships. Patrons are usually powerful figures in the higher echelons of management. The patron might be a manager's direct boss, or his boss's boss, or someone several levels higher in the chain of command. In either case, the manager is still bound by the immediate, formal authority and fealty patterns of his position but he also acquires new, though more ambiguous, fealty relationships with his highest-ranking patron. Patrons play a crucial role in advancement, a point that I shall discuss later.

It is characteristic of this authority system that details are pushed down and credit is pulled up. Superiors do not like to give detailed instructions to subordinates. The official reason for this is to maximize subordinates' autonomy. The underlying reason is, first, to get rid of tedious details. Most hierarchically organized occupations follow this pattern; one of the privileges of authority is the divestment of humdrum intricacies. This also insulated higher bosses from the peculiar pressures that accompany managerial work at the middle levels and below; the lack of economy over one's time because of continual interruption from one's subordinates, telephone calls from customers and clients, and necessary meetings with colleagues; the piecemeal fragmentation of issues both because of the discontinuity of events and because of the way subordinates filter news; and the difficulty of minding the store while sorting out sometimes unpleasant personnel issues. Perhaps more important, pushing details down protects the privilege of authority to declare that a mistake has been made. A high-level executive in Alchemy Inc. explains:

> If I tell someone what to do—like do A, B, or C—the inference and implication is that he will succeed in accomplishing the objective. Now, if he doesn't succeed, that means that I have invested part of myself in his work and I lose any right I have to chew his ass out if he doesn't succeed. If I tell you what to do, I can't bawl you out if things don't work. And this is why a lot of bosses don't give explicit directions. They just give a statement of objectives, and then they can criticize subordinates who fail to make their goals.

Moreover, pushing down details relieves superiors of the burden of too much knowledge, particularly guilty knowledge. A superior will say to a subordinate, for instance: "Give me your best thinking on the problem with [X]." When the subordinate makes his report, he is often told: "I think you can do better than that," until the subordinate has worked out all the details of the boss's predetermined solution, without the boss being specifically aware of "all the eggs that have to be broken." It is also not at all uncommon for very bald and extremely general edicts to emerge from on high. For example, "Sell the plant in [St. Louis]; let me know when you've struck a deal," or "We need to get higher prices for [fabric X]; see what you can work out," or "Tom, I want you to go down there and meet with those guys and make a deal and I don't want you to come back until you've got one." This pushing down of details has important consequences.

First, because they are unfamiliar with—indeed deliberately distance themselves from— entangling details, corporate higher echelons tend to expect successful results without messy complications. This is central to top executives' well-known aversion to bad news and to the resulting tendency to kill the messenger who bears the news.

Second, the pushing down of details creates great pressure on middle managers not only to transmit good news but, precisely because they know the details, to act to protect their corporations, their bosses, and themselves in the process. They become the "point men" of a given strategy and the potential "fall guys" when things go wrong. From an organizational standpoint, overly conscientious managers are particularly useful at the middle levels of the structure. Upwardly mobile men and women, especially those from working-class origins who find themselves in higher-status milieux, seem to have the requisite level of anxiety, and perhaps tightly controlled anger and hostility, that fuels an obsession with detail. Of course, such conscientiousness is not necessarily, and is certainly not systematically, rewarded; the real organizational premiums are placed on other, more flexible, behavior.

Credit flows up in this structure and is usually appropriated by the highest-ranking officer involved in a successful decision or resolution of a problem. There is, for instance, a tremendous competition for ideas in the corporate world; authority provides a license to steal ideas, even in front of those who originated them. Chairmen routinely appropriate the useful suggestions made by members of their committees or task forces; research directors build their reputations for scientific wizardry on the bricks laid down by junior researchers and directors of departments. Presidents of whole divisions as well are always on the lookout for "fresh ideas" and "creative approaches" that they can claim as their own in order to put themselves "out in front" of their peers. A subordinate whose ideas are appropriated is expected to be a good sport about the matter; not to balk at so being used is one attribute of the good team player. The person who appropriates credit redistributes it as he chooses, bound essentially and only by a sensitivity to public perceptions of his fairness. One gives credit, therefore, not necessarily where it is due, although one always invokes this old saw, but where prudence dictates. Customarily, people who had nothing to do with the success of a project can be allocated credit for their exemplary efforts. At the middle levels, there-fore, credit for a particular idea or success is always a type of refracted social honor; one cannot claim credit even if it is earned. Credit has to be given, and acceptance of the gift implicitly involves a reaffirmation and strengthening of fealty. A superior may share some credit with subordinates in order to deepen fealty relationships and induce greater efforts on his behalf. Of course, a different system obtains in the allocation of blame.

Because of the interlocking character of the commitment system, a CEO carries enormous influence in his corporation. If, for a moment, one thinks of the presidents of operating companies or divisions as barons, then the CEO of the corporation is the king. His word is law; even the CEO's wishes and whims are taken as commands by close subordinates on the corporate staff, who turn them into policies and directives. A typical example occurred in Weft Corporation a few years ago when the CEO, new at the time, expressed mild concern about the rising operating costs of the company's fleet of rented cars. The following day, a stringent system for monitoring mileage replaced the previous casual practice. Managers have a myriad of aphorisms that refer to how the power of CEOs, magnified through the zealous efforts of subordinates, affects them. These range from the trite "When he sneezes, we all catch colds" to the more colorful "When he says 'Go to the bathroom,' we all get the shits."

Great efforts are made to please the CEO. For example, when the CEO of Covenant Corporation visits a plant, the most significant order of business for local management is a fresh paint job, even when, as in several cases, the cost of paint alone exceeds $100,000. If a paint job has already been scheduled at a plant, it is deferred along with all other cosmetic maintenance until just before the CEO arrives; keeping up appearances without recognition for one's efforts is pointless. I am told that similar anecdotes from other corporations have been in circulation since 1910, which suggests a certain historical continuity of behavior toward top bosses.

The second order of business for the plant management is to produce a book fully describing the plant and its operations, replete with photographs and illus-trations, for presentation to the CEO; such a book costs about $10,000 for the single copy. By any standards of budgetary stringency, such expenditures are irrational. But by the social standards of the corporation, they make perfect sense. It is far more important to please the king today than to worry about the future economic state of one's fief, since, if one does not please the king, there may not be a fief to worry about or indeed vassals to do the worrying.

By the same token, all of this leads to an intense interest in everything the CEO does and says. In all the companies that I studied, the most common topic of conversation among managers up and down the line is speculation about their respective CEO's plans, intentions, strategies, actions, style, public image, and ideological leanings of the moment. Even the metaphorical temper of a CEO's language finds its way down the hierarchy to the lower reaches of an organization. In the early stages of my fieldwork at Covenant Corporation, for example, I was puzzled by the inordinately widespread usage of nautical terminology, especially in a corporation located in a landlocked site. As it happens, the CEO is devoted to sailboats and prefers that his aides call him "Skipper." Moreover, in every corporation that I studied, stories and rumors circulate constantly about the social world of the CEO and his immediate subordinates—who, for instance, seems to have the CEO's ear at the moment; whose style seems to have gained approbation; who, in short, seems to be in the CEO's grace and who seems to have fallen out of favor. In the smaller and more intimate setting of Images Inc., the circulation of favor takes an interesting, if unusual, tack. There, the CEO is known for attaching younger people to himself as confidants. He solicits their advice, tells them secrets, gets their assessments of developments further down in the hierarchy, gleans the rumors and gossip making the rounds about himself. For the younger people selected for such attention, this is a rare, if fleeting, opportunity to have a place in the sun and to share the illusion if not the substance of power. In time, of course, the CEO tires of or becomes disappointed with particular individuals and turns his attention to others. "Being discarded," however, is not an obstacle to regaining favor. In larger organizations, impermeable structural barriers between top circles and junior people prevent this kind of intimate interchange and circulation of authoritative regard. Within a CEO's circle, however, the same currying and granting of favor prevails, always amidst conjectures from below about who has edged close to the throne.

But such speculation about the CEO and his leanings of the moment is more than idle gossip, and the courtlike atmosphere that I am describing more than stylized diversion. Because he stands at the apex of the corporation's bureaucratic and patrimonial structures and locks the intricate system of commitments between bosses and subordinates into place, it is the CEO who ultimately decides whether those commitments have been satisfactorily met. The CEO becomes the actual and the symbolic keystone of the hierarchy that constitutes the defining point of the managerial experience. Moreover, the CEO and his trusted associates determine the fate of whole business areas of a corporation.

Within the general ambiance established by a CEO, presidents of individual operating companies or of divisions carry similar, though correspondingly reduced, influence within their own baronies. Adroit and well-placed subordinates can, for instance, borrow a president's prestige and power to exert great leverage. Even chance encounters or the occasional meeting or lunch with the president can, if advertised casually and subtly, cause notice and the respect among other managers that comes from uncertainty. Knowledge of more clearly established relationships, of course, always sways behavior. A middle manager in one company, widely known to be a very close personal friend of the president, flagged her copious memoranda to other managers with large green paperclips, ensuring prompt attention to her requests. More generally, each major division of the core textile group in Weft Corporation is widely thought to reflect the personality of its leader—one hard-driving, intense, and openly competitive; one cool, precise, urbane, and proper; and one gregarious, talkative, and self-promotional. Actually, market exigencies play a large role in shaping each division's tone and tempo. Still, the popular conception of the dominance of presidential personalities not only points to the crucial issue of style in business, a topic to be explored in depth later, but it underlines the general tendency to personalize authority in corporate bureaucracies.

Managers draw elaborate cognitive maps to guide them through the thickets of their organizations. Because they see and experience authority in such personal terms, the singular feature of these maps is their biographical emphasis. Managers carry around in their heads thumbnail sketches of the occupational history of virtually every other manager of their own rank or higher in their particular organization. These maps begin with a knowledge of others' occupational expertise and specific work experience, but focus especially on previous and present reporting relationships, patronage relationships, and alliances. Cognitive maps incorporate memories of social slights, of public embarrassments, of battles won and lost, and of people's behavior under pressure. They include as well general estimates of the abilities and career trajectories of their colleagues. I should mention that these latter estimates are not necessarily accurate or fair; they are, in fact, often based on the flimsiest of evidence. For instance, a general manager at Alchemy Inc. describes the ephemeral nature of such opinions:

> It's a feeling about the guy's perceived ability to run a business—like he's not a good people man, or he's not a good numbers man. This is not a quantitative thing. It's a gut feeling that a guy can't be put in one spot, but he might be put in another spot. These kinds of informal opinions about others are the lifeblood of an organization's advancement system. Oh, for the record, we've got the formal evaluations; but the real opinions—the ones that really count in determining people's fates—are those which are traded back and forth in meetings, private conferences, chance encounters, and so on.

Managers trade estimates of others' chances within their circles and often color them to suit their own purposes. This is one reason why it is crucial for the aspiring young manager to project the right image to the right people who can influence others' sketches of him. Whatever the accuracy of these vocabularies of description, managers' penchant for biographical detail and personal histories contrasts sharply with their disinclination for details in general or for other kinds of history. Details, as I have mentioned, get pushed down the ladder; and a concern with history, even of the short-run, let alone long-term, structural shifts in one's own organization, constrains the forward orientation and cheerful optimism highly valued in most corporations. Biographical detail, however, constitutes crucial knowledge because managers know that, in the rough-and-tumble politics of the corporate world, individual fates are made and broken not necessarily by one's accomplishments but by other people.

One must appreciate the simultaneously monocratic and patrimonial character of business bureaucracies in order to grasp the personal and organizational significance of political struggles in managerial work. As it happens, political struggles are a constant and recurring feature in business, shaping managers' experience and outlooks in fundamental ways. Of course, such conflicts are usually cloaked by typically elaborate organizational rhetorics of harmony and teamwork. However, one can observe the multiple dimensions of these conflicts during periods of organizational upheaval, a regular feature of American business where mergers, buyouts, divestitures, and especially "organizational restructuring" have become commonplace occurrences. As Karl Mannheim, among others, has pointed out, it is precisely when a social order begins to fall apart that one can discern what has held it together in the first place. A series of shake-ups that occurred in Covenant Corporation, all within a period of a few years, present a focused case study of political processes basic to all big corporations.

II

In 1979, a new CEO took power in Covenant Corporation. The first action of most new CEOS is some form of organizational change. On the one hand, this prevents the inheritance of blame for past mistakes; on the other, it projects an image of bare-knuckled aggressiveness much appreciated on Wall Street. Perhaps most important, a shake-up rearranges the fealty structure of the corporation, placing in power those barons whose style and public image mesh closely with that of the new CEO and whose principal loyalties belong to him. Shortly after the new CEO of Covenant was named, he reorganized the whole business, after a major management consulting firm had "exhaustively considered all the options," and personally selected new presidents to head each of the five newly formed companies of the corporation—Alchemy, Energy, Metals, Electronics, and Instruments. He ordered the presidents to carry out a thorough reorganization of their separate companies complete with extensive "census reduction," or firing as many people as possible. The presidents were given, it was said, a free hand in their efforts, although in retrospect it seems that the CEO insisted on certain high-level appointments.

The new president of Alchemy Inc.—let's call him Smith[3]—had risen from a marketing background in a small but important specialty chemicals division in the former company. Specialty chemicals are produced in relatively small batches and command high prices, showing generous profit margins; they depend on customer loyalty and therefore on the adroit cultivation of buyers through professional marketing. Upon promotion to president, Smith reached back into his former division, indeed back to his own past work in a particular product line, and systematically elevated many of his former colleagues, friends, clients, and allies. Powerful managers in other divisions, particularly in a rival process chemicals division, whose commodity products, produced in hugh quantities, were sold only by price and who exemplified an old-time "blood, guts, and courage" management style were forced to take big demotions in the new power structure; put on "special assignment"—the corporate euphemism for Siberia, sent to a distant corner office where one looks for a new job (the saying is: "No one ever comes back from special assignment"); fired; or given "early retirement," a graceful way of doing the same thing. What happened in Alchemy Inc. was typical of the pattern in the other companies of the conglomerate. Hundreds of people throughout the whole corporation lost their jobs in what became known as "Bloody Thursday," the "October Revolution," or in some circles, the "Octoberfest." I shall refer back to this event as the "big purge."

Up and down the chemical company, former associates of Smith were placed in virtually every important position. Managers in the company saw all of this as an inevitable fact of life. In their view, Smith simply picked those managers with whom he was comfortable. The whole reorganization could easily have gone in a completely different direction had another CEO been named, or had the one selected picked someone besides Smith, or had Smith come from a different work group in the old organization. Fealty is the mortar of the corporate hierarchy, but the removal of one well-placed stone loosens the mortar throughout the pyramid. And no one is ever quite sure, until after the fact, just how the pyramid will be put back together.

The year after the "big purge," Alchemy prospered and met its financial commitments to the CEO, the crucial coin of the realm to purchase continued autonomy. Smith consolidated his power and, through the circle of the mostly like-minded and like-mannered men and women with whom he surrounded himself, further weeded out or undercut managers with whom he felt uncomfortable. At the end of the year, the mood in the company was buoyant not only because of high profits but because of the expectation of massive deregulation and boom times for business following President Reagan's first election. On the day after the election, by the way, managers, in an unusual break with normal decorum, actually danced in the corridors.

What follows might be read as a cautionary tale on the perils of triumph in a probationary world where victory must follow victory. Elated by his success in 1980, and eager to make a continued mark with the CEO vis-à-vis the presidents of the other four companies, all of whom were vying for the open presidency of Covenant Corporation, Smith became the victim of his own upbeat marketing optimism. He overcommitted himself and the chemical company financially for the coming year just as the whole economy began to slide into recession. By mid-1981, profit targets had to be readjusted down and considerable anxiety pervaded Smith's circle and the upper-middle levels of management, whose job it became both to extract more profits from below and to maintain a public facade of cheerful equanimity. A top executive at Alchemy Inc. describes this anxiety:

> See, the problem with any change of CEO is that any credibility you have built up with the previous guy all goes by the board and you have to begin from scratch. This CEO thinks that everybody associated with the company before him is a dummy. And so you have to prove yourself over and over again. You can't just win some and lose

some. You have to keep your winning record at least at 75 percent if not better. You're expected to take risks. At least the CEO says that, but the reality is that people are afraid to make mistakes.

Toward the end of the year, it became clear that the chemical company would reach only 60 percent of its profit target and that only by remarkable legerdemain with the books. Publicly, of course, managers continued to evince a "cautious optimism" that things would turn around; privately, however, a deepening sense of gloom and incipient panic pervaded the organization. Stories began to circulate about the CEO's unhappiness with the company's shortfall. To take but one example, managers in chemical fertilizers were told by the CEO never again to offer weather conditions or widespread farmer bankruptcy as excuses for lagging sales. Rumors of every sort began to flourish, and a few of these are worth recounting.

Smith was on his way out, it was feared, and would take the whole structure of Alchemy Inc. with him. In fact, one of the CEO's most trusted troubleshooters, a man who "eats people for breakfast," was gunning for Smith and his job. (This man distinguished himself around this time by publicly accusing those who missed a 9:00 A.M. staff meeting, held during one of the worst snowstorms in two decades, of being disloyal to Covenant.)

Smith would survive, it was said, but would be forced to sacrifice all of his top people, alter his organization's structure, and buckle under to the increasingly vigorous demands of the CEO.

The CEO, it was argued, was about to put the whole chemical company on the block; in fact, the real purpose of creating supposedly self-contained companies in the first place might have been to package them for sale. At the least, the CEO would sell large portions of Alchemy Inc., wreaking havoc with its support groups at corporate headquarters.

There were disturbing rumors too about the growth of personal tension and animosity between Smith and the CEO. The CEO was well known for his propensity for lording it over his subordinates, a behavioral pattern that often emerges in top authority figures after years of continual suppression of impulses. He was now said to have targeted Smith for this kind of attention. Managers up and down the line knew instinctively that, if the personal relationship between Smith and the CEO were eroding, the inevitable period of blame and retribution for the bad financial year might engulf everyone, and not just well-targeted individuals. Managers began to mobilize their subordinates to arrange defenses, tried to cement crucial alliances, and waited. In the meantime, they joked that they were updating their résumés and responding graciously to the regular phone calls of headhunters.

While reorganizations by CEOs have the broadest impact in a corporation, such shake-ups are not made by CEOs alone. Shake-ups are in fact the first line of defense against a CEO's demands by presidents of operating companies or divisions in trouble. At Alchemy Inc., invoking a commissioned study by management consultants, Smith eliminated a layer of top management early in 1982 to give himself and his top aides "greater access to the business areas." In the process, he got rid of Brown, the chemical company's executive vice-president. Brown was an anomaly in the higher circles of the company. Although his formal training had been in marketing, he had ended up performing a financial function in the executive vice-president slot—that is, riding herd on business managers about costs. His principal rise had been through the old specialty chemicals division; however, his original roots in the corporation were in the Energy Division where he had been a friend and close associate of the man who later rose to the presidency of that company in the "big purge." This biographical history made Brown suspect, especially when the tension between the CEO and Smith intensified and some of the presidents of the other companies were thought to be seizing the chance to extend their own influence. Brown's straitlaced personal style was also out of keeping with the back-slapping bonhomie that marked Smith's inner circle. Managers often note that one must stay at least three drinks behind one's boss at social functions; this meant that Brown's subordinates might never drink at all on such occasions. As it happens, however, the CEO, himself a financial man, saved Brown and appointed him an executive vice-president of the electronics company, in charge of what had become known as the "corporate graveyard," a place with decaying businesses that one buries by selling off.

Many managers were amused at Brown's reassignment. They felt that, as soon as he had succeeded in disposing of the unwanted businesses, he would be out of a job. He was, in effect, being told to dig his own grave in an appropriate location. Some managers, however, were more wary; they saw the move as a complicated gambit, in fact as a cover-up by the CEO himself who had invested heavily in several businesses in the electronics area only to have them expire. In any case, Brown had not been popular at Alchemy and his departure was greeted, as one manager describes it, "by a lot of people standing on the sidelines, hooting, and hollering, and stamping our feet. We never thought we'd see old [Brown] again."

In Brown's place, Smith appointed two executive vice-presidents, one a trusted aide from his favorite product group in the old specialty chemicals division and the other an outsider whose expertise was, it was said, in selling off commodity businesses, that is, what was left of the old process chemicals division. Though badly scarred, Smith managed to deflect blame for the bad year onto the heads of a few general managers, all from the old process division, whom he fired. One ominous note was Smith's loss of administrative control of the corporate headquarters site, a function that had fallen to the chemical company during the "big purge." A fundamental rule of corporate politics is that one never cedes control over assets, even if the assets are administrative headaches. More ominous was the CEO's gift of responsibility for headquarters to the man "who eats people for breakfast," mentioned earlier. On the whole, however, managers felt that not only had Smith reasserted the supremacy of his own alliances but that he had in the bargain bought himself eight months—time enough perhaps for the economy to turn around.

As it happened, however, the economy continued to worsen and the CEO's pressure on Smith increased. In the late spring of 1982, the CEO began sending a series of terse notes to company executives accompanied by photocopied articles written by a well-known management consultant in the *Wall Street Journal* about the necessity of trimming staff to streamline operations. Only companies that aggressively cut staff during the recession, the articles argued, would emerge lean and poised for the economic recovery. The CEO's notes usually said simply: "This article merits your careful attention." Smith's aides privately referred to the CEO as a "tinhorn tyrant" and muttered about his "henchmen" being sent to extract information from them to be used against Smith. One executive describes the chemical company's growing feeling toward corporate staff: "The boys he [the CEO] has over there are not very nice . . . they never miss a chance to stomp on you when you're down." As time passed, this feeling became more acerbic. Another executive describes how he sees "internal auditors," that is, the CEO's people who were overlooking Alchemy's operations:

> Have I ever told you my definition of an auditor? An auditor is someone who situates himself up on a hill overlooking a battle, far from the noise of the guns and the smoke of the explosions. And he watches the battle from afar, and when it is over and the smoke is cleared, he goes down onto the battlefield and walks among the wounded. And he shoots them.

Finally, in the early summer, the CEO demanded a 30 percent cut in staff in the chemical company, even asking for the names of those to be terminated. Smith had little choice but to go along and he fired 200 people. Most of these, however, were technical support people, Indians rather than chiefs. Smith was thus able to maintain a basic rule of management circles, namely that management takes care of itself, at least of other known managers, in good times and bad.

As the economy continued to flounder throughout the summer, Alchemy's earnings dipped even further, and the CEO's demands on Smith became relentless. By this point, the watchword in the corporation had become "manage for cash" and the CEO wanted some businesses sold, others cut back, still others milked, and costs slashed. Particular attention began to be focused on the chemical company's environmental protection staff, a target of hostility not only from the CEO's people but from line managers within Alchemy itself. In response to an environmental catastrophe in the late 1970s, and to the public outrage about chemical pollution in general, Smith had erected, upon his ascendancy to the presidency, an elaborate and relatively free-roaming envirnomental staff. Though costly, Smith felt that this apparatus was the best defense against another severely embarrassing and even more expensive environmental debacle. The company had, in fact, won an industrial award and wide public recognition for its program; the CEO himself, of course, had been a principal beneficiary of all this public praise and he basked in that attention. But, as the political atmosphere in the country changed with the conservative legislative, budgetary, and regulatory triumphs after President Reagan's election, line managers in Alchemy began chafing under staff intrusions. They blamed the environmental staff for creating extra work and needless costs during a period of economic crisis. The CEO agreed with these sentiments, and his opinion helped deepen the splits in the chemical company. In the early fall, faced with unremitting pressure because of the company's declining fortunes, internal warring factions, and, worse, the prospect of public capitulation to the CEO on the structure of his supposedly autonomous company, Smith chose to resign to "pursue other interests," pulling the cord on his "golden parachute" (a fail-safe plan ensuring comfortable financial landing) as he left.

His parting letter to the company typifies the peculiar combination of in-house humor, personal jauntiness in the face of adversity, and appeals to some of the classical legitimations of managerial work that one may observe among high-ranking managers. It reads in part:

> Hi!
>
> Someone from the stockroom just called and said there were reams of my stationery left downstairs—what did I want to do with it? Not only have I relocated myself to a distant corner office, but it appears that I've also freed up space on the stockroom shelves as well! Since I will be leaving on October 15, I want to take this opportunity to thank each and every one of you for the never-failing support and understanding you have given me throughout my years with [Alchemy]. I have had the privilege of knowing many of you personally, and the greatest satisfaction in my job here has been, throughout the years, to be able to walk down the hall and have so many of you say "Hi, [Joe]."
>
> I would like to invite you to have a drink with me after work on October 6th. My first inclination was that it would be great to pitch a tent in the front parking lot and have hotdogs, too, but somehow I don't think that one would fly. So the [nearby hotel] it is, and I promise you—no speeches, no presentations, no formalities. Just a chance to personally say thank you for being part of a great team—one that I will never forget.

It is important to note that many managers were deeply moved by Smith's letter and particularly by the social occasion to which he invited them. It became not only a farewell party for a fallen leader, but was seen as a small act of rebellion against the CEO.

Alchemy Inc. went into a state of shock and paralysis at Smith's resignation, and the rumor mills churned out names of possible replacements, each tied to a scenario of the future. Once again, the mortar of fealty loosened throughout the pyramid even as it bound managers to their pasts. Managers know that others' cognitive maps afford little escape from old loyalties, alliances, and associations. At the same time, they realize that they must be poised to make new alliances in a hurry if their areas get targeted for "restructuring."

As things turned out, a great many managers found themselves in exactly that position. To almost everyone's astonishment, and to the trepidation of many, the CEO brought Brown back from the electronics graveyard after a "thorough assessment of all the candidates," which took two days, and made him the new president of Alchemy. No laughter or jeering was heard in the corridors, although some wags suggested nominating Brown as the "Comeback Player of the Year." Whatever Brown's previous affiliations, there was no doubt about where his fealty now lay. He became known throughout the corporation as the "CEO's boy" and everyone recognized that he had a mandate to "wield a meat axe" and to wreak whatever mayhem was necessary to cut expenditures. At every level of the company, managers began furiously to scramble—writing position papers, holding rushed meetings, making deals—to try to secure their domains against the coming assault. Within a short time, Brown had fired 150 people, mostly at the managerial level, focusing particular attention on "streamlining" the environmental staff, slashing it by 75 percent. The survivors from the environmental staff were "moved close to the action," that is, subordinated to the business units, each of which was made more "free-standing," and thus the staff was effectively neutralized. The official rationale was as follows. The company had gone through an extraordinary learning experience on environmental issues and had benefited greatly from the expertise of the environmental staff. It had, however, by this point fully integrated and institutionalized that knowledge into its normal operations. Moreover, since there were no longer any environmental problems facing the company, a modest reduction in this area made good business sense. Privately, of course, the assessments were different. Brown himself said at a managerial meeting that good staff simply create work to justify their own existence. Many line managers echoed this opinion. More to the point, the feeling was that work on environmental issues had lost any urgency in the Reagan era. The Environmental Protection Agency (EPA) was dead. Moreover, the only real threat to corporations on environmental issues was in the courts, which, however, judge past actions, not present practices. By the time the courts get to cases generated by contemporary practices, typically in fifteen years, those executives presently in charge will have moved on, leaving any problems their policies might create to others. Managers noted, some ruefully, some with detached bemusement, the irony of organizational reform. The public outcry against Covenant after the environmental disaster of the late 1970s produced thoroughgoing internal reform designed to ward off such incidents in the future. But the reforms also unintentionally laid down the bases of resentment among managers who did not benefit from the staff increase. During a crisis, these managers grasped the chance to clamor for dismantling the safeguards that might prevent future catastrophes.

Brown's "housecleaning" created extreme anxiety throughout Alchemy. Even managers who agreed with Brown's attack on the staff and his wholesale pruning of other areas expressed astonishment and sometimes outrage that mostly persons of managerial rank had been fired. This seemed an ominous violation of the managerial code. Those that survived were "looking over their shoulders" and "listening for footsteps behind them." Bitter jokes circulated freely, like: "Opening Day at the chemical company; Brown comes in and throws out the first employee." Some managers even passed around among their colleagues a list of thirteen tough questions to throw at Brown at an internal news conference.

Throughout this entire period, the CEO had been pursuing an aggressive policy of acquisitions, picking up small and medium-sized companies and adding them to one or another of the operating companies' holdings. No one could discern the pattern of the acquisitions. High-technology industries with rapid growth potential were the officially stated targets; in fact, however, mostly mature businesses were purchased and unsuccessful bids were made for several others. Suddenly, in the midst of Alchemy's crisis, the CEO announced the acquisition, publicly called a merger, of another major corporation with mostly mature businesses and large, complicated corporate and company staffs. The announcement precipitated both consternation and excitement throughout Covenant Corporation; up and down the ladder of every company both line and staff managers began to mobilize their forces and to gear their troops for the inevitable and dangerous showdown with the personnel of the newly acquired firm. Showdowns following the acquisition of a smaller company are wholly predictable and are virtually no contest. The apprehension of Covenant managers in this case stemmed from their wariness of the bureaucratic battle skills of their opposite numbers in the firm acquired. Everything, of course, would depend on which leaders emerged from the crucible.

In the meantime, Alchemy Inc. staggered into the following year. Six months after the national economy took an upswing, its own fortunes began to improve, a typical pattern for industrial supply companies. Suddenly, in the spring of 1983, the CEO announced another major reorganization in order to integrate the newly acquired corporation, citing yet another thorough appraisal by a management consulting firm. Once again the entire corporation was divided into several "sectors," each section with different companies. This time, the Industrial Supplies Sector incorporated Alchemy, Metals, and Plastics. Brown did not get the call to head the whole Industrial Supplies Sector but remained as the president of Alchemy. The leadership of the whole sector fell instead to a man who had emerged out of the Metals company where he had been president in the old order. He in turn gave the presidencies of Metals and Plastics to metals people, and a new cycle of ascendancy with its own patterns of fealty, patronage, and power cliques began. Managers noted, with some satisfaction, the irony of Brown being passed over by the CEO for the sector presidency after performing the CEO's dirty work. Their satisfaction was short-lived. After a stint at the helm of chemicals, Brown returned to his original home in the corporation as the aide-de-camp of the president of the new Energy Sector—his old mentor. When the latter retired, Brown assumed control of that sector.

III

This sequence of events is remarkable only for its compactness. One need only regularly read the *Wall Street Journal*, the business section of the *New York Times*, any of the leading business magazines, let alone more academic publications, to see that these sorts of upheavals and political struggles are commonplace in American business. In Weft Corporation, one could observe exactly similar patterns, though played out over a much longer period of time. For instance, more than a decade ago, a new CEO was brought into the company to modernize and professionalize what had been up to that point a closely held family business. His first act was to make a rule that no executives over sixty years old could hold posts above a certain high-ranking management grade. In one stroke, he got rid of a whole cohort of executives who had ruled the company for a generation. He then staffed all key posts of each division, as well as his own inner circle, either with people who had served under him in the Army during World War II, or with whom he had worked in another corporation, or with former consultants who had advised him on how to proceed with the reorganization, or with people from the old organization with whom he felt comfortable. All of these managers in turn brought in their own recruits and protégés. They established a corporate order notable for its stability for many years. As the CEO and his subordinates grew older, of course, he eliminated the rule governing age. Eventually, however, retirement time did come. The new CEO was handpicked by the outgoing boss from the high reaches of another corporation where he had been vice-chairman and thus effectively dead-ended. He graciously bided his time until the old CEO had entirely left the scene and then moved decisively to shape the organization to his liking. The most important move in this regard was the rapid elevation of a man who had been a mere vice-president of personnel, normally the wasteland of the corporate world. Within a year of the new CEO's ascendancy, this manager was given control over all other staff functions. He then moved into an executive vice-president post as the closest aide and confidant to the CEO on the Central Management Committee, with decisive say-so over financial issues and thus over operations. Tough, seasoned managers in the operating divisions—men and women of great drive and ambition—began to see their own chances for future ascendancy possibly blocked. Many began to depart the corporation. The posts of those who left were filled by men and women whose loyalties and futures lay with the new regime. Thus, the compressed sequence of events at Covenant Corporation simply allows one to be particularly attentive to ongoing, and usually taken for granted, structural and psychological patterns of corporate life.

Here I want to highlight a few of these basic structures and experiences of managerial work, those that seem to form its essential framework. First of all, at the psychological level, managers have an acute sense of organizational contingency. Because of the interlocking ties between people, they know that a shake-up at or near the top of a hierarchy can trigger a widespread upheaval, bringing in its wake startling reversals of fortune, good and bad, throughout the structure. Managers' cryptic aphorism, "Well, you never know . . . ," repeated often and regularly, captures the sense of uncertainty created by the constant potential for social reversal. Managers know too, and take for granted, that the personnel changes brought about by upheavals are to a great extent arbitrary and depend more than anything else on one's social relationships with key individuals and with groups of managers. Periods of organizational quiescence and stability still managers' wariness in this regard, but the foreboding sense of contingency never entirely disappears. Managers' awareness of the complex levels of conflict in their world, built into the very structure of bureaucratic organizations, constantly reminds them that things can very quickly fall apart.

The political struggles at Covenant Corporation, for instance, suggest some immediately observable levels of conflict and tension.

First, occupational groups emerging from the segmented structure of bureaucratic work, each with different expertise and emphasis, constantly vie with one another for ascendancy of their ideas, of their products or services, and of themselves. It is, for instance, an axiom of corporate life that the greatest satisfaction of production people is to see products go out the door; of salesmen, to make a deal regardless of price; of marketers, to control salesmen and squeeze profits out of their deals; and of financial specialists, to make sure that everybody meets budget. Despite the larger interdependence of such work, the necessarily fragmented functions performed day-to-day by managers in one area often put them at cross purposes with managers in another. Nor do competitiveness and conflict result only from the broad segmentation of functions. Sustained work in a product or service area not only shapes crucial social affiliations but also symbolic identifications, say, with particular products or technical services, that mark managers in their corporate arenas. Such symbolic markings make it imperative for managers to push their particular products or services as part of their overall self-promotion. This fuels the constant scramble for authoritative enthusiasm for one product or service rather than another and the subsequent allocation or reallocation of organizational resources.

Second, line and staff managers, each group with different responsibilities, different pressures, and different bailiwicks to protect, fight over organizational resources and over the rules that govern work. The very definition of staff depends entirely on one's vantage point in the organization. As one manager points out: "From the perspective of the guy who actually pushes the button to make the machine go, everyone else is staff." However, the working definition that managers use is that anyone whose decisions directly affect profit and loss is in the line; all others in an advisory capacity of some sort are staff. As a general rule, line managers' attitudes toward staff vary directly with the independence granted staff by higher management. The more freedom staff have to intervene in the line, as with the environmental staff at Alchemy or Covenant's corporate staff, the more they are feared and resented by line management. For line managers, independent staff represent either the intrusion of an unwelcome "rules and procedures mentality" into situations where line managers feel that they have to be alert to the exigencies of the market or, alternatively, as power threats to vested interests backed by some authority. In the "decentralized" organizations prevalent today in the corporate world, however, most staff are entirely dependent on the line and must market their technical, legal, or organizational skills to line managers exactly as an outside firm must do. The continual necessity for staff to sell their technical expertise helps keep them in check since line managers, pleading budgetary stringency or any number of other acceptable rationales, can thwart or ignore proffered assistance. Staff's dependent position often produces jealous respect for line management tinged with the resentment that talented people relegated to do "pine time" (sit on the bench) feel for those in the center of action. For instance, an environmental manager at Weft Corporation comments on his marginal status and on how he sees it depriving him of the recognition he feels his work deserves:

> I also want recognition. And usually the only way you get that is having a boss near you who sees what you do. It rubs me raw in fact. . . . For instance, you know they run these news releases when some corporate guy gets promoted and all? Well, when I do something, nothing ever gets said. When I publish papers, or get promoted, and so on, you never see any public announcement. Oh, they like me to publish papers amd I guess someone reads them, but that's all that's ever said or done. . . . I can get recognition in a variety of arenas, like professional associations, but if they're

going to recognize the plant manager, why not me? If we walked off, would the plants operate? They couldn't. We're *essential*.

This kind of ambivalent resentment sometimes becomes vindictiveness when a top boss uses staff as a hammer.

Staff can also become effective pitchmen; line managers' anxious search for rational solutions to largely irrational problems, in fact, encourages staff continually to invent and disseminate new tactics and schemes. Alternatively, social upheavals that produce rapid shifts in public opinion—such as occurred in the personnel or environmental areas in the aftermath of the 1960s—may encourage proliferation of staff. In either circumstance, staff tend to increase in an organization until an ideological cycle of "organizational leanness" comes around and staff, at least those of lower rank, get decimated.

Third, powerful managers in Alchemy Inc., each controlling considerable resources and the organizational fates of many men and women, battle fiercely with one another to position themselves, their products, and their allies favorably in the eyes of their president and of the CEO. At the same time, high-ranking executives "go to the mat" with one another striving for the CEO's approval and a coveted shot at the top. Bureaucratic hierarchies, simply by offering ascertainable rewards for certain behavior, fuel the ambition of those men and women ready to subject themselves to the discipline of external exigencies and of their organization's institutional logic, the socially constructed, shared understanding of how their world works. However, since rewards are always scarce, bureaucracies necessarily put people against each other and inevitably thwart the ambitions of some. The rules of such combat vary from organization to organization and depend largely on what top management countenances either openly or tacitly.

Nor are formal positions and perquisites the only objects of personal struggle between managers. Even more important on a day-to-day basis is the ongoing competition between talented and aggressive people to see whose will prevails, who can get things done their way. The two areas are, of course, related since one's chances in an organization depend largely on one's "credibility," that is, on the widespread belief that one can act effectively. One must therefore prevail regularly, though not always, in small things to have any hope of positioning oneself for big issues. The hidden agenda of seemingly petty disputes may be a struggle over long-term organizational fates.

At the same time, all of these struggles take place within the peculiar tempo and framework each CEO establishes for an organization. Under an ideology of thorough decentralization—the gift of authority with responsibility—the CEO at Covenant actually centralizes his power enormously because fear of derailing personal ambitions prevents managers below him from acting without his approval. A top official at Alchemy comments:

What we have now, despite rhetoric to the contrary, is a very centralized system. It's [the CEO] who sets the style, tone, tempo of all the companies. He says: "Manage for cash," and we manage for cash. The original idea . . . was to set up free-standing companies with a minimum of corporate staff. But . . . we're moving toward a system that is really beyond what we used to have, let alone modeled on a small corporate staff and autonomous divisions. What we used to have was separate divisions reporting to a corporate staff. I think we're moving away from that idea too. I think what's coming is a bunch of separate businesses reporting to the corporation. It's a kind of portfolio management. This accords perfectly with [the CEO's] temperament. He's a financial type guy who is oriented to the bottom line numbers. He doesn't want or need intermediaries between him and his businesses.

In effect, the CEO of Covenant, who seems to enjoy constant turmoil, pits himself and his ego against the whole corporation even while he holds it in vassalage. Other CEOs establish different frameworks and different tempos, depending on self-image and temperament. The only firm rule seems to be that articulated by a middle-level Covenant manager: "Every big organization is set up for the benefit of those who control it; the boss gets what he wants."

Except during times of upheaval, the ongoing conflicts that I have described are usually hidden behind the comfortable and benign social ambiance that most American corporations fashion for their white-collar personnel. Plush carpets, potted trees, burnished oak wall paneling, fine reproductions and sometimes originals of great art, mahogany desks, polished glass tables and ornaments, rich leather upholstery, perfectly coiffured, attractive, and poised receptionists, and private, subsidized cafeterias are only a few of the pleasant features that grace the corporate headquarters of any major company. In addition, the corporations that I studied provide their employees with an amazing range and variety of services, information, and social contacts. Covenant Corporation, for instance, through its daily newsletter and a variety of other internal media, offers information about domestic and international vacation packages; free travelers' checks; discounted tickets for the ballet, tennis matches, or art exhibits; home remedies for the common cold, traveling clinics for diagnosing high blood pressure, and advice on how to save one's sight; simple tests for gauging automotive driving habits; tips on home vegetable gardening; advice on baby-sitters; descriptions of business courses at a local college; warning articles on open fireplaces and home security; and directions for income tax filing. The newsletter also offers an internal market for the sale, rental, or exchange of a myriad of items ranging from a Jamaican villa, to a set of barbells, to back issues of *Fantasy* magazine. Covenant offers as well intracompany trapshotting contests, round-robin tennis and golf tournaments, running clinics, and executive fitness programs. Weft Corporation's bulletin is even more elaborate, with photographic features on the "Great Faces" of Weft employees; regular reports on the company's 25- and 50-year clubs; personal notes on all retirees from the company; stories about the company's sponsorship of art exhibits; human-interest stories about employees and their families—from a child struggling against liver cancer to the heroics of a Weft employee in foiling a plane hijacker; and, of course, a steady drumbeat of corporate ideology about the necessity for textile import quotas and the desirability of "buying American."

My point here is that corporations are not presented nor are they seen simply as places to work for a living. Rather the men and women in them come to fashion an entire social ambiance that overlays the antagonisms created by company politics; this makes the nuances of corporate conflict difficult to discern. A few managers, in fact, mistake the first-name informality, the social congeniality, and the plush exterior appointments for the entire reality of their collective live and are surprised when hard structural jolts turn their world upside down. Even battle-scarred veterans evince, at times, an ambivalent half-belief in the litany of rhetorics of unity and cohesive legitimating appeals. The latter are sometimes accompanied by gala events to underline the appeal. For instance, not long after the "big purge" at Covenant Corporation when 600 people were fired, the CEO spent $1 million for a "Family Day" to "bring everyone together." The massive party was attended by over 14,000 people and featured clowns, sports idols, and booths complete with bean bag and ring tosses, foot and bus races, computer games, dice rolls, and, perhaps appropriately, mazes. In his letter to his "Fellow Employees" following the event, the CEO said:

> I think Family Day made a very strong statement about the [Covenant] "family" of employees at [corporate headquarters]. And that is that we can accomplish whatever we set out to do if we work together; if we share the effort, we will share the rewards. The "New World of [Covenant]" has no boundaries, only frontiers, and each and everyone can play a role, for we need what *you* have to contribute.

The very necessity for active involvement in such rituals often prompts semi-credulity. But wise and ambitious managers resist the lulling platitudes of unity, though they invoke them with fervor, and look for inevitable clash of interests beneath the bouncy, cheerful surface of corporate life. They understand implicitly that the suppression of open conflict simply puts a premium on the mastery of the socially accepted modes of waging combat.

The continuous uncertainty and ambiguity of managerial hierarchies, exacerbated over time by masked conflict, causes managers to turn toward each other for cues for behavior. They try to learn from each other and to master the shared assumptions, the complex rules, the normative codes, the underlying institutional logic that governs their world. They thus try to control the construction of their everyday reality. Normally, of course, one learns to master the managerial code in the course of repeated, long-term social interaction with other managers, particularly in the course of shaping the multiple and complex alliances essential to organizational survival and success.

Alliances are ties of quasiprimal loyalty shaped especially by common work, by common experiences with the same problems, the same friends, or the same enemies, and by favors traded over time. Although alliances are rooted in fealty and patronage relationships, they are not limited by such relationships since fealty shifts with changing work assignments or with organizational upheavals.

Making an alliance may mean, for instance, joining or, more exactly, being included in one or several of the many networks of managerial associates that crisscross an organization. Conceptually, networks are usually thought of as open-ended webs of association with a low degree of formal organization and no distinct criteria of membership. One becomes known, for instance, as a trusted friend of a friend; thought of as a person to whom one can safely refer a thorny problem; considered a "sensible" or "reasonable" or, especially, a "flexible" person, not a "renegade" or a "loose cannon rolling around the lawn"; known to be a discreet person attuned to the nuances of corporate etiquette, one who can keep one's mouth shut or who can look away and pretend to notice nothing; or considered a person with sharp ideas that break deadlocks but who does not object to the ideas being appropriated by superiors.

Alliances are also fashioned in social coteries. These are more clublike groups of friends that, in Weft Corporation, forge ties at the cocktail hour over the back fence on Racquet Drive, the road next to the company's tennis courts where all important and socially ambitious executives live; or in Friday night poker sessions that provide a bluff and hearty setting where managers can display their own and unobtrusively observe others' mastery of public faces, a clue to many managerial virtues. In other companies, coteries consist of "tennis pals" who share an easy camaraderie over salad and yogurt lunches following hard squash games or two-mile jogs at noon. They are also made up of posthours cronies who, in midtown watering holes, weld private understandings with ironic bantering, broad satire, or macabre humor, the closest some managers ever get to open discussion of their work with their fellows; or gatherings of the smart social set where business circles intersect with cliques from intellectual and artistic worlds and where glittering, poised, and precisely vacuous social conversation can mark one as a social lion. In one company, a group of "buddies" intertwine their private lives with their organizational fates in the most complete way by, for example, persuading an ambitious younger colleague to provide a woodsy cabin retreat and local girls for a collegial evening's entertainment while on a business trip. At the managerial and professional levels, the road between work and life is usually open because it is difficult to refuse to use one's influence, patronage, or power on behalf of another regular member of one's social coterie. It therefore becomes important to choose one's social colleagues with some care and, of course, know how to drop them should they fall out of organizational favor.

Alliances are also made wholly on the basis of specific self-interests. The paradigmatic case here is that of the power clique of established, well-placed managers who put aside differences and join forces for a "higher cause," namely their own advancement or protection. Normally, though not always, as Brown's case at Covenant shows, one must be "plugged into" important networks and an active participant in key coteries in order to have achieved an organizational position where one's influence is actively counted. But the authority and power of a position matter in and of themselves. Once one has gained power, one can use one's influence in the organization to shape social ties. Such alliances often cut across rival networks and coteries and can, in fact, temporarily unite them. Managers in a power clique map out desired organizational tacks and trade off the resources in their control. They assess the strengths and weaknesses of their opponents; they plan coups and rehearse the appropriate rationales to legitimate them. And, on the other hand, they erect requisite barriers to squelch attempted usurpations of their power. Cliques also introduce managers to new, somewhat more exclusive networks and coteries. Especially at the top of a pyramid, these social ties extend over the boundaries of one's own corporation and mesh one's work and life with those of top managers in other organizations.

I shall refer to all the social contexts that breed alliances, fealty relationships, networks, coteries, or cliques, as circles of affiliation, or simply managerial circles. Now, the notion of "circles," as it has been used in sociological literature as well as colloquially, has some drawbacks for accurately delineating the important features of the web of managerial interaction. Specifically, a circle suggests a quasiclosed social group made up of members of relatively equal status without defined leadership and without formal criteria for membership or inclusion. In a bureaucratic hierarchy, nuances of status are, of course, extremely important. Moreover, since business cannot be conducted without formal authorization by appropriate authorities, one's formal rank always matters even though there is ample scope for more informal charismatic leadership. Finally, the most crucial features of managerial circles of affiliation is precisely their establishment of informal criteria for admission, criteria that are, it is true, ambiguously defined and subject to constant, often arbitrary, revision. Nonetheless, they are criteria that managers must master. At bottom, all of the social contexts of the managerial world seek to discover if one "can feel comfortable" with another manager, if he is someone who "can be trusted," if he is "our kind of guy," or, in short, if he is "one of the gang." The notion of gang, in fact, insofar as it suggests the importance of leadership, hierarchy, and probationary mechanisms in a bounded but somewhat amorphous group, may more accurately describe relationships in the corporation than the more genteel, and therefore preferable, word "circle." In any event, just as managers must continually please their boss, their boss's boss, their patrons, their president, and their CEO, so must they prove themselves again and again to each other. Work becomes an endless round of what might be called probationary crucibles. Together with the uncertainty and sense of contingency that mark managerial work, this constant state of probation produces a profound anxiety in managers, perhaps the key experience of managerial work. It also breeds, selects, or elicits certain traits in ambitious managers that are crucial to getting ahead.

NOTES

1. Brackets within quotations represent words or phrases changed or added by the author, either to protect identity or to provide grammatical fluency.
2. Henceforth, I shall generally use only "he" or "his" to allow for easier reading.
3. All personal names in the field data throughout the book are pseudonyms.

Shooting an Elephant

GEORGE ORWELL

In Moulmein, in lower Burma, I was hated by large numbers of people—the only time in my life that I have been important enough for this to happen to me. I was subdivisional police officer of the town, and in an aimless, petty kind of way anti-European feeling was very bitter. No one had the guts to raise a riot, but if a European woman went through the bazaars alone somebody would probably spit betel juice over her dress. As a police officer I was an obvious target and was baited whenever it seemed safe to do so. When a nimble Burman tripped me up on the football field and the referee (another Burman) looked the other way, the crowd yelled with hideous laughter. This happened more than once. In the end the sneering yellow faces of young men that met me everywhere, the insults hooted after me when I was at a safe distance, got badly on my nerves. The young Buddhist priests were the worst of all. There were several thousands of them in the town and none of them seemed to have anything to do except stand on street corners and jeer at Europeans.

All this was perplexing and upsetting. For at that time I had already made up my mind that imperialism was an evil thing and the sooner I chucked up my job and got out of it the better. Theoretically—and secretly, of course—I was all for the Burmese and all against their oppressors, the British. As for the job I was doing, I hated it more bitterly than I can perhaps make clear. In a job like that you see the dirty work of Empire at close quarters. The wretched prisoners huddling in the stinking cages of the lock-ups, the gray, cowed faces of the long-term convicts, the scarred buttocks of the men who had been flogged with bamboos—all these oppressed me with an intolerable sense of guilt. But I could get nothing into perspective. I was young and ill educated and I had had to think out my problems in the utter silence that is imposed on every Englishman in the East. I did not even know that the British Empire is dying, still less did I know that it is a great deal better than the younger empires that are going to supplant it. All I knew was that I was stuck between my hatred of the empire I served and my rage against the evil-spirited little beasts who tried to make my job impossible. With one part of my mind I thought of the British Raj as an unbreakable tyranny, as something clamped down, in *saecula saeculorum,* upon the will of prostrate peoples; with another part I thought that the greatest joy in the world would be to drive a bayonet into a Buddhist priest's guts. Feelings like these are the normal by-products of imperialism; ask any Anglo-Indian official, if you can catch him off duty.

One day something happened which in a roundabout way was enlightening. It was a tiny incident in itself, but it gave me a better glimpse than I had had before of the real nature of imperialism—the real motives for which despotic govern-ments act. Early one morning the subinspector at a police station the other end of the town rang me up on the phone and said that an elephant was ravaging the bazaar. Would I please come and do something about it? I did not know what I could do, but I wanted to see what was happening and I got on to a pony and started out. I took my rifle, an old .44 Winchester and much too small to kill an elephant, but I thought the noise might be useful *in terrorem*. Various Burmans stopped me on the way and told me about the elephant's doings. It was not, of course, a wild elephant, but a tame one which had gone "must." It had been chained up, as tame elephants always are when their attack of "must" is due, but on the previous night it had broken its chain and escaped. Its mahout, the only person who could manage it when it was in that state, had set out in pursuit, but had taken the wrong direction and was now twelve hours' journey away, and in the morning the elephant had suddenly reappeared in the town. The Burmese population had no weapons and were quite helpless against it. It had already destroyed somebody's bamboo hut, killed a cow and raided some fruit-stalls and devoured the stock; also it had met the municipal rubbish van and, when the driver jumped out and took to his heels, had turned the van over and inflicted violences upon it.

The Burmese subinspector and some Indian constables were waiting for me in the quarter where the elephant had been seen. It was a very poor quarter, a labyrinth of squalid bamboo huts, thatched with palm-leaf, winding all over a steep hillside. I remember that it was a cloudy, stuffy morning at the beginning of the rains. We began questioning the people as to where the elephant had gone and, as usual, failed to get any definite information. That is invariably the case in the East; a story always sounds clear enough at a distance, but the nearer you get to the scene of events the vaguer it becomes. Some of the people said that the elephant had gone in one direction, some said that he had gone in another, some professed not even to have heard of any elephant. I had almost made up my mind that the whole story was a pack of lies, when we heard yells a little distance away. There was a loud, scandalized cry of "Go away, child! Go away this instant!" and an old woman with a switch in her hand came round the corner of a hut, violently shooing away a crowd of naked children. Some more women followed, clicking their tongues and exclaiming; evidently there was something that the children ought not to have seen. I rounded the hut and saw a man's dead body sprawling in the mud. He was an Indian, a black Dravidian coolie, almost naked, and he could not have been dead many minutes. The people said that the elephant had come suddenly upon him round the corner of the hut, caught him with its trunk, put its foot on his back and ground him into the earth. This was the rainy season and the ground was soft, and his face had scored a trench a foot deep and a couple of yards long. He was lying on his belly with arms crucified and head sharply twisted to one side. His face was coated with mud, the eyes wide open, the teeth bared and grinning with an expression of unendurable agony. (Never tell me, by the way, that the dead look peaceful. Most of the corpses I have seen looked devilish.) The friction of the great beast's foot had stripped the skin from his back as neatly as one skins a rabbit. As soon as I saw the dead man I sent an orderly to a friend's house nearby to borrow an elephant rifle. I had already sent back the pony, not wanting it to go mad with fright and throw me if it smelled the elephant.

The orderly came back in a few minutes with a rifle and five cartridges, and meanwhile some Burmans had arrived and told us that the elephant was in the paddy fields below, only a few hundred yards away. As I started forward practically the whole population of the quarter flocked out of the houses and followed me. They had seen the rifle and were all shouting excitedly that I was going to shoot the elephant. They had not shown much interest in the elephant when he was merely ravaging their homes, but it was different now that he was going to be shot. It was a bit of fun to them, as it would be to an English crowd; besides they wanted the meat. It made me vaguely uneasy. I had no intention of shooting the elephant—I had merely sent for the rifle to defend myself if necessary—and it is always unnerving to have a crowd following you. I marched down the hill, looking and feeling a fool, with the rifle over my shoulder and an ever-growing army of people jostling at my heels. At the bottom, when you got away from the huts, there was a metaled road and beyond that a miry waste of paddy fields a thousand yards across, not yet plowed but soggy from the first rains and dotted with coarse grass. The elephant was standing eight yards from the road, his left side toward us. He took not the slightest notice of the crowd's approach. He was tearing up bunches of grass, beating them against his knees to clean them, and stuffing them into his mouth.

I had halted on the road. As soon as I saw the elephant I knew with perfect certainty that I ought not to shoot him. It is a serious matter to shoot a working elephant—it is comparable to destroying a huge and costly piece of machinery—and obviously one ought not to do it if it can possibly be avoided. And at that distance, peacefully eating, the elephant looked no more dangerous than a cow. I thought then and I think now that his attack of ''must'' was already passing off; in which case he would merely wander harmlessly about until the mahout came back and caught him. Moreover, I did not in the least want to shoot him. I decided that I would watch him for a little while to make sure that he did not turn savage again, and then go home.

But at that moment I glanced round at the crowd that had followed me. It was an immense crowd, two thousand at the least and growing every minute. It blocked the road for a long distance on either side. I looked at the sea of yellow faces above the garish clothes—faces all happy and excited over this bit of fun, all certain that the elephant was going to be shot. They were watching me as they would watch a conjurer about to perform a trick. They did not like me, but with the magical rifle in my hands I was momentarily worth watching. And suddenly I realized that I should have to shoot the elephant after all. The people expected it of me and I had got to do it; I could feel their two thousand wills pressing me forward, irresistibly. And it was at this moment, as I stood there with the rifle in my hands, that I first grasped the hollowness, the futility of the white man's dominion in the East. Here was I, the white man with his gun, standing in front of the unarmed native crowd—seemingly the leading actor of the piece; but in reality I was only an absurd puppet pushed to and fro by the will of those yellow faces behind. I perceived in this moment that when the white man turns tyrant it is his own freedom that he destroys. He becomes a sort of hollow, posing dummy, the conventionalized figure of a sahib. For it is the condition of his rule that he shall spend his life in trying to impress the "natives," and so in every crisis he has got to do what the "natives" expect of him. He wears a mask, and his face grows to fit it. I had got to shoot the elephant. I had committed myself to doing it when I sent for the rifle. A sahib has got to act like a sahib; he has got to appear resolute, to know his own mind and do definite things. To come all that way, rifle in hand, with two thousand people marching at my heels, and then to trail feebly away, having done nothing—no, that was impossible. The crowd would laugh at me. And my whole life, every white man's life in the East, was one long struggle not to be laughed at.

But I did not want to shoot the elephant. I watched him beating his bunch of grass against his knees with that preoccupied grandmotherly air that elephants have. It seemed to me that it would be murder to shoot him. At that age I was not squeamish about killing animals, but I had never shot an elephant and never wanted to. (Somehow it always seems worse to kill a *large* animal.) Besides, there was the beast's owner to be considered. Alive, the elephant was worth at least a hundred pounds; dead, he would only be worth the value of his tusks, five pounds, possibly. But I had got to act quickly. I turned to some experienced-looking Burmans who had been there when we arrived, and asked them how the elephant had been behaving. They all said the same thing: he took no notice of you if you left him alone, but he might charge if you went too close to him.

It was perfectly clear to me what I ought to do. I ought to walk up to within, say, twenty-five yards of the elephant and test his behavior. If he charged, I could shoot; if he took no notice of me, it would be safe to leave him until the mahout came back. But also I knew that I was going to do no such thing. I was a poor shot with a rifle and the ground was soft mud into which one would sink at every step. If the elephant charged and I missed him, I should have about as much chance as a toad under a steam-roller. But even then I was not thinking particularly of my own skin, only of the watchful yellow faces behind. For at that moment, with the crowd watching me, I was not afraid in the ordinary sense, as I would have been if I had been alone. A white man mustn't be frightened in front of "natives"; and so, in general, he isn't frightened. The sole thought in my mind was that if anything went wrong those two thousand Burmans would see me pursued, caught, trampled on, and reduced to a grinning corpse like that Indian up the hill. And if that happened it was quite probable that some of them would laugh. That would never do. There was only one alternative. I shoved the cartridges into the magazine and lay down on the road to get a better aim.

The crowd grew very still, and a deep, low, happy sigh, as of people who see the theater curtain go up at last, breathed from innumerable throats. They were going to have their bit of fun after all. The rifle was a beautiful German thing with cross-hair sights. I did not then know that in shooting an elephant one would shoot to cut an imaginary bar running from ear-hole to ear-hole. I ought, therefore, as the elephant was sideways on, to have aimed straight at his ear-hole; actually I aimed several inches in front of this, thinking the brain would be further forward.

When I pulled the trigger I did not hear the bang or feel the kick—one never does when a shot goes home—but I heard the devilish roar of glee that went up from the crowd. In that instant, in too short a time, one would have thought, even for the bullet to get there, a mysterious, terrible change had come over the elephant. He neither stirred nor fell, but every line of his body had altered. He looked suddenly stricken, shrunken, immensely old, as though the frightful impact of the bullet had paralyzed him without knocking him down. At last, after what seemed a long time—it might have been five seconds, I dare say—he sagged flabbily to his knees. His mouth slobbered. An enormous senility seemed to have settled upon him. One could have imagined him thousands of years old. I fired again into the same spot. At the second shot he did not collapse but climbed with desperate slowness to his feet and stood weakly upright, with legs sagging and head drooping. I fired a third time. That was the shot that did for him. You could see the agony of it jolt his whole body and knock the last remnant of strength from his legs. But in falling he seemed for a moment to rise, for as his hind legs collapsed beneath him he seemed to tower upward like a huge rock toppling, his trunk reaching skyward like a tree. He trumpeted, for the first and only time. And then down he came, his belly toward me, with a crash that seemed to shake the ground even where I lay.

I got up. The Burmans were already racing past me across the mud. It was obvious that the elephant would never rise again, but he was not dead. He was breathing very rhythmically with long rattling gasps, his great mound of a side painfully rising and falling. His mouth was wide open—I could see far down into caverns of pale pink throat. I waited a long time for him to die, but his breathing did not weaken. Finally I fired my two remaining shots into the spot where I thought his heart must be. The thick blood welled out of him like red velvet, but still he did not die. His body did not even jerk when the shot hit him, the tortured breathing continued without a pause. He was dying, very slowly and in great agony, but in some world remote from me where not even a bullet could damage him further. I felt that I had got to put an end to that dreadful noise. It seemed dreadful to see the great beast lying there, powerless to move and yet powerless to die, and not even to be able to finish him. I sent back for my small rifle and poured shot after shot into his heart and down his throat. They seemed to make no impression. The tortured gasps continued as steadily as the ticking of a clock.

In the end I could not stand it any longer and went away. I heard later that it took him half an hour to die. Burmans were bringing dahs and baskets even before I left, and I was told they had stripped his body almost to the bones by the afternoon.

Afterward, of course, there were endless discussions about the shooting of the elephant. The owner was furious, but he was only an Indian and could do nothing. Besides, legally I had done the right thing, for a mad elephant has to be killed, like a mad dog, if its owner fails to control it. Among the Europeans opinion was divided. The older men said I was right, the younger men said it was a damn shame to shoot an elephant for killing a coolie, because an elephant was worth more than any damn Coringhee coolie. And afterward I was very glad that the coolie had been killed; it put me legally in the right and it gave me a sufficient pretext for shooting the elephant. I often wondered whether any of the others grasped that I had done it solely to avoid looking a fool.

9

The Marginalized

The Black Masses

WILLIAM LANGER

We may safely assume that the standard of living of the peasantry had been miserably low ever since the dawn of sedentary society. In the eighteenth century the "common herd," the "black masses," were generally rated as not much higher in the social scale than the cows and pigs which shared their hovels. Yet the evidence leaves little doubt that in many parts of Europe their lot had become harder by the early nineteenth century. It is dangerous to generalize, because of the multiplicity of systems of land tenure and the varying conditions in different countries. But so much seems clear: that with the rapidly increasing population, the demand for food and clothing became urgent. Farming and grazing were increasingly profitable and it was perhaps inevitable that changes should take place. Improved breeds of cattle and sheep were introduced; the methods of agriculture were modernized; waste lands were drained. Above all, the larger landowners everywhere attempted to enlarge and consolidate their holdings, if only to increase efficiency of operation. The result was the abolition of the open fields and common lands by legal procedure, by chicanery, or by pressure. In England this was the process of "enclosure"; in Scotland of "clearance"; in eastern Germany of "regulation." The details might differ widely, but the result was in all instances much the same. By 1830 the rural scene had been profoundly altered. The poorer people had lost the right to glean the fields, to gather faggots in the forests, to run their cow or pig on the common. In return they had received small allotments of land, frequently so meager in size as to be unprofitable. In such cases there was no alternative to selling the land to the nearest landowner and becoming a landless farm laborer.

The results in most countries were strikingly similar. By the mid-nineteenth century there were in England and Wales some 700,000 families of landless agricultural laborers, representing about a fifth of the total population. In Scotland many Highland lairds showed little compunction in "clearing" the cotters from the land so as to run sheep. The heiress of Sutherland, who owned almost the entire county, established a record by expelling 15,000 people from her estates and burning their cottages, while "generously" providing them with a couple of acres per family on which to eke out a living on the coast.

In Ireland the condition of the peasants was perhaps worse than anywhere else in Europe. Some 6,000–7,000 English landlords, the "Protestant Ascendancy," held 90 percent of the land, in estates running to tens of thousands of acres. The natives rack-rented small farms or one- or two-acre potato patches in return for payment in "duty labor." Yet here, too, many landlords undertook "clearing" of their properties so as to run cattle for the British market.

On the Continent the same process was under way in all countries except France, where small holdings appear to have actually increased in number, though the peasants progressively lost some of their traditional rights. In Scandinavia the consolidation of landholdings was virtually complete by the midcentury. It left a fifth of the population of Sweden and Norway and two-fifths of the Finnish population landless. Similarly, the great estates of the Po valley and of central Sicily were gradually taking over the small holdings and reducing numerous peasant families to the status of day laborers. With regard to Germany there is still some controversy as to how many peasants were made landless through the laws of 1807 emancipating the serfs and "regulating" the peasantry. So much, however, is agreed upon: in return for abolition of feudal dues the peasants paid with one-third to one-half of their land, while in the enclosure of the common lands they received only 14 percent, mostly wasteland. Large numbers of small holdings were completely liquidated and absorbed in the large estates. Yet farther east, where the feudal system was still in operation, the peasants owned little if any land, and were completely at the mercy of the landowners. In Hungary, for example, the landowners, by hook or crook, appropriated the common pastures. By 1846 there were 825,000 peasant families without land as against 550,000 who still had small holdings.

Where they could, the peasants rented or leased land in return for labor and produce. The systems of tenure varied enormously and in Italy usually took the form of sharecropping. Elsewhere in Central Europe the peasants contributed a substantial part of their time to domestic or field work for their landlords. Sometimes the law specified the maximum amount, but such restrictions were always circumvented. In the Danubian Principalities (modern Rumania), where the legal limit was twelve days a year, peasants were devoting forty to sixty days to the service of their voracious lords; in Russia, the classic land of forced labor, the law specified three days a week of work for the lord, while in practice the peasants, especially at harvest time, were left only Sundays and moonlit nights to cultivate their own little holdings. In addition to labor, the peasants almost everywhere had to pay taxes and make contributions to the lord in grain or other produce. Furthermore, they were required to supply the needed tools, carts, and draft animals.

The condition of the peasantry in the midcentury was such as to appall many observers. Henry Colman, the American, saw the landless workers as condemned to labor without any prospect whatever of betterment: "They are not slaves, but they are not free. . . . They have no chains on their hands, but the iron enters

into their souls. Their limbs may be unshackled, but their spirits are bound.
. . . They are used, and thrown aside, as occasion may require, like mere
implements upon the farm.'' This was said with reference to the agricultural
laborers who were hired by the week or the day and consequently suffered long
winter months of unemployment. Their wages in England were between eight
and eleven shillings a week, which was not sufficient to support a family. Even
with the addition of the woman's of children's work it was barely possible to stay
alive. Traditionally the peasants had turned to home industry, especially spinning
and weaving, as winter occupations to supplement their incomes. But increasingly as the century advanced the machine was taking over these functions and
depriving the peasants of this last resource. The fate of the handloom workers was
everywhere incredibly hard, leading in 1844 to the insurrection in Silesia during
which factories were gutted and their owners beaten or murdered.

It takes but little imagination to envision the living conditions of the poorer
peasants and rural laborers. Many of them lived in half-buried hovels of mud or
wattle, with next to no furniture or bedding. Their food consisted largely of
potatoes, the culture of which had become universal in the late eighteenth century
and provided at least good food value. Potatoes might be supplemented by a little
milk or cheese and, in the autumn, when the pig was slaughtered, with occasional
pork or bacon. The time between potato planting and harvesting was the ''summer famine,'' when in many parts of Europe droves of half-starved, half-naked
men, women, and children plodded along the roads begging for food and rags. As
for the winter, that was made hideous not only by unemployment but by want of
fuel.

Hunger and cold let to a great increase in the consumption of hard liquor by the
lower classes of both country and town. In Ireland the production of distilled
liquor doubled between 1820 and 1830, while in 1830 Sweden produced 35
million gallons of *branvin* and *akvavit,* consumption reaching ten gallons per
capita in that year. In the northern countries it was, one might say, the golden age
of inebriation, so much so that heroic countermeasures became imperative.
Agents of American temperance societies were warmly received in Europe even
by monarchs and princes. By 1840 Europe was covered by local and national
temperance organizations and that amazing Irishman, Father Theobald Mathew,
was inspiring hundreds of thousands of people to take the oath of total abstinence.
Mathew was undoubtedly one of the truly charismatic leaders of his day, a man
whose deep concern for the suffering poor struck a responsive chord. Maria
Edgeworth, the Irish novelist, called him ''the greatest benefactor of his country,'' and the Boston Unitarian leader, William Ellery Channing, suggested that
his name be inserted in the calendar of saints just below those of the apostles. For
a time at least, in the 1840s, Mathew's efforts led to a marked reduction in liquor
consumption in the British Isles.

The Black Family in Slavery and Freedom
HERBERT GEORGE GUTMAN

Forty years passed between the recording of the 1925 New York State census (a document showing that family disorganization did not accompany poor southern black migrants to northern cities) and the publication of Daniel Patrick Moynihan's enormously controversial *The Negro Family: The Case for National Action* (a document which argued that it did). Although Moynihan emphasized the importance of unemployment as a cause of family disorganization among lower-class Afro-Americans, he confused the problems of poor blacks in the second half of the twentieth century with those of their great-grandparents in the first half of the nineteenth century. And he misperceived the history of both groups. "At the heart of the deterioration of the fabric of Negro society," said the controversial 1965 report, "is the deterioration of the Negro family," "the fundamental source of the weakness in the Negro community at the present time." "In its lasting effects on individuals and their children," American slavery was "indescribably worse than any recorded servitude, ancient or modern." Moynihan quoted approvingly from Nathan Glazer's summary of Stanley Elkins, from Thomas Pettigrew, and from E. Franklin Frazier to argue that "the slave household often developed a fatherless matrifocal (mother-centered) pattern," and that severe postemancipation rural and urban poverty meant that "the Negro family made but little progress toward the middle-class pattern of the present time." Migration to the North reinforced social and familial disorganization among southern blacks—a process similar to what had happened in "the wild Irish slums of the nineteenth century Northeast" where "drunkenness, crime, corruption, family disorganization, [and] juvenile delinquency" were "routine." "No one Negro problem" existed, and there was "no one solution." "Nevertheless," Moynihan said, "at the center of the tangle of pathology is the weakness of the family structure. . . . It was by destroying the Negro family that white America broke the will of the Negro people. . . . Three centuries of injustice have brought about deep-seated structural distortions in the life of the Negro American." Moynihan urged "a national effort . . . to strengthen the Negro family."

Much criticism greeted the "Moynihan Report." Critics bitterly debated what came to be called "the slavery-specific hypothesis." Had slavery bred among Afro-Americans what some call "a culture of poverty"? "The habit of analyzing data by color rather than by income levels," the sociologist Hylan Lewis pointed out in one of the most intelligent critiques, "has tended to support the slavery specific hypothesis." Lewis and others convincingly showed that "Negro-white differences in family structure diminish when controlled for income and that differences by income are more striking than differences by color. . . . Since a much larger proportion of Negroes than of whites are on the lowest income levels, what look like statistically significant differences between Negroes and whites may actually be differences between socioeconomic levels" (see table). Lewis argued that "since the job is a crucial determinant of where and how the family fits in the society and of the effectiveness of many of the society's rewards, probably the most important single clue to the quality of change in the Negro family and in the community, is . . . the job picture . . . for the male." Lewis later wrote: "The answer to the problem of family disorganization is not one of inculcating marriage and family values in young couples; there is ample evidence that they exist. The critical test is to find ways and means for the young adult male to meet the economic maintenance demands of marriage and family life." Lewis and others like him did not suggest that slavery had been less harsh than Moynihan had argued but denied that the difficulties encountered by poor urban Afro-Americans in the 1960s had their roots in a three-century "cycle of self-perpetuating pathology." "Pseudofacts," the sociologist Robert K. Merton warns, "have a way of inducing pseudoproblems which cannot be solved because matters are not as they purport to be." So does pseudohistory. A vast difference exists in dealing with a problem rooted in "three centuries of exploitation" and one caused by massive structural unemployment.

Few critics of the "Moynihan Report" disputed the accuracy of Moynihan's characterization of the enslaved Afro-American. Instead, they debated its relevance to late-twentieth-century urban America. Most shared his view of the "slave family." The few who disputed the conventional history of the "black

Male-Present Black and White Families, 1960

	Black families	White families
All families	79%	94%
All rural families	86	96
All urban families	77	93
FAMILIES UNDER $3000		
All families	64	78
All rural families	82	88
All urban families	53	62
FAMILIES $3000+		
All families	93	97
All rural families	95	98
All urban families	92	96

family" did not glorify slavery but instead emphasized the positive adaptive capacities of the slaves and their immediate descendants and the common misperception of them. Ralph Ellison wrote:

> [W]ithin the group, we act out, we make certain assertions, we make certain choices, and we have various social structures, which determine to a great extent how we act and what we desire. This is what we live. When we try to articulate it, all we have is sociology. And the sociology is loaded. The concepts which are brought to it are usually based on those of white, middle-class, Protestant values and life style.

Laura Carper made a similar point. Adult women, she said, had played powerful roles in the families of diverse oppressed groups, not just among Afro-Americans. She caricatured family life in the East European Jewish *shtetl* to make her point:

> [T]he father was frequently absent, either as a peddler on the road, as an immigrant in America, or as a permanent resident of the house of study who came home only to eat. Newly married couples usually moved into the home of the bride's parents. Among the Hassidic Jews (Hassidism was a movement initiated by the poor), it was common for the father to leave his wife and children without a kopek or a groshen in the house and depart for the Rebbe's court where he would dance and drink and spend all his money. As among the American poor, relations between husband and wife were cold and the roles of each clearly defined. The wife worked and assumed the main burden of supporting the family, and the children became adults before they had ever had an opportunity to be children. The man either struggled desperately to make a living with little success or withdrew entirely into a private male society based on discourse or ecstasy and left the family to shift for itself. What the Jewish man succeeded in doing that the Negro man has failed to do is place a positive value on family desertion and personal withdrawal.
>
> Since the Negro man does not rationalize his role as being a desirable religious achievement, it seems to me he would be easier to integrate into the surrounding culture than the Jew. After all, once integration became a viable possibility, even the Shtetl Jew cast off what no longer served him. And the depth and extent to which oppression and poverty reduced the Jew can be measured by the disintegrative effects of the widespread Messianic movements, two of which emphasized orgiastic sexual practices as a means of insuring the coming of the Messiah.
>
> I have chosen to detail the matriarchal organization of the Jewish family life not because it corresponds to the Negro family but because sociologists look upon Jewish family life as remarkably cohesive. Is the caricature I have drawn of the shtetl family accurate? Of course not. I have applied Mr. Moynihan's method of describing the Negro to a description of the Jew. I lumped a few hundred years of history together and failed to distinguish between people. Pathology is in the eye of the beholder. If one eliminates the positive social function of a cultural constellation, if one ignores the meaning personal relations have to the people involved, if one, in short, uses science to depersonalize, what emerges is always pathology. For health involves spontaneous human feelings of affection and tenderness which the Moynihan Report, like my deliberate caricature of Jewish family life, cannot encompass.
>
> People living under oppression always develop social formations which appear to the surrounding oppressive culture to be excessive or pathological. The form these so-called excesses take varies, from culture to culture and person to person within the

culture—but no matter how extreme the nature of the adjustment, once the social pressure which created it is removed, a new adjustment develops. A people is not destroyed by its history. What destroys a people is physical annihilation or assimilation, not its family life.

Carper's point bears directly on the "slavery-specific hypothesis." Enslavement was harsh and constricted the enslaved. But it did not destroy their capacity to adapt and sustain the vital familial and kin associations and beliefs that served as the underpinning of a developing Afro-American culture. The capacity of the emancipated slaves to adapt to the general emancipation is evidence of their earlier adaptation to enslavement. And the capacity of early twentieth-century southern black migrants to adapt to the northern city in 1905 and 1925 is evidence of the adaptive capacities of Afro-Americans living in the rural and urban South between 1880 and 1900. Their household arrangements do not mean that such persons were without "problems." A vast and painful record documents the economic and social—as well as the psychological—costs extracted from poor rural and urban blacks in the decades between the general emancipation and the Great Depression. But that record is not evidence that the black family crumbled or that a "pathological" culture thrived.

Nor is there reason to believe that the poor black family crumbled in the near half century that has passed since the onset of the Great Depression. That remains a little-studied subject, but the broad outlines detailing the vast social and economic processes and pressures affecting the black family in that half century seem clear. They first and most importantly involve a modern Enclosure Movement without parallel in the nation's history. Between 1940 and 1970, more than twenty million Americans—including over four million blacks—left the countryside for the cities. The magnitude of this internal migration is revealed in the fact that almost the same number left Europe for the United States in the entire century between 1820 and 1920. In 1940, half of the nation's blacks lived on the land; by 1965 four-fifths of them were urban. Between 1950 and 1965, "new machines and new methods increased farm output in the United States by 45 percent—and reduced farm employment by 45 percent." In 1945, the South had one tractor per farm, and twenty years later two tractors per farm. One study shows that in 1965 mechanical cotton pickers harvested 81 percent of the Mississippi Delta region's cotton crop. Such machines had harvested 27 percent in 1958. In seventeen Arkansas counties typical of the southern cotton economy, the number of cotton-picking machines increased from 482 to 5,061 between 1952 and 1963. Black tenant farmers in these counties declined from 21,862 to 6,587 between 1952 and 1959. A fine study of Humphrey County, Mississippi, blacks by Tony Dunbar describes something of the meaning of this mid-twentieth-century transformation and displacement:

> Until a few years ago, every family on a plantation was allowed a small patch of land to grow vegetables for its own use. Many tenants also raised hogs, chickens, and possibly a cow. Today only a few of the planters will allow even their full-time laborers to plant one or two rows of vegetables. For the rest a garden or coops or pens for poultry and livestock are impossible, because rows of cotton or soybeans now

push up to the tenant's doorstep. In their drive to get the greatest possible yield from their land, the planters may force the tenants to move their toilets right up to their homes, so that every possible foot of land can be seeded and so that the machines can run straight down the rows without having to detour around the tiny, rickety privies. Even where space does permit the growing of a little truck, most tenants are prohibited from doing so because planters fear that weeds from the garden will spread to the cotton and bean fields, which they like to keep meticulously clean by spraying down poisons from the air.

. . . The planter is out to make money, and, viewed in this way, he is coming of age [by mechanizing]. The last years in the Delta have seen tenants go homeless, truck patches on plantations prohibited or restricted, people dying or being permanently disabled because the planter would not send for a doctor, plantation huts being allowed to fall into complete disrepair, women and children by the thousands left with no way to earn money, women forced to do work for which they are physically unsuited in order to save their families from being told to move out, and countless other shameful events. This has happened, I think, not because the planters have decided to starve the black man out of the Delta, as some have said, but rather because the planters no longer care, except as it affects their own operations, what happens to the tenants on their farms; or, in a larger sense, they do not care whether the black man in the Delta starves or not. . . .

There is nothing predictable now about life on the plantation. No man knows if his home is secure, or if he will be given enough work to support his family. He does not know if he will be placed in a hospital if he is hurt on the job. He has no idea what he will do when he becomes too old to work. If he falls into debt to the planter, he does not know if he will be given enough work to get in the clear. He can no longer expect the planter to give him materials with which to repair his house. If he owes the planter or cannot accumulate any savings, he has no way to leave the plantation. If he can contemplate leaving, he, who has never been 100 miles from Louise, must face a move to Chicago, which he has seen on television but does not really believe in. And what will he do in Chicago? The plantation world is all uncertainty, and the tenant farmer is economically and politically unable to make it any less so.

Urban unemployment and underemployment greeted those driven from the land. The cities had too few jobs. A regular differential in the black-white unemployment rate (two-to-one) made adaptation to northern city life very difficult for migrant blacks, a point made by Daniel P. Moynihan but buried in the dispute over an alleged "tangle of pathology." "The fundamental overwhelming fact is that Negro *unemployment,* with the exception of the few years during World War Two and the Korean War," said Moynihan in 1965, *"has continued at disaster levels for thirty-five years."* (It was no different in the Bicentennial year.) A year later, the Department of Labor published its first "subemployment index," which included people sporadically unemployed and those working at very low wages. The nonwhite subemployment rate was 21.6 percent, three times the white rate. Subemployment rates in nine slum ghetto areas that same year were staggering—they averaged 33 percent.

These were the pressures operating on the mid-twentieth-century lower-class black family. Not surprisingly, the rate of family breakup (measured by male presence) increased between 1950 and 1970. But that "rate" had little if any connection to "a tangle of pathology" rooted in "deep-seated structural distortions in the life of Negro Americans.'' The behavior of poor southern black migrants to central Harlem, among others, in 1925 makes that clear. Poor migrant blacks responded to the devastating pressures of rural enclosure and urban unemployment in diverse but still little-studied ways. Some are revealed in Carol B. Stack's *All Our Kin: Strategies for Survival in a Black Community* (1974), a splendid work that shows how extensive networks of black kin and friends devise ways of dealing with severe deprivation. Elastic household boundaries, not small nuclear families, serve such purposes. So do affective quasi-kin relationships. Whites responded differently. As Frances Fox Piven and Richard A. Cloward have shown in *Regulating the Poor: The Functions of Public Welfare* (1971), the social crisis that accompanied the transformation of rural black unemployment into urban black unemployment was met by a loosening up of ''welfare'' regulations to contain the severe discontent accompanying that transformation. A new ''Poor Law'' matched the new Enclosure Movement.

Intense suffering resulted from the interaction between the late twentieth-century Enclosure Movement and Poor Law, but it has become fashionable, once again, to ''blame the victim.'' Herbert H. Hyman and John Shelton Reed, however, show that little evidence exists ''for any socio-psychological pattern of matriarchy peculiarly characteristic of the Negro family on the basis of which social theorizing or social policy could be formulated.'' And his interviews with black mothers and their children on welfare convince Leonard Goodwin that they want work, not ''welfare.'' ''Getting a job'' is far more important to these women than to middle-class white women. ''Welfare youths from fatherless homes,'' Goodwin's study discloses, ''show a strong work ethic, a willingness to take training and an interest in working even if it is not a financial necessity.'' ''Their mothers,'' Goodwin adds, ''favorably influence these positive orientations.'' But neither the economy nor those who dominate the political decision-making process have as a priority the creation of useful work for those driven in such great numbers from the land. Much has changed in the nation's history in the century following the general emancipation, but wealth and commonwealth still remain polar opposites.

Race Matters

CORNEL WEST

Recent discussions about the plight of African Americans—especially those at the bottom of the social ladder—tend to divide into two camps. On the one hand, there are those who highlight the *structural* constraints on the life chances of black people. Their viewpoint involves a subtle historical and sociological analysis of salvery, Jim Crowism, job and residential discrimination, skewed unemployment rates, inadequate health care, and poor education. On the other hand, there are those who stress the *behavioral* impediments on black upward mobility. They focus on the waning of the Protestant ethic—hard work, deferred gratification, frugality, and responsibility—in much of black America.

Those in the first camp—the liberal structuralists—call for full employment, health, education, and child-care programs, and broad affirmative action practices. In short, a new, more sober version of the best of the New Deal and the Great Society: more government money, better bureaucrats, and an active citizenry. Those in the second camp—the conservative behaviorists—promote self-help programs, black business expansion, and nonpreferential job practices. They support vigorous "free market" strategies that depend on fundamental changes in how black people act and live. To put it bluntly, their projects rest largely upon a cultural revival of the Protestant ethic in black America.

Unfortunately, these two camps have nearly suffocated the crucial debate that should be taking place about the prospects for black America. This debate must go far beyond the liberal and conservative positions in three fundamental ways. First, we must acknowledge that structures and behavior are inseparable, that institutions and values go hand in hand. How people act and live are shaped—though in no way dictated or determined—by the larger circumstances in which they find themselves. These circumstances can be changed, their limits attenuated, by positive actions to elevate living conditions.

Second, we should reject the idea that structures are primarily economic and political creatures—an idea that sees culture as an ephemeral set of behavioral attitudes and values. Culture is as much a structure as the economy or politics; it is rooted in institutions such as families, schools, churches, synagogues, mosques, and communication industries (television, radio, video, music). Similarly, the economy and politics are not only influenced by values but also promote particular cultural ideals of the good life and good society.

Third, and most important, we must delve into the depths where neither liberals nor conservatives dare to tread, namely, into the murky waters of despair and dread that now flood the streets of black America. To talk about the depressing statistics of unemployment, infant mortality, incarceration, teenage pregnancy, and violent crime is one thing. But to face up to the monumental eclipse of hope, the unprecedented collapse of meaning, the incredible disregard for human (especially black) life and property in much of black America is something else.

The liberal/conservative discussion conceals the most basic issue now facing black America: *the nihilistic threat to its very existence*. This threat is not simply a matter of relative economic deprivation and political powerlessness—though economic well-being and political clout are requisites for meaningful black progress. It is primarily a question of speaking to the profound sense of psychological depression, personal worthlessness, and social despair so widespread in black America.

The liberal structuralists fail to grapple with this threat for two reasons. First, their focus on structural constraints relates almost exclusively to the economy and politics. They show no understanding of the structural character of culture. Why? Because they tend to view poeple in egoistic and rationalist terms according to which they are motivated primarily by self-interest and self-preservation. Needless to say, this is partly true about most of us. Yet, people, especially degraded and oppressed people, are also hungry for identity, meaning, and self-worth.

The second reason liberal structuralists overlook the nihilistic threat is a sheer failure of nerve. They hesitate to talk honestly about culture, the realm of meanings and values, because doing so seems to lend itself too readily to conservative conclusions in the narrow way Americans discuss race. If there is a hidden taboo among liberals, it is to resist talking *too much* about values because such discussions remove the focus from structures and especially because they obscure the positive role of government. But this failure by liberals leaves the existential and psychological realities of black people in the lurch. In this way, liberal structuralists neglect the battered identities rampant in black America.

As for the conservative behaviorists, they not only misconstrue the nihilistic threat but inadvertently contribute to it. This is a serious charge, and it rests upon several claims. Conservative behaviorists talk about values and attitudes as if political and economic structures hardly exist. They rarely, if ever, examine the innumerable cases in which black people do act on the Protestant ethic and still remain at the bottom of the social ladder. Instead, they highlight the few instances in which blacks ascend to the top, as if such success is available to all blacks, regardless of circumstances. Such a vulgar rendition of Horatio Alger in blackface may serve as a source of inspiration to some—a kind of model for those already on the right track. But it cannot serve as a substitute for serious historical and social analysis of the predicaments of and prospects for all black people, especially the grossly disadvantaged ones.

Conservative behaviorists also discuss black culture as if acknowledging one's obvious victimization by white supremacist practices (compounded by sexism and class condition) is taboo. They tell black people to see themselves as agents, not victims. And on the surface, this is comforting advice, a nice cliché for downtrodden people. But inspirational slogans cannot substitute for substantive historical and social analysis. While black people have never been simply victims, wallowing in self-pity and begging for white giveaways, they have been—and are—*victimized*. Therefore, to call on black people to be agents makes sense only if we also examine the dynamics of this victimization against which their agency will, in part, be exercised. What is particularly naive and peculiarly vicious about the conservative behavioral outlook is that it tends to deny the lingering effect of black history—a history inseparable from though not reducible to victimization. In this way, crucial and indispensable themes of self-help and personal responsibility are wrenched out of historical context and contemporary circumstances—as if it is all a matter of personal will.

Harlem Teenagers Checkmate a Stereotype

JOHN TIERNEY

The Raging Rooks are getting a lot of attention this week, and they can understand why. These teenagers from Harlem have grown accustomed to incredulous stares in airports and hotels when they explain that, no, they are not a rap group, and no, the trophy is not for basketball.

"When we tell them we're a chess team," said Kasaun Henry, the fourteen-year-old captain, "people look baffled and say, 'What?' It's stupid, but we try not to let it upset us. We just concentrate on our chess."

Their concentration was evident last week in Dearborn, Michigan, where the Raging Rooks tied for first place in the National Junior High Chess Championship sponsored by the United States Chess Federation. The team, from Adam Clayton Powell Jr. Junior High School 43 beat sixty junior high school teams, including the defending champion and traditional powerhouse from the Upper East Side, the Dalton private school.

Their concentration was also evident at a victory celebration Wednesday evening at the Upper East Side townhouse of Bob Guccione. Mr. Guccione is best known as the publisher of *Penthouse* magazine, but this didn't mean much to the Raging Rooks. Most of the players—adolescent boys, every one—said they were not really familiar with the publication.

"Is it a magazine about penthouses?" asked Charu Robinson, fourteen years old. Upon learning that it was not, he said: "Whenever I have free time, I play chess. It's just chess, chess, chess."

His mother, Ruth Robinson, later explained that the Rooks had plenty of practice ignoring temptations. As she sat not far from Mr. Guccione's indoor pool, she talked about the neighborhood around the school at 129th Street and Amsterdam Avenue and about the four crack houses around the corner from her home.

"There's everything on the streets, but these kids walk right by it," she said. "All they do is play chess—once the homework's done. It's such a pleasure when they're playing at our house. It's quiet, and you hear the pieces clicking, and it's like being in another world. You can really feel your child will never get involved with all that out there."

The Rooks grew out of a chess club started twenty years ago at the school by Richard Gudonsky, a science teacher and casual player. Six years ago he and

Danny Botok, a school administrator, began taking the students to tournaments. Then, two years ago, the Manhattan Chess Club School, which sponsors chess teachers at 130 schools in the New York area, sent them a professional player, Maurice Ashley.

"ANSWER TO OUR DREAMS"

"He was the answer to our dreams," Mr. Gudonsky said. "Besides being a great coach and player, he's an African American, and he's just the kind of man these boys need in their lives. Watching them with him, it's like moths to a flame. He coaches them chess, and I take care of the logistics. He's the brains, and I'm the brawn."

Being the brawn means that Mr. Gudonsky is there at eight o'clock in the morning so the boys can play for an hour before school. His lunch hour goes to chess, and so do many afternoons and weekends, when he picks the youths up at home and drives them to tournaments.

"It's all been out of my own time and pocket," he explained when asked. "But it was such a beautiful thing happening that I had to go with it, no matter what it cost. My payback has been watching the boys succeed."

Mr. Ashley, a native of Jamaica who learned chess as a teenager in the Brownsville section of Brooklyn, is twenty-five years old and ranked as a senior master. One of his hopes, he said, is to become the world's first black grandmaster. Another is for one of the Raging Rooks to beat him one day.

ROLE MODELS SOUGHT

"When I started, there weren't a lot of good black chess players, so there wasn't a high ceiling for me to shoot for," he said. "Now I'm the ceiling for these kids, and I'm hoping they'll surpass me. I want them to become role models. Their victory already makes a major statement about the potential of kids in the inner city—and about the lost potential of those adults you see on street corners."

Some of the selective citywide public schools in New York have done well before in national chess competition, but the Rooks are the first team from a neighborhood school to go this far in the junior high nationals. They won three of their last four games to finish, on April 14, in a tie for first place with a team from the Masterman Laboratory and Demonstration School in Philadelphia.

It was the first time in four years that Dalton, a school in East 89th Street where the tuition is $12,000 a year, did not win the national title. Dalton's coach, Bruce Pandolfini, was impressed with how quickly the Rooks had improved in the last year.

"Nothing fazed them," he said. "Most kids under pressure will start hurrying a little bit or showing their feelings, but not them. They took their time, and they were absolutely poker-faced at the board. I've never seen kids that age so cool. They were like professionals."

BATHING IN CONGRATULATIONS

Since the victory, the Rooks have been busy accepting congratulations. At school there were standing ovations, a banner in a hall, and a pizza party. There were appearances on television, and they went to the Apollo Theater for a live radio interview.

The major celebration was at Mr. Guccione's home, which consists of two former town houses on East 67th Street turned into one villa. Mr. Guccione and his wife, Kathy Keeton, are chairman and vice-chairwoman, respectively, of General Media International, which has been supporting schools in Harlem and which helped pay for the Rooks' trip to the national championship.

The Rooks arrived with their parents and with Mr. Gudonsky. He gave a speech about how the Rooks had broadened their horizons, thanks to chess. He paused to wave admiringly around the cavernous living room, with its stone fireplace from Italy and golden Steinway piano that once belonged to Judy Garland.

"And now we're here in a mansion," he said. "Normally at our school, broadening experiences mean going to the zoo or a museum."

The Rooks listened to the speeches politely, and they did not try to argue with the many adults who were pointing to them as symbols of hope. Some of them said there might be something to the idea.

"Before this, I wouldn't even have thought myself that a national chess champion would come from Harlem," said Jonathan Nock, thirteen years old. "But now everyone has to give us respect. It proves that we may live in a bad neighborhood, but we can do things for ourselves."

But the Rooks were not all that interested in talking about symbols or themselves. They spent most of the evening playing chess on the livingroom table. Between moves and nibbles of shrimp, they briefly discussed their ambitions—doctor, corporate lawyer, business executive, or preferably a professional chess player like Mr. Ashley—but they soon returned to concentrate on gambits.

When the time came to thank everyone who had helped them, thirteen-year-old Michael Johnson bravely stood up, expressed the team's gratitude, said it was a very nice house and paid everyone a compliment. He looked around at the adults, whose eyes were not entirely dry, and said, "You are all Raging Rooks in our hearts."

If You Go . . .

R. B.

[O]n the Seimstrand from St. Vincent, check departure times beforehand at the dock next to the Geest line terminal. The schedule in January 1975 called for a round trip to Union on Mondays and Thursdays. Fidays and Sundays she sailed to Mustique and back. Every other Tuesday, the Seimstrand sailed to Barbados. She sailed to Bequia almost every day. Sample fares (one-way) were $1.50 to Bequia, $3 to Cannouan, $3.50 to Mayreau, and $4 to Union. No discounts for round trip.

You may elect to take the day-long trip to Union and back. Or get off on Bequia, spend the day there, and board the Seimstrand again on its return from Union to St. Vincent that afternoon or evening. You may also stay on Bequia, Mustique, or Union until the Seimstrand next passes through.

Besides the Seimstrand there are smaller, motorized schooners such as the Friendship Rose that also ply the Grenadines. They are cheaper than the Seimstrand and thus attract poorer passengers willing to put up with the crowding and occasional sinkings.

''If You Go . . .'' by Ralph Blumenthal, April 27, 1975. Copyright © 1975 by the New York Times Company. Reprinted by permission.

10

Power and Culture

Notes Toward the Definition of Culture

T. S. ELIOT

It would appear, according to the account of levels of culture put forward . . . that among the more primitive societies, the higher types exhibit more marked differentiations of function among their members than the lower types. At a higher stage still, we find that some functions are more honored than others, and this division promotes the development of *classes,* in which higher honor and higher privilege are accorded, not merely to the person as functionary but as member of the class. And the class itself possesses a function, that of maintaining that part of the total culture of the society which pertains to that class. We have to try to keep in mind, that in a healthy society this maintenance of a particular level of culture is to the benefit, not merely of the class which maintains it, but of the society as a whole. Awareness of this fact will prevent us from supposing that the culture of a ''higher'' class is something superfluous to society as a whole, or to the majority, and from supposing that it is something which ought to be shared equally by all other classes. It should also remind the ''higher'' class, insofar as any such exists, that the survival of the culture in which it is particularly interested is dependent upon the health of the culture of the people.

It has now become a commonplace of contemporary thinking, that a society thus articulated is not the highest type to which we may aspire; but that it is indeed in the nature of things for a progressive society eventually to overcome these divisions, and that it is also within the power of our conscious direction, and therefore a duty incumbent upon us, to bring about a classless society. But while it is generally supposed that class, in any sense which maintains associations of the past, will disappear, it is now the opinion of some of the most advanced minds that some qualitative differences between individuals must still be recognized, and that the superior individuals must be formed into suitable groups, endowed with appropriate powers, and perhaps with varied emoluments and honors. Those

From ''Notes Toward the Definition of Culture'' by T. S. Eliot. Reprinted by permission of Faber and Faber Ltd.

groups, formed of individuals apt for powers of government and administration, will direct the public life of the nation; the individuals composing them will be spoken of as "leaders." There will be groups concerned with art, and groups concerned with science, and groups concerned with philosophy, as well as groups consisting of men of action: and these groups are what we call elites.

It is obvious, that while in the present state of society there is found the voluntary association of likeminded individuals, and association based upon common material interest, or common occupation or profession, the elites of the future will differ in one important respect from any that we know: they will replace the classes of the past, whose positive functions they will assume.

. . . it would seem that as we perfect the means for identifying at an early age, educating for their future role, and settling into positions of authority, the individuals who will form the elites, all former class distinctions will become a mere shadow or vestige, and the only social distinction of rank will be between the elites and the rest of the community, unless, as may happen, there is to be an order of precedence and prestige among the several elites themselves.

Superficially, [this] appears to aim at no more than what we must all desire—that all positions in society should be occupied by those who are best fitted to exercise the functions of the positions. We have all observed individuals occupying situations in life for which neither their character nor their intellect qualified them, and so placed only through nominal education, or birth or consanguinity. No honest man but is vexed by such a spectacle. But the doctrine of elites implies a good deal more than the rectification of such injustice. It posits an *atomic* view of society. . . .

The case for a society with a class structure, the affirmation that it is, in some sense, the "natural" society, is prejudiced if we allow ourselves to be hypnotized by the two contrasted terms *aristocracy* and *democracy*. The whole problem is falsified if we use these terms antithetically. What I have advanced is not a "defense of aristocracy"—an emphasis upon the importance of one organ of society. Rather it is a plea on behalf of a form of society in which an aristocracy should have a peculiar and essential function, as peculiar and essential as the function of any other part of society. What is important is a structure of society in which there will be, from "top" to "bottom," a continuous gradation of cultural levels: it is important to remember that we should not consider the upper levels as possessing *more* culture than the lower, but as representing a more conscious culture and a greater specialization of culture. I incline to believe that no true democracy can maintain itself unless it contains these different levels of culture. The levels of culture may also be seen as levels of power, to the extent that a smaller group at a higher level will have equal power with a larger group at a lower level; for it may be argued that complete equality means universal irresponsibility; and in such a society as I envisage, each individual would inherit greater or less responsibility toward the commonwealth, according to the position in society which he inherited—each class would have somewhat different responsibilities. A democracy in which everybody had an equal responsibility in everything would be oppressive for the conscientious and licentious for the rest.

There are other grounds upon which a graded society can be defended; and I hope, in general, that this essay will suggest lines of thought that I shall not myself explore; but I must constantly remind the reader of the limits of my subject. If we agree that the primary vehicle for the transmission of culture is the family, and if we agree that in a more highly civilized society there must be different levels of culture, then it follows that to ensure the transmission of the culture of these different levels there must be groups of families persisting, from generation to generation, each in the same way of life.

And once again I must repeat, that the "conditions of culture" which I set forth do not necessarily produce the higher civilization: I assert only that when they are absent, the higher civilization is unlikely to be found.

The German Ideology

KARL MARX AND FRIEDRICH ENGELS

The ideas of the ruling class are in every epoch the ruling ideas: that is, the class which is the ruling *material* force of society is at the same time its ruling *intellectual* force. The class which has the means of material production at its disposal has control at the same time over the means of mental production, so that thereby, generally speaking, the ideas of those who lack the means of mental production are subject to it. The ruling ideas are nothing more than the ideal expression of the dominant material relationships, the dominant material relationships grasped as ideas; hence of the relationships which make the one class the ruling one, therefore, the ideas of its dominance. The individuals composing the ruling class possess among other things consciousness, and therefore think. Therefore, insofar as they rule as a class and determine the extent and compass of an epoch, it is self-evident that they do this in its whole range, hence among other things rule also as thinkers, as producers of ideas, and regulate the production and distribution of the ideas of their age: thus their ideas are the ruling ideas of the epoch. For instance, in an age and in a country where royal power, aristocracy, and bourgeoisie are contending for mastery and where, therefore, mastery is shared, the doctrine of the separation of powers proves to be the dominant idea and is expressed as an "eternal law."

The division of labor, which we already saw above as one of the chief forces of history up till now, manifests itself also in the ruling class as the division of mental and material labor, so that inside this class one part appears as the thinkers of the class (its active, conceptive ideologists, who make the perfecting of the illusion of the class about itself their chief source of livelihood), while the others' attitude to these ideas and illusions is more passive and receptive, because they are in reality the active members of this class and have less time to make up illusions and ideas about themselves. Within this class this cleavage can even develop into a certain opposition and hostility between the two parts, which, however, in the case of a practical collision, in which the class itself is endangered, automatically comes to nothing, in which case there also vanishes the semblance that the ruling ideas were not the ideas of the ruling class and had a power distinct from the power of this class. The existence of revolutionary ideas in a particular period presupposes the existence of a revolutionary class; about the premises for the latter sufficient has already been said above.

From *The German Ideology,* by Karl Marx and Friedrich Engels. Reprinted by permission of International Publishers.

If now in considering the course of history we detach the ideas of the ruling class from the ruling class itself and attribute to them an independent existence, if we confine ourselves to saying that these or those ideas were dominant at a given time, without bothering ourselves about the conditions of production and the producers of these ideas, if we thus ignore the individuals and world conditions which are the source of the ideas, we can say, for instance, that during the time that the aristocracy was dominant, the concepts honor, loyalty, and the like were dominant, during the dominance of the bourgeoisie the concepts freedom, equality, and the like. The ruling class itself on the whole imagines this to be so. This conception of history, which is common to all historians, particularly since the eighteenth century, will necessarily come up against the phenomenon that increasingly abstract ideas hold sway, that is, ideas which increasingly take on the form of universality. For each new class which puts itself in the place of one ruling before it, is compelled, merely in order to carry through its aim, to represent its interest as the common interest of all the members of society, that is, expressed in ideal form: it has to give its ideas the form of universality, and represent them as the only rational, universally valid ones. The class making a revolution appears from the very start, if only because it is opposed to a *class,* not as a class but as the representative of the whole of society; it appears as the whole mass of society confronting the one ruling class. It can do this because, to start with, its interest really is more connected with the common interest of all other nonruling classes, because under the pressure of hitherto existing conditions its interest has not yet been able to develop as the particular interest of a particular class. Its victory, therefore, benefits also many individuals of the other classes which are not winning a dominant position, but only insofar as it now puts these individuals in a position to raise themselves into the ruling class. When the French bourgeoisie overthrew the power of the aristocracy, it thereby made it possible for many proletarians to raise themselves above the proletariat, but only insofar as they became bourgeois. Every new class, therefore, achieves its hegemony only on a broader basis than that of the class ruling previously, whereas the opposition of the nonruling class against the new ruling class later develops all the more sharply and profoundly. Both these things determine the fact that the struggle to be waged against this new ruling class, in its turn, aims at a more decided and radical negation of the previous conditions of society than could all previous classes which sought to rule.

This whole semblance, that the rule of a certain class is only the rule of certain ideas, comes to a natural end, of course, as soon as class rule in general ceases to be the form in which society is organized, that is to say, as soon as it is no longer necessary to represent a particular interest as general or the ''general interest'' as ruling.

Once the ruling ideas have been separated from the ruling individuals and, above all, form the relationships which result from a given stage of the mode of production, and in this way the conclusion has been reached that history is always under the sway of ideas, it is very easy to abstract from these various ideas ''*the* idea,'' the notion and so on as the dominant force in history, and thus to understand all these separate ideas and concepts as ''forms of self-determination'' on the part of *the* concept developing in history. It follows then naturally, too, that all the relationships of men can be derived from the concept of man, man as conceived, the essence of man, *Man*. This has been done by the speculative philosophers. Hegel himself confesses at the end of the *Geschichtsphilosophie* that he "has considered the progress of the *concept* only, and has represented in history the 'true *theodicy.'*" Now one can go back again to the producers of the "concept," to the theorists, ideologists, and philosophers, and one comes then to the conclusion that the philosophers, the thinkers as such, have at all times been dominant in history: a conclusion, as we see, already expressed by Hegel. The whole trick of proving the hegemony of the spirit in history (hierarchy Stirner calls it) is thus confined to the following three efforts.

No. 1. One must separate the ideas of those ruling for empirical reasons, under empirical conditions and as empirical individuals, from these actual rulers, and thus recognize the rule of ideas or illusions in history.

No. 2. One must bring an order into this rule of ideas, probe a mystical connection among the successive ruling ideas, which is managed by understanding them as "acts of self-determination on the part of the concept" (this is possible because by virtue of their empirical basis these ideas are really connected with one another and because, conceived as *mere* ideas, they become self-distinctions, distinctions made by thought).

No. 3. To remove the mystical appearance of this "self-determining concept" it is changed into a person—"Self-Consciousness"—or, to appear thoroughly materialistic, into a series of persons, who represent the "concept" in history, into the "thinkers," the "philosophers," the ideologists, who again are understood as the manufacturers of history, as the "council of guardians," as the rulers. Thus the whole body of materialistic elements has been removed from history and now full rein can be given to the speculative steed.

While in ordinary life every shopkeeper is very well able to distinguish between what somebody professes to be and what he really is, our historians have not yet won even this trivial insight. They take every epoch at its word and believe that everything it says and imagines about itself is true.

This historical method which reigned in Germany, and especially the reason why, must be understood from its connection with the illusion of ideologists in general, for example, the illusions of the jurists, politicians (of the practical statesmen among them, too), for the dogmatic dreamings and distortions of these fellows; this is explained perfectly easily from their practical position in life, their job, and the division of labor.

11

Power, Culture, and Media

The Wrong Kind of Readers: The Fall and Rise of the New Yorker

BEN H. BAGDIKIAN

Nothing in American publishing approaches the profitable heresies of the *New Yorker* magazine.

In an era when magazine editors regard covers with eye-catching headlines and striking graphics as imperative for survival, *New Yorker* covers typically are subdued watercolors of idyllic scenes. While other magazines assume that modern Americans don't read, *New Yorker* articles are incredibly long and weighted with detail. The magazine's cartoons ridicule many of its readers, the fashionably affluent who are portrayed in their Upper East Side penthouses speaking Ivy League patois. Editorial doctrine on other leading magazines calls for short punchy sentences, but the *New Yorker* is almost the last repository of the style and tone of Henry David Thoreau and Matthew Arnold, its chaste, old-fashioned columns breathing the quietude of nineteenth-century essays.

New Yorker advertisements are in a different world. They celebrate the ostentatious jet set. Christmas ads offer gold, diamond-encrusted wristwatches without prices, the implied message being that if you have to ask you have no business looking. A display of Jaeger–Le Coulture advises that the wristwatch "can be pivoted to reveal . . . your coat of arms." One ad for Audemars Piguet watches suggests giving three to impress a woman while another ad does suggest a price, murmuring in fine print, "From $10,500."

There are some homely products, like a Jeep station wagon. But it is displayed with a polo field in the background and is redeemed by other ads like the one that shows a couple in evening clothes embracing in the cockpit of an executive jet. Even in advertisements for products that cost less than $5,000, the characters seem to come from adjacent ads where cuff links are offered at $675, earrings at $3,500, a bracelet at $6,000, a brooch at $14,000. A Jean Patou perfume ad has no vulgar listing of price but says in bold letters what the spirit of all *New Yorker* ads seems to proclaim: "So rare . . . and available to so few."

Despite its violation of the most commanding conventions of what makes a magazine sell, the *New Yorker* for decades has been a leader in making money.

Over the years, the magazine was the envy of the periodical industry in the standard measure of financial success—the number of advertising pages sold annually. Year after year, the *New Yorker* was first or second, so fixed in its reputation that other magazines promoting their effectiveness would tell prospective advertisers they were first or second "after the *New Yorker*," the implication being that, like the New York Yankees in 1950s baseball, the *New Yorker* was unassailably in first place.

That was true until 1967. The year before was a record one for the *New Yorker*. Most people in the industry believe that in 1966 the magazine attained the largest number of advertising pages sold in a year by any magazine of general circulation in the history of publishing. In 1966, the *New Yorker* sold 6,100 pages of ads. Its circulation was at its usual level, around 448,000.

In 1967, a strange disease struck. The *New Yorker*'s circulation remained the same, but the number of ad pages dropped disastrously. In a few years, 2,500 pages of ads disappeared, a loss of almost 50 percent. The magazine's net profits shrank from the 1966 level of $3 million to less than $1 million. Dividends per share, $10.93 in 1955, were down to $3.67 by 1970.

The disastrous loss of advertising occurred despite a continued high level of circulation which, to lay observers, would seem to be the only statistic needed to indicate a magazine's success. The popular assumption is that if enough people care enough about a publication or a television program to buy it or to turn to it, advertisers will beat a path to their doorway. That clearly was not happening at the *New Yorker*.

The onset of the *New Yorker*'s malady can be traced to July 15, 1967. That issue of the magazine carried a typically long report under the typically ambiguous title "Reporter at Large." This is the standing head for *New Yorker* articles dealing in depth with subjects as diverse as the history of oranges, the socialization of rats, and the culture of an Irish saloon. This time the subject was a report from the village of Ben Suc in Vietnam.

The author was Jonathan Schell, a recent Harvard graduate who, after commencement, visited his brother, Orville, in Taiwan, where Orville was doing Chinese studies. Once in Taiwan, Jonathan decided to take a trip to Vietnam, where, according to the standard press, the American war against the Vietcong was going well.

In Saigon, Schell was liked and "adopted" by the colonels, perhaps because he had proper establishment connections: he carried an expired *Harvard Crimson* press pass and his father was a successful Manhattan lawyer. The military gave him treatment ordinarily reserved for famous correspondents sympathetic to the war. In addition to attending the daily military briefing sessions in Saigon, the basis for most reports back to the United States, Schell was also taken on helicopter assaults and bombing and strafing missions and given ground transportation to battle scenes.

The assumption of his hosts was that the nice kid from Harvard would be impressed with the power and the purpose of the American mission. But Schell was appalled. The war, it seemed to him, was not the neat containment of Soviet-Chinese aggression that had been advertised at home or the attempt of humane Americans to save democracy-loving natives from the barbaric Vietcong. Like all wars, this one was mutually brutal. Americans shot, bombed, and uprooted civilians in massive campaigns that resulted in the disintegration of Vietnamese social structures. And the Americans were not winning the war.

Schell returned to the United States disturbed by his findings. He visited a family friend, William Shawn, the quiet, eccentric editor of the *New Yorker,* who had known the Schell children since childhood. Shawn listened to Schell's story and asked him to try writing about his experiences. Schell produced what Shawn called "a perfect piece of *New Yorker* reporting." The story, which ran in the July 15, 1967, issue, told in clear, quiet detail what the assault on one village meant to the villagers and to the American soldiers.

Shawn said he had serious doubts about the war before Schell appeared, "but certainly I saw it differently talking to him and reading what he wrote. That was when I became convinced that we shouldn't be there and the war was a mistake."

Thereafter, the *New Yorker* in issue after issue spoke simply and clearly against the war. It was not the first publication to do so, but at the time most important media followed the general line that the war was needed to stop international communism and save the Vietnamese, and that the United States was on the verge of victory. Most newspapers, including the two most influential dailies in the country, the *New York Times* and the *Washington Post,* editorially supported the war. There were growing popular protests, but the mass marches were yet to come. Neither the My Lai massacre nor the Tet offensive had occurred, and the exposure of the Pentagon Papers detailing a long history of government lying about Indochina was still four years away.

The *New Yorker* was the voice of the elite, the repository of advertisements for the hedonistic rich, of genteel essays on the first day of spring, of temperate profiles of aesthetes, of humor so sophisticated that it seemed designed solely for intelligent graduates of the best schools. The *Wall Street Journal* once labeled it "Urbanity, Inc." When the magazine spoke clearly against the war, it was a significant event in the course of public attitudes toward the American enterprise in Vietnam. If this apolitical organ of the elite said the war was morally wrong, it was saying it to the country's establishment.

At the same time, the magazine was giving the message to a quite different constituency. A *New Yorker* staff member recalled that in 1967, "Our writers would come back from speaking on campuses and say that the kids are reading the *New Yorker* out loud in the dormitories."

Ordinarily, this is a happy event in the life of a magazine. There is always a need for some younger readers so that when older subscribers die the magazine will not die with them. But advertisers live in the present. Throughout its crisis years after 1966, the *New Yorker* audience actually grew in numbers. But while the median age of readers in 1966 was 48.7—the age when executives would be at the peak of their spending power—by 1974, *New Yorker* subscribers' median age was 34, a number brought down by the infusion of college students in their late teens and early twenties. Many college students will form the affluent elite of the future, but at the moment they are not buying $10,500 wristwatches and $14,000 brooches. They were buying the magazine because of its clear, moral stand against the war and its quiet, detailed reporting from the scene.

It was then that ad pages began their drastic disappearance. An easy explanation would be that conservative corporations withdrew their ads in political protest. Some did. But the majority of the losses came from a more impersonal process, one of profound significance to the character of contemporary American mass media. The *New Yorker* had begun to attract "the wrong kind" of reader. Circulation remained the same, but the magazine had become the victim, as it had formerly been the beneficiary, of an iron rule of advertising-supported media: it is less important that people buy your publication (or listen to your program) than that they be "the right kind" of people.

The "right kind" usually means affluent consumers eighteen to forty-nine years of age, the heavy buying years, with above-median family income. Newspapers, magazines, and radio and television operators publicly boast of their audience size, which is a significant factor. But when they sit down at conferences with big advertisers, they do not present simple numbers but reams of computer printouts that show the characteristics of their audience in income, age, sex, marital status, ethnic background, social habits, residence, family structure, occupation, and buying patterns. These are components of demographics, the study of population characteristics.

The standard cure for "bad demographics" in newspapers, magazines, radio, and television is simple: change the content. Fill the publication or the programs with material that will attract the kind of people the advertisers want. The general manager of *Rolling Stone* expressed it when that magazine wanted to attract a higher level of advertiser: "We had to deliver a more high-quality reader. The only way to deliver a different kind of reader is to change editorial." If an editor refuses or fails to change, the editor is fired.

The *New Yorker* faced this problem but it did not fire the editor; nor did the editor "change editorial." It is almost certain that for conventional corporate ownership the "cure" would be quick and decisive. William Shawn would have "changed editorial," which would have meant dropping the insistent line on the war in Vietnam, or he would have been fired. In the place of the Vietnam reporting and commentary there would have been less controversial material that would adjust demographics back to the affluent population of buying age and assuage the anger of those corporations that disliked the magazine's position on the war.

But the *New Yorker* is not the property of a conglomerate nor is it insistent on trouble-free maximum profits. It is an idiosyncrasy in modern media, owned by heirs to the founders who regard it as an institution to be supported in foul weather as well as fair and who are wedded to an idea normally given only lip service: total freedom for the editors.

William Shawn, a Dickensian man, modest in manner and speech, reddens in indignation when asked whether, during the critical 1966–1974 period, the business leaders of the magazine informed him that his editorial content was attracting the wrong kind of reader.

"It would be unthinkable for the advertising and business people to tell me that," he says. "I didn't hear about it until the early 1970s. . . . It gradually sank in on me that the *New Yorker* was being read by young people. I didn't know it in any formal way. Who the readers are I really don't want to know. I don't want to know because we edit the magazine for ourselves and hope there will be people like ourselves and people like our writers who will find it interesting and worthwhile."

Shawn's words are standard rhetoric of publishers and editors when they are asked about separation of editorial independence and advertising. The rhetoric usually has little relation to reality. Increasingly, editorial content of publications and broadcasting is dictated by the computer printouts on advertising agency desks, not the other way around. When there is a conflict between the printouts and an independent editor, the printouts win. Were it not for the incontrovertible behavior of the *New Yorker* during the Vietnam war, it would be difficult not to regard Shawn's words as the standard mythic rhetoric.

"We never talk about 'the readers,'" Shawn said. "I won't permit that—if I may put it so arrogantly. I don't want to speak about our readers as a 'market.' I don't want them to feel that they are just consumers to us. I find that obnoxious."

The full-page ads of other newspapers, magazines, and broadcast networks in the *New York Times* and the *Wall Street Journal* are often puzzling to the lay reader. They do not urge people to read and listen. They seem to be filled with statistics of little interest to potential subscribers or viewers. They are intended to show the advertising industry that the demographics of the publication or station are "correct." But unlike the typical industry ad, *New Yorker* promotional ads are limited to stressing the quality of the writing.

Eventually during the 1967–1974 period Shawn did hear what he called "murmurings":

> There were murmurings in the background about three things: the magazine was getting too serious, the magazine was getting too much into politics, and the pieces were getting too long. My reaction was that we should do nothing about it. Whatever change took place did so gradually and spontaneously as we saw the world. . . . To be silent when something is going on that shouldn't be going on would be cowardly. . . . We published information we believed the public should have and we said what we believed. If the magazine was serious, it was no more serious than we were. If there was too much politics, it was because politics became more important and it was on our minds.

Shawn noted that the *Time-Life* and *Reader's Digest* empires succeeded because they were started by editors who expressed their own values regardless of the market and thereby established an identity that made for long-range success.

> Now the whole idea is that you edit for a market and if possible design a magazine with that in mind. Now magazines aren't started with the desire for someone to express what he believes. I think the whole trend is so destructive and so unpromising

so far as journalism is concerned that it is very worrisome. Younger editors and writers are growing up in that atmosphere. "We want to edit the magazine to give the audience what they want. What do we give them?"

There is a fallacy in that calculation. . . . The fallacy is if you edit that way, to give back to the readers only what they think they want, you'll never give them something new they didn't know about. You stagnate. It's just this back-and-forth and you end up with the networks, TV, and the movies. The whole thing begins to be circular. The new tendency is to discourage this creative process and kill originality.

We sometimes publish a piece that I'm afraid not more than one hundred readers will want. Perhaps it's too difficult, too obscure. But it's important to have. That's how people learn and grow. This other way is bad for our entire society and we're suffering from it in almost all forms of communications.

A magazine industry executive was asked if a magazine owned by a conventional corporation would have supported Shawn during the lean years. He answered: "Are you kidding? One bad year like the one the *New Yorker* had in 1967 and either the editorial formula would change or the editor would be out on his ear. It happens regularly."

By the 1980s, the *New Yorker* was economically healthy again. Its circulation in 1980 was over 500,000, it was running 4,220 pages of ads a year, fourth among all American magazines, and its profits were back above $3 million. That seems to be a heartwarming morality lesson in the rewards of integrity. But the *New Yorker* remains an anomaly in the world of American media of the 1980s. Newspapers and magazines in the main do not want merely readers; they want affluent readers. Broadcasters do not want just any listeners; they want rich ones.

Years after the near-fatal disease struck the *New Yorker*, when recovery had set in, the magazine's Market Research Department commissioned a professional survey to analyze its subscribers. For the edification of prospective advertisers in the *New Yorker*, its salespeople could display 134 pages of statistical tables that showed that the magazine's readers were 58.5 percent male, 63.8 percent married (6.6 percent widowed, 8.1 percent separated or divorced); 94.0 percent had attended college or had degrees (21.8 percent had Ph.D.'s); 71.0 percent were in business, industry, or professions; 19.3 percent were in top management; 16.6 percent were members of corporate boards of directors; 40.1 percent collected original paintings and sculptures; 26.1 percent bought wine by the case; 59.3 percent owned corporate stock, which had an average value of $75,000 (though a scrupulous footnote to this datum says, "In order not to distort the average . . . one respondent reporting $25,000,000 was omitted from the calculation"); and the median age was 48.4. In other words, the elite audience was "the right kind" for advertising expensive merchandise.

By 1981, the *New Yorker* had recovered enough of its high-quality demographics to make it a desirable carrier for a full-page advertisement by the Magazine Publishers Association. The ad pursued the theme that magazines are superior for advertising because they don't want readers who aren't going to buy. The headline on the ad read: A MAGAZINE DOESN'T WASTE WORDS ON WINDOW SHOPPERS.

Neither does any newspaper or broadcast station that makes most of its money from advertising.

Sex, Lies, and Advertising

GLORIA STEINEM

About three years ago, as *glasnost* was beginning and *Ms.* seemed to be ending, I was invited to a press lunch for a Soviet official. He entertained us with anecdotes about new problems of democracy in his country. Local Communist leaders were being criticized in their media for the first time, he explained, and they were angry.

"So I'll have to ask my American friends," he finished pointedly, "how more *subtly* to control the press." In the silence that followed, I said, "Advertising."

The reporters laughed, but later, one of them took me aside: How *dare* I suggest that freedom of the press was limited? How dare I imply that his news-weekly could be influenced by ads?

I explained that I was thinking of advertising's media-wide influence on most of what we read. Even newsmagazines use "soft" cover stories to sell ads, confuse readers with "advertorials," and occasionally self-censor on subjects known to be a problem with big advertisers.

But, I also explained, I was thinking especially of women's magazines. There, it isn't just a little content that's devoted to attracting ads, it's almost all of it. That's why advertisers—not readers—have always been the problem for *Ms.* As the only women's magazine that didn't supply what the ad world euphemistically describes as "supportive editorial atmosphere" or "complementary copy" (for instance, articles that praise food/fashion/beauty subjects to "support" and "complement" food/fashion/beauty ads), *Ms.* could never attract enough advertising to break even.

"Oh, *women's* magazines," the journalist said with contempt. "Everybody knows they're catalogs—but who cares? They have nothing to do with journalism."

I can't tell you how many times I've had this argument in twenty-five years of working for many kinds of publications. Except as moneymaking machines—"cash cows" as they are so elegantly called in the trade—women's magazines are rarely taken seriously. Though changes being made by women have been called more far-reaching than the industrial revolution—and though many editors try hard to reflect some of them in the few pages left to them after all the ad-related subjects have been covered—the magazines serving the female half of this

From "Sex, Lies and Advertising" by Gloria Steinem. *Ms. Magazine*, July/August 1990. Reprinted by permission.

country are still far below the journalistic and ethical standards of news and general interest publications. Most depressing of all, this doesn't even rate an exposé.

If *Time* and *Newsweek* had to lavish praise on cars in general and credit General Motors in particular to get GM ads, there would be a scandal—maybe a criminal investigation. When women's magazines from *Seventeen* to *Lear's* praise beauty products in general and credit Revlon in particular to get ads, it's just business as usual.

I

When *Ms.* began, we didn't consider *not* taking ads. The most important reason was keeping the price of a feminist magazine low enough for most women to afford. But the second and almost equal reason was providing a forum where women and advertisers could talk to each other and improve advertising itself. After all, it was (and still is) as potent a source of information in this country as news or TV and movie dramas.

We decided to proceed in two stages. First, we would convince makers of "people products" used by both men and women but advertised mostly to men— cars, credit cards, insurance, sound equipment, financial services, and the like— that their ads should be placed in a women's magazine. Since they were accustomed to the division between editorial and advertising in news and general interest magazines, this would allow our editorial content to be free and diverse. Second, we would add the best ads for whatever traditional "women's products" (clothes, shampoo, fragrance, food, and so on) that surveys showed *Ms.* readers used. But we would ask them to come in *without* the usual quid pro quo of "complementary copy."

We knew the second step might be harder. Food advertisers have always demanded that women's magazines publish recipes and articles on entertaining (preferably ones that name their products) in return for their ads; clothing advertisers expect to be surrounded by fashion spreads (especially ones that credit their designers); and shampoo, fragrance, and beauty products in general usually insist on positive editorial coverage of beauty subjects, plus photo credits besides. That's why women's magazines look the way they do. But if we could break this link between ads and editorial content, then we wanted good ads for "women's products," too.

By playing their part in this unprecedented mix of *all* the things our readers need and use, advertisers also would be rewarded: ads for products like cars and mutual funds would find a new growth market; the best ads for women's products would no longer be lost in oceans of ads for the same category; and both would have access to a laboratory of smart and caring readers whose response would help create effective ads for other media as well.

I thought then that our main problem would be the imagery in ads themselves. Carmakers were still draping blondes in evening gowns over the hoods like ornaments. Authority figures were almost always male, even in ads for products that only women used. Sadistic, he-man campaigns even won industry praise. (For instance, *Advertising Age* had hailed the infamous Silva Thin cigarette theme, "How to Get a Woman's Attention: Ignore Her," as "brilliant.") Even in medical journals, tranquilizer ads showed depressed housewives standing beside piles of dirty dishes and promised to get them back to work.

Obviously, *Ms.* would have to avoid such ads and seek out the best ones—but this didn't seem impossible. The *New Yorker* had been selecting ads for aesthetic reasons for years, a practice that only seemed to make advertisers more eager to be in its pages. *Ebony* and *Essence* were asking for ads with positive black images, and though their struggle was hard, they weren't being called unreasonable.

Clearly, what *Ms.* needed was a very special publisher and ad sales staff. I could think of only one woman with experience on the business side of magazines—Patricia Carbine, who recently had become a vice president of *McCall's* as well as its editor in chief—and the reason I knew her name was a good omen. She had been managing editor at *Look* (really *the* editor, but its owner refused to put a female name at the top of his masthead) when I was writing a column there. After I did an early interview with Cesar Chavez, then just emerging as a leader of migrant labor, and the publisher turned it down because he was worried about ads from Sunkist, Pat was the one who intervened. As I learned later, she had told the publisher she would resign if the interview wasn't published. Mainly because *Look* couldn't afford to lose Pat, it *was* published (and the ads from Sunkist never arrived).

Though I barely knew this woman, she had done two things I always remembered: put her job on the line in a way that editors often talk about but rarely do, and been so loyal to her colleagues that she never told me or anyone outside *Look* that she had done so.

Fortunately, Pat did agree to leave *McCall's* and take a huge cut in salary to become publisher of *Ms.* She became responsible for training and inspiring generations of young women who joined the *Ms.* ad sales force, many of whom went on to become "firsts" at the top of publishing. When *Ms.* first started, however, there were so few women with experience selling space that Pat and I made the rounds of ad agencies ourselves. Later, the fact that *Ms.* was asking companies to do business in a different way meant our saleswomen had to make many times the usual number of calls—first to convince agencies and then client companies besides—and to present endless amounts of research. I was often asked to do a final ad presentation, or see some higher decision maker, or speak to women employees so executives could see the interest of women they worked with. That's why I spent more time persuading advertisers than editing or writing for *Ms.* and why I ended up with an unsentimental education in the seamy underside of publishing that few writers see (and even fewer magazines can publish).

Let me take you with us through some experiences, just as they happened:

- Cheered on by early support from Volkswagen and one or two other car companies, we scrape together time and money to put on a major reception in

Detroit. We know U.S. carmakers firmly believe that women choose the upholstery, not the car, but we are armed with statistics and reader mail to prove the
contrary: a car is an important purchase for women, one that symbolizes mobility and freedom.

But almost nobody comes. We are left with many pounds of shrimp on the
table, and quite a lot of egg on our face. We blame ourselves for not guessing that
there would be a baseball pennant play-off on the same day, but executives go out
of their way to explain they wouldn't have come anyway. Thus begins ten years
of knocking on hostile doors, presenting endless documentation, and hiring a
full-time saleswoman in Detroit; all necessary before *Ms.* gets any real results.

This long saga has a semihappy ending: foreign and, later, domestic carmakers
eventually provided *Ms.* with enough advertising to make cars one of our top
sources of ad revenue. Slowly, Detroit began to take the women's market seriously enough to put car ads in other women's magazines, too, thus freeing a few
pages from the hothouse of fashion-beauty-food ads.

But long after figures showed a third, even a half, of many car models being
bought by women, U.S. makers continued to be uncomfortable addressing
women. Unlike foreign carmakers, Detroit never quite learned the secret of
creating intelligent ads that exclude no one, and then placing them in women's
magazines to overcome past exclusion. (*Ms.* readers were so grateful for a routine
Honda ad featuring rack and pinion steering, for instance, that they sent fan
mail.) Even now, Detroit continues to ask, "Should we make special ads for
women?" Perhaps that's why some foreign cars still have a disproportionate
share of the U.S. women's market.

- In the *Ms.* Gazette, we do a brief report on a congressional hearing into
chemicals used in hair dyes that are absorbed through the skin and may be
carcinogenic. Newspapers report this too, but Clairol, a Bristol-Myers subsidiary that makes dozens of products—a few of which have just begun to advertise in *Ms.*—is outraged. Not at newspapers or newsmagazines, just at us. It's
bad enough that *Ms.* is the only women's magazine refusing to provide the
usual "complementary" articles and beauty photos, but to criticize one of their
categories—*that* is going too far.

We offer to publish a letter from Clairol telling its side of the story. In an
excess of solicitousness, we even put this letter in the Gazette, not in Letters to
the Editors where it belongs. Nonetheless—and in spite of surveys that show *Ms.*
readers are active women who use more of almost everything Clairol makes than
do the readers of any other women's magazine—*Ms.* gets almost none of these
ads for the rest of its natural life.

Meanwhile, Clairol changes its hair coloring formula, apparently in response
to the hearings we reported.

- Our saleswomen set out early to attract ads for consumer electronics: sound
equipment, calculators, computers, vcrs, and the like. We know that our
readers are determined to be included in the technological revolution. We know

from reader surveys that *Ms.* readers are buying this stuff in numbers as high as those of magazines like *Playboy;* or "men 18 to 34," the prime targets of the consumer electronics industry. Moreover, unlike traditional women's products that our readers buy but don't need to read articles about, these are subjects they want covered in our pages. There actually *is* a supportive editorial atmosphere.

"But women don't understand technology," say executives at the end of ad presentations. "Maybe not," we respond, "but neither do men—and we all buy it."

"If women *do* buy it," say the decision makers, "they're asking their husbands and boyfriends what to buy first." We produce letters from *Ms.* readers saying how turned off they are when salesmen say things like "Let me know when your husband can come in."

After several years of this, we get a few ads for compact sound systems. Some of them come from JVC, whose vice president, Harry Elias, is trying to convince his Japanese bosses that there is something called a women's market. At his invitation, I find myself speaking at huge trade shows in Chicago and Las Vegas, trying to persuade JVC dealers that showrooms don't have to be locker rooms where women are made to feel unwelcome. But as it turns out, the shows themselves are part of the problem. In Las Vegas, the only women around the technology displays are seminude models serving champagne. In Chicago, the big attraction is Marilyn Chambers, who followed Linda Lovelace of *Deep Throat* fame as Chuck Traynor's captive and/or employee. VCRs are being demonstrated with her porn videos.

In the end, we get ads for a car stereo now and then, but no VCRs; some IBM personal computers, but no Apple or Japanese ones. We notice that office magazines like *Working Woman* and *Savvy* don't benefit as much as they should from office equipment ads either. In the electronics world, women and technology seem mutually exclusive. It remains a decade behind even Detroit.

- Because we get letters from little girls who love toy trains, and who ask our help in changing ads and box-top photos that feature little boys only, we try to get toy-train ads from Lionel. It turns out that Lionel executives *have* been concerned about little girls. They made a pink train, and were surprised when it didn't sell.

Lionel bows to consumer pressure with a photograph of a boy *and* a girl—but only on some of their boxes. They fear that, if trains are associated with girls, they will be devalued in the minds of boys. Needless to say, *Ms.* gets no train ads, and little girls remain a mostly unexplored market. By 1986, Lionel is put up for sale.

But for different reasons, we haven't had much luck with other kinds of toys either. In spite of many articles on child-rearing; an annual listing of nonsexist, multiracial toys by Letty Cottin Pogrebin; Stories for Free Children, a regular feature also edited by Letty; and other prizewinning features for or about children, we get virtually no toy ads. Generations of *Ms.* saleswomen explain to toy manufacturers that a larger proportion of *Ms.* readers have preschool children than do the readers of other women's magazines, but this industry can't believe feminists have or care about children.

▪ When *Ms.* begins, the staff decides not to accept ads for feminine hygiene sprays or cigarettes: they are damaging and carry no appropriate health warnings. Though we don't think we should tell our readers what to do, we do think we should provide facts so they can decide for themselves. Since the antismoking lobby has been pressing for health warnings on cigarette ads, we decide to take them only as they comply.

Philip Morris is among the first to do so. One of its brands, Virginia Slims, is also sponsoring women's tennis and the first national polls of women's opinions. On the other hand, the Virginia Slims theme, "You've come a long way, baby," has more than a "baby" problem. It makes smoking a symbol of progress for women.

We explain to Philip Morris that this slogan won't do well in our pages, but they are convinced its success with some women means it will work with *all* women. Finally, we agree to publish an ad for a Virginia Slims calendar as a test. The letters from readers are critical—and smart. For instance: Would you show a black man picking cotton, the same man in a Cardin suit, and symbolize the antislavery and civil rights movements by smoking? Of course not. But instead of honoring the test results, the Philip Morris people seem angry to be proven wrong. They take away ads for *all* their many brands.

This costs *Ms.* about $250,000 the first year. After five years, we can no longer keep track. Occasionally, a new set of executives listens to *Ms.* saleswomen, but because we won't take Virginia Slims, not one Philip Morris product returns to our pages for the next sixteen years.

Gradually, we also realize our naiveté in thinking we *could* decide against taking cigarette ads. They became a disporportionate support of magazines the moment they were banned on television, and few magazines could compete and survive without them; certainly not *Ms.,* which lacks so many other categories. By the time statistics in the 1980s showed that women's rate of lung cancer was approaching men's, the necessity of taking cigarette ads has become a kind of prison.

▪ General Mills, Pillsbury, Carnation, DelMonte, Dole, Kraft, Stouffer, Hormel, Nabisco: you name the food giant, we try it. But no matter how desirable the *Ms.* readership, our lack of recipes is lethal.

We explain to them that placing food ads *only* next to recipes associates food with work. For many women, it is a negative that works *against* the ads. Why not place food ads in diverse media without recipes (thus reaching more men, who are now a third of the shoppers in supermarkets anyway), and leave the recipes to specialty magazines like *Gourmet* (a third of whose readers are also men)?

These arguments elicit interest, but except for an occasional ad for a convenience food, instant coffee, diet drinks, yogurt, or such extras as avocados and almonds, this mainstay of the publishing industry stays closed to us. Period.

- Traditionally, wines and liquors didn't advertise to women: men were thought to make the brand decisions, even if women did the buying. But after endless presentations, we begin to make a dent in this category. Thanks to the unconventional Michel Roux of Carillon Importers (distributors of Grand Marnier, Absolut Vodka, and others), who assumes that food and drink have no gender, some ads are leaving their men's club.

Beermakers are still selling masculinity. It takes *Ms.* fully eight years to get its first beer ad (Michelob). In general, however, liquor ads are less stereotyped in their imagery—and far less controlling of the editorial content around them—than are women's products. But given the underrepresentation of other categories, these very facts tend to create a disproportionate number of alcohol ads in the pages of *Ms.* This in turn dismays readers worried about women and alcoholism.

- We hear in 1980 that women in the Soviet Union have been producing feminist *samizdat* (underground, self-published books) and circulating them throughout the country. As punishment, four of the leaders have been exiled. Though we are operating on our usual shoestring, we solicit individual contributions to send Robin Morgan to interview these women in Vienna.

The result is an exclusive cover story that includes the first news of a populist peace movement against the Afghanistan occupation, a prediction of *glasnost* to come, and a grass-roots, intimate view of Soviet women's lives. From the popular press to women's studies courses, the response is great. The story wins a Front Page award.

Nonetheless, this journalistic coup undoes years of efforts to get an ad schedule from Revlon. Why? Because the Soviet women on our cover *are not wearing makeup*.

- Four years of research and presentations go into convincing airlines that women now make travel choices and business trips. United, the first airline to advertise in *Ms.*, is so impressed with the response from our readers that one of its executives appears in a film for our ad presentations. As usual, good ads get great results.

But we have problems unrelated to such results. For instance: because American Airlines flight attendants include among their labor demands the stipulation that they could choose to have their last names preceded by "Ms." on their name tags—in a long-delayed revolt against the standard, "I am your pilot, Captain Rothgart, and this is your flight attendant, Cindy Sue"—American officials seem to hold the magazine responsible. We get no ads.

There is still a different problem at Eastern. A vice-president cancels subscriptions for thousands of copies on Eastern flights. Why? Becasue he is offended by ads for lesbian poetry journals in the *Ms.* Classified. A "family airline," as he explains to me coldly on the phone, has to "draw the line somewhere."

It's obvious that *Ms.* can't exclude lesbians and serve women. We've been trying to make that point ever since our first issue included an article by and about lesbians, and both Suzanne Levine, our managing editor, and I were lectured by such heavy hitters as Ed Kosner, then editor of *Newsweek* (and now of *New York Magazine*), who insisted that *Ms.* should "position" itself *against* lesbians. But our advertisers have paid to reach a guaranteed number of readers, and soliciting new subscriptions to compensate for Eastern would cost $150,000, plus rebating money in the meantime.

Like almost everything ad-related, this presents an elaborate organizing problem. After days of searching for sympathetic members of the Eastern board, Frank Thomas, president of the Ford Foundation, kindly offers to call Roswell Gilpatrick, a director of Eastern. I talk with Mr. Gilpatrick, who calls Frank Borman, then the president of Eastern. Frank Borman calls me to say that his airline is not in the business of censoring magazines: *Ms.* will be returned to Eastern flights.

- Women's access to insurance and credit is vital, but with the exception of Equitable and a few other ad pioneers, such financial services address men. For almost a decade after the Equal Credit Opportunity Act passes in 1974, we try to convince American Express that women are a growth market—but nothing works.

Finally, a former professor of Russian named Jerry Welsh becomes head of marketing. He assumes that women should be cardholders, and persuades his colleagues to feature women in a campaign. Thanks to this 1980s series, the growth rate for female cardholders surpasses that for men.

For this article, I asked Jerry Welsh if he would explain why American Express waited so long. "Sure," he said, "they were afraid of having a 'pink' card."

- Women of color read *Ms.* in disproportionate numbers. This is a source of pride to *Ms.* staffers, who are also more racially representative than the editors of other women's magazines. But this reality is obscured by ads filled with enough white women to make a reader snowblind.

Pat Carbine remembers mostly "astonishment" when she requested African American, Hispanic, Asian, and other diverse images. Marcia Ann Gillespie, a *Ms.* editor who was previously the editor in chief of *Essence,* witnesses ad bias a second time: having tried for *Essence* to get white advertisers to use black images (Revlon did so eventually, but L'Oréal, Lauder, Chanel, and other companies never did), she sees similar problems getting integrated ads for an integrated magazine. Indeed, the ad world often creates black and Hispanic ads only for black and Hispanic media. In an exact parallel of the fear that marketing a product to women will endanger its appeal to men, the response is usually, "But your [white] readers won't identify."

In fact, those we are able to get—for instance, a Max Factor ad made for *Essence* that Linda Wachner gives us after she becomes president—are praised by white readers, too. But there are pathetically few such images.

- By the end of 1986, production and mailing costs have risen astronomically, ad income is flat, and competition for ads is stiffer than ever. The 60/40 preponderance of edit over ads that we promised to readers becomes 50/50; children's stories, most poetry, and some fiction are casualties of less space; in order to get variety into limited pages, the length (and sometimes the depth) of articles suffers; and, though we do refuse most of the ads that would look like a parody in our pages, we get so worn down that some slip through. Still, readers perform miracles. Though we haven't been able to afford a subscription mailing in two years, they maintain our guaranteed circulation of 450,000.

Nonetheless, media reports on *Ms.* often insist that our unprofitability must be due to reader disinterest. The myth that advertisers simply follow readers is very strong. Not one reporter notes that other comparable magazines our size (say, *Vanity Fair* or the *Atlantic*) have been losing more money in one year than *Ms.* has lost in sixteen years. No matter how much never-to-be-recovered cash is poured into starting a magazine or keeping one going, appearances seem to be all that matter. (Which is why we haven't been able to explain our fragile state in public. Nothing causes ad-flight like the smell of nonsuccess.)

My healthy response is anger. My not-so-healthy response is constant worry. Also an obsession with finding one more rescue. There is hardly a night when I don't wake up with sweaty palms and pounding heart, scared that we won't be able to pay the printer or the post office; scared most of all that closing our doors will hurt the women's movement.

Out of chutzpah and desperation, I arrange a lunch with Leonard Lauder, president of Estée Lauder. With the exception of Clinique (the brainchild of Carol Phillips), none of Lauder's hundreds of products has been advertised in *Ms.* A year's schedule of ads for just three or four of them could save us. Indeed, as the scion of a family-owned company whose ad practices are followed by the beauty industry, he is one of the few men who could liberate many pages in all women's magazines just by changing his mind about "complementary copy."

Over a lunch that costs more than we can pay for some articles, I explain the need for his leadership. I also lay out the record of *Ms.:* more literary and journalistic prizes won, more new issues introduced into the mainstream, new writers discovered, and impact on society than any other magazine; more articles that became books, stories that became movies, ideas that became television series, and newly advertised products that became profitable; and, most important for him, a place for his ads to reach women who aren't reachable through any other women's magazine. Indeed, if there is one constant characteristic of the ever-changing *Ms.* readership, it is its impact as leaders. Whether it's waiting until later to have first babies, or pioneering PABA as sun protection in cosmetics, *whatever Ms.* readers are doing today, a third to a half of American women will be doing three to five years from now. It's never failed.

But, he says, *Ms.* readers are not *our* women. They're not interested in things like fragrance and blush-on. If they were, *Ms.* would write articles about them.

On the contrary, I explain, surveys show they are more likely to buy such things than the readers of, say, *Cosmopolitan* or *Vogue*. They're good customers because they're out in the world enough to need several sets of everything: home, work, purse, travel, gym, and so on. They just don't need to read articles about these things. Would he ask a men's magazine to publish monthly columns on how to shave before he advertised Aramis products (his line for men)?

He concedes that beauty features are often concocted more for advertisers than readers. But *Ms.* isn't appropriate for his ads anyway, he explains. Why? Because Estée Lauder is selling "a kept-woman mentality."

I can't quite believe this. Sixty percent of the users of his products are salaried, and generally resemble *Ms.* readers. Besides, his company has the appeal of having been started by a creative and hardworking woman, his mother, Estée Lauder.

That doesn't matter, he says. He knows his customers, and they would *like* to be kept women. That's why he will never advertise in *Ms.*

In November 1987, by vote of the Ms. Foundation for Education and Communication (*Ms.*'s owner and publisher, the media subsidiary of the Ms. Foundation for Women), *Ms.* was sold to a company whose officers, Australian feminists Sandra Yates and Anne Summers, raised the investment money in their country that *Ms.* couldn't find in its own. They also started *Sassy* for teenage women.

In their two-year tenure, circulation was raised to 550,000 by investment in circulation mailings, and, to the dismay of some readers, editorial features on clothes and new products made a more traditional bid for ads. Nonetheless, ad pages fell below previous levels. In addition, *Sassy,* whose fresh voice and sexual frankness were an unprecedented success with young readers, was targeted by two mothers from Indiana who began, as one of them put it, "calling every Christian organization I could think of." In response to this controversy, several crucial advertisers pulled out.

Such links between ads and editorial content were a problem in Australia, too, but to a lesser degree. "Our readers pay two times more for their magazines," Anne explained, "so advertisers have less power to threaten a magazine's viability."

"I was shocked," said Sandra Yates with characteristic directness. "In Australia, we think you have freedom of the press—but you don't."

Since Anne and Sandra had not met their budget's projections for ad revenue, their investors forced a sale. In October 1989, *Ms.* and *Sassy* were bought by Dale Lang, owner of *Working Mother, Working Woman,* and one of the few independent publishing companies left among the conglomerates. In response to a request from the original *Ms.* staff—as well as to reader letters urging that *Ms.* continue, plus his own belief that *Ms.* would benefit his other magazines by blazing a trail—he agreed to try the ad-free, reader-supported *Ms.* you hold now and to give us complete editorial control.

II

Do you think, as I once did, that advertisers make decisions based on solid research? Well, think again. "Broadly speaking," says Joseph Smith of Oxtoby-

Smith, Inc., a consumer research firm, "there is no persuasive evidence that the editorial context of an ad matters."

Advertisers who demand such "complementary copy," even in the absence of respectable studies, clearly are operating under a double standard. The same food companies place ads in *People* with no recipes. Cosmetics companies support the *New Yorker* with no regular beauty columns. So where does this habit of controlling the content of women's magazines come from?

Tradition. Ever since *Ladies Magazine* debuted in Boston in 1828, editorial copy directed to women has been informed by something other than its readers' wishes. There were no ads then, but in an age when married women were legal minors with no right to their own money, there was another revenue source to be kept in mind: husbands. "Husbands may rest assured," wrote editor Sarah Josepha Hale, "that nothing found in these pages shall cause her [his wife] to be less assiduous in preparing for his reception or encourage her to 'usurp station' or encroach upon prerogatives of men."

Hale went on to become the editor of *Godey's Lady's Book,* a magazine featuring "fashion plates": engravings of dresses for readers to take to their seamstresses or copy themselves. Hale added "how to" articles, which set the tone for women's service magazines for years to come: how to write politely, avoid sunburn, and—in no fewer than 1,200 words—how to maintain a goose quill pen. She advocated education for women but avoided controversy. Just as most women's magazines now avoid politics, poll their readers on issues like abortion but rarely take a stand, and praise socially approved life-styles, Hale saw to it that *Godey's* avoided the hot topics of its day: slavery, abolition, and women's suffrage.

What definitively turned women's magazines into catalogs, however, were two events: Ellen Butterick's invention of the clothing pattern in 1863 and the mass manufacture of patent medicines containing everything from colored water to cocaine. For the first time, readers could purchase what magazines encouraged them to want. As such magazines became more profitable, they also began to attract men as editors. (Most women's magazines continued to have men as top editors until the feminist 1970s.) Edward Bok, who became editor of the *Ladies' Home Journal* in 1889, discovered the power of advertisers when he rejected ads for patent medicines and found that other advertisers canceled in retribution. In the early twentieth century, *Good Housekeeping* started its institute to "test and approve" products. Its Seal of Approval became the grandfather of current "value-added" programs that offer advertisers such bonuses as product sampling and department store promotions.

By the time suffragists finally won the vote in 1920, women's magazines had become too entrenched as catalogs to help women learn how to use it. The main function was to create a desire for products, teach how to use products, and make products a crucial part of gaining social approval, pleasing a husband, and performing as a homemaker. Some unrelated articles and short stories were included to persuade women to pay for these catalogs. But articles were neither consumerist nor rebellious. Even fiction was usually subject to formula: if a woman had any sexual life outside marriage, she was supposed to come to a bad end.

In 1965, Helen Gurley Brown began to change part of that formula by bringing "the sexual revolution" to women's magazines—but in an ad-oriented way. Attracting multiple men required even more consumerism, as the Cosmo Girl made clear, than finding one husband.

In response to the workplace revolution of the 1970s, traditional women's magazines—that is "trade books" for women working at home—were joined by *Savvy, Working Woman,* and other trade books for women working in offices. But by keeping the fashion/beauty/entertaining articles necessary to get traditional ads and then adding career articles besides, they inadvertently produced the antifeminist stereotype of Super Woman. The male-imitative, dress-for-success woman carrying a briefcase became the media image of a woman worker, even though a blue-collar woman's salary was often higher than her glorified secretarial sister's, and though women at a real briefcase level are statistically rare. Needless to say, these dress-for-success women were also thin, white, and beautiful.

In recent years, advertisers' control over the editorial content of women's magazines has become so institutionalized that it is written into "insertion orders" or dictated to ad salespeople as official policy. The following are recent typical orders to women's magazines:

- Dow's Cleaning Products stipulates that ads for its Vivid and Spray 'n Wash products should be adjacent to "children or fashion editorial"; ads for Bathroom Cleaner should be next to "home furnishing/family" features; and so on for other brands. "If a magazine fails for ¹/₂ the brands or more," the Dow order warns, "it will be omitted from further consideration."

- Bristol-Myers, the parent of Clairol, Windex, Drano, Bufferin, and much more, stipulates that ads be placed next to "a full page of compatible editorial."

- S. C. Johnson & Son, makers of Johnson Wax, lawn and laundry products, insect sprays, hair sprays, and so on, orders that its ads *"should not be opposite extremely controversial features or material antithetical to the nature/copy of the advertised product"* (italics theirs).

- Maidenform, manufacturer of bras and other apparel, leaves a blank for the particular product and states: "The creative concept of the ____ campaign, and the very nature of the product itself appeal to the positive emotions of the reader/consumer. Therefore, it is imperative that all editorial adjacencies reflect that same positive tone. The editorial must not be negative in content or lend itself contrary to the ____ product imagery/message (e.g., *editorial relating to illness, disillusionment, large size fashion, etc.*)" (italics mine).

- The De Beers diamond company, a big seller of engagement rings, prohibits magazines from placing its ads with "adjacencies to hard news or anti/love-romance themed editorial."

- Procter & Gamble, one of this country's most powerful and diversified advertisers, stands out in the memory of Anne Summers and Sandra Yates (no mean feat in this context): its products were not to be placed in *any* issue that included *any* material on gun control, abortion, the occult, cults, or the disparagement of religion. Caution was also demanded in any issue covering sex or drugs, even for educational purposes.

Those are the most obvious chains around women's magazines. There are also rules so clear they needn't be written down: for instance, an overall "look" compatible with beauty and fashion ads. Even "real" nonmodel women photographed for a woman's magazine are usually made up, dressed in credited clothes, and retouched out of all reality. When editors do include articles on less-than-cheerful subjects (for instance, domestic violence), they tend to keep them short and unillustrated. The point is to be "upbeat." Just as women in the street are asked, "Why don't you smile, honey?" women's magazines acquire an institutional smile.

Within the text itself, praise for advertisers' products has become so ritualized that fields like "beauty writing" have been invented. One of its frequent practitioners explained seriously that "It's a difficult art. How many new adjectives can you find? How much greater can you make a lipstick sound? The FDA restricts what companies can say on labels, but we create illusion. And ad agencies are on the phone all the time pushing you to get their product in. A lot of them keep the business based on how many editorial clippings they produce every month. The worst are products," like Lauder's as the writer confirmed, "with their own name involved. It's all ego."

Often, editorial becomes one giant ad. Last November, for instance, *Lear's* featured an elegant woman executive on the cover. On the contents page, we learned she was wearing Guerlain makeup and Samsara, a new fragrance by Guerlain. Inside were full-page ads for Samsara and Guerlain antiwrinkle cream. In the cover profile, we learned that this executive was responsible for launching Samsara and is Guerlain's director of public relations. When the *Columbia Journalism Review* did one of the few articles to include women's magazines in coverage of the influence of ads, editor Frances Lear was quoted as defending her magazine because "this kind of thing is done all the time."

Often, advertisers also plunge odd-shaped ads into the text, no matter what the cost to the readers. At *Woman's Day,* a magazine originally founded by a supermarket chain, editor in chief Ellen Levine said, "The day the copy had to rag around a chicken leg was not a happy one."

Advertisers are also adamant about where in a magazine their ads appear. When Revlon was not placed as the first beauty ad in one Hearst magazine, for instance, Revlon pulled its ads from *all* Hearst magazines. Ruth Whitney, editor in chief of *Glamour,* attributes some of these demands to "ad agencies wanting to prove to a client that they've squeezed the last drop of blood out of a magazine." She also is, she says, "sick and tired of hearing that women's magazines are controlled by cigarette ads." Relatively speaking, she's right. To be as censoring as are many advertisers for women's products, tobacco companies would have to demand articles in praise of smoking and expect glamorous photos of beautiful women smoking their brands.

I don't mean to imply that the editors I quote here share my objections to ads: most assume that women's magazines have to be the way they are. But it's also true that only former editors can be completely honest. "Most of the pressure came in the form of direct product mentions," explains Sey Chassler, who was editor in chief of *Redbook* from the sixties to the eighties.

> We got threats from the big guys, the Revlons, blackmail threats. They wouldn't run ads unless we credited them.
>
> But it's not fair to single out the beauty advertisers because these pressures came from everybody. Advertisers want to know two things: What are you going to charge me? What *else* are you going to do for me? It's a holdup. For instance, management felt that fiction took up too much space. They couldn't put any advertising in that. For the last ten years, the number of fiction entries into the National Magazine Awards has declined.
>
> And pressures are getting worse. More magazines are more bottom-line oriented because they have been taken over by companies with no interest in publishing.
>
> I also think advertisers do this to women's magazines especially because of the general disrespect they have for women.

Even media experts who don't give a damn about women's magazines are alarmed by the spread of this ad-edit linkage. In a climate the *Wall Street Journal* describes as an unacknowledged depression for media, women's products are increasingly able to take their low standards wherever they go. For instance: newsweeklies publish uncritical stories on fashion and fitness. The *New York Times Magazine* recently ran an article on "firming creams," complete with mentions of advertisers. *Vanity Fair* published a profile of one major advertiser, Ralph Lauren, illustrated by the same photographer who does his ads, and turned the life-style of another, Calvin Klein, into a cover story. Even the outrageous *Spy* has toned down since it began to go after fashion ads.

And just to make us really worry, films and books, the last media that go directly to the public without having to attract ads first, are in danger, too. Producers are beginning to depend on payments for displaying products in movies, and books are now being commissioned by companies like Federal Express.

But the truth is that women's products—like women's magazines—have never been the subjects of much serious reporting anyway. News and general interest publications, including the "style" or "living" sections of newspapers, write about food and clothing as cooking and fashion, and almost never evaluate such products by brand name. Though chemical additives, pesticides, and animal fats are major health risks in the United States, and clothes, shoddy or not, absorb more consumer dollars than cars, this lack of information is serious. So is ignoring the contents of beauty products that are absorbed into our bodies through our skins, and that have profit margins so big they would make a loan shark blush.

III

What could women's magazines be like if they were as free as books? as realistic as newspapers? as creative as films? as diverse as women's lives? We don't know.

But we'll only find out if we take women's magazines seriously. If readers were to act in a concerted way to change traditional practices of *all* women's magazines and the marketing of *all* women's products, we could do it. After all, they are operating on our consumer dollars; money that we now control. You and I could:

- write to editors and publishers (with copies to advertisers) that we're willing to pay *more* for magazines with editorial independence, but will *not* continue to pay for those that are just editorial extensions of ads;
- write to advertisers (with copies to editors and publishers) that we want fiction, political reporting, consumer reporting—whatever is, or is not, supported by their ads;
- put as much energy into breaking advertising's control over content as into changing the images in ads, or protesting ads for harmful products like cigarettes;
- support only those women's magazines and products that take *us* seriously as readers and consumers.

Those of us in the magazine world can also use the carrot-and-stick technique. For instance: pointing out that, if magazines were a regulated medium like television, the demands of advertisers would be against FCC rules. Payola and extortion could be punished. As it is, there are probably illegalities. A magazine's postal rates are determined by the ratio of ad to edit pages, and the former costs more than the latter. So much for the stick.

The carrot means appealing to enlightened self-interest. For instance: there are many studies showing that the greatest factor in determining an ad's effectiveness is the credibility of its surroundings. The "higher the rating of editorial believability," concluded a 1987 survey by the *Journal of Advertising Research,* "the higher the rating of the advertising." Thus, an impenetrable wall between edit and ads would also be in the best interest of advertisers.

Unfortunately, few agencies or clients hear such arguments. Editors often maintain the false purity of refusing to talk to them at all. Instead, they see ad salespeople who know little about editorial, are trained in business as usual, and are usually paid by commission. Editors might also band together to take on controversy. That happened once when all the major women's magazines did articles in the same month on the Equal Rights Amendment. It could happen again.

It's almost three years away from life between the grindstones of advertising pressures and readers' needs. I'm just beginning to realize how edges got smoothed down—in spite of all our resistance.

I remember feeling put upon when I changed "Porsche" to "car" in a piece about Nazi imagery in German pornography by Andrea Dworkin—feeling sure Andrea would understand that Volkswagen, the distributor of Porsche and one of our few supportive advertisers, asked only to be far away from Nazi subjects. It's taken me all this time to realize that Andrea was the one with a right to feel put upon.

Even as I write this, I get a call from a writer for *Elle,* who is doing a whole article on where women part their hair. Why, she wants to know, do I part mine in the middle?

It's all so familiar. A writer trying to make something of a nothing assignment; an editor laboring to think of new ways to attract ads; readers assuming that other women must want this ridiculous stuff; more women suffering for lack of information, insight, creativity, and laughter that could be on these same pages.

I ask you: Can't we do better than this?

12

Bringing It Back Home

Learning about Education at the Workplace

BARRY CASTRO

Not long ago, I was using a small air hammer to pound vinyl strips around the edges of three hundred table tops a day. My hands were swollen. My movements, the energy I had to expend, the timing of my work, were all spoken for in detail. The twenty-minute lunch, in addition to eating, had to do for cleaning up, unwinding, and socializing. For the most part, the noise of the factory and the pace of the work enforced silence. Banter might break out occasionally—one-liners retold many times, sports talk, gossip—but nothing that needed real attention. I was glad to be there anyway.

I had been a teacher for twenty-five years, the last dozen of them in self-consciously innovative schools, and it had not come to much. The sense of purpose that had seemed so compelling when I began was gone. It was no longer clear that we were building anything that would remain, much less provide a model for others. There was a sense of hanging on, of waiting for the next defeat; a recognition that we had believed in a broader, more committed, and less polarized collegiality than we had achieved; an awareness of obstacles more persistent and powerful than we had imagined.

A speaker at my college described academicians as an endangered species, frolicking on collegiate game preserves and taking pride in the prowess that could be displayed there, while ignoring, or pretending to ignore, the poachers and land speculators gathering outside. We faculty nodded our heads remembering that our frolics had been increasingly interrupted by the thinning of our ranks and by the withdrawal of support for activities we valued. We knew that the courses our students were taking were increasingly those designated by specialized accrediting agencies. Our commitments to a common cultural heritage, to critical rigor, and to collegiate structure had all been deeply shaken by a readiness to sell something that ostensibly was professional training. New programs were ratio-

"Looking for the Real World" by Barry Castro. *Change,* May 1984. Published by Heldref Publications, Washington, D.C. Copyright 1984. Reprinted by permission of The Helen Dwight Reid Educational Foundation.

nalized and developed in direct response to the availability of federal support, and we found ourselves managed by career administrators increasingly difficult to describe as colleagues.

Most faculty had learned that to take much notice was to invite struggles we could not win, that the poachers and land speculators who undermined our institutions were difficult to distinguish from the legitimate conservationists whose compromises permitted our survival, and that whether we could tell them apart or not, there was little we could do. Beneath what might have seemed a frolic, there was a general confusion about goals, a lack of power, and the loss of an opportunity that a few years earlier had promised more than the moon.

ADOPTING BUSINESS VALUES

Many colleges, faced with declining enrollments, and many faculty, primarily concerned with job security, sought cover. A proper appearance was what counted. For individuals, that often meant adopting business values; for institutions, a mimicry of both marketing imagery and industrial process. Our understanding of to whom we were accountable, our sense of proper restraint, even our language, became more businesslike.

The substance of things, the content of our classes and the meaning of our scholarly work, was increasingly difficult to address. Electives disappeared. Close student-faculty advising relationships did not seem cost-effective. A conviction that academic policy might actually emerge from a collegial dialogue was regarded at best as quaint, more often as unrealistic, sometimes as suicidal. The brief resurgence of college-based liberal education in the public sector was incompatible with the bureaucratic context in which it had been set, and was almost entirely undone.

Business is seen (by faculty, students, and others) as being what academia is not: self-confident, up-to-date, competitive, well coordinated, regulated by close accountability, and compatible with mass-production technology. We are impressed with the power associated with being businesslike, but we do not attend to what workers or managers actually do. Simplistic associations with accounting and engineering are neater than actual corporate life and easier to use as moral guidelines. Clichés like team play, competitive spirit, stick-to-itiveness, and toughness under fire are brought to the campus with what appears to be innocent zeal.

Inside the corporation, these images are humanized and rendered recognizable by the half-humorous, half-confessional stories of waste and inefficiency workers and managers like to tell (though not to each other). Neither college faculty nor students get to hear such stories. Our points of view, whether probusiness or antibusiness, often result from our envy of the glamour and power of managerial life, an awareness that business and industry do indeed provide the material underpinnings of the civilization we share, and anxieties about the relative intangibility of academic work, the elusiveness of academic goals, and the demoralizingly meager institutional support that colleges ordinarily provide for teaching and scholarship. Corporate people have often seemed to me afraid to confront ideas head-on because of what might be revealed about their enterprises and themselves. Academics seem unwilling to encounter the workplace for similar reasons.

The academic reputation of corporate work and its impact on the campus was what concerned me. I did not think that workers and managers were the battle-hardened survivors of a competitive jungle anymore than faculty were the protected and naive inhabitants of an ivory tower. I did not think that the manufacture of luxury soap, office furniture, or automobile upholstery—the local industries I explored—was likely either to involve a more natural human activity or to fill a more basic human need than what I did as a teacher, even though my students and colleagues often slipped into calling that work the real world. I thought that corporate work's reputation for a stronger hold on reality primarily reflected the powerful position of business in American life.

Nonetheless, it was unmistakably academic work that had to be justified in coroporate terms—not the reverse. As we lost confidence in ourselves, we measured ourselves more and more against an ideal of business. As would likely be the case in any comparison with an ideal, we found ourselves wanting.

What I needed was to compare actual schools to actual workplaces, and to do this in very personal terms. I took a series of factory jobs finishing table tops, stamping out packing cartons, assisting in the operation of a panel saw, and boxing soap. During a sabbatical leave, I worked with managers in the training and development division of a local corporation, getting assessment training and then participating in the assessment of a wide range of corporate employees. I shadowed the shift representatives who held things together for the management of another local company at night. I attended many business meetings, conferences, and workshops, and hoped that what I learned might be useful to others.

ON THE JOB

Let me begin with an account of the reactions I and one of my co-workers had to the well-dressed visitors who regularly toured a plant at which I worked one summer. A few weeks earlier I could have been on tour with them. Now the visitors seemed to come from someplace far away: hurrying, staying close to one another, and avoiding eye contact with any of us. Their presence was a reminder that on-the-line work permitted neither comfort nor grace, that I was sweating and dirty and that others were not, and that there was no way I could expect or even welcome their sensitivity to my grievances. None of that was a surprise.

I had expected to be frustrated by the demands of industrial work. Underlying my grievances was a kind of pleasure at discovering that I could handle them. I also found that I could get along with my fellow workers. In terms of my own expectations, I was doing fine. I knew that I had only temporarily surrendered the ability to leave a personal mark on my work and that I would regain that when I returned to campus. Nevertheless, I found that my situation (having lost more power than faculty are accustomed to losing, even in hard times) made it difficult for me to be generous; I had unexpected scores to settle with those passing on the tour. I wanted to get back at them, to believe that somehow whatever they did lacked substance and cohesion. It was pleasant to reflect that their bodies seemed to be denied by their coats and ties; that their movements, which I imagined to be from one air-conditioned environment to another, appeared to be more fragile and tenuous than my own.

I saw my efforts as part of a larger whole, producing things that people would value, and intricately connected to the work of those around me. My respect for the tangible and physical grew to be almost monolithic. I distrusted those whose work could not be put in my terms, especially if I had reason to believe that their privileges were greater than my own. One of the workers had early on told me the ratio of them (white collars) to us (those who did real work) and though I knew reality was much more complicated than that, my fondness for his way of looking at things increased with each day on the line.

After only a few weeks on the line, I had gone a long way toward accepting a milieu in which language was relatively unimportant—in which subtlety might even be suspect. The notion that abstraction, nuance, and perhaps even serious conversation were effete privileges built on real work (and the backs of real workers) I had encountered often among working-class students. It was unsettling to note how quickly I began making it my own view.

There is a great sense of collective effort to factory work. It gives a meaning to corporate as opposed to social or personal identity that I have rarely been conscious of elsewhere. There were, however, clear lines delineating who could or could not be part of the corporate entity, and defensive armament against outsiders was impressive. Once, when a group being shown through the plant had just passed our station, a co-worker smiled and said, "They look as if they're afraid we might turn on them." We had both assumed them to be visiting managers or sales representatives. He had recognized their physical and moral vulnerability and affirmed our superiority on each count. Yet, his lack of interest in probing further was as memorable as his comment.

It seemed to me that the things my co-worker could not address silenced him. The differences between their pay and status and his; their long lunches and short Friday afternoons and his difficulty in taking an unscheduled break; the impossibility of his having any personal impact on his product and their opportunity to regard what they did as a personal challenge; the limits imposed by the very tangibility of his work; the differences between a career and a job: none of these could be acknowledged. He could easily feel patronized and outclassed by management, trapped by his obligations, and nervous about his worth. He did not believe that he could do anything to change his circumstances. He got what momentary pleasure he could from the passing group and went on with his work. The hurried pace and averted eyes of those on tour showed their own uncertainties. Privileges and power commanded some deference but their inability to easily justify themselves embarrassed them. Artificial barriers had to be erected between them and us lest awkward questons about relative contributions and relative rewards be raised.

There are silences in academic life too. The injunction "do not fold, spindle, mutilate, or bend" which served the Berkeley student movement twenty years ago pointed to an important one. Neither managers nor faculty have been associated with a drug problem. Both students and workers have. That may well be indicative of another. The differences between faculty and students are both more temporary and easier to legitimize than those between workers and managers. Yet as the number of students in a classroom rises, as faculty become less available for conferences and informal conversations, as examinations come to be machine graded, and as the self-interested requirements of professional societies wipe out the elective portion of the curriculum, student inability to participate in the development of their own work, student anonymity, and presumptive student homogeniety all connect them to on-the-line workers.

Academic administrators and faculty know about the passive resistance of students. We understand the difference between what education might be and what it has become, and do not generally believe that we can defend the way our institutions are organized. Our inability to act on our beliefs, even to acknowledge them, brings to mind the anxious managers who rushed past my work station. Like them, it seems we have been sufficiently doubtful of the value of our work to avoid thinking much about it, and sufficiently decent to have trouble looking in the eye those for whom we claim some responsibility.

PLAYING FOR POWER

The devices workers use to feel good about themselves were new to me. Once, shortly after I had been taught to use a machine which stapled together cartons, an assistant foreman came by to check on my progress. He discovered that I was being less than artful, and very patiently ran me through the procedure again. I listened and nodded my head while simultaneously taking in a silent but unmistakable message from a worker down the line. She was letting me know what she thought he could do with his good managerial technique. It affirmed our right, at $5.50 an hour, to be alienated if we chose to be. It also affirmed our moral power relative to the manager. Whatever our work required of us, it did not ask us to manipulate each other in the service of corporate goals. The assistant foreman's wages were not very much higher than our own. He was not one of them. Yet he was their man, and it put us one up on him in a way that we needed and used.

Managers lose power in other ways. They know that their status is ephemeral; it can be retained only so long as some corporation or other recognizes it, and it is contingent on the maintenance of the appropriate style. To whatever extent a manager's performance has been reduced to style, workers are likely to notice. Both the superficiality of the posture and the underlying desperation it suggests reduce managerial prestige. This is true whether the retreat to style is a self-imposed means of handling anxiety or a response to corporate high-handedness. A preoccupation with style will almost automatically follow from an inability to deal with whatever is at hand. It can harness managers or teachers to appearances in much the same way on-the-line workers are harnessed to their machine operations.

Managerial retaliation may take the form of an assumption that workers are less well motivated, less bright, less reliable than they are, but these assumptions are either left implicit or stated in very carefully screened contexts. Managerial power is gained by an assumption of greater responsibility for what is assumed to be the common good. One need only examine the materials used in corporate training and development to note that the approved tone is patronage. Two purposes seem to be served. First, the overt use of power (and the expected reaction to it in various forms of resistance) is avoided, and s cond, managers may help justify their positions by a self-identification with ge rosity, responsibility, greater understanding, and the like.

Workers seem to be both intimidated by all of this and amused by a sense that managers are deluding themselves. Knowing what white-collar people can do with their managerial techniques and, perhaps more generally, their good manners, produces a sense of worker solidarity. Knowing that they may recognize their feelings but will be unable to retaliate as long as you avoid explicit conflicts gives those being managed power. It can all make a teacher very nervous.

A decade and a half ago, I taught introductory economics to 250 students at a time, students whose names I would never learn, and whose understanding I could test but not otherwise engage. I could not take their work seriously enough to encourage them to take it seriously themselves. There was in fact little I could do that could not have been achieved as well through print or television. We were retaining a vestige of the face-to-face meeting for the same reasons that commercial bakeries have pictures of grandmotherly ladies on their products, or managerial workshops teach supervisors to simulate caring by responding to those working under them in positive terms—to get what we can as long as we can from a systematically cheapened version of something that had once earned respect. I hope that my students also exchanged knowing glances about what I could do with my good teaching techniques. It is sobering to think that their experience might have been a useful orientation to what the "real world" was going to be.

THE PLAN

I worked for a little while at a factory in which elaborate schemes for securing worker involvement and profit sharing had been developed. I had a long prior association with the human resources director, met with vice presidents, production managers, and so forth. I don't remember ever talking to any of them without hearing about some aspect of their efforts to broaden worker participation in the company (a form of Scanlon Plan). During the two weeks I worked on the floor of their factory, and had many opportunities to talk to workers, that plan was acknowledged in only two ways: in anticipating the size of the bonus with the current quarter's profits ("The only thing I care about is my pay"), and in teasing those worker representatives who got to sit around a table for a meeting every so often and nonetheless were paid as if they had been doing real work ("I work for a living—everything else is a rip-off").

Few details of the plan were known, and none seemed to matter, even to workers who were expecting to stay with the company to retirement. Workers took some pride in being with a firm that other people regarded as a good place to be employed—and they knew that the Scanlon Plan was part of that reputation—but their interest in the plan seemed to stop there. Even this limited pride in being part of the company could not be expressed openly. They could not allow themselves to come on like managers, in the first instance because that raised fears of looking foolish and, behind these fears, because "joining the team" would deprive them of access to their grievances and to ways in which they could feel morally superior to managers. Neither managers nor workers could deal explicitly with each other's view of the differences between them.

I am not sure that there can ever be a sustained real conversation between members of groups whose power, privilege, and status are sharply differentiated and destined to remain that way. Each is likely to be tempted to secure a negotiated peace and let well enough alone. This sort of truce may be a compelling need in industrial work: it seems much less necessary in schools. Students are on the way to something. They are not stuck where they are. Their work bears the stamp of their individual perceptions and expressions, and initiates them into a wider community of intellectual, scientific, and artistic enterprise. They should themselves be regarded as the primary consumers of their productive efforts. Their work need not be forced into a standardized mold and it need not be accommodated to preset time frames. Differences between their own faculty income, power, and status are temporary and can be legitimized by differential knowledge.

The whole meaning of the student-faculty relationship is bound up in its evolving collegiality. The differences from the workplace are substantial. The parallels between worker-manager relations and those between students and faculty, which are striking moving from one environment to the other, thus seem to represent an unnecessary cost—one that the colleges find it easier to pay because they are forever being told that the real world they are to emulate is that of the industrial system.

A few months after I had left my last job on the factory floor, I was meeting over lunch with a local manager to discuss ways in which his firm and my college could work together. He is a bright, well-educated man, and the corporation he works for is widely regarded as enlightened and progressive. We were talking about a position he was trying to fill. Ideally, applicants were to be intolerant of ambiguity, committed to making quick decisions, responsive to categorical measures, and not caught up in indivdual nuance. His purpose was to find someone who would help him in developing plans to reshape the organization of his company. Neither he nor the new employee he sought would be expected to devote much time to understanding the functioning of the preexisting organization.

The intention was to redesign from the top. The language of the contemplated design change was scientific and quantitative. The "native languages" of those who had been making the organization run in purchasing or sales or production, and the function of those languages, could not be much attended to. His frame of reference was powerful because it emphasized energy, logical consistency, and a centralized overview; dangerous because it did not recognize the presumption of denying experience and subtlety; radical because it was impatient with incremental change; and self-serving because it was well suited to generate approval from above.

The rigorously defined instrumental goals which dominate managerial decision making are accompanied by a looser and less consistent, but no less demanding, need to maintain appearances. No observer of managerial life can miss the terrific pressure to avoid being the first to go home. It's not so much that one needs to be working as it is that one cannot need to be somewhere else. Managers are supposed to be selfless in an easygoing, unselfconscious way, and maintain their family relations, community involvements, and friendships in their spare time. One can make little jokes about the impossibility of it but one is not really supposed to mind. The managerial life is full of gaming and sport metaphors. The players, like players in any game, cannot want to do something else instead.

Most managers would join my coworkers on the factory floor in regarding personal and cultural values as essentially irrelevant to the "real world." Education devoted to uniting avocation and vocation, increasing sensitivity to experience and tolerance of ambiguity, to strengthening an awareness of membership in a cultural and intellectual tradition: these goals would strike them as either irrelevant or counterproductive. An interest in liberal education would be regarded, at best, as necessary to the acquisition of skills which ease passage into polite society—at worst, as a distraction from real work. Both groups believe that they are being hardheaded pragmatists and that such pragmatism precludes attention to either personal growth or social utility. They do, however, have quite different commitments to leisure skills, and these too relate to their understanding of what higher education is supposed to achieve.

JOGGING?

Think about jogging. It is superficially more like factory work than management. Like factory work, it is incompatible with focused thought or extended conversation. Both jogging and factory work require physical presence and physical exertion but only partial attention.

Each can heighten an awareness of time and induce a sense of timeless personal reverie. The differences between them are easy for people like me to forget. Workers are held to a pace they cannot alter. Their efforts serve purposes which are not their own. Factory work is typically carried out in its own enclosed and often closely guarded space. Jogging is public. The jogger's efforts are celebrated by news stories, special purpose magazines, and a host of highly promoted community events.

Factory work provides very little occasion for celebration. It has no books or magazines or public events for its participants and no tradition of heroic achievement with which they are likely to identify. Jogging complements privilege and power. Managers do it. Factory workers do not. Factory work fosters bitterness about the privileges of others, frustrations with the perceived limits of one's own alternatives, and a feeling of powerlessness.

My students expect me to know something about jogging. It is the sort of thing higher education, and particularly liberal education, is supposed to be associated with—a leisure-related activity—a little precious, mildly taxing, a little threatening and alien. Even my minimal experience on a factory floor is a surprise to them. One works only because one has to. It is not something one ought to think much about. It is most fundamentally not the worker's business. Nevertheless, work is likely to be familiar, and many of my beginning students would welcome schooling which was more like it. They have inured themselves to doing more or less what they are told. They have learned that enthusiastic performance will only increase the demands placed on them, and that these demands are ultimately intended to benefit someone else. They have no reason to believe that work should be done thoughtfully: thought is supposed to be engineered out of work.

They do not expect anyone to be seriously interested in their insights and have little reason to invest them with rigor. Certainly no one is expected to be interested in the nuances of their particular situation. They often learn to seek shelter in the anonymity of impersonal routine. Friendliness and a commitment to good teaching may promote both short-term gratification and long-term anxiety. (If this is fun, can I be learning anything useful? If the faculty are friendly, can they be powerful?) Students who are unaccustomed to accepting responsibility for their own educations will be tempted to opt for educational structure where that responsibility is denied them. It will be businesslike and it may be cheap, but it is unlikely to accomplish much.

My sabbatical leave spent with a corporate training and development staff led me to recognize how easily I too could be attracted to such a structure. Corporate classrooms place great emphasis on accountability and planning. They use media well and pay sophisticated attention to group process, are often reviewed by expensive consultants, and are informed by elaborately staged conferences. Wasted time is primarily a cost to the organization and not, as is the case in collegiate settings, to the individual. The organization's best interest is served by making sure its personnel are not diverted from their operational tasks casually. The trainees themselves are often as powerfully placed as their trainers and are likely to act on whatever resentment they may feel about inappropriate demands on their time. There is no room for the petty abuses of authority one can find in college classrooms. The sense of discipline with which goals are developed, presentations worked out, and results assessed contrast favorably with the less strict norms that are routine in academic teaching.

However, there are trade-offs. College students can be asked to work on their own time, and when things are going well can often obtain profound personal benefit from what is being taught. The substance of their education comes closer to belonging to them and consequently, there is a much broader range within which they can respond, from meeting only the modest minimum the colleges demand, to making the most ambitious and strenuous demands on themselves.

More than either the worker or manager, they can shape their own behavior and be themselves shaped by the process. When collegiate curricula become businesslike—when the requirements are rigorously specified and progress is closely monitored—some of that will necessarily be lost.

The complement of the purposefulness of the corporate classroom was a general understanding of the limits of what could be achieved or even attempted there. The corporate student's time at work is no longer his own. It has already been surrendered, and the corporation is free to use it without much concern about competing personal demands. Almost everything that is going to be done, however, must be done in the classroom. There is no corporate equivalent to the serious term paper. Corporate managers may have a longer range and more exclusive commitment to their firm than students do to a college, but the line between the corporation and the manager is more clearly drawn. Corporate work does not in the end belong to the manager.

Corporate instruction is almost always short-term (generally a few days is the maximum for any particular instructional unit). The need for trainees to leave happy, combined with the limited time, often results in nothing being attempted beyond technical instruction and simple guidelines for human relations. Tricky, albeit relevant, subjects like stereotyping along racial or gender or class-based lines cannot be broached. Demands for analytic rigor pose similar risks of embarrassment and failure. The reality of the sophisticated presentation with very limited substance became obvious to me. It was disturbing to recognize that my confidence in my own work was sufficiently shaky for it to have taken me some months to discover that dissonant reality.

COMMITMENT AND RESPONSIBILITY

Faculty, like students and managers, have responsibilities they are unaccustomed to assuming. An advertising executive who was on an advisory board to my college reminded me of one. A few of us had been talking about the college's commitment to career-relevant liberal education, when he broke in. He told us that he had learned a great deal from his clients. An industrial firm he was then working with had introduced him to mechanics, electrics, hydraulics, and pneumatics—none of which he had studied before. He thought of his new knowledge not as a chance glimpse of the esoteric understanding of the engineer but as an important part of his general education, and knowingly asked whether it was part of our curriculum.

Our advisory board member had guessed that, like factory workers and managers, we faculty have a black box in which a considerable body of human knowledge can be categorized, trivialized, and dismissed. Ours is called technology; theirs liberal education. In both cases, the importance of the missing perspective is acknowledged in principle. In neither case is it seriously attended to.

The problem is not just working-class resistance to higher values or corporate commitment to instrumental goals. It also rests on a long-standing academic

involvement with preindustrial forms. Our advisor was suggesting that academicians are more likely to understand jogging than factory work, that we are closer
to the manager's leisure skills then to his function, and that we ought to consider
what that implies for our teaching.

It is not that we have ignored the perspectives of factory workers and managers. On the contrary, public higher education has come into its own in the wake
of the Industrial Revolution and we have applied industrial models to it as if they
were the exclusive exemplar of the real world. However, we emulate industry
better than we study it. We are not convined that such study is consistent with
liberal education, and are both troubled by the extent to which liberal education
has come to mean a conspicuous consumption of leisure skills, and reluctant to
tamper with that usage.

We protect our disciplinary enclaves and define the curriculum by dividing the
turf. It is neater if subjects are not much encountered outside the specific disciplinary contexts to which they have been assigned. We produce parts of a whole
as if some philosopher king *qua* great engineer had taken care of their synthesis
some time ago and it need no longer concern us.

We pretend to ivory towers we do not occupy as we pretend to job training we
cannot provide. A corporate personnel director once suggested to me that the
prime function of undergraduate management courses was a certification of student loyalty—of their propensity for not asking the wrong questions. His remark
may be extended to include a great deal of undergraduate education, particularly
in the public sector where the need to process very large numbers of students is an
important fact of academic life.

Students are hurried through tours of education. Their sense that a job is all
that need concern them is confirmed. Eye contact is avoided. Bottom-line language, production-based notions of accountability, marketing consciousness, a
reluctance to recognize that we share a culture and a community as well as an
economy, all shape the structure of the college as they do that of the office and the
factory.

As I come back to collegiate life, I am taken with both how difficult and how
necessary it is for us to resist these currents of mainstream realism. If we assume
that our traditional affirmations of faith, reason, and community are no longer
relevant; that the real world is somewhere else, and that we must attempt to
mimic it rather than learn from it and act on it, then we will have contributed to
making more than just the colleges a reserve where we can, for a time, frolic
unencumbered by reality. That it will be done in the name of practical realism
will not make it any less a radical abdication of responsibility.

III
ETHICS

13

A Dilemma to Begin With

The Prisoner's Dilemma and
the Evolution of Cooperation

DOUGLAS HOFSTADTER

Life is filled with paradoxes and dilemmas. Sometimes it even feels as if the essence of living is the sensing—indeed, the savoring—of paradox. Although all paradoxes seem somehow related, some paradoxes seem abstract and philosophical, while others touch on life very directly. A very lifelike paradox is the so-called Prisoner's Dilemma, discovered in 1950 by Melvin Dresher and Merrill Flood of the RAND Corporation. Albert W. Tucker wrote the first article on it, and in that article he gave it its now-famous name. I shall here present the Prisoner's Dilemma—first as a metaphor, then as a formal problem.

The original formulation in terms of prisoners is a little less clear to the uninitiated, in my experience, than the following one. Assume you possess copious quantities of some item (money, for example), and wish to obtain some amount of another item (perhaps stamps, groceries, diamonds). You arrange a mutually agreeable trade with the only dealer of that item known to you. You are both satisfied with the amounts you will be giving and getting. For some reason, though, your trade must take place in secret. Each of you agrees to leave a bag at a designated place in the forest, and to pick up the other's bag at the other's designated place. Suppose it is clear to both of you that the two of you will never meet or have further dealings with each other again.

Clearly, there is something for each of you to fear: namely, that the other one will leave an empty bag. Obviously, if you both leave full bags, you will both be satisfied; but equally obviously, getting something for nothing is even more satisfying. So you are tempted to leave an empty bag. In fact, you can even reason it through quite rigorously this way: "If the dealer brings a full bag, I'll be better off having left an empty bag, because I'll have gotten all that I wanted and

Selected excerpts from *Metamagical Themas: Questing for the Essence of Mind* by Douglas Hofstadter. Copyright © 1985 by Basic Books, Inc. Reprinted by permission of Basic Books, a division of HarperCollins Publishers, Inc.

given away nothing. If the dealer brings an empty bag, I'll be better off having left an empty bag, because I'll not have been cheated. I'll have gained nothing but lost nothing either. Thus it seems that *no matter what the dealer chooses to do, I'm better off leaving an empty bag. So I'll leave an empty bag.*"

The dealer, meanwhile, being in more or less the same boat (though at the other end of it), thinks analogous thoughts and comes to the parallel conclusion that it is best to leave an empty bag. And so both of you, with your impeccable (or impeccable-seeming) logic, leave empty bags, and go away empty-handed. How sad, for if you had both just cooperated, you could have each gained something you wanted to have. *Does logic prevent cooperation?* This is the issue of the Prisoner's Dilemma.

In case you're wondering why it is called "Prisoner's Dilemma," here's the reason. Imagine that you and an acomplice (someone you have no feelings for one way of the other) committed a crime, and now you've both been apprehended and thrown in jail, and are fearfully awaiting trials. You are being held in separate cells with no way to communicate. The prosecutor offers each of you the following deal (and informs you both that the identical deal is being offered to each of you—and that you both know *that* as well!): "We have a lot of circumstantial evidence on you both. So if you both claim innocence, we will convict you anyway and you'll both get two years in jail. But if you will help us out by admitting your guilt and making it easier for us to convict your accomplice—oh, pardon me, your *alleged* accomplice—why, then, we'll let you out free. And don't worry about revenge—your accomplice will be in for five years! How about it?" Warily you ask, "But what if we *both* say we're guilty?" "Ah, well, my friend—I'm afraid you'll both get four-year sentences, then."

Now you're in a pickle! Clearly, you don't want to claim innocence if your partner has sung, for then you're in for five long years. Better you should both have sung—then you'll only get four. On the other hand, if your partner claims innocence, then the best possible thing for you to do is sing, since then you're out scot-free! So at first sight, it seems obvious what you should do: Sing! But what is obvious to you is equally obvious to your opposite number, so now it looks like you both ought to sing, which means—Sing Sing for four years! At least that's what *logic* tells you to do. Funny, since if both of you had just been *illogical* and manitained innocence, you'd both be in for only half as long! Ah, logic does it again.

Let us now go back to the original metaphor and slightly alter its conditions. Suppose that both you and your partner very much want to have a regular supply of what the other has to offer, and so, before conducting your first exchange, you agree to carry on a lifelong exchange, once a month. You still expect never to meet face to face. In fact, neither of you has any idea how old the other one is, so you can't be very sure of how long this lifelong agreement may go on, but it seems safe to assume it'll go on for a few months anyway, and very likely for years.

Now, what do you do on your first exchange? Taking an empty bag seems fairly nasty as the opening of a relationship—hardly an effective way to build up trust. So suppose you take a full bag, and the dealer brings one as well. Bliss—for a month. Then you both must go back. Empty, or full? Each month, you have to decide whether to *defect* (take an empty bag) or to *cooperate* (take a full one). Suppose that one month, unexpectedly, your dealer defects. Now what do you do? Will you suddenly decide that the dealer can never be trusted again, and from now on always bring empty bags, in effect totally giving up on the whole project forever? Or will you pretend you didn't notice, and continue being friendly? Or— will you try to punish the dealer by some number of defections of your own? One? Two? A random number? An increasing number, depending on how many defections you have experienced? Just how mad will you get?

This is the so-called *iterated* Prisoner's Dilemma. It is a very difficult problem. It can be, and has been, rendered more quantitative and in that form studied with the methods of game theory and computer simulation. How does one quantify it? One builds a *payoff matrix* presenting point values for the various alternatives. A typical one is shown in the figure entitled the Prisoner's Dilemma. In this matrix, mutual cooperation earns both parties 2 points (the subjective value of receiving a full bag of what you need while giving up a full bag of what you have). Mutual defection earns you both 0 points (the subjective value of gaining nothing and losing nothing, aside from making a vain trip out to the forest that month). Cooperating while the other defects stings: you get—1 point while the rat gets 4 points! Why so many? Because it is so pleasurable to get something for nothing. And of course, should *you* happen to be a rat some month when the dealer has cooperated, then you get 4 points and the dealer loses 1.

It is obvious that in a *collective* sense, it would be best for both of you to always cooperate. But suppose you have no regard whatsoever for the other. There is no "collective good" you are both working for. You are both supreme egoists. Then what? The meaning of this term, "egoist," can perhaps be made clear by the following. Suppose you and your dealer have developed a trusting relationship of mutual cooperation over the years, when one day you receive secret and reliable information that the dealer is quite sick and will soon die, probably within a month or two. The dealer has no reason to suspect that you have heard this. Aren't you highly tempted to defect, all of a sudden, despite all your years of cooperating? You are, after all, out for yourself and no one else in this cruel, cruel world. And since it seems that this may very well be the dealer's last month, why not profit as much as possible from your secret knowledge? Your defection may never be punished, and at the worst, it will be punished by one last-gasp defection by the dying dealer.

The surer you are that this next turn is to be the very last one, the more you feel you *must* defect. Either of you would feel that way, of course, on learning that the other one was nearing the end of the rope. This is what is meant by "egoism." It means you have no feeling of friendliness or goodwill or compassion for the other player; you have no conscience; all you care about is amassing points, more and more and more of them.

What does the payoff matrix for the other metaphor, the one involving prisoners, look like? It is shown in the figure. The equivalence of this matrix to the

Dealer

	Cooperates	Defects
Cooperate	(2,2)	(−1,4)
Defect	(4,−1)	(0,0)

You

(a)

Your accomplice

	Stays mum	Sings
Stay mum	(−2,−2)	(−5,0)
Sing	(0,−5)	(−4,−4)

You

(b)

Player B

	Cooperates	Defects
Cooperates	(3,3)	(0,5)
Defects	(5,0)	(1,1)

Player A

(c)

The Prisoner's Dilemma.

In (a), a Prisoner's Dilemma payoff matrix in the case of a dealer and a buyer of commodities or services, in which both participants have a choice: to *cooperate* (i.e., to deliver the goods or the payment) or to *defect* (i.e., to deliver nothing). The numbers attempt to represent the degree of satisfaction of each partner in the transaction.

In (b), the formulation of the Prisoner's Dilemma to which it owes its name: in terms of prisoners and their opportunities for double-crossing or collusion. The numbers are negative because they represent punishments: the length of both prisoners' prospective jail sentences, in years. This metaphor is due to Albert W. Tucker.

In (c), a Prisoner's Dilemma formulation where all payoffs are nonnegative numbers. This is my canonical version, following the usage in Robert Axelrod's book *The Evolution of Cooperation*.

previous matrix is clear if you add a constant—namely, 4—to all terms in this one. Indeed, we could add any constant to either matrix and the dilemma would remain essentially unchanged. So let us add 5 to this one so as to get rid of all negative pay-offs. We get the canonical Prisoner's Dilemma payoff matrix, shown in the figure. The number 3 is called the *reward for mutual cooperation*, or

R for short. The number 1 is called the *punishment,* or *P.* The number 5 is *T,* the *temptation,* and 0 is *S,* the *sucker's payoff.* The two conditions that make a matrix represent a Prisoner's Dilemma situation are these:

$$(1) \quad T > R > P > S$$

$$(2) \quad (T+S)/2 < R$$

The first one simply makes the argument go through for each of you, that "it is better for me to defect no matter what my counterpart does." The second one simply guarantees that if you two somehow get locked into out-of-phase alternations (that is, "you cooperate, I defect" one month and "you defect, I cooperate" the next), you will not do better—in fact, you will do worse—than if you were cooperating with each other each month.

Well, what would be your best strategy? It can be shown quite easily that there is no universal answer to this question. That is, there is no strategy that is better than all other strategies under all circumstances. For consider the case where the other player is playing *ALL D*—the strategy of defecting each round. In that case, the best you can possibly do is to defect each time as well, including the first. On the other hand, suppose the other player is using the *Massive Retaliatory Strike* strategy, which means "I'll cooperate until you defect and thereafter I'll defect forever." Now if you defect on the very first move, then you'll get one *T* and all *P*'s thereafter until one of you dies. But if you had waited to defect, you could have benefited from a relationship of mutual cooperation, amassing many *R*'s beforehand. Clearly that bunch of *R*'s will add up to more than the single *T* if the game goes on for more than a few moves. This means that against the *ALL D* strategy, *ALL D* is the best counterstrategy, whereas "Always cooperate unless you learn that you or the other player is just about to die, in which case defect" is the best counterstrategy against *Massive Retaliatory Strike.* This simple argument shows that *how* you should play depends on *whom* you're playing.

The whole concept of the "quality" of a strategy takes on a decidedly more operational and empirical meaning if one imagines an ocean populated by dozens of little beings swimming around and playing Prisoner's Dilemma over and over with each other. Suppose that each time two such beings encounter each other, they recognize each other and remember how previous encounters have gone. This enables each one to decide what it wishes to do this time. Now if each organism is continually swimming around and bumping into the others, eventually each one will have met every other one numerous times, and thus all strategies will have been given the opportunity to interact with each other. By "interact," what is meant here is certainly not that anyone knocks anyone else out of the ocean, as in an elimination tournament. The idea is simply that each organism gains zero or more points in each meeting, and if sufficient time is allowed to elapse, everybody will have met with everybody else about the same number of times, and now the only question is, Who has amassed the most points? Amassing points is truly the name of the game.

It doesn't matter if you have "beaten" anyone, in the sense of having gained more from interacting with them than they gained from interacting with you. That kind of "victory" is totally irrelevant here. What matters is not the number of "victories" rung up by any individual, but the individual's *total point count*— a number that measures the individual's overall viability in this particular "sea" of many strategies. It sounds nearly paradoxical, but you could lose many— indeed, *all*—of your individual skirmishes, and yet still come out the overall winner.

As the image suggests very strongly, this whole situation is highly relevant to questions in evolutionary biology. Can totally selfish and unconscious organisms living in a common environment come to evolve reliable cooperative strategies? Can cooperation emerge in a world of pure egoists? In a nutshell, *can cooperation evolve out of noncooperation?* If so, this has revolutionary import for the theory of evolution, for many of its critics have claimed that this was one place that it was hopelessly snagged.

Well, as it happens, it has now been demonstrated rigorously and definitively that such cooperation can emerge, and it was done through a computer tournament conducted by political scientist Robert Axelrod of the Political Science Department and the Institute for Public Policy Studies of the University of Michigan in Ann Arbor. More accurately, Axelrod first studied the ways that cooperation evolved by means of a computer tournament, and when general trends emerged, he was able to spot the underlying principles and prove theorems that established the facts and conditions of cooperation's rise from nowhere. Axelrod has written a fascinating and remarkably thought-provoking book on his findings, called *The Evolution of Cooperation,* published in 1984 by Basic Books. (Quoted sections below are taken from an early draft of that book.) Furthermore, he and evolutionary biologist William D. Hamilton have worked out and published many of the implications of these discoveries for evolutionary theory. Their work has won much acclaim—including the 1981 Newcomb Cleveland Prize, a prize awarded annually by the American Association for The Advancement of Science for "an outstanding paper published in *Science.*"

There are really three aspects of the question "Can cooperation emerge in a world of egoists?" The first is: How can it get started at all? The second is: Can cooperative strategies survive better than their noncooperative rivals? The third one is: Which cooperative strategies will do the best, and how will they come to predominate?

To make these issues vivid, let me describe Axelrod's tournament and its somewhat astonishing results. In 1979, Axelrod sent out invitations to a number of professional game theorists, including people who had published articles on the Prisoner's Dilemma, telling them that he wished to pit many strategies against one another in a round-robin Prisoner's Dilemma tournament, with the overall goal being to amass as many points as possible. He asked for strategies to be encoded as computer programs that could respond to the "C" or "D" of another player, taking into account the remembered history of previous interactions with that same player. A program should always reply with a "C" or a "D," of course, but its choice need not be deterministic. That is, consultation of a random-number generator was allowed at any point in a strategy.

Fourteen entries were submitted to Axelrod, and he introduced into the field one more program called RANDOM, which in effect flipped a coin (computationally simulated, to be sure) each move, cooperating if heads came up, defecting otherwise. The field was a rather variegated one, consisting of programs ranging from as few as four lines to as many as seventy-seven lines (of Basic). Every program was made to engage each other program (and a clone of itself) 200 times. No program was penalized for running slowly. The tournament was actually run five times in a row, so that ppseudo-effects caused by statistical fluctuations in the random-number generator would be smoothed out by averaging.

The program that won was submitted by the old Prisoner's Dilemma hand, Anatol Rapoport, a psychologist and philosopher from the University of Toronto. His was the shortest of all submitted programs, and is called TIT FOR TAT. TIT FOR TAT uses a very simple tactic:

Cooperate on move 1; thereafter, do whatever the other player did the previous move.

That is all. It sounds outrageously simple. How in the world could such a program defeat the complex stratagems devised by other experts?

Well, Axelrod claims that the game theorists in general did not go far enough in their analysis. They looked ''only two levels deep,'' when in fact they should have looked *three* levels deep to do better. What precisely does this mean? He takes a specific case to illustrate this point. Consider the entry called JOSS (submitted by Johann Joss, a mathematician from Zurich, Switzerland). JOSS's strategy is very similar to TIT FOR TAT's, in that it begins by cooperating, always responds to defection by defecting and *nearly* always responds to cooperation by cooperating. The hitch is that JOSS uses a random-number generator to help it decide when to pull a ''surprise defection'' on the other player. JOSS is set up so that it has a 10 percent probability of defecting right after the other player has cooperated.

In playing TIT FOR TAT, JOSS will do fine until it tries to catch TIT FOR TAT off guard. When it defects, TIT FOR TAT retaliates with a single defection, while JOSS ''innocently'' goes back to cooperating. Thus we have a ''DC'' pair. On the next move, the ''C'' and ''D'' will switch places since each program in essence echoes the other's latest move, and so it will go: CD then DC, CD, DC, and so on. There may ensue a long reveration set off by JOSS's D, but, sooner or later, JOSS will randomly throw in *another* unexpected D after a C from TIT FOR TAT. At this point, there will be a ''DD'' pair, and that determines the entire rest of the match. Both will defect forever, now. The ''echo'' effect resulting from JOSS's first attempt at exploitation and TIT FOR TAT's simple punitive act lead ultimately to complete distrust and lack of cooperation.

This may seem to imply that both strategies are at fault and will suffer for it at the hands of others, but in fact the one that suffers from it most is JOSS, since JOSS tries out the same trick on partner after partner, and in many cases this leads to the same type of breakdown of trust, whereas TIT FOR TAT, never defecting first, will never be the initial cause of a breakdown of trust. Axelrod's technical term for a strategy that never defects before its opponent does is *nice*. TIT FOR TAT is a nice strategy, JOSS is not. Note that "nice" does not mean that a strategy *never* defects! TIT FOR TAT defects when provoked, but that is still considered being "nice."

Axelrod summarizes the first tournament this way:

> A major lesson of this tournament is the importance of minimizing echo effects in an environment of mutual power. A sophisticated analysis must go at least three levels deep. First is the direct effect of a choice. This is easy, since a defection always earns more than a cooperation. Second are the indirect effect, taking into account that the other side may or may not punish a defection. This much was certainly appreciated by many of the entrants. But third is the fact that in responding to the defections of the other side, one may be repeating or even amplifying one's own previous exploitative choice. Thus a single defection may be successful when analyzed for its direct effects, and perhaps even when its secondary effects are taken into account. But the real costs may be in the tertiary effects when one's own isolated defections turn into unending mutual recriminations. Without their realizing it, many of these rules actually wound up punishing themselves. With the other player serving as a mechanism to delay the self-punishment by a few moves, this aspect of self-punishment was not perceived by the decision rules. . . .
>
> The analysis of the tournament results indicates that there is a lot to be learned about coping in an environment of mutual power. Even expert strategists from political science, sociology, economics, psychology, and mathematics made the systematic errors of being too competitive for their own good, not forgiving enough, and too pessimistic about the responsiveness of the other side.

Axelrod not only analyzed the first tournament, he even performed a number of "subjunctive replays" of it, that it, replays with different sets of entries. He found, for instance, that the strategy called TIT FOR TWO TATS, which tolerates two defections before getting mad (but still only strikes back once), *would* have won, had it been in the line-up. Likewise, two other strategies he discovered, one called REVISED DOWNING and one called LOOK-AHEAD, would have come in first had they been in the tournament.

In summary, the lesson of the first tournament seems in to have been that it is important to be *nice* ("don't be the first to defect") and *forgiving* ("don't hold a grudge once you've vented your anger"). TIT FOR TAT possesses both these qualities, quite obviously.

14

Conscience

The Corporation as Community

ROBERT SOLOMON

> To argue, in the manner of Machiavelli, that there is one rule for business and
> another for private life, is to open the door to an orgy of unscrupulousness
> before which the mind recoils. To argue that there is no difference at all is to
> lay down a principle which few men who have faced the difficulty in practice
> will be prepared to endorse as of invariable application, and incidentally to
> expose the ideas of morality itself to discredit by subjecting it to an almost
> intolerable strain.
>
> R. H. TAWNEY, *Religion and the Rise of Capitalism*

I want to organize my introduction to the Aristotelean approach to business by
summarizing the essential parameters that circumscribe and define the virtues in
business ethics, a half-dozen concerns typically ignored in the more abstract and
principle-bound discussions of ethics and policy discussions that so dominate the
field. Together, they form an integrative structure in which the individual, the
corporation, and the community, self-interest and the public good, the personal
and the professional, business and virtues all work together instead of against one
another. I will discuss each of the following six parameters in turn:

- community
- excellence
- membership
- integrity
- judgment
- holism

From *Ethics and Excellence: Cooperation and Integrity in Business* by Robert Solomon. Copyright
© 1992 by Oxford University Press. Reprinted by permission.

THE CORPORATION AS COMMUNITY

> It is not at all bad being a businessman. There is a spirit of trust and coopera-
> tion here. Everyone jokes about such things, but if businessmen were not
> trusting of each other the country would collapse tomorrow.
>
> WALKER PERCY, *The Moviegoer*

The Aristotelean approach begins with the idea that we are, first of all, members
of organized groups, with shared histories and established practices governing
everything from eating and working to worshiping. We are not, as our favorite
folklore would have it, first of all *individuals*—that is, autonomous, self-
sustaining, self-defining creatures who, ideally, think entirely for ourselves and
determine what we are. The "self-made man" (or woman) is a social creature,
and he or she "makes it" by being an essential part of society, however, innovative or eccentric he or she may be. To say that we are communal creatures is to
say that we have shared interests, that even in the most competitive community
our self-interests are parasitic on and largely defined in terms of our mutual
interests. To think of the corporation as a community is to insist that it cannot be,
no matter how vicious its internal politics, a mere collection of self-interested
individuals. To see business as a social activity is to see it as a practice that both
thrives on competition and presupposes a coherent community of mutually concerned as well as self-interested citizens.

To be sure, communities in the contemporary "Western" world are anything
but homogeneous or harmonious, and the heterogeneity and cacophony of different voices and cultures is what gives the urgency to our insistence on community.
Corporations are not (or should not be) "melting pots," but neither can they long
contain factions of mutually resentful minorities.[1] It seems to be one of the
staples of conservative social thinking that communities are and ought to be
uniform and defined by consensus. But it seems to me that there have been few
such communities of more than tribal size and that every community from the
rural South to the northeastern ghetto has had to accommodate minorities and
class differences, flourishing by virtue of rather than in spite of a mixture of
cultures, customs, and mores. I do not pretend that we could or should go back to
the imaginary good old days of authoritarian homogeneity. The claim I am
making here is metaphysical rather than nostalgic, and the claim is that what we
call "the individual" is socially constituted and socially situated. "The in-
vidual" today is the product of a particularly mobile and entrepreneurial society
in which natural groups (notably the extended family or tribe) have been replaced
by artificial organizations such as schools and corporations. Movement among
them is not only possible (as it is usually not among tribes and families) but
encouraged, even required. But as traditional bonds are broken, the person who
was once defined simply as "the daughter of Yanni" or "the son of Zeke" now
becomes known as "the expert from Reno" and "the new vice-president." Our
credits and credentials accumulate, making us not so much unique as the product
of a dozen or more competing and overlapping social groups and influences. That

is "the individual," not an ontological atom but part of a complex interwoven metaphysical social fabric.

"The individual" was an invention of the eleventh and twelfth centuries in Europe, when families were separated by war and the tightly arranged structures of feudalism were breaking apart. The individual became increasingly important partly with the advent of capitalist and consumer society, but (as so often in the overly materialist history of economics) mainly because of changing religious conceptions during the Reformation, with increased emphasis on personal faith and individual salvation. But "the individual" was always a relative, context-dependent designation. An individual in one society would be a sociopath in another. ("The nail that sticks out is the one that gets hammered," says a traditional Japanese proverb.) But what we call "the individual" is, from even the slightest outside perspective, very much a social, even a conformist, conception as well. To show one's individuality in the financial world, for example, it may be imperative for men to wear ties of certain colors or patterns that they might not have chosen on their own. To further emphasize individuality (which connotes creativity, even genius), one might sport a mustache or beard (though the range of styles is very strictly circumscribed). But getting beyond trivial appearances, even our thoughts and feelings are for the most part defined and delineated by our society, in our conversations and confrontations with other people. Princeton anthropologist Cliffort Geertz once wrote that a human being all alone in nature would not be a noble, autonomous being but a pathetic, quivering creature with no identity and few defenses or means of support. Our heroic conception of "the individual"—often exemplified by the lone (usually male) hero—is a bit of bad but self-serving anthropology. There are exceptional individuals, to be sure, but they are social creations and become exceptional just because they serve the needs of their society, more often than not by exemplifying precisely those forms of excellence most essential to that society.[2]

We find our identities and our meanings only within communities, and for most of us that means at work in a company or an institution. However we might prefer to think of ourselves, however we (rightly) insist on the importance of family and friends, however much we might complain about our particular jobs or professional paths, we define ourselves largely in terms of them, even if, in desperation, in opposition to them. Whether a person likes or hates his or her job more often than not turns on relationships with the people one works for and works with, whether there is mutual repsect or animosity and callousness or indifference. Even the lone entrepreneur—the sidewalk jeweler or the financial wizard—will succeed only if he or she has social skills, enjoys (or seems to) his or her customers or clients.

The philosophical myths that have grown almost cancerous in many business circles, the neo-Hobbesian view that business is "every man for himself" and the Darwinian view that "it's a jungle out there," are direct denials of the Aristotelean view that we are first of all members of a community and our self-interest is for the most part identical to the larger interests of the group. Competition presumes, it does not replace, an underlying assumption of mutual interest and cooperation. Whether we do well, whether we like ourselves, whether we lead happy productive lives, depends to a large extent on the companies we choose. As the Greeks used to say, "to live the good life one must live in a great city." To my business students today, who are all too prone to choose a job on the basis of salary and start-up bonus alone, I always say, "to live a decent life choose the right company." In business ethics the corporation becomes one's immediate community and, for better or worse, the institution that defines the values and the conflicts of values within which one lives much of one's life. A corporation that encourages mutual cooperation and encourages individual excellence as an essential part of teamwork is a very different place to work and live than a corporation that incites "either/or" competition, antagonism, and continuous jostling for status and recognition. There is nothing more "natural" about the latter, which is at least as much the structuring of an organization (whether intended or not) as the cooperative ambience of the former.

The first principle of business ethics is that the corporation is itself a citizen, a member of the larger community, and inconceivable without it. This is the idea that has been argued over the past few decades as the principle of "social responsibility," but the often attenuated and distorted arguments surrounding that concept have been more than enough to convince me that the same idea needed a different foundation. The notion of "responsibility" (a version of which will, nevertheless, be central to my argument here too) is very much a part of the atomistic individualism that I am attacking as inadequate, and the classic arguments for "the social responsibilities of business" all too readily fall into the trap of *beginning* with the assumption of the corporation as an autonomous, independent entity, which *then* needs to consider its obligations to the surrounding community. But corporations, like individuals, are part and parcel of the communities that created them, and the responsibilities that they bear are not the products of arguments or implicit contracts but intrinsic to their very existence as social entities. There are important and sometimes delicate questions about what the social responsibilities of business or of a particular corporation might be, but the question whether they have such responsibilities is a nonstarter, a bit of covert nonsense. Friedman's now-infamous idea that "the social responsibility of business is to increase its profits" betrays a willful misunderstanding of the very nature of both social responsibility and business. (Not surprisingly, the author of that doctrine has elsewhere protested, alienating his friends along with his critics, that he is "not pro-business but pro-free enterprise.")

These claims are closely akin to the ideas captured in the punlike notion of a *stakeholder,* that broadening conception of the corporate constituency that includes a variety of affected (and effective) groups and all sorts of different obligations and responsibilities. The term has become something of a coverall, and so what considerable advantages it has provided in terms of breadth are to some extent now compromised by the uncritical overuse of the word. for example, the notion of "stakeholder" suggests discrete groups or entities whereas the primary source of dilemmas in business ethics is the fact that virtually all of us wear (at least) two hats, for example, as employees and as members of the larger community, as consumers and as stockholders, as a manager and as a friend, and these roles can come into conflict with one another. As a program for ethical analysis in business, the standard list of stakeholders is notoriously incomplete where it concerns one's competitors rather than one's constituents. In an obvious sense, no one is more affected by one's actions (and, sometimes, no one is more effective in determining one's actions) than one's competitors. "Good sportsmanship" and fair play are essential obligations in business ethics. And yet it seems odd to say that the competition "has a stake" in the company. The idea of community thus goes beyond the idea of particular responsibilities and obligations, although it embraces the same impetus toward larger thinking and citizenship endorsed by stakeholder analysis.

If we consider corporations first of all as communities—not legal fictions, not monolithic entities, not faceless bureaucracies, not matrices of price/earnings ratios, net assets and liabilities—then the activities and the ethics of business become much more comprehensible and much more human. Shareholders are, of course, part of the community, but most of them are only marginally rather than, as in some now-classic arguments, the sole recipients of managerial fiduciary obligations. The concept of community also shifts our conception of what makes a corporation "work" or not. What makes a corporation efficient or inefficient is not a series of well-oiled mechanical operations but the working interrelationships, the coordination and rivalries, team spirit and morale of the many people who work there and are in turn shaped and defined by the corporation. So, too, what drives a corporation is not some mysterious abstraction called "the profit motive" (which is highly implausible even as a personal motive, but utter nonsense when applied to a fictitious legal entity or a bureaucracy). It is the collective will and ambitions of its employees, few of whom (even in profit-sharing plans or in employee-owned companies) work for a profit in any obvioius sense. Employees of a corporation do what they must to fit in, to perform their jobs, and to earn both the respect of others and self-respect. They want to prove their value in their jobs, they try to shoe their independence or their resentment, they try to please (or intentionally aggravate) their superiors, they want to impress (or intimidate) their subordinates, they want to feel good about themselves or they try to make the best of a bad situation. And, of course, they want to bring home a paycheck. To understand how corporations work (and don't work) is to understand the social psychology and sociology of communities, not the logic of a flowchart or the organizational workings of a cumbersome machine.

I have already commented on the great deal of finger pointing concerning the supposed loss of competitiveness, noting that the real problem is lack of cooperation and a coordinated business community. It is within the context of a discussion of community, accordingly, that one should raise the usually restricted set of questions about the desirability of much of the recent mergers and acquisitions activity. The primary defense of "hostile takeovers"—often articulated by such masters of the craft as T. Boone Pickens and popularized by the fictitious but infamous Gordon Gekko in *Wall Street*—is the need to spur competition, get rid of bad management, and, of course, "to be fair to the stockholders." But competition is not the "bottom line" of corporate success, and management (even bad management) is not simply extraneous or contingent to the corporation. Managers, with some reason, typically identify themselves *as* the corporation, and what has received far too little attention in the debate over the public interest of unfriendly mergers and takeovers and the distraction of "golden parachutes" for a few top executives is the utter disaster precipitated by the disruption of corporate communities. It is no surprise that a good many of the new entities created (or "liberated") by takeover activity fail, and not just because of the mountain of debt typically accumulated in the process. What work force can keep its morale in the face of the continuous threat of layoffs? What manager can function as either an authority or as a team player when his or her authority is clearly contingent and it is not even clear what "team" he or she is playing for? Such threats may encourage the *appearance* of hard work (and a great deal of derrière covering) but it cannot possibly encourage dedication or loyalty. By virtue of the excessive emphasis on competition to the exclusion of cooperation, by ignoring such "intangible" features of business life as company morale and coordination in favor of the measurable quantities listed in the financial pages, we are destroying the corporation as a community and, consequently, as a fully functional human institution. As one Japanese executive said to me recently, "We don't have to compete with American companies. They do themselves in all by themselves."

What is a corporate community? To begin with, it is heterogeneous conglomerate that is bound to be riddled with personality clashes, competing aims and methodologies, cliques and rivalries, and crisscrossed loyalties. The very fact that a corporation requires specialization and the division of labor makes inevitable such heterogeneity. Two young men working in a garage, pooling their resources and their knowledge to produce a successful commodity, may, in the throes and thrills of development and struggle, experience an uninterrupted sense of oneness that would impress even a Buddhist. But once the product is launched and marketing people and managers are brought in to do the job, that primeval corporate unity is shattered and, as in the most famous recent case of this kind, one or both of the founders of the company may find themselves displaced or even fired by the assistants they brought in to help them. There is an intrinsic antagonism—to be explained in terms of social class rather than economics and in terms of our mythologies of work rather than the nature of the work itself— between the shop floor and the managerial office, just as there is an obvious opposition (not entirely financial) between those divisions of the corporation that always need to spend more money (advertising and research and development teams, for example) and those whose job it is to save it. Add to this the many different characters and personalities who populate even the most seemingly homogeneous company (although these differences too are already preestablished in the social types and classes who tend to one or the other position or profession) and one can appreciate the foolishness in our popular treatment of corporations as monolithic entities with a single mind and a single motive.

And yet there is an emergent phenomenon that does often speak with a single voice and deserves to be treated (and not just by the law) as a singular entity, "the corporation." Groups have personalities just as individuals do, the heterogeneous, even fragmented groups can nevertheless have a singluar character just as conflicted people do. it is a mistake to speak of corporations as only collections of individuals, both because the "individuals" in question are themselves the creatures of the corporation and because the corporation is one of those sums that is nevertheless greater than its many constituent parts. Aristotelean ethics takes both the corporation and the individual seriously without pretending thast either is an autonomous entity unto itself. Corporations are made up of people, and the people in corporations are defined by the corporation. Business ethics thus becomes a matter of corporate ethics, emphatically *not* in the sense that what counts is the ethics of the corporation, considered as an autonomous, autocratic agent, ruling over its employees (perhaps exemplified by its ''corporate code''), nor in the more innocent but naive sense that the ethics of the corporation is nothing but the product of the collective morality of its employees. The morals of the executives, particularly the exemplary morals of those who are most visible in the corporation, are an important influence on corporate morality, but it is the nature and power of institutions—particularly those in which a person spends half of his or her adult waking life—to shape and sanction the morals of the individual. There may well be (and often is) a gap or dichotomy between a persons' sense of ethics on the job and his or her sense of right and wrong with friends and family. There may well be real ethical differences within a company, particularly between its various departments and divisions. But even in diversity and conflict the ethics of a corporation becomes clearly and often soon visible to those most closely attached to, affiliated with, or affected by it. Corporations can (and often do) get a bad rap, an institutional black eye caused by a tiny percentage of its employees. (Hertz Rent-a-Car was caught up in a monumental car-repair scandal a year or so ago, which turned out to involve some twenty dealers out of twenty thousand. Nevertheless, it was the name ''Hertz'' that took the brunt of the abuse, and numbers were simply not the issue.) Such apparent injustices throw a revealing light on a company and its ethical standards, however, and give the best corporations a chance to show their moral mettle. Communities are essential units of morality, and corporations are ultimately judged not by the numbers but by the coherence and cooperation both within their walls and with the larger communities in which they play such an essential social as well as economic role.

NOTES

1. There is a substantial but often ignored problem here concerning affirmative action and justice. We argue for a meritocracy, but the truth is that interviewers are looking for someone they would enjoy working with, and for the most part that means someone like them. In the typical, mostly white male corporation, there is a natural block against women and minorities, and anyone who would raise the discomfort level. ''Merit'' often refers to comfort. How to develop pluralistic communities is critical here, but neither the shrill multiculturalism and ethnic identity debate nor the equally obstinate assimilationist success rhetoric is going to help us here.

2. There is always the *Star Trek* myth, of course, the benign ''outsider'' who brings to a civilization some virtue that is sorely missing but wholly lacking (e.g., Kirk's courage, Spock's rationality), and the more generic Joseph Campbell myth of the hero who leaves his society and wanders off on his own, later returning with new virtues to save the society. But the fact that these are *myths* should already tell us something about their sociological status. The virtues supposedly imported are already celebrated as such.

How Do They Live with Themselves?

ROGER ROSENBLATT

People who wonder how tobacco company executives can live with themselves conclude that they must be in denial. That would explain how they deal with their responsibility for a product that kills more than 420,000 Americans a year—surpassing the combined deaths from homicide, suicide, AIDS, automobile accidents, alcohol and drug abuse. But to be in denial implies that one may not be held accountable, in psychological terms, for one's actions. Tobacco people squarely face the accusation of accountability, and reject it.

They reject the overwhelming epidemiological evidence in the Surgeon General's Report of 1989, connecting smoking with lung and throat cancers, emphysema and heart disease, insisting that direct causation has not been proved. They dismiss the Food and Drug Administration's suggestion that cigarettes could be banned as an addictive drug, calling smoking merely a habit that has already been broken by tens of millions. They ridicule people who say they are pushing a drug, noting that their product is legal, that the same government that posts health warnings on cigarette packs subsidizes tobacco farmers and that what they are really promoting is freedom of choice.

In other words, if they experience denial as a psychological response, they also use denial as an aggressive tactic. This mirrors the way they live with themselves in general. Individually, they remove themselves from most of the rest of the country and create their own moral universe of explanations and justifications. Collectively, they embrace the country directly, involving as much of America as possible in their enormous success.

My case in point is Philip Morris, the largest tobacco company in America and the largest consumer-products company in the world, owner of Kraft General Foods, Jacobs Suchard, and Miller beer and maker of Marlboro, the best-selling cigarette in America and the best-selling packaged product in the world. The connection of the company to the American economy is so deep and secure that if one were to remove Philip Morris without first finding something equally valuable to fill the hole, much of the country would cave in.

The company paid 4.5 billion in taxes in 1992 (on revenues of $59 billion) and billions more in employees' and excise taxes—making it the largest taxpayer in the country and, outside of government, the largest tax collector. Also in 1992 it contributed $4 billion toward the balance of payments. It directly employs

161,000 people worldwide (92,000 of them in this country), not including those who sell the product or make the paper and the filters or who lobby in Washington or who advertise the product.

Philip Morris is also a mainstay of American farming. In Blackstone, Virginia, about fifty miles southwest of Richmond, I met with John Bledsoe, a tobacco farmer in his early thirties. Bledsoe believes there is a health risk in smoking, but he has to earn a living. "There's nothing that will ever replace tobacco as a cash crop," he said. "And the farther south you go from here, the more impact tobacco has. The local car store, the clothing store . . . people don't realize. And Philip Morris has always been on our side. They've sent us on trips to places like Canada and Brazil to meet other tobacco farmers. They've helped us to stand up for what they represent." . . .

Philip Morris contends with Procter & Gamble for the title of the largest advertiser in the world, supporting advertising agencies and the mass media. The introduction of Marlboro Medium in 1991 cost $60 million, the most ever spent by the company on a single new product. The company has not only advertised itself, it has advertised against its attackers. In 1988 it spent $5 million on a campaign to emphasize the economic power of smokers. One newspaper ad read: "Today, 21 million American smokers will go out to eat. That's a market you can sink your teeth into." . . .

Cigarette advertising has been a mainstay of the magazine business since 1971, when Congress prohibited tobacco advertising on radio and television. This prohibition did not hurt Philip Morris, since Marlboro ads were more effective as still pictures of the Marlboro cowboy (the most widely recognized advertising image in the world), either on billboards or in magazine pages. In 1992 the company spent over $2 billion on media advertising—of food, beer, and tobacco products—including nearly $18 million in daily newspapers and over $215 million in magazines. Many publishers and editors who welcome cigarette advertising also run health-hazard articles that omit or minimize the dangers of smoking.

The company's connection to journalistic enterprises is widening. Philip Morris has recently made an agreement with the *Time* magazine group to test a system for sending magazines with tobacco ads only to subscribers who smoke. Philip Morris has also used its own data base to enlist smokers in campaigns against increased cigarette taxes. The company places a great deal of advertising with Time Inc., as it does with the New York Times Company, the Washington Post Company, Hearst Publications, and Condé Nast. One member of the Philip Morris board of directors is Rupert Murdoch, owner of such publications as *TV Guide,* the *New York Post,* and the *Times of London.*

The composition of the board of directors itself suggests the extent of the company's connections to American business, banking, arts, education, government, intellectual, and health institutions, including hospitals and even cancer research centers. Besides Murdoch, outside members of the board, who are paid about $40,000 a year, include Harold Brown, the former defense secretary and a director of IBM, Mattel, and CBS; William H. Donaldson, chairman of the New York Stock Exchange, former dean of the Graduate School of Management at Yale and a director of Aetna Life and Casuality and the Carnegie Endowment for

World Peace; Richard D. Parsons, chief executive of the Dime Savings Bank, a director of Time Warner and the Metropolitan Museum of Art, and a trustee of Howard University; Roger S. Penske, head of the Penske Truck Leasing Company in Detroit and a director of American Express; John S. Reed, chairman of Citicorp and a trustee of the Massachusetts Institute of Technology, the Rand Corporation, and the Russell Sage Foundation and a member of the board of the Memorial Sloan-Kettering Cancer Center.

The mutually useful relationship between the company and the government may be illustrated by the Clinton administration's proposed excise tax on cigarettes. The tax is said to pose a menace to the tobacco industry by pricing the product off the market. Philip Morris and the other companies will, naturally, fight the tax. Yet does it matter if they lose? "You know, I don't really care about the excise tax at all," a company vice-president told me. "I wouldn't mind making the government a little more dependent on the habit."

While the president works to pass his excise tax, others in his White House have had relationships with the company that might affect their enthusiasm. When he was a lawyer in California, Mickey Kantor, the administration's trade representative, assisted restaurant owners who were fighting antismoking ordinances. His law firm also represented Philip Morris. Such relationships with the White House are common. After he left the Reagan administrastion, Michael Deaver represented Philip Morris in its efforts to penetrate the rich South Korean market. After he left the Bush administration, Craig L. Fuller joined the company as senior vice president for corporate affairs.

Encouraged by Michael A. Miles, the corporate chief executive officer, Fuller helped the Clinton administration promote the North American Free Trade Agreement. Free trade is in the company's interests, but "this is because we care about the issue," Fuller says. "Mike is willing to give time to public policies that matter." A corporate senior vice president, Murray H. Bring, former partner in the Washington law firm of Arnold & Porter, alludes to the White House connection when he says, only half-jokingly: "To ban a product that is used so widely by so many people doesn't make any sense . . . certainly not from a political point of view. There are more smokers in the United States than there are people who voted for Clinton."

In 1991–1992 (the most recent figures available) the tobacco industry contributed $2.39 million to Congress, including PAC money and donations from executives. Of that, Philip Morris gave about one-quarter, or $640,000. Connections to individuals include Representatives like Charlie Rose, Democrat of North Carolina, known as Mr. Tobacco, and Scotty Baesler, Democrat of Kentucky, who represents tobacco-growing states, and Charles Rangel, a New York Democrat whose campaigns and communities have benefited from Philip Morris donations. Rangel has been under fire for his opposition to the excise tax, especially since he has crusaded against drugs and because blacks have been found to suffer from smoking-related diseases at a higher rate than other groups.

I visited Rangel, who seems to be in something of a turmoil about the smoking issue. Before I could get out a question, he exploded that his opposition to the excise tax was perfectly consistent with his opposition to all regressive taxes.

Then he complained that poor people in his Harlem community would suffer nervous breakdowns because they would not be able to afford cigarettes. Finally he said that he was likely to change his mind on the tax to help pass the Clinton health package.

Philip Morris's involvement with social projects and the arts ranges from donations to a variety of organiztions and communities to efforts toward minority employment and civil liberties within the company. Under the former leadership of Joseph F. Cullman 3d and George Weissman, Philip Morris became the first tobacco company to hire blacks in high positions. For that the company was boycotted in the South. The white supremacist publication *White Sentinel* wrote that Philip Morris had the "worst race mixing record" of any large company in the nation. The company was among the first to advertise in black and Hispanic newspapers and magazines. It has been vigorous in its employment of women.

Philip Morris makes large and frequent contributions to the National Urban League, the NAACP, the United Negro College Fund, Goodwill Industries, the National Puerto Rican Forum, the Asian Pacific American Legal Consortium, the Boy Scouts, Girl Scouts, United Way, YMCA, hospitals all over America, the Legal Aid Society, the National Multiple Sclerosis Society, the Salk Institute, the National Association on Drug Abuse. In 1990–1991 it sponsored a 200th anniversary national tour of the original document of the Bill of Rights.

The company has supported teacher education and adult literacy, backed reform in elementary and secondary schools, and helped minority students go to college. In 1993 it donated more than $1.3 million to hunger relilef organizations and over $1 million to AIDS. When I asked Stephanie French, vice-president for corporate contributions and cultural affairs, whether any of the gift recipients ever expressed reservations or unhappiness about taking tobacco money, she pointed out that grantees apply to the company, not the other way around.

As for the arts, Philip Morris is not only the largest tobacco company contributor but one of the largest corporate contributors of any kind. Nor does it give its money only to the "safer" arts projects; it has long supported the Next Wave Festival at the Brooklyn Academy of Music and as early as 1965 it supported the well-received exhibition of "Pop and Op" art. A report on 35 years of its arts contributions runs to 130 pages and lists grants to the Joffrey Ballet, Morgan Library, Jewish Museum, the Guggenheim, the Yaddo artists' colony, the Whitney (a branch of which is located in its corporate headquarters building in New York), the American Museum of Natural History, and the National Gallery of Art in Washington.

George Weissman, the chief executive after Joe Cullman and before Hamish Maxwell, has been chairman of Lincoln Center since 1986. French serves on the board of the Joffrey. William Campbell, president of Philip Morris USA, the domestic tobacco company, is a member of the board of the Brooklyn Academy of Music and the MacDowell Colony.

Perhaps the company's single most-publicized arts donation was a $3 million-plus grant for the Vatican art treasures exhibition at the Metropolitan Museum of Art in 1983. When Terence Cardinal Cooke, then the Roman Catholic archbishop of New York, offered a benediction at a banquet celebrating the exhibition, Frank

Saunders, a Philip Morris vice-president, remarked: "We are probably the only cigarette company on this earth to be blessed by a Cardinal."

The company enjoys its association with art and artists on philosophical as well as aesthetic grounds. French believes that art fosters creative risk-taking within the company. Philip Morris may also like to relate the independent thinking of artists with its promotion of freedom of choice for smokers. The freedom to choose to smoke is the company's main philosophical, and legal, position, one which it links to other American freedoms. Usually, however, it does not advertise this linkage. In a pamphlet available to the public, the company announces: "We seek to lift the human spirit." In a set of in-house guidelines, it sounds more pragmatic: "We believe that business activities must make social sense, and social activities must make business sense. . . . Alexis de Tocqueville gave a name to this concept . . . 'the principle of self-interest rightly understood.'"

Every time one raises a spoonful of Jell-O or Post Raisin Bran or Breyers ice cream or pours Log Cabin maple syrup or squirts Miracle Whip or spreads Parkay Margarine or Philadelphia Cream Cheese or Cheez Whiz or takes a bite of an Oscar Mayer weiner or an Entenmann's cookie or a Toblerone chocolate or sips Maxwell House coffee or Kool-Aid or Miller Beer—whether or not one also lights up a Marlboro, Benson & Hedges, Parliament, Merit, Alpine, Chesterfield or a Virginia Slims—he or she is proving the principle of self-interest rightly understood.

All of Philip Morris's connections to the country have produced, and are sustained by, a corporate culture that gives company executives immense, if guarded, self-confidence and helps them do battle with opponents. The culture is nurtured in their New York City corporate headquarters, a tall gray stone-and-steel building largely unnoticeable where it stands on Park Avenue between 41st and 42nd Streets because that is where the Grand Central Terminal auto ramp dominates the avenue. After the World Trade Center bombing, many New York office buildings had to make protective structural alterations; this had already been done at Philip Morris.

The building is clean, quiet and decorated in the not-tasteless taste of most office buildings—grays, off-whites and tans; egg-box light fixtures; plants in the offices, fabric on the walls. Large works of contemporary art are on display. Except for the blown-up photos of cigarette brands and omnipresent ashtrays, 120 Park might be taken for any prosperous business tower. Well-dressed women and men in shirt sleeves make self-conscious chatter on the elevators and small, quick jokes in the halls, which are not smoke-filled.

Not long ago I visited the Philip Morris headquarters on several occasions and spoke with upper-level executives. Leery of journalists, they were nonetheless forthcoming in describing what they do and how they feel about it, though, to be sure, they are shrewd and, in terms of legal jeopardy, know what they can and cannot say. All of them are intelligent and companionable; most are family-oriented and community-minded. All feel beleaguered by portions of society (one vice-president complained of being accosted at a cocktail party in his hometown by someone calling him a "mass murderer") and by the news media and the "antis," whom they alternately call "Nazis" or "smoking police." All are well paid, but not much more than executives at other large companies. Every one of them expresses enormous affection and respect for the company.

Steven C. Parrish, who turns 44 in April, grew up in Moberly, Missouri, a town of thirteen thousand once known as the home of Banquet Foods TV dinners. His father was a railroad cop; his great-uncle a lawyer involved in state Democratic politics. Originally, Parrish thought he would go into politics himself. But after graduating from the University of Missouri, where he made Phi Beta Kappa, and from the University of Missouri Law School, where he was an editor of the law review, he joined the Kansas City law firm of Shook, Hardy & Bacon. Five years later, he was made a partner. He represented Philip Morris and Lorillard in the noted Cipollone case, in which the Liggett Group, Philip Morris, and other companies were sued for contributing to the death by lung cancer of Rose Cipollone, who had smoked from an early age. An initial judgment of $400,000 against Liggett was eventually overrturned and the case was never retried.

Parrish, who smokes, is a small, neat, compact man, young in manner and appearance in spite of graying hair. In a blue shirt with a white collar, he looks slightly overfashionable. His voice rises and falls like a boy's in the process of changing. Everything about him suggests that he had to struggle his way through the likable country boy demeanor to assert ability, sophistication, and authority. He is general counsel and senior vice-president for external affairs, Philip Morris USA. He and his wife live in Westport, Connecticut, with their daughter, eleven, and son, almost four.

> The Cipollone trial took several months. As soon as it was over, I took a sabbatical, and when I came back, Philip Morris approached me about working for them exclusively. I took the job because I liked being a trial lawyer. I enjoy the ego rush you get when you're up and performing in court. And there's something about being an in-house lawyer that had always intrigued me. Philip Morris is a great company in terms of its business success, its reputation, and all that sort of thing. The people really impressed me. And I really like representing the tobacco workers, who run the machinery and make the cigarettes. Really good people—the kind I thought I'd represent when I was growing up. I also had always wanted to live on the East Coast. My friends in Kansas City think I'm nuts.
>
> I didn't have any qualms about joining a tobacco company, partly because I had dealt with the issue already in the Cipollone case. We got nasty letters and a lot of confrontational things. My biggest qualm was: "Gee, I have a very successful practice here in the Midwest. My wife is from the Midwest. I've always been very happy here. You never know. I may go to Philip Morris and they might think I'm terrible and then what am I gonna do." That's what I thought. But I didn't have other qualms. I'd worked it out.
>
> And I certainly didn't divide my job and my feelings in the Cipollone case. I didn't attempt to keep myself from feeling bad for Mrs. Cipollone, who was a really neat lady. I met her a couple of times before she died. She was sort of spunky, you know. And Mr. Cipollone was a very nice man. So I didn't try not to feel bad for Antonio Cipollone, because number 1, I didn't think I could do it, and number 2, what would that say about me? But I really did feel strongly that he was not entitled to get money

because his wife chose to smoke. I mean, she was very clear about that. That she liked it. How it made her feel glamorous. That she enjoyed the taste of it. And never made a serious attempt to quit until she was told she had a problem. So when I met Mr. Cipollone, when he told about how his wife died, it was a very moving thing. It was a terrible thing. But she chose to smoke.

But I wouldn't be honest with you if I didn't tell you that when I see Sam Donaldson, for example, on "This Week with David Brinkley," as he did a few months ago, say "I don't see how an executive with a tobacco company can look himself in the mirror in the morning." . . . It troubles me. The day that happened I was sitting on a couch with my wife and my kids. We'd just gotten home from church. I love that show, so as soon as we get home I flip it on, and there's Sam Donaldson saying that. And it was upsetting.

Obviously, one way to deal with that is to say: "OK, I'm not going to work for a cigarette company. Then they wouldn't be saying those things about me." But I feel good about what I do, both in how I go about my job and what my role in the company is, so I try not to let it bother me. But anybody would feel hurt if somebody says you are a merchant of death and you shouldn't be able to look yourself in the mirror in the morning. I wish they wouldn't say things like that.

During the trial, I got to be pretty good friends with the plaintiff's lawyer. We used to get together every once in a while after the case was over, and he told me once . . . he and I were screaming at each other in front of the judge about something and he was calling me every name in the book and the company every name in the book and then I got up to do my response. And as he walked by, he said: "You take this too seriously. You take this too personally." And he was right.

My philosophy about everyday life is that you really have to constantly reexamine everything. Your convictions, I mean, your religious beliefs or whatever. And if you don't, you're not doing the right thing. And I ask myself the question: "Are you one of these people that just says, I make a nice salary. I have a job. There are a lot of people that don't have jobs at all. And so have you rationalized your way into saying, yeah, this is what I ought to be doing?" I ask myself that a lot, along with a lot of other questions that don't have anything to do with Philip Morris. And I don't think I do. I don't think I do.

A year or two ago, my daughter came home from school, and said: "I have a homework assignment I need you to help me with. Tomorrow we're going to talk about drugs like marijuana, cocaine, and alcohol. We're also going to talk about cigarettes and whether they're addictive. I want to know what you think about cigarettes." And I told her that a lot of people believe that cigarette smoking is addictive but I don't believe it. And I told her the surgeon general says some 40 million people have quit smoking on their own. But if she asked me about the health consequences, I would tell her that I certainly don't think it's safe to smoke. It's a risk factor for lung cancer. For heart disease. But it's a choice. We're confronted with choices all the time. Still, I'd have to tell her that it might be a bad idea. I don't know. But it might be.

Is the affection that people have for one another in this company based partly on the fact that we're all in the bunker together? I don't think so, and I'll tell you why. The atmosphere here is not really different than it was at my law firm in Kansas City. There is stress, there's pressure . . . but that was true there as well. I notice more people locking arms and getting together behind a business strategy than I see worrying about the externalities of charges about tobacco and health and things like that.

But that other lawyer was right about me. I do take things personally. My wife constantly tells me: "You worry too much about what other people think. You're doing fine." So, while in some ways the worst thing about me is that I take things personally, part of the reason that I think I do a good job or see things through is also because I take things personally. And I say to myself: "If I could just sit down with Sam Donaldson, he's not going to change his attitudes about smoking, but doggone, he'd probably realize that this guy's not a bad guy. He's got two little kids. He worries about all the issues that a parent worries about with their kids—drugs, AIDS, violence, all that stuff."

You might say that we ought to do everything we can do reasonably to make sure that nobody ever smokes another cigarette. But you wouldn't say that people who work for tobacco companies can't look at themselves in the mirror because they're somehow lesser human beings than people who work for a drug company or a steel company.

David E. R. Dangoor, forty-four, was appointed executive vice-president for Philip Morris International in 1992. He has spent virtually his entire working life with Philip Morris, having served the company in Switzerland, Germany, England, and Canada. Reared and educated in Sweden, he has the easy, gracious manner and unidentifiable accent of the fictional character known as "the Continental"—wire-rimmed glasses, iron-gray hair combed straight back, a blue-and-red striped tie over a blue-and-white striped shirt, and a gray double-breasted suit with a white handkerchief peeking up from the jacket pocket. Slightly jowly and soft-looking, he nonetheless has one of those faces that says, "I will beat you with sheer brainpower, and I will do it so deftly and politely that you will love every minute of it."

Imagine me, growing up in Sweden in 1976, extremely frustrated by a country where socialism was really going too far, where equality was everything but equality meaning everything should be average, rather than quality at a high end. And then I got an opportunity to get interviewed by Philip Morris, in Switzerland. I had no interest in working for them. I had an antipathy toward smoking. I must tell you, I met five executives and after that I walked out and the only thing on my mind was how am I going to land a job in this company. I had met people that spoke to me about the business, life, family, in a way that I had never been exposed to in school. I realized that I wasn't talking to a rigid company, where everybody had to toe the party line. It was a company where one could remain an individualist.

I don't believe I would do anything that would benefit me if I thought at the same time that I was cheating society, that I was lying to society, that I was doing something truly immoral. Everybody knows that smoking must be a terrible idea, I mean, it's not a secret. In actual fact, we live in a perfect world. We are allowed to conduct our business, and the press and the antis are allowed to rip us apart and kill us. The debate is in the forefront. And this is a shocking statement to make, but I'm sure that people think smoking is even more dangerous than it ever could be. Yet they do it. Why? Is it an addiction issue? I don't believe it. People do all sorts of things to express their individuality and to protest against society. And smoking is one of them, and not the worst.

When you are in the business, and when you're confronted with all the issues, I promise you, you come out of it saying, "I don't feel that bad about doing this."

Is this denial? My wife says I'm a specialist in denial, and so does my doctor. Let me try to answer you in the following way. If people are staying with the company because of denial, they must be incredibly resilient. I had a tremendous amount of job offers; a lot of our people did. I could have gone into the cereal business, the cosmetics business. I must tell you, the people you have around you every day, and the kind of environment that you live in every day, become an incredibly important part of the quality of your life. The issues that you refer to become less important, not because you deny the problems but because as a whole it's not the question of making more money. It's the question of being very happy at doing what you're doing.

You know, actually, it sounds crude and simplistic, but ultimately it's not up to the tobacco industry to deal with the cigarette issue. The final solution to the cigarette issue, that's up to society. If they want to ban cigarettes, you know, we live in a democracy, it should be done in a democratic way and discussed how the hell to deal with the economic consequences, and that's not meant as a threat. It's just a fact.

I'll tell you what I like about the business. First, there are no surprises. There is nothing more to be said or discovered about the cigarette business or the industry. And there's no way to write an article that could do us any more harm than what has already been written. Second, no new company wants to get into the tobacco business. That's great. Third, we have the best partners in the world: the governments. In a lot of countries, it's incredibly important to the whole welfare state that we sell our products to collect taxes. When you sit with a finance minister or deputy of any government to discuss taxation, he's much cruder about the financial analysis of that taxing than we are. He asks, "How much can I put up the tax, to make sure that the demand is not going to go down so much so that my net intake goes down?" Amazing. So no matter how you look at the cigarette business, it's incredibly predictable, it's extremely secure as an investment vehicle and, therefore, it's a great business to be in—if you can deal with the fact that some people are not going to like you.

As senior vice-president for corporate affairs, Craig L. Fuller, forty-three, helps to shape and superintend the company's definition and image. Fuller came to the company in January 1992, after having served as assistant for Cabinet affairs for President Ronald Reagan from 1981 to 1985, chief of staff for Vice-President George Bush from 1985 to 1988 and chief executive of Hill & Knowlton USA, the public relations firm. He has spent most of his career moving between public relations and politics. His first full-time job was as manager of public affairs for the Pacific Mutual Life Insurance Company; his second, with Michael Deaver's firm, Deaver & Hannaford. He grew up in the late 1960s in Walnut Creek, California, and went to UCLA.

Fuller and his wife, Karen, still keep their home in Virginia from their Washington days. He is about six feet tall, has a large belly, an open merry face and is slightly bucktoothed. His dark brown hair is slick and neatly cut, like a teenager's of the 1950s.

My wife, Karen, has—had—more concerns about joining a tobacco company than I did. I smoke cigars. She's a nonsmoker. But Mike Miles [the corporate chief executive] was the first to tell me, "Think it through." I was very interested in understanding what the company's point of view was. I was impressed with programs that existed before I came here, about "accommodation." We think smokers and nonsmokers alike have rights. And that they ought to be accommodated. So I was concerned to take time to understand what the company's point of view was, and it was consistent with my own. I think that it's important to have a match with respect to some basic values.

The link between working for George Bush and working for Philip Morris is that not only must you believe, you have to make the others believe in themselves. My job with Bush was telling him, in effect, "This is who you are and this is what you believe." I've always thought of myself as a good listener and a good communicator between and among groups. I'd like to have people better understand what we're about. I don't know if I ever said to myself, "What I really want to go do is represent people who might not be able to represent themselves as well," but I sort of have done it.

My corporate job is a little different—and I'm not sliding away from the tobacco issue. But my job is to help the company work through how you can have a great deal of pride and respect, and care a lot, and nurture a very, very successful tobacco business, while recognizing that you are a global leader in the food business. If you analyze constituencies or audiences, you find out that the general public, the media, opinion leaders, business leaders, investors really don't understand this company very well. And regardless of how they feel about tobacco, I'd like them to judge us for what we actually are—a company of some of the world's best brands. Among our strongest brands is Marlboro; that, I think, is going to be the case for a long time to come. It gives us a chance to do a lot of other things and it gives us a strength that other companies don't enjoy. It gives us cash flow, a financial base to invest in food businesses and expand the beer businesses. And so I'm for a strong tobacco identity.

People under attack here sometimes say, "Why don't we change our name to Kraft?" I think that would be wrong, because that would be stepping away from the world's largest tobacco company and a business that succeeds because people know that folks on this floor, and shareholders and others, have a great deal of respect for what it is that they do. And they are a wonderful group of people. Again, I have to help people figure out who they are.

You know, there's been a deep reluctance here about talking to the press. We almost never do it. I say we should. My thinking is: if there's one more negative story, so what? I mean, if we can't describe what we think and feel and how we go about our business and we're not willing to share some of the challenges and some of the human dimensions to it and the pride, well what are we doing? Once you know what you're doing, you've got to believe it.

When I first came here, Fortune magazine did a story on us, and it's funny because, at the time, people thought it was a terrible story. I told them, I think it's a terrific story. If you open the magazine, you see a big full-page picture of Mike Miles. He looks terrific, like Clint Eastwood. Next to it is this bar chart that shows our cash flow. Just looking at it, within 10 seconds, you know that our cash flow is greater than the next ten companies combined. I said, I'll take it. We now use that article to recruit people.

Ellen Merlo, a self-described social smoker, has worked for Philip Morris for twenty-five years. Born in 1940 in the Bronx, she grew up in West New York, New Jersey, a town on the Palisades cliffs that overlooks the Hudson. Her parents were in the embroidery business. "I hated New Jersey and I hated West New York," she says matter-of-factly. "I used to look at Manhattan across the river and say to myself, 'I'm a New Yorker.'" After high school, she spent two years

studying at Katharine Gibbs, then found employment first with Young &
Rubicam, then at Revlon, Ziff Davis, and Petersen Publishing. Starting out as a
secretary at Young & Rubicam, she rose at Petersen to be managing editor of
Motor Trend magazine, though she had little interest in cars.

Joining Philip Morris in Canada in 1969, she later transferred to New York
where she was brand manager successively for Parliament, Virginia Slims, and
Benson & Hedges. She moved up further in various executive marketing positions and today is vice-president for corporate affairs for Philip Morris USA. Her
work focuses on government relations and supervising lobbying interests.

Merlo dresses business-stylishly, has dark brown hair and dark brown eyes,
and carries herself with the self-assurance of someone who has worked long and
hard to get where she is. She is steadfastly loyal to her colleagues, though she
speaks wistfully of the days when . . . everyone knew most everyone else.
"Now we have a Christmas party for two thousand people at the Metropolitan
Museum." A lifelong liberal Democrat, her fondest memory is of shaking hands
with Eleanor Roosevelt. She lives in the heart of Manhattan:

> Dealing with government, state or national, the first thing you have to think about is
> what are the company objectives, overall. Secondly, what legislation is out there that
> is either positive or negative for the company. Then you put a strategy together to deal
> with various legislators or issues.
>
> The way you win the most battles is to have information. Contrary to what people
> think, it's not having influence. Yes, it's knowing who the legislators are and having
> a good relationship and having access. But once you have access, you have to be able
> to deliver a message that makes sense. If it's a tax that we're against, then we have to
> be able to prove that there are going to be job losses, that it's not going to produce the
> revenue that is being projected, that if a state raises its taxes so high and it's next to
> another state that has low taxes, there are going to be cross-border sales and those
> sales will not only be a loss in tobacco revenue, but once someone goes over a border
> to buy their tobacco or their liquor or something else, they're probably making a lot of
> other purchases.
>
> You ask, "What if Rangel changes his position and supports on the excise tax?"
> If he does change his mind, we will show him the facts and figures—that an excise tax
> will not produce the revenue. Philip Morris supports health care reform. I don't know
> anybody who's against health care reform. But it's a matter of how extensive it is,
> how quickly it's implemented and how it's paid for. What we're saying is that an
> excise tax is an unreliable way of paying for health care. Number 1, it will not
> produce the revenue to pay for the plan, so there's going to have to be other taxation,
> and number 2, it's going to play economic havoc, because it probably will cost the
> country 275,000 jobs. So we will talk to Charlie Rangel, not to dissuade him from
> supporting health care reform but to get him and others to think about alternative
> ways of funding and reducing costs.
>
> We really don't care how people feel about smoking; we're not asking anyone to
> endorse our product. It's not a smoking issue. We say: "This is what an excise tax
> will do to this city, state, to people in your district. This is what a smoking ban will do
> to restaurants, the impact it'll have on revenue." It's not about the tobacco.
>
> Of course, the economic and the smoking issue are related. I'll tell you an
> interesting story about a Philip Morris employee. This was in California. He was
> taking a group of business associates to a restaurant, and when they got there—there

were six or seven of them—he said we'd like a table in the smoking section. They said, "Sorry, but this is a no-smoking restaurant. We don't allow smoking anywhere in the restaurant."

He turned to his guests and said: "I'd just as soon not stay here. Do you mind if we go to another restaurant?" After all, it was Philip Morris money. So his guests said no problem, and they went down the block and they had a lovely time and he paid the bill, which was about $500 for everybody. And he got a copy of the bill and sent it to the first restaurant with a note: "Just thought you should know. Here is the receipt of the funds that I spent that night, that could have gone to you. Multiply it by all of the other people who might want to come in and have a cigarette."

Two days later, he gets a phone call—and he never put his phone number in the letter. "We just want you to know that we received your letter and we thought about it, and we decided that we are going to employ an accommodation in our restaurant from now on, so we hope that the next time you go out to dinner, you and your smoking friends will think about us again."

William I. Campbell was born in Regina, Saskatchewan, and grew up in the oil boom town of Edmonton, Alberta. His father's family goes back several generations in Canada; his mother came over from Scotland. Campbell's grandfather had been a small-town grocer but got wiped out in the Depression. Neither of his parents went to college. They invested their hopes in their one son—they also had two older daughters—and were pleased when he studied economics at the University of Alberta and considered pursuing a Ph.D., with the idea of becoming a college professor.

But a mentor saw in Campbell a flair for business, and Campbell felt that was right. He had, he says, an ability to "see through the data." He went east to an M.B.A. from the University of Western Ontario ("that was my rebellion"). He went directly to work for Philip Morris, first in the marketing division of Benson & Hedges, Canada, then in a number of increasingly higher marketing and sales positions. In September 1990 he was appointed president and chief executive officer of Philip Morris USA, placing him in charge of everything in the tobacco company.

The conference room beside his office displays photos with dignitaries, awards, a souvenir medal from President Clinton, and a mug from the Clinton inauguration. Like Steve Parrish, Campbell is thin, smallish, and young-looking. He turns fifty in May. He has sharp blue eyes, wavy silver hair, and a face that looks both rugged and malleable. He has a ready, explosive laugh and he frequently talks with his hands. Campbell is divorced. His two young daughters live with their mother.

You know, even today I go out with the sales reps. There are things that you can learn at that level of contact that you just can't learn any other way. You can't read it off the computer or in the reports. Especially at the early stages of a launch. Sales reps are a continuous source of real, hands-on information. And of how you're really being perceived. They react a lot like consumers. So you can get a sense of where you are, what kind of adjustments you should make and so on.

So I still go out with the sales force. Because any good leader has to be able to see the data as something else. If the skills are purely objective, at some point they'll tend to falter. And if the skills are purely subjective, where they'll falter typically is in the people area. The principal responsibilities are people-related. In a decision like Marlboro Friday, you have a tremendous obligation to your employees, your customers, your shareholders. [On April 2, 1993, called "Marlboro Friday," Philip Morris rattled the stock market when it cut the retail price of a pack of Marlboros by forty cents to compete with the cheaper generic cigarettes, which had cut its market share to 22 percent. The move cost the company an instant $2 billion, but now, not a year later, the stock is up and the market share, at almost 27 percent, is at its highest point ever.]

You know, you just can't take the responsibility lightly. And people did feel good about that. And particularly my ex-boss, Hamish Maxwell. Early in my career, I was describing to Hamish my new plan for the Canadian sales organization. And I was going on blah-blah-blah. And I said, "You know, the morale will be much better," et cetera, et cetera. And he said: "Bill, you go ahead with that. I'm sure you're right. But all in all, through the years, I've found that there's nothing better for morale than a sales curve going up."

I'm a smoker. Not a heavy smoker. I like it. Smoking slows me down, gives me a pause. I'm very active and I tend to sometimes jump. A cigarette will sort of slow me down to that level of not jumping around quite so much. My girls ask why I smoke. And I can only answer that I enjoy it, and I think I'm informed about it. And I tell them, "You'll be facing decisions like this one, when you're an adult." It requires thought. I think that people do have to take a step back and say, "Isn't individual freedom and individual choice an important characteristic of our society?" And that's more philosophical than "Don't."

But the attacks on the company are hard on the people. I feel deeply for our sales people across the country. They go into some very hostile environments, and because they're sales people, without any escape, they basically have to take what's given to them. And, you know, some people can be downright rude if they think that right is on their side. And we always have to try to be as well-mannered as we can be, because it only makes us look bad when we're not. And yet nobody in this company I know, including the time that I've been president, and before, has ever come and said: "I don't believe this any more. I want out." Never. In twenty-seven years. That's a lot of people we're talking about. All over the world.

This company is a town, and a city, a large town. It has shared values. It's a centrist town, but it's surprisingly liberal. If you added the town up, you would still statistically be on the right side of center, but the liberal attitude is significant. It's not sophisticated enough to be real Northeast. And it's not Southern, like its roots. But it's an interesting combination of South and North and probably more East than West. It's not New York, although there are some very New York elements about it. Cultural stuff and so forth. Something different. It's an American town. Yeah. An American town.

If I had asked any of the Philip Morris executives directly, "How do you live with yourself?" each would have taken the question personally. None of these executives think of themselves as morally bankrupt, and I do not think of them individually in that way, either. What often happens to people who work for a large, immensely successful company, however, is that they tend to adopt the values of the company, regardless of its product. Loyalty supersedes objectivity.

How good, smart, decent individuals manage to contribute to a wicked enterprise is a question that has been applied to murderous governments as well as to industries. The best answer, which isn't particularly satisfying, is that people in groups behave differently, and usually worse, than they do singly. In speaking with these Philip Morris executives, I felt the presence of the company within the person. In the end, I felt that I was speaking with more company than person, or perhaps to a person who could no longer distinguish between the two. In this situation, in which the company has effectively absorbed its employees in its moral universe, the more responsible employees are the company and thus are to blame.

What the company feels, then, is what its people feel. And these days Philip Morris is on top of the world. Like all tobacco companies, it operates under monopoly conditions, raising and lowering prices at will and using billions in monopoly profits to buy up other businesses. While functioning as a monopoly, it cannot be touched by the government because, as Dangoor said, other companies could get in the business if they wanted to, but, given the risk of liability, they don't.

Also, recent polls suggest that more young people—women and teen-agers especially—are smoking cigarettes these days. The number of blacks who smoke is on the rise. Articles are beginning to appear on the pure pleasure of smoking— how a cigarette eases tension, aids thought, delineates the best moments of a day. Several executives mentioned the idea of "pleasure revenge"—a term coined by Faith Popcorn, a specialist in identifying pop business trends. They relate an upsurge in smoking to a rebellion against what they perceive as the country's neopuritanical attitude toward health. Several executives see in such cultural phenomena as the return of cigarette smoking in movies the signs of such a revival.

The company takes the position that it does not seek to make smokers of nonsmokers. But when I asked Bill Campbell and Ellen Merlo, "Why not?"— that is, if they believe in free choice why shouldn't nonsmokers be free to choose and why shouldn't the company, like any other, seek new customers?—they responded simply that it is not industry policy. In a climate where smoking appears to be growing more attractive, that may change. But, as many of them point out, even if the total domestic market shrinks to nothing there is still the rest of the world.

The company plant in Cabarrus County, North Carolina, is undergoing a $400 million expansion to increase production by 25 percent. The 1.6-million square-foot plant in Richmond, which I visited, houses a network of tubes, pipes, and rollers, resembling a vast model train exhibit, which is being geared up to produce between 580 million and 600 million cigarettes a day.

In short, the company is feeling as robust and secure as it ever has. It continues to face attacks, like a recent $5 billion lawsuit brought by Stanley M. Rosenblatt (no relation) on behalf of flight attendants who claim to have been afflicted by secondary smoke. Yet increasingly it is taking the offensive. Last June, the company sued the Environmental Protection Agency for citing secondary smoke as a carcinogen. Last month it sued the city of San Francisco to overturn its anti-smoking ordinance, one of the strictest in the country. On March 9, it helped organize a tobacco workers march on Washington against the proposal to raise the cigarette tax.

These executives think of themselves as the best company, and with much of the country acting on their side, they are also in the best company. Of course, there is also the evidence of illness and death that result from their product, but they do not accept that and, so far, neither does the country, formally. If it did, tobacco companies would be illegal. One might say that this absolves the company of special responsibility, since the responsibility is so widespread. But a tobacco company is where the entire process begins. It often ends elsewhere.

On an icy Wednesday afternoon, Victor L. Crawford sits in the conference room of his law office in a colonial house in Rockville, Maryland. The cold sun shoots bright light into the room without warming it. Photographs of Crawford, who was once a Maryland state senator, hang on the walls. The house, said to be the oldest in Rockville, dates from the 1780s. "See these?" Crawford points to the stone fireplace and the white chips in its mortar. "They're oyster shells," he says. "That's what they used to fill the holes." His voice sounds raspy like Sinatra's.

He is sixty-one years old, about six feet in height, gaunt, and he wears a three-piece sharkskin suit; the vest hangs loose. He also wears a light gray wig—noticeable but well made and by no means comical. A trial lawyer today, he served five years as a lobbyist for the Tobacco Institute and was instrumental in defeating major antismoking bills in Maryland:

> At that point, I had no particular feelings about smoking. I had stopped smoking cigarettes about fifteen, eighteen years earlier. I was fifty-two then. So I'd stopped smoking in my mid-thirties. But I still smoked pipes and cigars. I inhaled a little bit on the pipe, unfortunately. Not on the cigars. I smoked pipes and cigars right up until the time that I was diagnosed. And, of course, I'd smoked cigarettes all those years, since I was thirteen.
>
> One day I was sitting in one of the smoke-filled rooms in the Tobacco Institute—they all smoked—and thinking, "My God, maybe we're on the wrong side of this issue, because I can hardly breathe." But I was very impressed with the institute—their expertise in P.R. and lobbying. The fees were great, and I was useful to them. I knew everybody in Maryland politics. So I served them well, from the mid-80s till 1991.
>
> And '91 is when I started getting the problems. Pains in the head, pains in the eustachean tube. My biopsy was in right before Christmas '91. And January 3 of '92 I got the diagnosis of throat cancer. Originally, I stopped cigarettes because I was having trouble breathing. Too late, maybe. It's the most insidious habit, an addiction. I was an addictive personality. I'd stop six or eight weeks. Then I'd have one cigarette and the next day I was back up to two packs and the next day I was back up to three. It is highly addictive.
>
> I am undergoing chemotherapy. You can tell by the wig. I started off with radiation first, because they wanted to reduce the tumor before they operated. And they operated on me in the first week in April of 1992. They took away everything there in my lower neck and left shoulder, all of the muscles. You can't see the scar. They did a magnificent job.
>
> I've aged ten years in six months. This chemotherapy has really just torn the hell

out of me, worse than the operation. . . . There's no cure, of course. There is a chance—a good chance, since I've had such a tremendous response lately—that they can put it in remission. It might give me anywhere up to five years. When you're sixty-one, five years looks petty good.

I have no animosity, though. I've got nobody to blame but myself. I knew what it was. But the tobacco companies were culpable, too. I had some twinges when I was lobbying for them. Why don't they have a feeling of responsibility? Maybe it's the corporate mentality. I defend criminals. And the biggest charge of criminal law is to get a hopeless case and win. The reason it's hopeless is because the son of a bitch is *guilty*. Because he did it. And by putting him out on the street, I might help him do it again.

For thirty-three years, I've been doing this. Just like these hard-nosed tobacco execs say that they have a perfect right to do what they do. But they must know. They *have* to know. Because they're brilliant people. And they're tough, hard business-men. They know. But they're able to sublimate it, I'm convinced, because of the similar mentality that we lawyers have. ''Freedom of choice is more important than anything!'' Well, that's not necessarily true. But it offers a way that you can live with yourself.

I'm not proud of having lobbied for them. I think it's ironic. And in a way, I think I got my just deserts, because, in my heart, I knew better. But I rationalized and denied, because the money was so good and because I could always rationalize it. That's how you make a living, by rationalizing that black is not black; it's white, it's green, it's yellow. But I knew, in my heart, that what the surgeon general said was right. I think these people know that.

Do I feel guilty about that I did? Yeah. Would I do it again, knowing what I know now? No. Would I do it again *not* knowing what I know now? Yes. Why? Because it might be unhealthy, but it will never happen to me. And after all, there's freedom of choice. And it's a free country. And if you want to make an ass out of yourself, you have the right. It sounds good. But the fact of the matter is that it's a killer.

15

Law

On Commerce

MONTESQUIEU

The following material would require more extensive treatment, but the nature of this work does not permit it. I should like to glide on a tranquil river; I am dragged along by a torrent.

Commerce cures destructive prejudices, and it is an almost general rule that everywhere there are gentle mores, there is commerce and that everywhere there is commerce, there are gentle mores.

Therefore, one should not be surprised if our mores are less fierce than they were formerly. Commerce has spread knowledge of the mores of all nations everywhere; they have been compared to each other, and good things have resulted from this.

One can say that the laws of commerce perfect mores for the same reason that these same laws ruin mores. Commerce corrupts pure mores, and this was the subject of Plato's complaints; it polishes and softens barbarous mores, as we see every day. . . . The natural effect of commerce is to lead to peace. Two nations that trade with each other become reciprocally dependent; if one has an interest in buying, the other has an interest in selling, and all unions are founded on mutual needs.

But, if the spirit of commerce unites nations, it does not unite individuals in the same way. We see that in countries where one is affected only by the spirit of commerce, there is traffic in all human activities and all moral virtues; the smallest things, those required by humanity, are done or given for money.

The spirit of commerce produces in men a certain feeling for exact justice, opposed on the one hand to banditry and on the other to those moral virtues that make it so that one does not always discuss one's own interests alone and that one can neglect them for those of others.

By contrast, total absence of commerce produces the banditry that Aristotle

From *The Spirit of the Laws* by Montesquieu. Reprinted by permission of Cambridge University Press.

puts among the ways of acquiring. Its spirit is not contrary to certain moral virtues; for example, hospitality, so rare among commercial countries, is notable among bandit peoples.

It is a sacrilege among the Germans, says Tacitus, to close one's house to any man whether known or unknown. Anyone who has offered hospitality to a stranger will point him to another house where there is similar hospitality, and he will be received there with the same humanity. But, after the Germans had founded kingdoms, hospitality became burdensome to them. This is shown by two laws in the code of the Burgundians: the one imposes a penalty on any barbarian who would point a stranger to the house of a Roman and the other rules that anyone who receives a stranger will be compensated by the inhabitants, each according to his share.

16

Environment

The Tragedy of the Commons

GARRETT HARDIN

At the end of a thoughtful article on the future of nuclear war, Wiesner and York[1] concluded that: "Both sides in the arms race are . . . confronted by the dilemma of steadily increasing military power and steadily decreasing national security. *It is our considered professional judgment that this dilemma has no technical solution.* If the great powers continue to look for solutions in the area of science and technology only, the result will be to worsen the situation."

I would like to focus your attention not on the subject of the article (national security in a nuclear world) but on the kind of conclusion they reached, namely that there is no technical solution to the problem. An implicit and almost universal assumption of discussions published in professional and semipopular scientific journals is that the problem under discussion has a technical solution. A technical solution may be defined as one that requires a change only in the techniques of the natural sciences, demanding little or nothing in the way of change in human values or ideas of morality.

In our day (though not in earlier times) technical solutions are always welcome. Because of previous failures in prophecy, it takes courage to assert that a desired technical solution is not possible. Wiesner and York exhibited this courage; publishing in a science journal, they insisted that the solution to the problem was not to be found in the natural sciences. They cautiously qualified their statement with the phrase, "It is our considered professional judgment." Whether they were right or not is not the concern of the present article. Rather, the concern here is with the important concept of a class of human problems which can be called "no technical solution problems," and, more specifically, with the identification and discussion of one of these.

It is easy to show that the class is not a null class. Recall the game of tick-tack-toe. Consider the problem, "How can I win the game of tick-tack-toe?" It is well

"The Tragedy of the Commons" by Garrett Hardin, based on a presidential address presented before the meeting of the Pacific Division of the American Association for the Advancement of Science at Utah State University, Logan, 25 June 1968. Reprinted with permission of Garrett Hardin.

known that I cannot, if I assume (in keeping with the conventions of game theory) that my opponent understands the game perfectly. Put another way, there is no "technical solution" to the problem. I can win only by giving a radical meaning to the word "win." I can hit my opponent over the head; or I can drug him; or I can falsify the records. Every way in which I "win" involves, in some sense, an abandonment of the game, as we intuitively understand it. (I can also, of course, openly abandon the game—refuse to play it. This is what most adults do.)

The class of "No technical solution problems" has members. My thesis is that the "population problem," as conventionally conceived, is a member of this class. How it is conventionally conceived needs some comment. It is fair to say that most people who anguish over the population problem are trying to find a way to avoid the evils of overpopulation without relinquishing any of the privileges they now enjoy. They think that farming the seas or developing new strains of wheat will solve the problem—technologically. I try to show here that the solution they seek cannot be found. The population problem cannot be solved in a technical way, any more than can the problem of winning the game of tick-tack-toe.

Population, as Malthus said, naturally tends to grow "geometrically," or, as we would now say, exponentially. In a finite world this means that the per capita share of the world's goods must steadily decrease. Is ours a finite world?

A fair defense can be put forward for the view that the world is infinite; or that we do not know that it is not. But, in terms of the practical problems that we must face in the next few generations with the foreseeable technology, it is clear that we will greatly increase human misery if we do not, during the immediate future, assume that the world available to the terrestrial human population is finite. "Space" is no escape.[2]

A finite world can support only a finite population; therefore, population growth must eventually equal zero. (The case of perpetual wide fluctuations above and below zero is a trivial variant that need not be discussed.) When this condition is met, what will be the situation of mankind? Specifically, can Bentham's goal of "the greatest good for the greatest number" be realized?

No—for two reasons, each sufficient by itself. The first is a theoretical one. It is not mathematically possible to maximize for two (or more) variables at the same time. This was clearly stated by von Neumann and Morgenstern,[3] but the principle is implicit in the theory of partial differential equations, dating back at least to D'Alembert (1717–1783).

The second reason springs directly from biological facts. To live, any organism must have a source of energy (for example, food). This energy is utilized for two purposes: mere maintenance and work. For man, maintenance of life requires about 1,600 kilocalories a day ("maintenance calories"). Anything that he does over and above merely staying alive will be defined as work, and is supported by "work calories" which he takes in. Work calories are used not only for what we call work in common speech; they are also required for all forms of enjoyment, from swimming and automobile racing to playing music and writing poetry. If our goal is to maximize population, it is obvious what we must do: we must make the work calories per person approach as close to zero as possible. No gourmet meals, no vacations, no sports, no music, no literature, no art. . . . I think that everyone will grant, without argument or proof, that maximizing population does not maximize goods. Bentham's goal is impossible.

In reaching this conclusion I have made the usual assumption that it is the acquisition of energy that is the problem. The appearance of atomic energy has led some to question this assumption. However, given an infinite source of energy, population growth still produces an inescapable problem. The problem of the acquisition of energy is replaced by the problem of its dissipation, as J. H. Fremlin has so wittily shown.[4] The arithmetic signs in the analysis are, as it were, reversed; but Bentham's goal is still unobtainable.

The optimum population is, then, less than the maximum. The difficulty of defining the optimum is enormous; so far as I know, no one has seriously tackled this problem. Reaching an acceptable and stable solution will surely require more than one generation of hard analytic work—and much persuasion.

We want the maximum good per person; but what is good? To one person it is wilderness, to another it is ski lodges for thousands. To one it is estuaries to nourish ducks for hunters to shoot; to another it is factory land. Comparing one good with another is, we usually say, impossible because goods are incommensurable. Incommensurables cannot be compared.

Theoretically this may be true; but in real life incommensurables *are* commensurable. Only a criterion of judgment and a system of weighting are needed. In nature the criterion is survival. Is it better for a species to be small and hideable, or large and powerful? Natural selection commensurates the incommensurables. The compromise achieved depends on a natural weighting of the values of the variables.

Man must imitate this process. There is no doubt that in fact he already does, but unconsciously. It is when the hidden decisions are made explicit that the arguments begin. The problem for the years ahead is to work out an acceptable theory of weighting. Synergistic effects, nonlinear variation, and difficulties in discounting the future make the intellectual problem difficult, but not (in principle) insoluble.

Has any cultural group solved this practical problem at the present time, even on an intuitive level? One simple fact proves that none has: there is no prosperous population in the world today that has, and has had for some time, a growth rate of zero. Any people that has intuitively identified its optimum point will soon reach it, after which its growth rate becomes and remains zero.

Of course, a positive growth rate might be taken as evidence that a population is below its optimum. However, by any reasonable standards, the most rapidly growing populations on earth today are (in general) the most miserable. This association (which need not be invariable) casts doubt on the optimistic assumption that the positive growth rate of a population is evidence that it has yet to reach its optimum.

We can make little progress in working toward optimum population size until we explicity exorcise the spirit of Adam Smith in the field of practical demography. In economic affairs, *The Wealth of Nations* (1776) popularized the "invisible hand," the idea that an individual who "intends only his own gain," is, as it were, "led by an invisible hand to promote . . . the public interest."[5] Adam Smith did not assert that this was invariably true, and perhaps neither did any of his followers. But he contributed to a dominant tendency of thought that has ever since interfered with positive action based on rational analysis, namely, the tendency to assume that decisions reached individually will, in fact, be the best decisions for an entire society. If this assumption is correct, it justifies the continuance of our present policy of laissez-faire in reproduction. If it is correct, we can assume that men will control their individual fecundity so as to produce the optimum population. If the assumption is not correct, we need to reexamine our individual freedoms to see which ones are defensible.

TRAGEDY OF FREEDOM IN A COMMONS

The rebuttal to the invisible hand in population control is to be found in a scenario first sketched in a little-known pamphlet[6] in 1833 by a mathematical amateur named William Forster Lloyd (1794–1852). We may well call it "the tragedy of the commons," using the word "tragedy" as the philosopher Whitehead used it:[7] "The essence of dramatic tragedy is not unhappiness. It resides in the solemnity of the remorseless working of things." He then goes on to say, "This inevitableness of destiny can only be illustrated in terms of human life by incidents which in fact involve unhappiness. For it is only by them that the futility of escape can be made evident in the drama."

The tragedy of the commons develops in this way. Picture a pasture open to all. It is to be expected that each herdsman will try to keep as many cattle as possible on the commons. Such an arrangement may work reasonably satisfactorily for centuries because tribal wars, poaching, and disease keep the numbers of both man and beast well below the carrying capacity of the land. Finally, however, comes the day of reckoning, that is, the day when the long-desired goal of social stability becomes a reality. At this point, the inherent logic of the commons remorselessly generates tragedy.

As a rational being, each herdsman seeks to maximize his gain. Explicitly or implicitly, more or less consciously, he asks, "What is the utility *to me* of adding one more animal to my herd?" This utility has one negative and one positive component.

1. The positive component is a function of the increment of one animal. Since the herdsman receives all the proceeds from the sale of the additional animal, the positive utility is nearly $+1$.
2. The negative component is a function of the additional overgrazing created by one more animal. Since, however, the effects of overgrazing are shared by all the herdsmen, the negative utility for any particular decision-making herdsman is only a fraction of -1.

Adding together the component partial utilities, the rational herdsman concludes that the only sensible course for him to pursue is to add another animal to his herd. And another; and another. . . . But this is the conclusion reached by each and every rational herdsman sharing a commons. Therein is the tragedy. Each man is locked into a system that compels him to increase his herd without limit—in a world that is limited. Ruin is the destination toward which all men rush, each pursuing his own best interest in a society that believes in the freedom of the commons. Freedom in a commons brings ruin to all.

Some would say that this is a platitude. Would that it were! In a sense, it was learned thousands of years ago, but natural selection favors the forces of psychological denial.[8] The individual benefits as an individual from his ability to deny the truth even though society as a whole, of which he is a part, suffers. Education can counteract the natural tendency to do the wrong thing, but the inexorable succession of generations requires that the basis for this knowledge be constantly refreshed.

A simple incident that occurred a few years ago in Leominster, Massachusetts, shows how perishable the knowledge is. During the Christmas shopping season the parking meters downtown were covered with plastic bags that bore tags reading: "Do not open until after Christmas. Free parking courtesy of the mayor and city council." In other words, facing the prospect of an increased demand for already scarce space, the city fathers reinstituted the system of the commons. (Cynically, we suspect that they gained more votes than they lost by this retrogressive act.)

In an approximate way, the logic of the commons has been understood for a long time, perhaps since the discovery of agriculture or the invention of private property in real estate. But it is understood mostly only in special cases which are not sufficiently generalized. Even at this late date, cattlemen leasing national land on the western ranges demonstrate no more than an ambivalent understanding, in constantly pressuring federal authorities to increase the head count to the point where overgrazing produces erosion and weed-dominance. Likewise, the oceans of the world continue to suffer from the survival of the philosophy of the commons. Maritime nations still respond automatically to the shibboleth of the "freedom of the seas." Professing to believe in the "inexhaustible resources of the oceans," they bring species after species of fish and whales closer to extinction.[9]

The National Parks present another instance of the working out of the tragedy of the commons. At present, they are open to all, without limit. The parks themselves are limited in extent—there is only one Yosemite Valley—whereas population seems to grow without limit. The values that visitors seek in the parks are steadily eroded. Plainly, we must soon cease to treat the parks as commons or they will be of no value to anyone.

What shall we do? We have several options. We might sell them off as private property. We might keep them as public property, but allocate the right to enter them. The allocation might be on the basis of wealth, by the use of an auction system. It might be on the basis of merit, as defined by some agreed-upon standards. It might be by lottery. Or it might be on a first-come, first-served basis, administered to long queues. These, I think, are all the reasonable possibilities. They are all objectionable. But we must choose—or acquiesce in the destruction of the commons that we call our National Parks.

POLLUTION

In a reverse way, the tragedy of the commons reappears in problems of pollution. Here it is not a question of taking something out of the commons, but of putting something in—sewage, or chemical, radioactive, and heat wastes into water; noxious and dangerous fumes into the air; and distracting and unpleasant advertising signs into the line of sight. The calculations of utility are much the same as before. The rational man finds that his share of the cost of the wastes he discharges into the commons is less than the cost of purifying his wastes before releasing them. Since this is true for everyone, we are locked into a system of "fouling our own nest," so long as we behave only as independent, rational, free-enterprisers.

The tragedy of the commons as a food basket is averted by private property, or something formally like it. But the air and waters surrounding us cannot readily be fenced, and so the tragedy of the commons as a cesspool must be prevented by different means, by coercive laws or taxing devices that make it cheaper for the polluter to treat his pollutants than to discharge them untreated. We have not progressed as far with the solution of this problem as we have with the first. Indeed, our particular concept of private property, which deters us from exhausting the positive resources of the earth, favors pollution. The owner of a factory on the bank of a stream—whose property extends to the middle of the stream—often has difficulty seeing why it is not his natural right to muddy the waters flowing past his door. The law, always behind the times, requires elaborate stitching and fitting to adapt it to this newly perceived aspect of the common.

The pollution problem is a consequence of population. It did not much matter how a lonely American frontiersman disposed of his waste. "Flowing water purifies itself every ten miles," my grandfather used to say, and the myth was near enough to the truth when he was a boy, for there were not too many people. But as population became denser, the natural chemical and biological recycling processes became overloaded, calling for a redefinition of property rights.

HOW TO LEGISLATE TEMPERANCE?

Analysis of the pollution problem as a function of population density uncovers a not generally recognized principal of morality, namely: *the morality of an act is a function of the state of the system at the time it is performed.*[10] Using the commons as a cesspool does not harm the general public under frontier conditions, because there is no public; the same behavior in a metropolis is unbearable. A hundred fifty years ago a plainsman could kill an American bison, cut out only the tongue for his dinner, and discard the rest of the animal. He was not in any important sense being wasteful. Today, with only a few thousand bison left, we would be appalled at such behavior.

In passing, it is worth noting that the morality of an act cannot be determined from a photograph. One does not know whether a man killing an elephant or setting fire to the grassland is harming others until one knows the total system in which his act appears. "One picture is worth a thousand words," said an ancient Chinese; but it may take ten thousands words to validate it. It is as tempting to ecologists as it is to reformers in general to try to persuade others by way of the photographic shortcut. But the essence of an argument cannot be photographed: it must be presented rationally—in words.

That morality is system-sensitive escaped the attention of most codifiers of ethics in the past. "Thou shalt not . . ." is the form of traditional ethical directives which make no allowance for particular circumstances. The laws of our society follow the pattern of ancient ethics, and therefore are poorly suited to governing a complex, crowded, changeable world. Our epicyclic solution is to augment statutory law with administrative law. Since it is practically impossible to spell out all the conditions under which it is safe to burn trash in the back yard or to run an automobile without smog control, by law we delegate the details to bureaus. The result is administrative law, which is rightly feared for an ancient reason—*Quis custodiet ipsos custodes?*—"Who shall watch the watchers themselves?" John Adams said that we must have "a government of laws and not men." Bureau administrators, trying to evaluate the morality of acts in the total system, are singularly liable to corruption, producing a government by men, not laws.

Prohibition is easy to legislate (though not necessarily to enforce); but how do we legislate temperance? Experience indicates that it can be accomplished best through the mediation of administrative law. We limit possibilities unnecessarily if we suppose that the sentiment of *Quis custodiet* denies us the use of administrative law. We should rather retain the phrase as a perpetual reminder of fearful dangers we cannot avoid. The great challenge facing us now is to invent the corrective feedbacks that are needed to keep custodians honest. We must find ways to legitimate the needed authority of both the custodians and the corrective feedbacks.

FREEDOM TO BREED IS INTOLERABLE

The tragedy of the commons is involved in population problems in another way. In a world governed solely by the principle of "dog eat dog"—if indeed there ever was such a world—how many children a family had would not be a matter of public concern. Parents who bred too exuberantly would leave fewer descendants, not more, because they would be unable to care adequately for their children. David Lack and others have found that such a negative feedback demonstrably controls the fecundity of birds.[11] But men are not birds, and have not acted like them for millenniums, at least.

If each human family were dependent only on its own resources; *if* the children of improvident parents starved to death; *if,* thus, overbreeding brought its own "punishment" to the germ line—*then* there would be no public interest in controlling the breeding of families. But our society is deeply committed to the welfare state,[12] and hence is confronted with another aspect of the tragedy of the commons.

In a welfare state, how shall we deal with the family, the religion, the race, or the class (or indeed any distinguishable and cohesive group) that adopts over-breeding as a policy to secure its own aggrandizement?[13] To couple the concept of freedom to breed with the belief that everyone born has an equal right to the commmons is to lock the world into a tragic course of action.

Unfortunately this is just the course of action that is being pursued by the United Nations. In late 1967, some thirty nations agreed to the following:[14]

> The Universal Declaration of Human Rights describes the family as the natural and fundamental unit of society. It follows that any choice and decision with regard to the size of the family must irrevocably rest with the family itself, and cannot be made by anyone else.

It is painful to have to deny categorically the validity of this right; denying it, one feels as uncomfortable as a resident of Salem, Massachusetts, who denied the reality of witches in the seventeenth century. At the present time, in liberal quarters, something like a taboo acts to inhibit criticism of the United Nations. There is a feeling that the United Nations is "our last and best hope," that we shouldn't find fault with it; we shouldn't play into the hands of the archconserva-tives. However, let us not forget what Robert Louis Stevenson said: "The truth that is suppressed by friends is the readiest weapon of the enemy." If we love the truth we must openly deny the validity of the Universal Declaration of Human Rights, even though it is promoted by the United Nations. We should also join with Kingsley Davis [15] in attempting to get Planned Parenthood–World Popula-tion to see the error of its ways in embracing the same tragic ideal.

CONSCIENCE IS SELF-ELIMINATING

It is a mistake to think that we can control the breeding of mankind in the long run by an appeal to conscience. Charles Galton Darwin made this point when he spoke on the centennial of the publication of his grandfather's great book. The argument is straightforward and Darwinian.

People vary. Confronted with appeals to limit breeding, some people will undoubtedly respond to the plea more than others. Those who have more children will produce a larger fraction of the next generation than those with more suscep-tible consciences. The difference will be accentuated, generation by generation.

In C. G. Darwin's words: "It may well be that it would take hundreds of generations for the progenitive instinct to develop in this way, but if it should do so, nature would have taken her revenge, and the variety *Homo contracipiens* would become extinct and would be replaced by the variety *Homo progeni-tivus.*"[16]

The argument assumes that conscience or the desire for children (no matter which) is hereditary—but hereditary only in the most general formal sense. The result will be the same whether the attitude is transmitted through germ cells, or exosomatically, to use A. J. Lotka's term. (If one denies the latter possibility as well as the former, then what's the point of education?) The argument has here been stated in the context of the population problem, but it applies equally well to any instance in which society appeals to an individual exploiting a commons to restrain himself for the general good—by means of his conscience. To make such an appeal is to set up a selective system that works toward the elimination of conscience from the race.

PATHOGENIC EFFECTS OF CONSCIENCE

The long-term disadvantage of an appeal to conscience should be enough to condemn it, but it has serious short-term disadvantages as well. If we ask a man who is exploiting a commons to desist "in the name of conscience," what are we saying to him? What does he hear?—not only at the moment but also in the wee small hours of the night when, half asleep, he remembers not merely the words we used but also the nonverbal communication cues we gave him unawares? Sooner or later, consciously or subconsciously, he senses that he has received two communications, and that they are contradictory: (i) (intended communication) "If you don't do as we ask, we will openly condemn you for not acting like a responsible citizen"; (ii) (the unintended communication) "If you *do* behave as we ask, we will secretly condemn you for a simpleton who can be shamed into standing aside while the rest of us exploit the commons."

Everyman then is caught in what Bateson has called a "double bind." Bateson and his co-workers have made a plausible case for viewing the double bind as an important causative factor in the genesis of schizophrenia.[17] The double bind may not always be so damaging, but it always endangers the mental health of anyone to whom it is applied. "A bad conscience," said Nietzsche, "is a kind of illness."

To conjure up a conscience in others is tempting to anyone who wishes to extend his control beyond the legal limits. Leaders at the highest level succumb to this temptation. Has any president during the past generation failed to call on labor unions to moderate voluntarily their demands for higher wages, or to steel companies to honor voluntary guidelines on prices? I can recall none. The rhetoric used on such occasions is designed to produce feelings of guilt in noncooperators.

For centuries it was assumed without proof that guilt was a valuable, perhaps even an indispensable, ingredient of the civilized life. Now, in this post-Freudian world, we doubt it.

Paul Goodman speaks from the modern point of view when he says: "No good has ever come from feeling guilty, neither intelligence, policy, nor compassion. The guilty do not pay attention to the object but only to themselves, and not even to their own interests, which might make sense, but to their anxieties."[18]

One does not have to be a professional psychiatrist to see the consequences of anxiety. We in the Western world are just emerging from a dreadful two-centuries-long Dark Ages of Eros that was sustained partly by prohibition laws, but perhaps more effectively by the anxiety-generating mechanisms of education. Alex Comfort has told the story well in *The Anxiety Makers;*[19] it is not a pretty one.

Since proof is difficult, we may even concede that the results of anxiety may sometimes, from certain points of view, be desirable. The larger question we should ask is whether, as a matter of policy, we should ever encourage the use of a technique the tendency (if not the intention) of which is psychologically pathogenic. We hear much talk these days of responsible parenthood; the coupled words are incorporated into the titles of some organizations devoted to birth control. Some people have proposed massive propaganda campaigns to instill responsibility into the nation's (or the world's) breeders. But what is the meaning of the word responsibility in this context? Is it not merely a synonym for the word conscience? When we use the word responsibility in the absence of substantial sanctions are we not trying to browbeat a free man in a commons into acting against his own interest? Responsibility is a verbal counterfeit for a substantial *quid pro quo*. It is an attempt to get something for nothing.

If the word responsibility is to be used at all, I suggest that it be in the sense Charles Frankel uses it.[20] "Responsibility," says this philosopher, "is the product of definite social arrangements." Notice that Frankel calls for social arrangements—not propaganda.

MUTUAL COERCION MUTUALLY AGREED UPON

The social arrangements that produce responsibility are arrangements that create coercion, of some sort. Consider bank robbing. The man who takes money from a bank acts as if the bank were a commons. How do we prevent such action? Certainly not by trying to control his behavior solely by a verbal appeal to his sense of responsibility. Rather than rely on propaganda we follow Frankel's lead and insist that a bank is not a commons; we seek the definite social arrangements that will keep it from becoming a commons. That we thereby infringe on the freedom of would-be robbers we neither deny nor regret.

The morality of bank robbing is particularly easy to understand because we accept complete prohibition of this activity. We are willing to say "Thou shalt not rob banks," without providing for exceptions. But temperance also can be created by coercion. Taxing is a good coercive device. To keep downtown shoppers temperate in their use of parking space we introduce parking meters for short periods, and traffic fines for longer ones. We need not actually forbid a citizen to park as long as he wants to; we need merely make it increasingly expensive for him to do so. Not prohibition, but carefully biased options are what we offer him. A Madison Avenue man might call this persuasion; I prefer the greater candor of the word coercion.

Coercion is a dirty word to most liberals now, but it need not forever be so. As with the four-letter words, its dirtiness can be cleansed away by exposure to the light, by saying it over and over without apology or embarrassment. To many, the word coercion implies arbitrary decisions of distant and irresponsible bureaucrats; but this is not a necessary part of its meaning. The only kind of coercion I recommend is mutual coercion, mutually agreed upon by the majority of the people affected.

To say that we mutually agree to coercion is not to say that we are required to enjoy it, or even to pretend we enjoy it. Who enjoys taxes? We all grumble about them. But we accept compulsory taxes because we recognize that voluntary taxes would favor the conscienceless. We institute and (grumblingly) support taxes and other coercive devices to escape the horror of the commons.

An alternative to the commons need not be perfectly just to be preferable. With real estate and other material goods, the alternative we have chosen is the institution of private property coupled with legal inheritance. Is this system perfectly just? As a genetically trained biologist I deny that it is. It seems to me that, if there are to be differences in individual inheritance, legal possession should be perfectly correlated with biological inheritance—that those who are biologically more fit to be the custodians of property and power should legally inherit more. But genetic recombination continually makes a mockery of the doctrine of "like father, like son" implicit in our laws of legal inheritance. An idiot can inherit millions, and a trust fund can keep his estate intact. We must admit that our legal system of private property plus inheritance is unjust—but we put up with it because we are not convinced, at the moment, that anyone has invented a better system. The alternative of the commons is too horrifying to contemplate. Injustice is preferable to total ruin.

It is one of the peculiarities of the warfare between reform and the status quo that it is thoughtlessly governed by a double standard. Whenever a reform measure is proposed it is often defeated when its opponents triumphantly discover a flaw in it. As Kingsley Davis has pointed out,[21] worshippers of the status quo sometimes imply that no reform is possible without unanimous agreement, an implication contrary to historical fact. As nearly as I can make out, automatic rejection of proposed reforms is based on one of two unconscious assumptions: (i) that the status quo is perfect; or (ii) that the choice we face is between reform and no action; if the proposed reform is imperfect, we presumably should take no action at all, while we wait for a perfect proposal.

But we can never do nothing. That which we have done for thousands of years is also action. It also produces evils. Once we are aware that the status quo is action, we can then compare its discoverable advantages and disadvantages with the predicted advantages and disadvantages of the proposed reform, discounting as best we can for our lack of experience. On the basis of such a comparison, we can make a rational decision which will not involve the unworkable assumption that only perfect systems are tolerable.

RECOGNITION OF NECESSITY

Perhaps the simplest summary of this analysis of man's population problems is this: the commons, if justifiable at all, is justifiable only under conditions of low-population density. As the human population has increased, the commons has had to be abandoned in one aspect after another.

First we abandoned the commons in food gathering, enclosing farmland and restricting pastures and hunting and fishing areas. These restrictons are still not complete throughout the world.

Somewhat later we saw that the commons as a place for waste disposal would also have to be abandoned. Restrictions on the disposal of domestic sewage are widely accepted in the Western world; we are still struggling to close the commons to pollution by automobiles, factories, insecticide sprayers, fertilizing operations, and atomic energy installations.

In a still more embryonic state is our recognition of the evils of the commons in matters of pleasure. There is almost no restriction on the propagation of sound waves in the public medium. The shopping public is assaulted with mindless music, without its consent. Our government is paying out billions of dollars to create supersonic transport which will disturb fifty thousand people for every one person who is whisked from coast to coast three hours faster. Advertisers muddy the airwaves of radio and television and pollute the view of travelers. We are a long way from outlawing the commons in matters of pleasure. Is this because our Puritan inheritance makes us view pleasure as something of a sin, and pain (that is, the pollution of advertising) as the sign of virtue?

Every new enclosure of the commons involves the infringement of somebody's personal liberty. Infringements made in the distant past are accepted because no contemporary complains of a loss. It is the newly proposed infringements that we vigorously oppose; cries of "rights" and "freedom" fill the air. But what does "freedom" mean? When men mutually agreed to pass laws against robbing, mankind became more free, not less so. Individuals locked into the logic of the commons are free only to bring on universal ruin; once they see the necessity of mutual coercion, they become free to pursue other goals. I believe it was Hegel who said, "Freedom is the recognition of necessity."

The most important aspect of necessity that we must now recognize, is the necessity of abandoning the commons in breeding. No technical solution can rescue us from the misery of overpopulation. Freedom to breed will bring ruin to all. At the moment, to avoid hard decisions many of us are tempted to propagandize for conscience and responsible parenthood. The temptation must be resisted, because an appeal to independently acting consciences selects for the disappearance of all conscience in the long run, and an increase in anxiety in the short.

The only way we can preserve and nurture other and more precious freedoms is by relinquishing the freedom to breed, and that very soon. "Freedom is the recognition of necessity"—and it is the role of education to reveal to all the necessity of abandoning the freedom to breed. Only so, can we put an end to this aspect of the tragedy of the commons.

REFERENCES

1. J. B. Wiesner and H. F. York, *Sci. Amer.* 211 (No. 4), 27 (1964).
2. G. Hardin, *J. Hered.* 50, 68 (1959); S. von Hoernor, *Science* 137, 18 (1962).

3. J. von Neumann and O. Morgenstern, *Theory of Games and Economic Behavior* (Princeton Univ. Press, Princeton, N.J., 1947), p. 11.

4. J. H. Fremlin, *New Sci.*, No. 415 (1964), p. 285.

5. A. Smith, *The Wealth of Nations* (Modern Library, New York, 1937), p. 423.

6. W. F. Lloyd, *Two Lectures on the Checks to Population* (Oxford Univ. Press, Oxford, England, 1833), reprinted (in part) in *Population, Evolution, and Birth Control*, G. Hardin, Ed. (Freeman, San Francisco, 1964), p. 37.

7. A. N. Whitehead, *Science and the Modern World* (Mentor, New York, 1948), p. 17.

8. G. Hardin, Ed. *Population, Evolution, and Birth Control* (Freeman, San Francisco, 1964), p. 56.

9. S. McVay, *Sci. Amer.* 216 (No. 8), 13 (1966).

10. J. Fletcher, *Situation Ethics* (Westminster, Philadelphia, 1966).

11. D. Lack, *The Natural Regulation of Animal Numbers* (Clarendon Press, Oxford, 1954).

12. H. Girvetz, *From Wealth to Welfare* (Stanford Univ. Press, Stanford, Calif., 1950).

13. G. Hardin, *Perspec. Biol. Med.* 6, 366 (1963).

14. U. Thant, *Int. Planned Parenthood News,* No. 168 (February 1968), p. 3.

15. K. Davis, *Science* 158, 730 (1967).

16. S. Tax, Ed., *Evolution after Darwin* (Univ. of Chicago Press, Chicago, 1960), vol. 2, p. 469.

17. G. Bateson, D. D. Jackson, J. Haley, J. Weakland, *Behav. Sci.* 1, 251 (1956).

18. P. Goodman, *New York Rev. Books* 10 (8), 22 (23 May 1968).

19. A. Comfort, *The Anxiety Makers* (Nelson, London, 1967).

20. C. Frankel, *The Case for Modern Man* (Harper, New York, 1955), p. 203.

21. J. D. Roslansky, *Genetics and the Future of Man* (Appleton-Century-Crofts, New York, 1966), p. 177.

The Idea of Wilderness

MAX OELSCHLAEGER

The early agriculturists (10000–3500 B.C.E.) reveal a slowly dawning awareness of distinctions between culture and nature. Hunting mythologies, which did not explicitly distinguish between the human and animal worlds, were forsaken and replaced by religions that centered on the worship of gods, especially gods conceptualized as incarnate in such animals as the bull. These early religions tended to be polytheistic, idolatrous, and focused on fertility—plant, animal, and human. The pinnacle of polytheistic, animalistic worship occurred in ancient Egypt and Sumeria, where people first conceived of the natural world as an abode designed for the human species. Yet even in the very geographical and historical midst of the Egyptians and Sumerians (Canaan lies astride the travel routes between the Fertile Crescent and Egypt) arose a tradition avowing an ideology that rejected naturalistic polytheism and, after an internal struggle with lingering remnants of fertility cults, embraced a monotheistic supernaturalism. The Hebrews believed themselves to be Yahweh's chosen people living in a land expressly designed for them to civilize. The Pentateuch, as reflected in the many accreted layers of meaning that constitute the text, thus represents the grandest rationalization of an agriculturist mode of existence ever conceived.

Penultimately in chronology, but not in importance and subsequent influence on the idea of wilderness, was the rise of logocentrism in Attica. Greek rationalism abandoned mythopoetry for explicit theory and definition; it was later spread throughout the Mediterranean world by first-century B.C.E. Hellenistic culture and the Romans. Whereas the Hebrews remained content with the metaphorical, allegorical, and symbolic, the New Testament of Paul and the patristic fathers used the theoretical edifice of Platonism (as some one thousand years later Aquinas used Aristotle) to create the concept of humanity and nature that has ruled the West for nearly two thousand years. Yet Christianity did not contradict but rather redefined earlier conceptions of the earth as a designed abode for humankind. What was radical in both Hebrew and early Christian thought was its profound anthropocentrism and its abandonment of a cyclical for a linear conception of time. Hellenism and Judeo-Christianity in combination introduced an unprecedented direction to human intercourse with the earth, for *nature was conceived as valueless until humanized.*

From *The Idea of Wilderness* by Max Oelschlaeger. Yale University Press, 1991. Reprinted by permission of Yale University Press.

ANIMAL IDOLATRY, POLYTHEISM, AND
THE RISE OF FERTILITY CULTS

A transitional phase of some six thousand years stretches between the lower Neolithic and the advent of the hieratic city states in Mesopotamia and Egypt. Only an extended study could account for the many significant ideological, sociological, and technological modifications of this era. Tribes and villages replaced bands and campsites as the dominant forms of social organization; domesticated livestock supplanted wild animals as a food source; human knowledge proliferated, as in metallurgy, ceramics, architecture, and mathematics. Further, the agricultural revolution fundamentally transformed the relations between humankind and nature. To say that prehistoric people were passive in relation to nature is inaccurate, for hunting-gathering exemplifies the perpetuation of life through environmental transaction. In contrast to most agricultures, however, the exchange for hunter-foragers is balanced and harmonious. Cynegetic (hunting-foraging) cultures alter neither the natural firmament nor the animals and plants that share the land with them. Agricultural people abandon the hunt and the spear, settle in villages, and take up the hoe and shepherd's staff. Animals are domesticated and herded, woodlands cleared, swamps and wetlands drained, the soil turned, planted, and tilled.

Materialists and idealists anguish over metaphysical priorities in this sequence, but most likely is simultaneous evolution in ideology, sociology, and technology—a rippling, interpenetrating process of cultural transition unknown to the early agriculturists who were living in medias res, living the agricultural revolution, perhaps as we are now living in an "age of ecology." Human beings were no longer tender carnivores in search of sacred game: domesticated livestock and planted crops were the focus of material life. Inevitably, the shaman of Paleolithic culture gave way to the priest. Religious life centered no longer on maintaining harmony and integrity but on fertility (although harmony with the eternal order was sometimes thought essential to fertility). Totemism, where the totem imaginatively mediated between humankind and the rest of nature, was supplanted by animal idolatry—the worship of icons fashioned in the image of animals, especially the Mediterranean bull. The Magna Mater of Paleolithic culture became the Earth Mother, now a goddess of fertility rather than an all-embracing mother of creation.

Slowly but inexorably, as centuries turned into millennia, change compounded upon change, and even the ways of the early agriculturists were modified. The village gave way to the city, and loose confederations of villages and cities to nation-states. Sociological changes were institutionalized, and politics and organized religion became a reality. Priestly classes appeared, ensconced in the temples of new cities, part of a socioeconomic elite that increasingly controlled the surrounding countryside. Humankind became more and more conscious of itself as an agent of environmental change, and rationalizations of the new ways proliferated. Cultivated grains and domesticated livestock became familiar artifacts of culture, predictable supplies of food. Wild plant and animal species were increasingly devoid of mystery and unworthy of veneration; animal gods were replaced by gods with human forms. Human beings became conscious of a mastery, however tenuous, over wild nature, and it occurred to them that the world was perhaps designed for their ends by divine forces.

Agriculturists initially (10000 B.C.E.) retained mobility to the extent that camps or villages were semipermanent and could be relocated as rivers changed course and shifted the desirable crop and pasture lands; but permanent settlement was probably inevitable once the turn from hunting-gathering was made. Çatal-Hüyük (the ruins are located in Turkey approximately four hundred miles northeast of Jerusalem) is among the first permanent Mediterranean settlements of size, dating from 8400 B.C.E. Research at this site had added greatly to our understanding of the ecological transition from the Paleolithic to the Neolithc. Situated at the foot of a mountain range, where each year run-off from melting snow replenished fields with silt and nutrients, permanent settlement was possible since relocation was not required to ensure fertility. In economic terms, Çatal-Hüyük represents a transitional form of life from hunting-foraging to agriculture, as indicated by abundant evidence of animal idolatry. Animal idolatry is arguably a transitional form of totemism; the clan no longer identifies itself with an animal but literally worships an animal statue as a god.

Archaic peoples the world over revere the animals and plants essential to survival: at Çatal-Hüyük this object was the great Mediterranean bull. About one-third of the rooms in the settlement are shrines, decorated with bull's heads carved into and clay heads built out from the walls. Inside these rooms are altars decorated with smaller bull's heads made of mud, and occasionally frontal portions of actual skulls. By all available evidence the bull itself was worshiped by these ancients, a veritable god incarnate, contrary to the thesis that the animal was sacrificed to transcendent gods. Repeating the apostasy of Paleolithic people, the cattle-gods were also consumed as food. Smaller female-shaped figurines are also found, implying that a female Earth Mother image played prominently in the fertility cult, sustaining the thesis that the early agriculturists represent a zone of ecological transition from the Paleolithic to the Neolithic: the legacy of Paleolithic culture—artistic, religious, intellectual—cannot be denied. Marija Gimbutas argues that not only are Neolithic goddesses composites of agricultural and preagricultural images, but so, too, "the water bird, deer, bear, fish, snake, toad, turtle, and the notion of hybridization of animal and man, were inherited from the Palaeolithic era and continued to serve as avatars of goddesses and gods. There was no such thing as a religion or mythical imagery newly created by agriculturists at the beginning of the food-producing period." And perhaps even more important, Merlin Stone suggests, "the most obvious fact may be of greatest interest to people of today—that in the lands that brought forth Judaism, Christianity, and Islam, God was once worshiped in the form of woman."

The transition *from* totemic, hunter mythology and rituals, representing above all else the belief in the sacrality of existence and the endeavor to maintain cosmic harmony, *to* the animal idolatry and fertility cults of agriculture is a comprehensible development. Settled cultivators and herders, unlike wandering hunting-gatherers, depend on the everlasting fruitfulness of field and animal. Whereas hunting-foraging people accepted the bounty of the world as they found it and identified with this natural universe of being, agricultural people—through the very reality of an ecological transition—experienced a new phenomenal-existential field of meaning. If the rains failed and the grass was stunted, the herds were imperiled; if insects descended in a plague, the crops were lost; and so on through myriad permutations of disaster. Such failings had serious consequences: starvation loomed continually. Little wonder the rise of fertility sects and the associated festivals, rituals, and other ceremonies, including plant and animal sacrifice. However barbaric such cultic fertility practices seem to the modern mind, such religions continued well into the Middle Ages. (Mithraism, for example, one of many Mediterranean bull cults, rivaled if not exceeded Christianity in popularity—that is, converts or believers—well into the third century c.e.) All were part of a complex of behaviors and ideas intended to ensure fecundity and productivity. A religiopolitico elite almost necessarily arose, serving the social functions of organization, control, and above all the rationalization of existence. The priest and chief supplanted the Paleolithic animal master, and society was slowly stratified. These new elites helped to explain the changing order of existence and thereby justify their own power.

By 4500 b.c.e. the stage was set for the emergence of civilization.

The Historical Roots of Our Ecologic Crisis

LYNN WHITE, JR.

A conversation with Aldous Huxley not infrequently put one at the receiving end of an unforgettable monologue. About a year before his lamented death he was discoursing on a favorite topic: man's unnatural treatment of nature and its sad results. To illustrate his point he told how, during the previous summer, he had returned to a little valley in England where he had spent many happy months as a child. Once it had been composed of delightful grassy glades; now it was becoming overgrown with unsightly brush because the rabbits that formerly kept such growth under control had largely succumbed to a disease, myxomatosis, that was deliberately introduced by the local farmers to reduce the rabbits' destruction of crops. Being something of a Philistine, I could be silent no longer, even in the interests of great rhetoric. I interrupted to point out that the rabbit itself had been brought as a domestic animal to England in 1176, presumably to improve the protein diet of the peasantry.

All forms of life modify their contexts. The most spectacular and benign instance is doubtless the coral polyp. By serving its own ends, it has created a vast undersea world favorable to thousands of other kinds of animals and plants. Ever since man became a numerous species he has affected his environment notably. The hypothesis that his fire-drive method of hunting created the world's great grasslands and helped to exterminate the monster mammals of the Pleistocene from much of the globe is plausible, if not proved. For six millennia at least, the banks of the lower Nile have been a human artifact rather than the swampy African jungle which nature, apart from man, would have made it. The Aswan Dam, flooding five thousand square miles, is only the latest stage in a long process. In many regions terracing or irrigation, overgrazing, and the cutting of forests—by Romans to build ships to fight Carthaginians or by Crusaders to solve the logistics problems of their expeditions—have profoundly changed some ecologies. Observation that the French landscape falls into two basic types, the open fields of the north and the *bocage* of the south and west, inspired Marc Bloch to undertake his classic study of medieval agricultural methods. Quite unintentionally, changes in human ways often affect nonhuman nature. It has been noted, for example, that the advent of the automobile eliminated huge flocks of sparrows that once fed on the horse manure littering every street.

The history of ecologic change is still so rudimentary that we know little about what really happened, or what the results were. The extinction of the European

---

aurochs as late as 1627 would seem to have been a simple case of overenthusiastic hunting. On more intricate matters it often is impossible to find solid information. For a thousand years or more the Frisians and Hollanders have been pushing back the North Sea, and the process is culminating in our own time in the reclamation of the Zuider Zee. What, if any species of animals, birds, fish, shore life, or plants have died out in the process? In their epic combat with Neptune have the Netherlanders overlooked ecological values in such a way that the quality of human life in the Netherlands has suffered? I cannot discover that the questions have ever been asked, much less answered.

People, then, have often been a dynamic element in their own environment, but in the present state of historical scholarship we usually do not know exactly when, where, or with what effects man-induced changes came. As we enter the last third of the twentieth century, however, concern for the problem of ecologic backlash is mounting feverishly. Natural science, conceived as the effort to understand the nature of things, had flourished in several eras and among several peoples. Similarly there had been an age-old accumulation of technological skills, sometimes growing rapidly, sometimes slowly. But it was not until about four generations ago that western Europe and North America arranged a marriage between science and technology, a union of the theoretical and the empirical approaches to our natural environment. The emergence in widespread practice of the Baconian creed that scientific knowledge means technological power over nature can scarcely be dated before about 1850, save in the chemical industries, where it is anticipated in the eighteenth century. Its acceptance as a normal pattern of action may mark the greatest event in human history since the invention of agriculture, and perhaps in nonhuman terrestrial history as well.

Almost at once the new situation forced the crystallization of the novel concept of ecology; indeed, the word *ecology* first appeared in the English language in 1873. Today, less than a century later, the impact of our race upon the environment has so increased in force that it has changed in essence. When the first cannons were fired, in the early fourteenth century, they affected ecology by sending workers scrambling to the forests and mountains for more potash, sulfur, iron ore, and charcoal, with some resulting erosion and deforestation. Hydrogen bombs are of a different order: a war fought with them might alter the genetics of all life on this planet. By 1285 London had a smog problem arising from the burning of soft coal, but our present combustion of fossil fuels threatens to change the chemistry of the globe's atmosphere as a whole, with consequences which we are only beginning to guess. With the population explosion, the carcinoma of planless urbanism, the now geological deposits of sewage and garbage, surely no creature other than man has ever managed to foul its nest in such short order.

There are many calls to action, but specific proposals, however worthy as individual items, seem too partial, palliative, negative: ban the bomb, tear down the billboards, give the Hindus contraceptives and tell them to eat their sacred cows. The simplest solution to any suspect change is, of course, to stop it, or, better yet, to revert to a romanticized past: make those ugly gasoline stations look like Anne Hathaway's cottage or (in the Far West) like ghost-town saloons. The "wilderness area" mentality invariably advocates deep-freezing an ecology, whether San Gimignano or the High Sierra, as it was before the first Kleenex was dropped. But neither atavism nor prettification will cope with the ecologic crisis of our time.

What shall we do? No one yet knows. Unless we think about fundamentals, our specific measures may produce new backlashes more serious than those they are desined to remedy.

As a beginning we should try to clarify our thinking by looking, in some historical depth, at the presuppositions that underlie modern technology and science. Science was traditionally aristocratic, speculative, intellectual in intent; technology was lower-class, empirical, action-oriented. The quite sudden fusion of these two, towards the middle of the nineteenth century, is surely related to the slightly prior and contemporary democratic revolutions which, by reducing social barriers, tended to assert a functional unity of brain and hand. Our ecologic crisis is the product of an emerging, entirely novel, democratic culture. The issue is whether a democratized world can survive its own implications. Presumably we cannot unless we rethink our axioms.

THE WESTERN TRADITIONS OF TECHNOLOGY AND SCIENCE

One thing is so certain that it seems stupid to verbalize it: both modern technology and modern science are distinctively *Occidental*. Our technology has absorbed elements from all over the world, notably from China; yet everywhere today whether in Japan or in Nigeria, successful technology is Western. Our science is the heir to all the sciences of the past, especially perhaps to the work of the great Islamic scientists of the Middle Ages, who so often outdid the ancient Greeks in skill and perspicacity: al-Rāzī in medicine, for example; or ibn-al-Haytham in optics; or Omar Khay-yám in mathematics. Indeed, not a few works of such geniuses seem to have vanished in the original Arabic and to survive only in medieval Latin translations that helped to lay the foundations for later Western developments. Today, around the globe, all significant science is Western in style and method, whatever the pigmentation or language of the scientists.

A second pair of facts is less well recognized because they result from quite recent historical scholarship. The leadership of the West, both in technology and in science, is far older than the so-called Scientific Revolution of the seventeenth century or the so-called Industrial Revolution of the eighteenth century. These terms are in fact outmoded and obscure the true nature of what they try to describe—significant stages in two long and separate developments. By A.D. 1000 at the latest—and perhaps, feebly, as much as two hundred years earlier—the West began to apply water power to industrial processes other than milling grain. This was followed in the late twelfth centry by the harnessing of wind power. From simple beginnings, but with remarkable consistency of style, the West rapidly expanded, its skills in the development of power machinery, labor-saving devices, and automation. Those who doubt should contemplate that most monumental achievement in the history of automation: the weight-driven mechanical clock, which appeared in two forms in the early fourteenth century. Not in craftsmanship but in basic technological capacity, the Latin West of the later Middle Ages far outstripped its elaborate, sophisticated, and aesthetically magnificent sister cultures, Byzantium and Islam. In 1444 a great Greek ecclesiastic, Bessarion, who had gone to Italy, wrote a letter to a prince in Greece. He is amazed by the superiority of Western ships, arms, textiles, glass. But above all he is astonished by the spectacle of waterwheels sawing timbers and pumping the bellows of blast furnaces. Clearly, he had seen nothing of the sort in the Near East.

By the end of the fifteenth century the technological superiority of Europe was such that its small, mutually hostile nations could spill out over all the rest of the world, conquering, looting, and colonizing. The symbol of this technological superiority is the fact that Portugal, one of the weakest states of the Occident, was able to become, and to remain for a century, mistress of the East Indies. And we must remember that the technology of Vasco da Gama and Albuquerque was built by pure empiricism, drawing remarkably little support or inspiration from science.

In the present-day vernacular understanding, modern science is supposed to have begun in 1543, when both Copernicus and Vesalius published their great works. It is no derogation of their accomplishments, however, to point out that such structures as the *Fabrica* and the *De revolutionibus* do not appear overnight. The distinctive Western tradition of science, in fact, began in the late eleventh century with a massive movement of translation of Arabic and Greek scientific works into Latin. A few notable books—Theophrastus, for example—escaped the West's avid new appetite for science, but within less than two hundred years effectively the entire corpus of Greek and Muslim science was available in Latin, and was being eagerly read and criticized in the new European universities. Out of criticism arose new observation, speculation, and increasing distrust of ancient authorities. By the late thirteenth century Europe had seized global scientific leadership from the faltering hands of Islam. It would be as absurd to deny the profound originality of Newton, Galileo, or Copernicus as to deny that of the fourteenth century scholastic scientists like Buridan or Oresme on whose work they built. Before the eleventh century, science scarcely existed in the Latin West, even in Roman times. From the eleventh century onward, the scientific sector of Occidental culture has increased in a steady crescendo.

Since both our technological and our scientific movements got their start, acquired their character, and achieved world dominance in the Middle Ages, it would seem that we cannot understand their nature or their present impact upon ecology without examining fundamental medieval assumptions and developments.

MEDIEVAL VIEW OF MAN AND NATURE

Until recently, agriculture has been the chief occupation even in "advanced" societies; hence, any change in methods of tillage has much importance. Early plows, drawn by two oxen, did not normally turn the sod but merely scratched it. Thus, cross-plowing was needed and field tended to be squarish. In the fairly light soils and semiarid climates of the Near East and Mediterranean, this worked well. But such a plow was inappropriate to the wet climate and often sticky soils of northern Europe. By the latter part of the seventh century after Christ, however, following obscure beginnings, certain northern peasants were using an entirely new kind of plow, equipped with a vertical knife to cut the line of the furrow, a horizontal share to slice under the sod, and a moldboard to turn it over. The friction of this plow with the soil was so great that it normally required not two but eight oxen. It attacked the land with such violence that cross-plowing was not needed, and fields tended to be shaped in long strips.

In the days of the scratch-plow, fields were distributed generally in units capable of supporting a single family. Subsistence farming was the presupposition. But no peasant owned eight oxen: to use the new and more efficient plow, peasants pooled their oxen to form large plow-teams, originally receiving (it would appear) plowed strips in proportion to their contribution. Thus, distribution of land was based no longer on the needs of a family but, rather, on the capacity of a power machine to till the earth. Man's relation to the soil was profoundly changed. Formerly man had been part of nature; now he was the exploiter of nature. Nowhere else in the world did farmers develop any analogous agricultural implement. Is it coincidence that modern technology, with its ruthlessness toward nature, has so largely been produced by descendants of these peasants of northern Europe?

This same exploitive attitude appears slightly before A.D. 830 in Western illustrated calendars. In older calendars the months were shown as passive personifications. The new Frankish calendars, which set the style for the Middle Ages, are very different: they show men coercing the world around them—plowing, harvesting, chopping trees, butchering pigs. Man and nature are two things, and man is master.

These novelties seem to be in harmony with larger intellectual patterns. What people do about their ecology depend on what they think about themselves in relation to things around them. Human ecology is deeply conditioned by beliefs about our nature and destiny—that is, by religion. To Western eyes this is very evident in, say, India or Ceylon. It is equally true of ourselves and of our medieval ancestors.

The victory of Christianity over paganism was the greatest psychic revolution in the history of our culture. It has become fashionable today to say that, for better or worse, we live in "the post-Christian age." Certainly the forms of our thinking and language have largely ceased to be Christian, but to my eye the substance often remains amazingly akin to that of the past. Our daily habits of action, for example, are dominated by an implicit faith in perpetual progress which was unknown either to Greco-Roman antiquity or to the Orient. It is rooted in, and is indefensible apart from, Judeo-Christian teleology. The fact that Communists share it merely helps to show what can be demonstrated on many other grounds: that Marxism, like Islam, is a Judeo-Christian heresy. We continue today to live, as we have lived for about seventeen hundred years, very largely in a context of Christian axioms.

What did Christianity tell people about their relations with the environment?

While many of the world's mythologies provide stories of creation, Greco-Roman mythology was singularly incoherent in this respect. Like Aristotle, the intellectuals of the ancient West denied that the visible world had had a beginning. Indeed, the idea of a beginning was impossible in the framework of their cyclical notion of time. In sharp contrast, Christianity inherited from Judaism not only a concept of time as nonrepetitive and linear but also a striking story of creation. By gradual stages a loving and all-powerful God had created light and darkness, the heavenly bodies, the earth and all its plants, animals, birds, and fishes. Finally, God had created Adam and, as an afterthought, Eve to keep man from being lonely. Man named all the animals, thus establishing his dominance over them. God planned all of this explicitly for man's benefit and rule: no item in the physical creation had any purpose save to serve man's purposes. And, although man's body is made of clay, he is not simply part of nature: he is made in God's image.

Especially in its Western form, Christianity is the most anthropocentric religion the world has seen. As early as the second century both Tertullian and Saint Irenaeus of Lyons were insisting that when God shaped Adam he was foreshadowing the image of the incarnate Christ, the Second Adam. Man shares in great measure, God's transcendence of nature. Christianity, in absolute contrast to ancient paganism and Asia's religious (except, perhaps, Zoroastrianism), not only established a dualism of man and nature but also insisted that it is God's will that man exploit nature for his proper ends.

At the level of the common people this worked out in an interesting way. In antiquity every tree, every spring, every stream, every hill had its own *genius loci,* its guardian spirit. These spirits were accessible to men, but were very unlike men; centaurs, fauns, and mermaids show their ambivalence. Before one cut a tree, mined a mountain, or dammed a brook, it was important to placate the spirit in charge of that particular situation, and to keep it placated. By destroying pagan animism, Christianity made it possible to exploit nature in a mood of indifference to the feelings of natural objects.

It is often said that for animism the Church substituted the cult of saints. True; but the cult of saints is functionally quite different from animism. The saint is not *in* natural objects; he may have special shrines, but his citizenship is in heaven. Moreover, a saint is entirely a man; he can be approached in human terms. In addition to saints, Christianity of course also had angels and demons inherited from Judaism and perhaps, at one remove, from Zoroastrianism. But these were all as mobile as the saints themselves. The spirits *in* natural objects, which formerly had protected nature from man, evaporated. Man's effective monopoly on spirit in this world was confirmed, and the old inhibitions to the exploitation of nature crumbled.

When one speaks in such sweeping terms, a note of caution is in order. Christianity is a complex faith, and its consequences differ in differing contexts. What I have said may well apply to the medieval West, where in fact technology made spectacular advances. But the Greek East, a highly civilized realm of equal Christian devotion, seems to have produced no marked technological innovation after the late seventh century, when Greek fire was invented. The key to the contrast may perhaps be found in a difference in the tonality of piety and thought which students of comparative theology find between the Greek and the Latin churches. The Greeks believed that sin was intellectual blindness, and that salvation was found in illumination, orthodoxy—that is, clear thinking. The Latins, on the other hand, felt that sin was moral evil, and that salvation was to be found in right conduct. Eastern theology has been intellectualist. Western theology has been voluntarist. The Greek saint contemplates; the Western saint acts. The implications of Christianity for the conquest of nature would emerge more easily in the Western atmosphere.

The Christian dogma of creation, which is found in the first clause of all the Creeds, had another meaning for our comprehension of today's ecologic crisis. By revelation, God had given man the Bible, the Book of Scripture. But since God had made nature, nature also must reveal the divine mentality. The religious study of nature for the better understanding of God was known as natural theology. In the early church, and always in the Greek East, nature was conceived primarily as a symbolic system through which God speaks to men: the ant is a sermon to sluggards; rising flames are the symbol of the soul's aspiration. This view of nature was essentially artistic rather than scientific. While Byzantium preserved and copied great numbers of ancient Greek scientific texts, science as we conceive it could scarcely flourish in such an ambience.

However, in the Latin West by the early thirteenth century natural theology was following a very different bent. It was ceasing to be the decoding of the physical symbols of God's communication with man and was becoming the effort to understand God's mind by discovering how his creation operates. The rainbow was no longer simply a symbol of hope first sent to Noah after the Deluge: Robert Grosseteste, Friar Roger Bacon, and Theodoric of Freiberg produced startlingly sophisticated work on the optics of the rainbow, but they did it as a venture in religious understanding. From the thirteenth century onward, up to and including Leibnitz and Newton, every major scientist, in effect, explained his motivations in religious terms. Indeed, if Galileo had not been so expert an amateur theologian he would have got into far less trouble: the professionals resented his intrusion. And Newton seems to have regarded himself more as a theologian than as a scientist. It was not until the late eighteenth century that the hypothesis of God became unnecessary to many scientists.

It is often hard for the historian to judge, when men explain why they are doing what they want to do, whether they are offering real reasons or merely culturally acceptable reasons. The consistency with which scientists during the long formative centuries of Western science said that the task and the reward of the scientist was "to think God's thoughts after him" leads one to believe that this was their real motivation. If so, then modern Western science was cast in a matrix of Christian theology. The dynamism of religious devotion, shaped by the Judeo-Christian dogma of creation, gave it impetus.

AN ALTERNATIVE CHRISTIAN VIEW

We would seem to be headed toward conclusions unpalatable to many Christians. Since both *science* and *technology* are blessed words in our contemporary vocabulary, some may be happy at the notions, first, that, viewed historically, modern science is an extrapolation of natural theology and, second, that modern technology is at least partly to be explained as an Occidental, voluntarist realization of the Christian dogma of man's transcendence of, and rightful mastery over, nature. But, as we now recognize, somewhat over a century ago science and technology—hitherto quite separate activities—joined to give mankind powers which, to judge by many of the ecologic effects, are out of control. If so, Christianity bears a huge burden of guilt.

I personally doubt that disastrous ecologic backlash can be avoided simply by applying to our problems more science and more technology. Our science and technology have grown out of Christian attitudes toward man's relation to nature which are almost universally held not only by Christians and neo-Christians but also by those who fondly regard themsleves as post-Christians. Despite Copernicus, all the cosmos rotates around our little globe. Despite Darwin, we are *not,* in our hearts, part of the natural process. We are superior to nature, contemptuous of it, willing to use it for our slightest whim. The newly elected governor of California, like myself a churchman but less troubled than I, spoke for the Christian tradition when he said (as is alleged), ''when you've seen one redwood tree, you've seen them all.'' To a Christian a tree can be no more than a physical fact. The whole concept of the sacred grove is alien to Christianity and to the ethos of the West. For nearly two millennia Christian missionaries have been chopping down sacred groves, which are idolatrous because they assume spirit in nature.

What we do about ecology depends on our ideas of the man-nature relationship. More science and more technology are not going to get us out of the present ecologic crisis until we find a new religion, or rethink our old one. The beatniks, who are the basic revolutionaries of our time, show a sound instinct in their affinity for Zen Buddhism, which conceives of the man-nature relationship as very nearly the mirror image of the Christian view. Zen, however, is as deeply conditioned by Asian history as Christianity is by the experience of the West, and I am dubious of its viability among us.

Possibly we should ponder the greatest radical in Christian history since Christ: Saint Francis of Assisi. The prime miracle of Saint Francis is the fact that he did not end at the stake, as many of his left-wing followers did. He was so clearly heretical that a general of the Franciscan Order, Saint Bonaventura, a great and perceptive Christian, tried to suppress the early accounts of Franciscanism. The key to an understanding of Francis is his belief in the virtue of humility—not merely for the individual but for man as a species. Francis tried to depose man from his monarchy over creation and set up a democracy of all God's creatures. With him the ant is no longer simply a homily for the lazy, flames a sign of the thrust of the soul toward union with God; now they are Brother Ant and Sister Fire, praising the Creator in their own ways as Brother Man does in his.

Later commentators have said that Francis preached to the birds as a rebuke to men who would not listen. The records do not read so: he urged the little birds to praise God, and in spiritual ecstasy they flapped their wings and chirped rejoicing. Legends of saints, especially the Irish saints, had long told of their dealings with animals but always, I believe, to show their human dominance over creatures. With Francis it is different. The land around Gubbio in the Apennines was being ravaged by a fierce wolf. Saint Francis, says the legend, talked to the wolf and persuaded him of the error of his ways. The wolf repented, died in the odor of sanctity, and was buried in consecrated ground.

What Sir Steven Ruciman calls "the Franciscan doctrine of the animal soul" was quickly stamped out. Quite possibly it was in part inspired, consciously or unconsciously, by the belief in reincarnation held by the Cathar heretics who at that time teemed in Italy and southern France, and who presumably had got it originally from India. It is significant that at just the same moment, about 1200, traces of metempsychosis are found also in western Judaism, in the Provençal *Cabbala*. But Francis held neither to transmigration of souls nor to pantheism. His view of nature and of man rested on a unique sort of pan-psychism of all things animate and inanimate, designed for the glorification of their transcendent Creator, who, in the ultimate gesture of cosmic humility, assumed flesh, lay helpless in a manger, and hung dying on a scaffold.

I am not suggesting that many contemporary Americans who are concerned about our ecologic crisis will be either able or willing to counsel with wolves or exhort birds. However, the present increasing disruption of the global environment is the product of a dynamic technology and science which were originating in the Western medieval world against which Saint Francis was rebelling in so original a way. Their growth cannot be understood historically apart from distinctive attitudes toward nature which are deeply grounded in Christian dogma. The fact that most people do not think of these attitudes as Christian is irrelevant. No new set of basic values has been accepted in our society to displace those of Christianity. Hence we shall continue to have a worsening ecologic crisis until we reject the Christian axiom that nature has no reason for existence save to serve man.

The greatest spiritual revolutionary in Western history, Saint Francis, proposed what he thought was an alternative Christian view of nature and man's relation to it: he tried to substitute the idea of the equality of all creatures, including man, for the idea of man's limitless rule of creation. He failed. Both our present science and our present technology are so tinctured with orthodox Christian arrogance toward nature that no solution for our ecologic crisis can be expected from them alone. Since the roots of our trouble are so largely religious, the remedy must also be essentially religious, whether we call it that or not. We must rethink and refeel our nature and destiny. The profoundly religious, but heretical, sense of the primitive Franciscans for the spiritual autonomy of all parts of nature may point a direction. I propose Francis as a patron saint for ecologists.

The Women in the Cowshed: A Review of
An Inquiry into Well-Being and Destitution
by Partha Dasgupta

ALAN RYAN

1

Had I not met Professor Dasgupta, I might have wondered from reading his book whether "Dasgupta" was the name of a large committee or a small research institution. *An Inquiry into Well-Being and Destitution* is a work of encyclopedic learning and matching ambition. It is not just the title of this book that recalls the beginnings of the modern disciplines of economics in Adam Smith's *Inquiry into the Nature and Causes of the Wealth of Nations*. Smith was a moral philosopher, a historian, and a political theorist; *The Wealth of Nations* is among other things a tract on moral philosophy, social change, and the duties of government as well as what we now call economics. *An Inquiry into Well-Being and Destitution,* as well as being a contribution to development economics, is among other things a tract on moral philosophy and political theory, on the duties of government in developing countries, and on the connections between economic analysis and such disciplines as the science of nutrition. The bibliography runs to eighty densely packed pages, and anyone who had mastered even a small part of that literature would be a distinguished practitioner of modern economics and well informed about a great deal else.

Professor Dasgupta teaches at Cambridge but wants to be read by many people besides graduate students in economics. He therefore spreads his net wide. He is concerned with the economics of extreme poverty, and has a lot to say about undernourishment as both a cause and an effect of poverty, as well as about the problems of soil erosion, the consequences of poorly defined property rights, the place of women's education in tackling problems of overpopulation, and the fate of the unemployed worker in India.

Because he is an economist who understands that economics is often reviled for its narrow view of human motivation—reducing all our hopes, wishes, and fears to the pursuit of "rational self-interest"—Professor Dasgupta wants to incorporate a richer understanding of human experience within economic analysis. And since economists are often complained of for trying to apply "Western" techniques of analysis to societies whose economies are built on habit, tradition, and personal ties rather than the fluid and flexible impersonal transactions of the developed marketplace, he tries to show how the economist's analytical methods illuminate the predicament of landless laborers and villagers facing crop failure in the Indian subcontinent and sub-Saharan Africa. All this is done with an unusual combination of boldness and subtlety.

An Inquiry into Well-Being and Destitution raises many questions. One is why books like this are so rare, and so hard to bring off successfully. I should say at once that to the extent that Professor Dasgupta aims at a general audience, he is not wholly successful. His *Inquiry* is a difficult book; it is neither pretentious nor willfully obscure, but it is stiff going. Dasgupta packs the mathematical demonstration of his results into "starred" chapters, but he expects a lot from his readers elsewhere. He gives the impression that he dreams in algebra, and one would do well to read him within reach of a good library.

It is in many ways a sad state of affairs that economics has become so technically forbidding that economists and the lay public have lost touch with each other. Keynes, to look no further back, was no mean logician—his first work was a treatise on probability—but he remained a skeptic about the role of mathematics in economic analysis. It is not irrelevant that he was also a powerful polemicist in public affairs. Dasgupta himself thinks that the contemporary divorce between economics and ethics is particularly unfortunate. Economics began as one of the "moral sciences"—the eighteenth-century term for the human sciences. In nineteenth-century Cambridge the "moral sciences" sheltered philosophy, psychology, politics, and economics. John Stuart Mill discussed the problems of the social sciences under the rubric of "the logic of the moral sciences," and when he wrote his own *Principles of Political Economy,* he added "with some of their applications to social philosopy" to the title.

In Cambridge, Alfred Marshall separated economics from other social studies at the turn of the century, but the economics faculty still shelters political scientists and sociologists. Oxford has never thought it right to allow undergraduates to study economics divorced from philosophy and politics (save in conjunction with engineering and management); the London School of Economics is properly the "London School of Economics and Political Science." In the United States, the emancipation of economics from philosophy, history, and sociology took many years. The domination of the "Chicago School" of Hayek and Milton Friedman during the past thirty years is a wry commentary on the economists of the turn-of-the-century Midwest. They practiced Christian economics, institutional and historical economics, and whatever the most apt label might be for the mordantly skeptical social commentary of Thorstein Veblen.

That economics ought to have some direct bearing on ethical issues seems obviously right and obviously wrong. It is obviously right because ethics is concerned with the human search for what does us good; we are constantly trading one good thing for another, trying to get the best possible outcome for ourselves, our families, those to whom we owe duties of various kinds. Economists claim to study rational action. It would be alarming to think that morality had no rational basis.

Yet moral argument is concerned to get people to change their ideas about what is good and bad; economics has no such concern. If Americans become still more frightened of violent crime and buy even more guns, the American Gross National Product will rise; the moralist may complain that the rise in GNP corresponds to no increase in human happiness, but the economist could say that his professional business is only to show how—paradoxically enough—crime can "pay," not just for crooks, but generally.

This division of labor between economics and ethical commentary is not enough for Partha Dasgupta. One of his purposes—he devotes the first hundred and forty pages of the *Inquiry* to it—is to clear economics of the charge that it fosters a passive and "consumerist" moral vision. The charge is made not because economists roundly defend consumerism but because they assume that what matters about human beings is their capacity both to experience pleasure and to make choices that will increase pleasure. The idea that human beings are rational "utility-maximizers" suggests a certain passivity in the economist's idea of the good life, as though a successful life were nothing more than a stream of agreeable sensations. Nobody believes this as a matter of moral conviction; it comes with the disciplines, in the way unexamined assumptions usually do. A *reductio ad absurdum* of such theories of the good life was offered by Robert Nozick in one of the more striking images of his *Anarchy, State and Utopia*. If what matters is agreeable sensation, he asked, what would be wrong with a world in which we turned out not to be human beings after all, but brains in vats of an appropriate fluid, wired to have nice sensations? What went on in these brains would include deluded beliefs about the world, but so what?

The hideousness of the image provides the answer. Plainly what we mind about includes truth, engagement with the world, and freedom. Like Amartya Sen, who has also attacked economics' obsession with a passive conception of "welfare," Dasgupta makes much of the idea that "agency"—or freedom—is an indisputable component of the good life. Dasgupta argues not only for the importance of civil liberties, and the "negative" freedoms of liberal, constitutional states, but also for the importance of "positive" liberty—capacities and abilities, the resources people need to make something of their own lives.

Among the payoffs of broadening the range of economic analysis to include these things some are obvious enough. The passive and acquiescent peasants and landless laborers in underdeveloped countries may appear more or less content with their lot. But they are poor in resources; they lack information, energy, access to employment, credit, materials, and markets. More interestingly, perhaps concentrating on positive liberty underlines for the analyst the importance of the distribution of power within poor households and shifts our gazes from the male head of the family to the capacities and resources of women and children. As we have recently begun to learn, it is there that we have to look for answers to problems of overpopulation and environmental degradation. Simple measures of income per head give us a rough indication of the well-being of families in richer societies, but they tell the development economist very much less than she or he needs to know.

If one of Professor Dasgupta's purposes is to reconnect economics with moral common sense, another is to show that some of the sacrifices that have often been thought necessary for the sake of economic development are not necessary, and that societies that have made them have not profited from them. The most glaring is the sacrifice of civil liberties and the rule of law for the sake of economic growth. A comparison often made is between India and China; in India, democracy has continued to work during the fifty years since independence; famine has been avoided, but economic growth has been slow, and the threat of overpopulation and environmental disaster increasingly hangs over the country. In China, there have been several man-made catastrophes during the past half-century costing millions of lives, but economic growth has recently been rapid and population growth is not wholly out of control.

Drawing on some not very elaborate statistical data, Dasgupta shows that even if constitutional government and the rule of law are not indispensable to economic development—the nineteenth-century liberals' optimistic view—it is clear that they do not retard it. The Indian balance sheet does not look at all bad alongside China's, even if we allow only a small weight to the importance of civil liberties. The real disasters in the developing world have been in sub-Saharan Africa, where civil liberties have been almost nonexistent and where many countries have experienced substantial negative growth in income per head. Reading John Rawls's *Theory of Justice,* many students have drawn from his discussion of civil liberties and material well-being the impression that political repression is likely to help economic growth. But it isn't so. Something that Amartya Sen seems to have been the first to notice must give us particular pause. In no country with a modicum of political liberty and a free press has there been a famine such as those that killed millions in Bengal in 1943, and more recently in Ethiopia and Somalia.

Moreover, any assessment of how well people are living must include the freedoms they enjoy and the things their income is spent on. Among "middle-income" societies, Dasgupta points out, the citizens of Costa Rica have rather less income per person than those of Iraq, and only two thirds the income of those of Iran. Happily for them, they spend none of it on an army, while Iraq and Iran have wasted vast amounts of money fighting each other, a folly that Iraq compounded by provoking a war with the United States. Unsurprisingly, life expectancy in Costa Rica is eleven years greater than in Iraq and Iran and infant mortality less than one third as great.

2

The economics of very poor societies is extremely difficult to understand for a great many reasons. The vast cultural divide between most of the observers and most of the observed raises the obvious questions whether the behavior of poor villagers in the third world is governed by norms and values that outsiders may find hard to comprehend. If that is the case, how can they alter it in any reasonable fashion? Dasgupta acknowledges the importance of such considerations. As he observes, the norms that govern local behavior "can be exploitative, or just plain silly." For instance,

In rural communities in the foothills of the Himalayas in the state of Uttar Pradesh in India, women give birth to their children in cowsheds and remain there for one to two weeks. They aren't permitted to return to their homes any earlier because they are regarded as impure. The (Indian) Centre for Science and Environment . . . reports that village folk in those parts believe cowdung and urine to be good disinfectants. They also believe that the mother and child are protected by the cows from evil spirits. Infant and maternal mortality rates are significantly higher on account of this practice, cowsheds being notoriously unhygienic.

One benefit of educating women is that they cease to believe in such practices.

Sometimes what is at issue is the decay of ethical and social standards that once served a useful purpose. One of the sadder instances is the erosion of the self-restraint that once averted "the tragedy of the commons." It is an axiom in economics that a resource that is owned in common, or available for use without a rent reflecting that use, will be overexploited. The North Atlantic fisheries are a good example. What any one boat does makes no decisive difference to the stocks of fish, so each fisherman feels he has every reason to catch all he can. Restraint only lowers his own catch without preserving total stocks to an appreciable extent. On that basis, you'd expect common land always to be overgrazed; if other people put all the cows they can on the land, I'd better do so too. The interesting fact, however, is not that there is extensive overgrazing in the third world, but that until recently there was little. Partly, this reflected less pressure from population growth than is now the case. But it also reflected the ability of village communities to enforce norms of self-restraint that protected the continued use of common property.

To be concerned with the place of norms and values in economic life raises wider questions than most economists wish to deal with; but these concerns are relevant to the conditions not only of the very poor but of many others as well.

Once Dasgupta concentrates on the lives of the very poorest people, the consequences for economic analysis are intriguing. In advanced societies, there is a clear line between consumption and savings; savings are the result of consumption forgone today for the sake of greater consumption tomorrow. In really poor households, however, consumption is itself a form of investment; when poor people eat better, they are better and produce more. Their health and strength improve.

This is not a small point; the conventional wisdom for forty years after World War II was that rapid industrialization was the way forward and high rates of savings were needed to support it. It was a view that had the imprimatur of the Nobel Prize-winner W. A. Lewis. But it was wrong. Diverting resources away from the consumption of poor people has been a bad bargain; their productivity has been so low that sub-Saharan Africa has invested something like 18 percent of GNP for a growth rate of 1.4 percent. The moral, as Dasgupta puts it, is that "increases in the consumption of basic needs are a form of investment with high returns in poor countries."

This conclusion raises the question of the role of government in the economic development of the poorest societies. In recent years skeptics have argued both that the overseas aid given by the developed world has been wasted and that the governments of underdeveloped countries have at best pursued foolish policies and at worst predatory ones. Others have pointed to the success of Japan, Taiwan, Korea, and Singapore as evidence that governments can foster industry, reform agriculture, and create an energetic, ambitious, disciplined work force into the bargain. Professor Dasgupta takes a careful but not an equivocal middle position. He is no enthusiast for wholesale intervention. Governments that try to support particular industries in a way the market will not—trying to "spot winners"—will run unjustified risks. Moreover, they are too likely to throw good money after bad and prop up ailing enterprises long after they should have been allowed to expire.

There are also problems of "moral hazard," which are familiar in developed countries' welfare systems but are particularly acute in countries that cannot afford to waste resources. "Moral hazard" arises wherever a policy gives people an incentive to behave in a way that does economic or social damage. Thus broadly applied food subsidies that lower food prices reduce the incentive to work, while the food may also end up disproportionately in the hands of the better-off. There is evidence that this has happened in Egypt. If food is handed out cheaply, entrepreneurs will be tempted to buy it and resell it. If free public health care is as good in quality as private fee-paid health care, the rich benefit needlessly, and too much is spent on health care for the good it does. People who do not need the benefits being offered will be able to exploit the system. In poor countries, moreover, the state is often seen as an alien force so that exploiting whatever loopholes it leaves is seen as legitimate resistance.

The response cannot be to throw up our hands. The Indian government, as Dasgupta writes, has at various times dealt with the problem of food subsidies by subsidizing only coarse grains; the rich won't eat them, so the poor get all the benefit. If health care is supplied in overcrowded clinics in the slums or in poor villages, the long wait for treatment is enough of a deterrent to those who can afford private medicine. If we worry that the availability of free food will encourage the rural poor to withdraw from the labor market, we can, Dasgupta writes, provide free food only during the periods when there is almost no employment to be had. One of Dasgupta's most original thoughts is that poor countries need "liberalization" but not so much in the sense that they need to be free from government controls. Instead their people need to acquire a sharper sense of the distinction between private interest and public interest.

Like other recent writers on development, Dasgupta looks to a change in the balance of power inside the poor household to do some good. Prosperity and a fairer deal for women reinforce each other. Much has recently been made of the correlation between increased education for woman and the control of fertility. The one thing that appears to be guaranteed to reduce the birthrate in most poor societies is educating women. Dasgupta mentions a qualification to this. Either independently or in conjunction with more education, a woman's ability to work outside the household has a powerful effect on fertility. Here we can see a virtuous circle in operation. Where a woman can work, the household does not need so many children to keep its members alive; conversely, the cost (in income forgone) of pregnancy, childbirth, and child rearing is increased.

In the absence of female employment we can, as Dasgupta often and gloomily emphasizes, see at work a vicious circle. There is, he points out, an interaction between poverty, overpopulation, and environmental decay that appears to have no self-correcting features. Really poor families certainly think of children as a provision against old age and as a form of investment, which is one reason why boys are so valued; but children may be even more important as an immediate source of labor: in rural households in the Himalaya foothills, "children in the age range 10–15 years work one-and-a-half times the number of hours adult males do, their tasks consisting of collecting fuelwood, dung, and fodder, grazing domestic animals, performing household chores, and marketing." Such families are caught in a bind: their productivity is very low so they need all the hands they can muster. If all families have many children, the environment is destroyed, so more children are needed to gather fuel and fodder, to graze animals, and so on. Since fertility only diminishes when human beings are very close to starving to death, the prospect of this downward spiral curing itself is not good.

Dasgupta is a calm critic, but he is something less than friendly to writers like J. L. Simon who have argued that a rising population is good for economic growth even in poor countries. Most poor women want access to birth control; but even if they have that access, they may be overwhelmed by the family's need for labor. Finding ways of educating girls, and employing women, works in favor of controlling fertility since it can relieve the pressure to have more children by altering the economic demands of the family.

Dasgupta has much to say about another matter in which government policy can make a difference—agrarian reform. "Land reform," he shows, has often been a disaster, because just expropriating the holdings of large landowners has rarely increased agricultural output. What is needed is family farms; in poor countries they are more productive than larger farms, and they provide the most direct ways to produce the food that poor villagers need. Equality as such is not a goal; we have seen how easy it is to turn privately owned estates into collective farms and end up with equality of starvation.

Families need to own their farms, or to have the sort of control over them that is equivalent to ownership. Only then can they get credit, and only then will they have an incentive to treat their resources intelligently. It takes governments to establish a legal system that will protect their rights, and it takes intelligent politics to put in place a scheme of reform that provides adequate compensation for those who lose land when family farms are created. All of which brings us back once more to the centrality of civil liberties and open government. Unless there is a free press and mechanisms of political responsibility, policies cannot be evaluated and improved, and private squalor is merely reinforced with public squalor.

There is much in Professor Dasgupta's *Inquiry* that I have not mentioned. His passing remarks on how many recalcitrant facts a theory can decently leave unexplained would provoke a class in the philosophy of science. His discussion of recent ideas about the duties one generation owes to the next would provoke another. I suspect that there are more economists who can appreciate Dasgupta's moral philosophy than philosophers who can appreciate his economics, but both will surely benefit from reading his arguments. In spite of the grimness of much of his subject matter, the book yields the pleasure that only a very clever thinker can give his readers. I wish that Dasgupta would now bend his talents to the politically much needed task of giving the nonspecialist reader an idea of why the path of economic development has been so painfully slow for so much of the world, and why there is reason to think we can do better.

17

An Overview

Rival Interpretations of Market Society: Civilizing, Destructive, or Feeble?

ALBERT O. HIRSCHMAN

Once upon a time, not all that long ago, the social, political, and economic order under which men and women were living was taken for granted. Among the people of those idyllic times many of course were poor, sick, or oppressed, and consequently unhappy; no doubt, others managed to feel unhappy for seemingly less cogent reasons; but most tended to attribute their unhappiness either to concrete and fortuitous happenings—ill luck, ill health, the machinations of enemies, an unjust master, lord, or ruler—or to remote, general, and unchangeable causes, such as human nature or the will of God. The idea that the social order—intermediate between the fortuitous and the unchangeable—may be an important cause of human unhappiness became widespread only in the modern age, particularly in the eighteenth century. Hence Saint-Just's famous phrase: "The idea of happiness is new in Europe"—it was then novel to think that happiness could be *engineered* by changing the social order, a task he and his Jacobin companions had so confidently undertaken.

Let us note in passing that the idea of a perfectible social order arose at about the same time as that of the unintended effects of human actions and decisions. The latter idea was in principle tailor-made to neutralize the former: it permitted one to argue that the best intentioned institutional changes might lead, via those unforeseen consequences or "perverse effects," to all kinds of disastrous results. But the two ideas were not immediately matched up for this purpose. In the first place, the idea of the perfectibility of the social order arose primarily in the course of the French Enlightenment while that of the unintended consequences was a principal contribution of the contemporary Scottish moralists. Also, the form

"Rival Interpretations of Market Society: Civilizing, Destructive, or Feeble?" by Albert O. Hirschman. *Journal of Economic Literature*, December 1982; republished as Chapter 5 in Hirshman, *Rival Views of Market Society and Other Recent Essays*, Viking, 1986, and Harvard University Press (paper), 1992. Reprinted by permission.

which the latter idea took initially was to stress the happy and socially desirable outcome of self-serving individual behavior that was traditionally thought to be reprehensible, rather than to uncover the unfortunate consequences of well-intentioned social reforms. In any event, the idea of a perfectible society was not to be nipped in the bud; to the contrary, it experienced a most vigorous development and, soon after the French Revolution, reappeared in the guise of powerful critiques of the social and economic order—capitalism—emerging at the beginning of the nineteenth century.

In the present essay I shall be concerned with several such critiques and their interrelations. First I shall show the close relationship and direct contradiction between an early argument *in favor of* market society and a subsequent principal *critique* of capitalism. Next, I shall point to the contradictions between this critique and another diagnosis of the ills from which much of modern capitalist society is said to suffer. And finally the tables will be turned on this second critique by yet another set of ideas. In all three cases, there was an almost total lack of communication between the conflicting theses. Intimately related intellectual formations unfolded at great length, without ever taking cognizance of each other. Such ignoring of close kin is no doubt the price paid by ideology for the self-confidence it likes to parade.

I. THE DOUX-COMMERCE THESIS

To begin, let me briefly evoke the complex of ideas and expectations which accompanied the expansion of commerce and the development of the market from the sixteenth to the eighteenth centuries. Here I must return to a principal theme of *The Passions and the Interests* (Hirschman, 1977), with the hope of placating at least partially those of my readers who complained that, with the book tracing ideological developments in some detail only up to Adam Smith, they were left guessing what happened next, in the age—our own—that *really* mattered to them. My book dwelt on the favorable side effects that the emerging economic system was imaginatively but confidently expected to have, with respect to both the character of citizens and the characteristics of statecraft. I stressed particularly the latter—the expectation, entertained by Montesquieu and Sir James Steuart, that the expansion of the market would restrain the arbitrary actions and excessive power plays of the sovereign, both in domestic and in international politics. Here I shall emphasize instead the expected effects of commerce on the *citizen* and *civil society*. At mid-eighteenth century it became the conventional wisdom—Rousseau of course rebelled against it—that commerce was a civilizing agent of considerable power and range. Let me again cite Montesquieu's key sentence, which he placed at the very beginning of his discussion of economic matters in the *Spirit of the Laws:*

> it is almost a general rule that wherever manners are gentle (*moeurs douces*) there is commerce; and wherever there is commerce, manners are gentle. (1749, 1961, vol. 2, p. 8)

Here the relationship between "gentle manners" and commerce is presented as mutually reinforcing, but a few sentences later Montesquieu leaves no doubt about the predominant direction of the causal link:

> Commerce . . . polishes and softens [*adoucit*] barbaric ways as we can see every day. (p. 81)

This way of viewing the influence of expanding commerce on society was widely accepted throughout most of the eighteenth century. It is stressed in two outstanding histories of progress—then a popular genre—William Robertson's *View of the Progress of Society in Europe* (1769) and Condorcet's *Esquisse d'un tableau historique du progrès de l'esprit humain* (1793–1794). Robertson repeats Montesquieu almost word by word:

> Commerce . . . softens and polishes the manners of men. (p. 67)

and Condorcet, while elsewhere critical of Montesquieu's political ideas, also followed his lead in this area quite closely:

> Manners [*moeurs*] have become more gentle [*se sont adoucies*] . . . through the influence of the spirit of commerce and industry, those enemies of the violence and turmoil which cause wealth to flee. . . . (Condorcet, 1795, p. 238)

One of the strongest statements comes from Thomas Paine, in *The Rights of Man* (1792):

> [Commerce] is a pacific system, operating to cordialise mankind, by rendering Nations, as well as individuals, useful to each other. . . . The invention of commerce . . . is the greatest approach towards universal civilization that has yet been made by any means not immediately flowing from moral principles. (p. 215)

What was the concrete meaning of all this *douceur,* polish, gentleness, and even cordiality? Through what precise mechanisms was expanding commerce going to have such happy effects? The eighteenth-century literature is not very communicative in this regard, perhaps because it all seemed so obvious to contemporaries. The most detailed account I have been able to find appears in a technical book on commerce first published in 1704 that must have been highly successful as it was reedited repeatedly through the next eighty years.

> Commerce attaches [men] one to another through mutual utility. Through commerce the moral and physical passions are superseded by interest. . . . Commerce has a special character which distinguishes it from all other professions. It affects the feelings of men so strongly that it makes him who was proud and haughty suddenly turn supple, bending and serviceable. Through commerce, man learns to deliberate, to be honest, to acquire manners, to be prudent and reserved in both talk and action. Sensing the necessity to be wise and honest in order to succeed, he flees vice, or at least his demeanor exhibits decency and seriousness so as not to arouse any adverse judgement on the part of present and future acquaintances; he would not dare make a spectacle of himself for fear of damaging his credit standing and thus society may well avoid a scandal which it might otherwise have to deplore. (Ricard, 1781, p. 463)

Commerce is here seen as a powerful moralizing agent which brings many nonmaterial improvements to society even though a bit of hypocrisy may have to be accepted into the bargain. Similar modifications of human behavior and perhaps even of human nature are later credited to the spread of commerce and industry by David Hume and Adam Smith: the virtues they specifically mention as being enhanced or brought into the world by commerce and manufacturing are industriousness and assiduity (the opposite of indolence), frugality, punctuality, and, most important perhaps for the functioning of market society, probity (Rosenberg, 1964, pp. 59–77).

There is here then the insistent thought that a society where the market assumes a central position for the satisfaction of human wants will produce not only considerable new wealth because of the division of labor and consequent technical progress, but would generate as a by-product, or external economy, a more "polished" human type—more honest, reliable, orderly, and disciplined, as well as more friendly and helpful, ever ready to find solutions to conflicts and a middle ground for opposed opinions. Such a type will in turn greatly facilitate the smooth functioning of the market. In sum, according to this line of reasoning, capitalism which in its early phases led a rather shaky existence, having to contend with a host of precapitalist mentalities left behind by the feudal and other "rude and barbarous" epochs, would create, in the course of time and through the very practice of trade and industry, a set of compatible psychological attitudes and moral dispositions, that are both desirable in themselves and conducive to the further expansion of the system. And at certain epochs, the speed and vigor displayed by that expansion lent considerable plausibility to the conjecture.

II. THE SELF-DESTRUCTION THESIS

Whatever became of this brave eighteenth-century vision? I shall reserve this topic for later and turn now to a body of thought which is far more familiar to us than the *doux-commerce* thesis—and happens to be its obverse. According to that view which first became prominent in the nineteenth century, capitalist society, far from fostering *douceur* and other fine attitudes, exhibits a pronounced proclivity toward undermining the moral foundations on which any society, including the capitalist variety, must rest. I shall call this the self-destruction thesis.

This thesis has a fairly numerous ancestry, among both Marxist and conservative thinkers. Moreover, a political economist who was neither has just recently given it renewed prominence and sophisticated treatment. So I shall first present his point of view and then go back to the earlier exponents. In his influential book, *Social Limits to Growth* (1976), Fred Hirsch dealt at length with what he called "The Depleting Moral Legacy" of capitalism.[1] He argues that the market *undermines* the moral values that are its own essential underpinnings, values that are now said to have been inherited from *preceding* socioeconomic regimes, such as the feudal order. The idea that capitalism depletes or "erodes" the moral foundation needed for its functioning is put forward in the following terms:

> The social morality that has served as an understructure for economic individualism has been a legacy of the precapitalist and preindustrial past. This legacy has dimin-

ished with time and with the corrosive contact of the active capitalist values—and
more generally with the greater anonymity and greater mobility of industrial society.
The system has thereby lost outside support that was previously taken for granted by
the individual. As individual behavior has been increasingly directed to individual
advantage, habits and instincts based on communal attitudes and objectives have lost
out. The weakening of traditional social values has made predominantly capitalist
economies more difficult to manage. (pp. 117–18)

Once again, one would like to know in more detail how the market acts on
values, this time in the direction of "depletion" or "erosion," rather than *douceur*. In developing his argument Hirsch makes the following principal points:

1. The emphasis on self-interest typical of capitalism makes it more difficult to
   secure the collective goods and cooperation increasingly needed for the proper
   functioning of the system in its later stages. (chapter 11)

2. With macromanagement, Keynesian or otherwise, assuming an important role in
   the functioning of the system, the macromanagers must be motivated by "the
   general interest" rather than by their self-interest, and the system, being based on
   self-interest, has no way of generating the proper motivation; to the extent such
   motivation does exist, it is a residue of previous value systems that are likely to
   "erode." (p. 128)

3. Social virtues such as "truth, trust, acceptance, restraint, obligation," needed
   for the functioning of an "individualistic, contractual economy" [p. 141] are
   grounded, to a considerable extent, in religious belief, but "the individualistic,
   rationalistic base of the market undermines religious support." (p. 143)

The last point stands in particularly stark contrast to the earlier conception of
commerce and of its beneficial side effects. In the first place, thinkers of the
seventeenth and eighteenth centuries took it for granted that they have to make do
with "man as he really is" and that meant to them with someone who has been
proven to be largely impervious to religious and moralistic precepts. With this
realistic-pessimistic appraisal of human nature, those thinkers proceeded to discover in "interest" a principle that could replace "love" and "charity" as the
basis for a well-ordered society. Secondly, and most important in the present
context, to the extent that society is in need of moral values such as "truth, trust,
etc." for its functioning, these values were confidently expected to be *generated,*
rather than eroded, by the market, its practices and incentives.

As already noted, Hirsch is only the latest representative of the idea that the
market and capitalism harbor self-destructive proclivities. Let us now trace it
back, if only to find out whether contact was ever made between the two opposite
views about the moral effects of commerce and capitalism that have been spelled
out.

The idea that capitalism as a socioeconomic order somehow carries within
itself "the seed of its own destruction" is of course a cornerstone of Marxian
thought. But for Marx, this familiar metaphor related to the social and economic
working of the system: some of its properties, such as the tendency to concentration of capital, the falling rate of profit, the periodic crises of overproduction,
would bring about, with the help of an ever-more numerous and more class-

conscious and combative proletariat, the socialist revolution. Thus Marx had little need to discover a more indirect and insidious mechanism that would operate as a sort of fifth column, by undermining the moral foundations of the capitalist system from within. Marx did, however, help in forging one key link in the chain of reasoning that would eventually lead to that conception: in the *Communist Manifesto* and other early writings, Marx and Engels make much of the way in which capitalism corrodes all traditional values and institutions such as love, family, and patriotism. Everything was passing into commerce, all social bonds were dissolved through money. This perception is by no means original with Marx. Over a century earlier it was the essence of the *conservative* reaction to the advance of market society, voiced during the 1730s in England by the opponents of Walpole and Whig rule, such as Bolingbroke and his circle (Hirschman, 1977, pp. 55–56). The theme was taken up again, from the early nineteenth century on, by the romantic and conservative critics of the Industrial Revolution. Coleridge, for example, wrote in 1817 that the "true seat and sources" of the "existing distress" are to be found in the "Overbalance of the Commercial Spirit" in relation to "natural counter-forces" such as the "ancient feelings of rank and ancestry."

This ability of capitalism to "overbalance" all traditional and "higher" values was not taken as a threat to capitalism itself, at least not right away. The opposite is the case: even though the world shaped by it was often thought to be spiritually and culturally much impoverished, capitalism was viewed as an all-conquering, irresistible force. Its rise was widely expected to lead to a thorough remaking of society: custom was to be replaced by contract, gemeinschaft by gesellschaft, the traditional by the modern. All spheres of social life, from the family to the state, from traditional hierarchy to longtime cooperative arrangements, were to be vitally affected: metaphors often used to describe this action of capitalism on ancient social forms ranged from the outright "dissolving" to "erosion," "corrosion," "contamination," "penetration," and "intrusion" by the "juggernaut market."

But once capitalism was thus perceived as an unbridled force, terrifyingly successful in its relentless forward drive, the thought arose naturally enough that, like all great conquerors, it just might break its neck. Being a blind force (recall the expression the "blind market forces") as well as a wild one, capitalism might corrode, not only traditional society and its moral values, but even those essential to its own success and survival. In this manner, to credit capitalism with extraordinary powers of expansion, penetration, and disintegration may in fact have been an adroit ideological maneuver for intimating that it was headed for disaster. The maneuver was especially effective in an age which had turned away from the idea of progress as a leading myth and was on the contrary much taken with various myths of self-destruction, from the Nibelungen to Oedipus.[2]

The simplest model for the self-destruction of capitalism might be called, in contrast to the self-reinforcing model of *doux-commerce,* the *dolce vita* scenario. The advance of capitalism requires, so this story begins, that capitalists save and lead a frugal life so that accumulation can proceed apace. However, at some ill-defined point, increases in wealth resulting from successful accumulation will tend to enervate the spirit of frugality. Demands will be made for *dolce vita*, that is for instant, rather than delayed, gratification and when that happens capitalist progress will grind to a halt.

The idea that successful attainment of wealth will undermine the process of wealth-generation is present throughout the eighteenth century from John Wesley (Weber, 1958, p. 175) to Montesquieu (1961, vol. 1, p. 52) and Adam Smith (1937, p. 578). With Max Weber's essay on *The Protestant Ethic,* reasoning along such lines became fashionable once again: any evidence that the repressive ethic, alleged to be essential for the development of capitalism, may be faltering was then interpreted as a serious threat to the system's survival. Observers as diverse as Herbert Marcuse (1965) and Daniel Bell (1976, p. 21) have written in this vein, unaware, it would appear, that they were merely refurbishing a well-known, much older morality tale: how the republican virtues of sobriety, civic pride, and bravery—in ancient Rome—led to victory and conquest which brought opulence and luxury, which in turn undermined those earlier virtues and destroyed the republic and eventually the empire.

While appealing in its simple dialectic, that tale has long been discredited as an explanation of Rome's decline and fall. The attempt to account for or to predict the present or future demise of capitalism in almost identical terms richly deserves a similar fate, and that for a number of reasons. Let me just point out one: the key role in this alleged process of capitalism's rise and decline is attributed first to the generation and then to the decline of personal savings so that changes in much more strategic variables, such as corporate savings, technical innovation, and entrepreneurial skill, not to speak of cultural and institutional factors, are totally left out of account.

There are less mechanical, more sophisticated forms of the self-destruction thesis. The best known is probably the one put forward by Joseph Schumpeter in *Capitalism, Socialism, and Democracy* (1942), whose second part is entitled *Can Capitalism Survive?* Schumpeter's answer to that question was rather negative, not so much, he argued, because of insuperable economic problems encountered or generated by capitalism as because of the growing hostility capitalism meets with on the part of many strata, particularly among the intellectuals. It is in the course of arguing along these lines that Schumpeter writes:

> Capitalism creates a critical frame of mind which, after having destroyed the moral authority of so many other institutions, in the end turns against its own; the bourgeois finds to his amazement that the rationalist attitude does not stop at the credentials of kings and popes but goes on to attack private property and the whole scheme of bourgeois values. (p. 143)

In comparison to the *dolce vita* scenario, this is a much more general argument on self-destruction. But is it more persuasive? Capitalism is here cast in the role of the sorcerer-apprentice who does not know how to stop a mechanism once set in motion—so it demolishes itself along with its enemies. This sort of vision may have appealed to Schumpeter who, after all, came right out of the Viennese *fin-de-siècle* culture for which self-destruction had become something totally familiar, unquestioned, *selbstverständlich*. Those not stepped in that tradition might not find the argument so compelling and might timidly raise the objection that, in addition to the mechanism of self-destruction, elementary forces of reproduction and *self-preservation* also ought to be taken into account. Such forces have certainly appeared repeatedly in the history of capitalism, from the first enactments of factory legislation to the introduction of social security schemes and the experimentation with countercyclical macroeconomic policies.

Schumpeter's point is made more persuasive if it can be argued that the ideological currents unleashed by capitalism are corroding the moral foundations of capitalism *inadvertently*. In other words, if the capitalist order is somehow beholden to previous social and ideological formations to a much greater extent than is realized by the conquering bourgeoisie and their ideologues, then their demolition work will have the *incidental* result of weakening the foundation on which they themselves are sitting. This idea was developed at about the time Schumpeter wrote by a very different group of European intellectuals who had also come to the United States during the thirties: the Frankfurt School of critical theory which, while working in the Marxist tradition, paid considerable attention to ideology as a crucial factor in historical development. In fact, a purely idealistic account of the disasters through which Western civilization was passing at the time is given by Max Horkheimer, a leading member of the group, in wartime lectures subsequently published under the title *Eclipse of Reason* (1947).

According to Horkheimer (1947), the commanding position of self-interest in capitalist society and the resulting agnosticism with regard to ultimate values downgraded reason to a mere instrument that would decide about the *means* to be used for reaching arbitrarily given ends, but would have nothing to say about those ends. Previously, reason and revelation had been called upon to define the ends as well as the means of human action and reason was credited with being able to shape such guiding concepts as liberty or equality or justice. But with utilitarian philosophy and self-interest-oriented capitalist practice in the saddle, reason came to lose this power, and thus

> the progress of subjective reason destroyed the theoretical basis of mythological, religious, and rationalistic ideas [and yet] *civilized society has up until now been living on the residue of these ideas.* (p. 34)

And Horkheimer speaks movingly of "all these cherished ideas" and values, from freedom and humanity, to "enjoyment of a flower or of the atmosphere of a room . . . that, in addition to physical force and material interest, hold society together . . . but have been *undermined* by the formalization of reason" (1947, p. 36, my emphases).

Here, then, are some early versions of Hirsch's thesis on the "depleting moral legacy" of capitalism. It is no mystery why the idea was almost forgotten in the thirty-year interval between Schumpeter-Horkheimer and Hirsch: during that era the Western world passed through a remarkably long period of sustained growth and comparative political stability. Capitalist market society, suitably modified by Keynesianism, planning, and welfare state reforms, seemed to have escaped from its self-destructive proclivities and to generate, once again, if not *douceur*, at least considerable confidence in its ability to solve the problems which it would encounter along its way. But the sense of pervasive crisis which had characterized the thirties and forties reappeared in the seventies, in part as an aftereffect of the still poorly understood mass movements of the late sixties and in part as an immediate reaction to contemporary shocks and disarray.

Moreover, the analytical exploration of social interaction along the logic of self-interest had by then uncovered situations, such as the prisoner's dilemma, in which strict allegiance to self-interest was shown to bring far-from-optimal results *unless* some exogenous norms of cooperative behavior were adhered to by the actors. Now, since human behavior, allegedly guided by self-interest, had not yet had clearly disastrous effect, it was tempting to conclude: (a) that such norms, in effect, have been adhered to tacitly; (b) that they must somehow predate the market society in which self-interest alone rules; and (c) that the survival of such norms is now threatened. In the circumstances, the idea that capitalism lived on time (and morals) borrowed from earlier ages surfaced naturally enough once again.

NOTES

1. This is the general heading of chapters 8 to 11.
2. On the important place the theme of self-destruction held in Richard Wagner's political and economic thought, see L. J. Rather, 1979, and Erik Eugène, 1973.

REFERENCES

Bell, Daniel. (1976). *The Cultural Contradictions of Capitalism.* New York: Basic Books.

Eugène, Eric. (1973). *Les Idées Politiques de Richard Wagner.* Paris: Publications Universitaires.

Hirsch, Fred. (1976). *Social Limits to Growth.* Cambridge, Mass.: Harvard University Press.

Hirschman, Albert O. (1970). *Exit, Voice and Loyalty: Responses to Decline in Firms, Organizations, and States.* Cambridge, Mass.: Harvard University Press.

———. (1977). *The Passions and the Interests: Arguments for Capitalism Before Its Triumph.* Princeton, N.J.: Princeton University Press.

Horkheimer, Max. (1947). *Eclipse of Reason.* New York: Oxford University Press.

Marcuse, Herbert. (1965). "Industrialization and Capitalism." *New Left Review,* no. 30, pp. 3–17.

Montesquieu, Charles Louis. (1961/1748). *De l'Esprit des Lois,* vol. 1. Paris: Garnier, p. 52.

Rather, L. J. (1979). *The Dream of Self-Destruction: Wagner's Ring and the Modern World.* Baton Rouge: Louisiana State University Press.

Ricard, Samuel. (1781). *Traité Général du Commerce.* Amsterdam: Chez E. Van Harrevelt et Soeters.

Rosenberg, Nathan. (1964). "Neglected Dimensions in the Analysis of Economic Change." *Oxford Bulletin of Economic Statistics* 26, 1: 59–77.

Schumpeter, Joseph. (1942). *Capitalism, Socialism, and Democracy*. New York: Harper and Row.

Smith, Adam. (1937/1776). *An Inquiry into the Wealth of Nations*. New York: Modern Library, p. 578.

Weber, Max. (1958/1904–5). *The Protestant Ethic and the Spirit of Capitalism*. New York: Scribners.

18

Bringing It Back Home

Business Ethics: Knowing Ourselves

BARRY CASTRO

I

Self-knowledge has been thought to be both illusive and important by a great many people for a long time. Pre-Socratic Greeks and moderns, romantics and rationalists, radicals and conservatives, foundationalists and deconstructionists, differing about a great deal, have agreed on both the critical importance of ridding ourselves of self-delusion and the impossibility of doing that. They have understood that what any of us can truly know is limited, distorted by self-interest and social convention, and constrained by our awareness of the difficulties which would likely follow from an effort to convince others of the value of new understandings we might come to. Nevertheless, they believed that at least some of us, whatever our own defenses and the defenses of those with whom we could communicate, are obliged to acknowledge our ignorance, and to struggle, however incompletely, for greater understanding.

Just who those some of us are, and are not, has always been troubling. Plato, for example, heroically affirmed his commitment to the quest for self-knowledge because it served the God, but was also willing to have most people forgo such a struggle in the interest of social utility. "The many" were to be kept from examining their lives, made to believe they were of baser stuff than their leaders, perhaps because they could not be trusted to think well enough, but certainly also because they were needed for more mundane tasks. Descartes too seemed to consign most people to something less ambitious than the examined life. He notes, in a letter to a friend from his long retreat in Holland, "where everybody but myself is in business and so engrossed with his profits that I could live here all my life without being noticed by anyone," that all their toil "helps to adorn the place of my abode and supplies all my wants." He did not seek to help them to question either their occupations or their preoccupations. Adam Smith, in a

This article first appeared in *Business Ethics Quarterly,* The Journal of the Society for Business Ethics, April 1995, vol. 4, no. 3. Reprinted by permission.

famous passage from *The Wealth of Nations*, worried that the specialization of function he recommended was likely to create a "man who has no occasion to exert his understanding, or to exercise his invention in finding expedients for removing difficulties which never occur." Smith expected that such a man would naturally "become as stupid and ignorant as it is possible for a human creature to become." That was a cost he was concerned about but was nevertheless willing to accept on the specialized worker's behalf.

Gilbert (1991) has argued that management theorists, in focusing on the power of the CEO, have analogously consigned most corporate people to access to less than a full sense of the corporation, and that business ethicists generally have acquiesced in this arrangement. Gilbert suggests that business ethicists have not protested against most people simply being encouraged to get on with their work; that we have granted quiet exemptions from the effort to see that work in a larger perspective to those needed for less intellectually challenging tasks; that we have, in effect, passively reflected Nietzsche's contention that lying to ourselves about needing to lie comes very easily to human beings and is at the heart of "the terrifying and problematic character of existence." It certainly seems to me true that business ethicists have left unstated whatever discomfort we may have had with questions about where and how the lines between self-questioning and the absence of such questioning should be drawn—left unstated any inquiry into the senses in which business ethics itself reflects the Nietzschean necessity of lying— and contented ourselves with a loose concern with the narrowness of corporate life.

Veblen (1904)) called this narrowness "trained incapacity." Marcuse (1964) meant much the same thing by managerial "one-dimensionality." Kanter (1977) suggested that corporate blind spots are acquired through a mostly unconscious process of adaptation, which she calls homosocial reproduction. Braverman (1974) and Levitan and Johnson (1983), in a tradition that goes back to Marx and Engels, argued that what appears to be one-dimensionality (the displacement of substance with process) is centrally a means of co-opting blue-collar people. Ellul (1954), and following him, Scott and Hart (1973) thought of this narrowness as a technologically induced spiritual abdication. Arendt called it the banality of evil in 1964 and seems to have argued later (1979) that such banality would inevitably be widespread in a world where most people were focused on doing rather than thinking. Maccoby (1976) and Jackall (1988) saw the pretense of technical expertise and the affect of superficial optimism required to play the managerial game as substantial barriers to the contemplative life. Many commentators have suggested that the day-to-day demands of the work—the very long hours and continuing small crises—also have this effect.

Among these writers, overwhelmingly professors, only Veblen undertook a parallel critique of the university. The business ethics literature suggests that it has been easier for us too to focus on the constraints imposed by corporate life than it has been to look inward at our own institutions and disciplines. Descartes, as I have noted, believed that the role of merchants and artisans was to do rather than to think; Smith, that industrial work was incompatible with a developed consciousness; Plato, that most people needed to learn to not think too much—to be given to understand that they were men of brass. I wonder if many of us have not in a parallel way given up on passing the virtues of the contemplative life and dialogue to our students—if some of us, under the pressure to get things done, have given up on it for ourselves. Both Mulligan (1987) and Bowie (1991) have argued that the business school, like the corporation, is apt to see contemplation as philosophic and anything philosophic as suspect. I have suggested in Castro (1989) that there are a number of reasons, not all of them bad, that business faculty may have rejected contemplation for narrowly based empiricism.

Some of the preliminary findings from a study of the business literature in which I am now involved speak to the reluctance of business faculty to wax philosophic. I have been particularly interested in the business ethics literature, an area where breadth of perspective and contemplation generally has clear relevance. I first looked at a sample of sixty articles drawn from the 1985, 1988, and 1991 volumes of the *Journal of Business Ethics,* half by faculty affiliated with management departments and half by faculty in departments of philosophy. The eight reports of survey data were all written by management faculty. Eight of the ten articles which essentially described corporate behavior were also by authors affiliated with management departments. Articles which spoke to the underlying questions at issue or sought to analyze policy questions were over-whelmingly drawn from philosophy departments (twenty-three of twenty-seven) and several of the remaining four were by authors affiliated with management departments but trained in philosophy. Campbell (1969) identifies this sort of disciplinary single-mindedness as a training-based ethnocentrism. DeGeorge (1991) suggests that it may simply be indicative of the lack of philosophic competence on the part of business faculty. I expect that it is partially both—and something else too.

It seems to me that business faculty properly see themselves as attempting both to serve the business community and to study it—that business students properly see themselves as being in school to learn to fit in as well as to learn from a more detached perspective, that Nietzsche was right in suggesting that we cannot wish away the messiness of these sorts of often contradictory goals, but that he was also right in affirming the possibility of working to make ourselves conscious of them. Schumpeter (1949) argued that if we were to be good academics we could not avoid doing so. I believe that business ethicists can help their business faculty colleagues to be good in precisely this sense—that our task is to maintain that the struggle for heightened consciousness is both a necessary undertaking and one that will and ought to be resisted, that the Nietzschean dilemma is especially difficult in a practitioner oriented context like that of the business school but that it cannot be ignored. I am arguing that in order to play their part, faculty, especially those of us who teach business ethics, both have to be willing to understand the legitimate sources of resistance to knowing ourselves and to insist that they be explicitly balanced against the legitimate objections to too much self-scrutiny. The integrity of business ethics as an academic field seems to me to hinge on whether or not we can do that. There is a good deal of reason to believe that the injunction to attempt it is, as I have suggested, at the heart of ethical inquiry.

My intention here is to share my thoughts as to how we ought to proceed. I want to begin by stating my understanding of the reasons self-questioning may not be easy to recommend to corporate people—the reasons it may even be prohibitively dangerous to the organization. I will then go on to explore the various surrogates for moral power that may be developed in the absence of self-questioning, proceed to an analysis of the reasons it may also be absolutely necessary, and finally, say what I can about the implications of all this for academic inquiry into business ethics.

II

Let me start by acknowledging that corporate life requires a complex balancing of responsibilities. There are subordinates, collaborators, and superiors toward whom one has undertaken a variety of obligations. There are customers and suppliers, large and small, long-term and recent, actual and potential. There are staff people and various other co-workers ranging from new hires to corporate old timers, from casual acquaintances to those with whom one shares a long history. There is an ideal of long-term corporate well-being variously defined in terms of market share, profitability, technological sophistication, financial solidity, and standing in the larger community. There are also the immediate pressures of stockholder attention to short-term return on investment, the requirements of regulatory agencies, and perhaps the demands of collective bargaining. To the degree the corporation is able to function as a coherent whole, it is because it is able to maintain some orderly balance in the way its managers attend to the exercise of these various responsibilities.

We know that this balance cannot be the concern of each manager. We understand that most managers have reason to believe that they cannot, in important senses, ought not, inquire very deeply into whether or not they should do what they normally do. We understand that they, like us, know that they have to routinize most of what they do in order to function—that they have to refer many decisions they might like to make to specialists, that coordinated action requires a disciplined deference to authority—and yet we are also aware that they must hold themselves responsible for their own behavior if they are to have moral integrity and that they, for the most part, understand this to be true. Both personal honor and the moral legitimacy of organizational leadership require such integrity.

The pivotal problem may come not for top leadership regarding whom the importance of at least the appearance of moral probity seems essential—see Bennis and Nanus (1985), and DePree (1989)—but for entry level and middle managers. If ethical leadership at the top is important, it must also be important to ask whether or not lower-on-the-ladder organizational needs inhibit its practice and development. Whether it is important at the top or not, we need to encounter the difficult ethical questions raised for the occupants of positions in highly coordinated hierarchical enterprises where career success is a pivotal goal and where that success is often dependent on narrowly defined performance measures. These middle and lower management positions are necessary to corporate function. Most business students aspire to them. However, these positions constrain decision-making discretion and make powerful calls on obedience and loyalty. They often make open-ended dialogue impolitic, translate questioning into negativism, and make normative a work load that renders contemplation an indication of lack of discipline. This milieu, both in the corporation and in the business school where our students are socialized into it, is a good deal closer to home than the ethos of top management. It seems to me to clearly deserve more of our attention.

Rapid changes in top management, growing gaps between the earnings of top managers and those of middle managers, reorganizations, mergers and acquisitions, job shifts—all increasingly general, and all weakening whatever passes for corporate tradition—will exacerbate these difficulties by undermining whatever ability lower-level managers may have had earlier to rely on corporate norms as a substitute for wider self-questioning. Moreover, managers on the rise can rarely rely on the bonding made possible by a compelling sense of common purpose. The pressure to climb the next step of the ladder, the pervasive sense that any abstention from the fast track is an implicit declaration of an inability to keep up to speed, the self-conscious subordination of purposefulness to gamesmanship, all make things worse.

Part of our task, it seems to me, is to take note of all of this. Euphemistic language may provide some comfort to those who want to keep their jobs and avoid some anxiety. So may a veneer of ethical concern or an expression of sentimental loyalty. Corporate people may cultivate an ascetic self-discipline that provides them with self-affirmation too. Managerial propensities to keep trim, to jog the extra mile, to go in for high-tech fitness rituals, to maintain sobriety without seeming concerned about it, to be careful about self-disclosure, neither complaining nor explaining, initially to others, and probably eventually to themselves—all can be seen as responses to the frustrations inevitable in any large coordinated enterprise. One function of studying business ethics in a business school is to learn both that all of these may be natural adaptations to corporate work and that they may also be potentially dangerous obfuscations of important moral issues.

It is relevant that temptations to trust the decision-making process and involve one's self in the little organizational rituals that seem to affirm that one belongs—to accept the technical jargon of corporate communication as if it were an index of a compelling higher rationality, to take privileged access to the occasional splash of corporate life as an expression of the esteem in which one is personally held, to embrace the perhaps substantial material rewards that the work may yield, or at least the prospect of such rewards, as a personal bottom line—at least be named. The likelihood that they are all thin soup needs to be discussed too. I have written something about their unsatisfying lack of substance (Castro, 1984, 1985). So have Jackall (1988) and, in an interesting Kafkaesque vein, Walker (1985).

Middle-management self-affirmation, however it is structured, seems to me to be potentially fragile and, perhaps relatedly, unlikely to depend much on what ethicists mean by self-knowledge. The effort to know ourselves, however, as consultants going at least as far back as the Delphic oracle have noted, gives us dignity, power, and a good deal of our ability to tell right from wrong. Individuals or organizations which leave relatively little room for it have been regarded as both morally and intellectually suspect for a long time.

Such suspicions, amounting really to an indictment, have been almost routinely associated with studies of corporate life. I think about Veblen (1904, 1918), Mannheim (1936), Schumpeter (1942), Mills (1956), Whyte (1956), Argyris (1957), Moore (1962), Presthus (1962), Crozier (1964), Hacker (1964), Marcuse (1964), Maccoby (1976), Kanter (1977), Scott and Hart (1973), Jackall (1988), and Zaleznik (1989). Their observations are tied to an ancient body of complaints about the amorality of the marketplace—complaints which go back to the very beginnings of commerce. Whether or not managers are in sympathy with the indictment, they cannot but be generally aware that it has been made, and be impressed by the prestige and power of those from whom the charges come. We cannot shelter either our corporate colleagues or our students from an awareness of those charges. Our task, it seems to me, is to help them to understand the indictment, to understand its limits, and to come to terms with the difficult tensions living with that awareness requires. We have, I believe, been too anxious about what corporate managers were to do with such knowledge—and, perhaps more to the point, too concerned about what such knowledge implies for schools of business.

III

The Socratic tradition suggests that ethics be pursued through an insistence on confronting both personal and institutionally mediated defenses against recognizing what would otherwise be clearly visible. Ethics, defined in this way, is likely to open sensitive wounds which neither corporate managers nor business faculty are likely to be in a position to heal. That is intrusive stuff which can leave not just managers, but any of us with substantive action agendas, profoundly uncomfortable. Because of this, it seems to me especially important for academic people to legitimize their inquiries into what is in the end other people's business, by undertaking a parallel inquiry into their own.

I have in mind something close to what Gouldner (1970) meant by reflexive sociology: an inward-turning departure from the positivist detachment normative in both management and academia. Looking at our own organizations, our own work, and our own professioanl socializations, would help us to learn more about ourselves and, critically, about the ways in which we increase the difficulty of self-scrutiny by building defenses against it. It is also a way of seeing more subtle nuances in the thought and action of those others we are studying. We are liable to be capable of understanding the functionality of the ways in which we shield ourselves from inconvenient truths and that should raise our sensitivity to analogous function in others—perhaps even enhancing our judgment about how to tell them what we see. (I do not think we can legitimately decide not to share what we see at all but perhaps that too is something that needs to be worked through.) In the end, subjecting ourselves to rigorous self-inquiry is modeling ethics, and is likely to increase the probability that others will pay some attention to our conclusions.

Gouldner seems to me to have been importantly correct when he suggested that it is necessary to acknowledge that "much of our noble talk about the importance of 'truth for its own sake' is often a tacit way of saying that we want the truth about others, at whatever cost is may be to them" and that we can only acquire legitimacy as an ethical enterprise if we struggle "to see ourselves as we see others . . . recognizing the depth of kinship with those whom we study" (p. 490).

We in the schools of business, in taking Gouldner's admonition to heart, for example, might ask in what ways the business school reflects and perhaps even magnifies the ethical dilemmas of the corporation. We might ask whether our schools ordinarily encourage our students to take responsibility for their own educations, to reflect on them, to do much more than simply meet requirements, presented to them as if they came from on high. We might ask whether we help students to consider the opportunity costs of their own curricula; to blow the whistle on wastefulness in their own classrooms. We might ask whether they could or should attempt to do these things. We might ask why there is so little of the self-referential in business education; so little awareness of institutional evolution; so little inquiry into the sources of managerial legitimacy; why we offer almost nothing by way of social or political theory; almost nothing to support academic contemplation generally.

We might look at our research in parallel ways, taking up the suggestions to do so that Peters and Waterman (1982), Schmotter (1984), Ouchi (1985), and Weis (1990) have made, and inquire into whether we may be creating a management literature that includes too many articles that no one will read and too many surveys from which nothing of value can be learned. Bowie (1991) and Freeman and Gilbert (1992) note that our literature, more than other academic literature, may be burdened with a scientistic tone that discourages either academic dialogue or practical application. Might we not follow up by asking whether our own research helps to reveal the reality it purports to study or merely mirrors it; whether our curricula are too much textbook-mediated and training-directed; whether our case-study approach, like the literature and the textbooks, simulates the narrow focus of the manager, and whether it ought to? Is it not the responsibility of business ethicists to seriously inquire into such questions?

IV

This is in many respects a dangerous line of inquiry, even in the realtively tolerant atmosphere of the university, but if it cannot be pursued there, do we not need to face up to the much larger difficulties in the way of such an inquiry in the corporation, and thus to questions about the possibility of actually using business ethics anywhere—or at least anywhere below the level of the CEO and the board room. My sense is that we must either risk the effort of lower-level self-scrutiny in the university, or surrender whatever moral power our efforts may have in the corporation—that we must acknowledge that business ethics itself can be not only a means of confronting the partial, illusory, and merely convenient qualities of our perceptions, but also a means of merely pretending to do that, a subtle layer of self-protection with which we shield ourselves from what could be the too-close-to-home questions ethical inquiry can raise.

It seems to me that we must encounter the inherent murkiness as directly as we can—and, finally, that in so doing we must make it plain who the "we" who are to undertake such an inquiry are, and who is to be excused from the effort. Are undergraduate students, for example, to be invited into an inquiry into the organization and function of their business curricula? To what degree does smooth organizational function in a bureaucratized university environment require a negative answer to that question? To what degree does our mandate to provide our students with appropriate socialization for corporate work also impose that requirement? Does one need to at least acknowledge any such negative answers to teach business ethics or can the inquiry itself be built on what generously may be assumed to be a noble lie?

Such questions, terribly difficult to answer, nevertheless seem to me to lie at the heart of our work. They suggest that business ethics, like any other branch of ethics, must enjoin us to go on trying to know ourselves, in the face of the certain knowledge that, in so doing, we must also be deceiving ourselves—to affirm that we cannot, at least for more than a passing moment, see truth directly, but that we have to go on trying anyway.

It may be that we, like Plato, must acknowledge that we will, on occasion, need lies to be built into the underlying structure of the society. Like him, we may also have to acknowledge that we can require analogous intrapsychic lies of ourselves when we act as guardians of our own values. However, it seems to me that we must at least accept his admonition to allow that part of us that aspires to be godlike to attack those same lies more or less simultaneously. The need to delude ourselves and also to purge ourselves of delusion—to live the examined life and to permit ourselves to live by not examining life—can then together be seen as central to the human condition. The need for the one does not deny the need for the other. They coexist in uneasy tension and the study of business ethics, I want to maintain, can be seen as the study of that tension.

Business ethics, regarded in this light, must fundamentally confront Cartesian dualism. It must be built on an effort to see ourselves and the objects of our inquiry in context, and it must deny the premise that we can carry on our examination at a safe distance. To study business ethics may then involve being enjoined to come fact to face with our interest in and penchant for distraction—to include in our appreciation of ethics an understanding that the desire to escape from both reason and responsibility can be both real and functional, but also to note that this desire is one that can be exploited organizationally and politically, one that can be marketed, and one that can be used to allay anxieties that ought not be allayed. Hannah Arendt's (1964) famous discussion of banality comes to mind.

My purpose has been to suggest that a consideration of the defensive redefinition of reality by various economic actors, and of the institutional and ideological support structure that supports these defenses, may belong at the center of business ethics. I have not, however, meant to simply condemn self-delusion. It seems to me that we need to explore both the functional and the dysfunctinal qualities of the lies we tell ourselves, first in our own contexts, and only then in a related effort to make some sense of the dissonance between the functional lies corporate life seems to require, and the struggle for fuller consciousness which I take to be at the center of any serious inquiry. I do not know how we can pursue this line of thinking very far without encountering a need to become more truly members of our own universities, more seriously responsible to our students and our colleagues, and more conscious of the costs associated with the bureaucratic compartmentalization within our own precincts.

BIBLIOGRAPHY

Arendt, Hannah. (1964). *Eichmann in Jerusalem: A Report on the Banality of Evil*. Viking Press, New York.

———. (1979). "On Hannah Arendt," in Melvyn A. Hill (editor), *Hannah Arendt: The Recovery of the Public World*. St. Martin's Press, New York.

Argyris, Chris. (1957). *Organizations and Personality*. Harper and Brothers, New York.

Bennis, Warren, and B. Nanus. (1985). *Leaders*. Harper and Row, New York.

Bowie, Norman E. (1991). "Business Ethics as a Discipline: The Search for Legitimacy," in R. Edward Freeman (editor), *Business Ethics: The State of the Art*. Oxford University Press, New York.

Braverman, Harry. (1974). *Labor and Monopoly Capital*. Monthly Review Press, New York.

Campbell, Donald T. (1969). "Ethnocentrism of Disciplines and the Fish-Scale Model of Omniscience," in Sherif and Sherif (editors), *Interdisciplinary Relationships in the Social Sciences*. Aldine Publishing Company, Chicago.

Castro, Barry. (1984). "Back in the Workforce: Learning about Education at the Workplace." *Change* 16, 4: 35–41.

———. (1985). "Middle-Management Blues: Notes from Hill Street." *Soundings* 68, 4: 435–42.

———. (1989). "Business Ethics and Business Education: A Report from a Regional State University." *Journal of Business Ethics* 8: 479–86.

———. (1990). "Socrates in Dallas: Managing the Facilities." *Bridges* 2, 3–4: 143–53.

Crozier, M. (1964). *The Bureaucratic Phenomenon*. University of Chicago Press, Chicago.

DeGeorge, Richard T. (1991). "Will Success Spoil Business Ethics?" in R. Edward Freeman (editor), *Business Ethics: The State of the Art*. Oxford University Press, New York.

DePree, Max. (1989). *Leadership Is an Art*. Doubleday, New York.

Ellul, Jacques. (1954). *The Technological Society*. Alfred A. Knopf, New York.

Freeman, R. Edward, and Daniel R. Gilbert, Jr. (1992). "Business, Ethics and Society: A Critical Agenda." *Business and Society* 31, 1: 9–17.

Gilbert, Daniel R., Jr. (1991). "Respect for Persons, Management Theory, and Businss Ethics," in R. Edward Freeman (editor), *Business Ethics: The State of the Art*. Oxford University Press, New York.

Goodpaster, Kenneth E. (1991). "Ethical Imperatives and Corporate Leadership," in R. Edward Freeman (editor), *Business Ethics: The State of the Art*. Oxford University Press, New York.

Gouldner, Alvin W. (1970). *The Coming Crisis of Western Sociology*. Basic Books, New York.

Hacker, Andrew. (1964). "Politics and the Corporation," in *The Corporation Take-Over*. Anchor Books, Garden City, New York.

Hill, Melvin A. (1979). "On Hannah Arendt," in Melvin A. Hill (editor), *Hannah Arendt: The Recovery of the Public World*. St. Martin's Press, New York.

Jackall, Robert. (1988). *Moral Mazes: The World of Corporate Management*. Oxford, New York.

Kanter, Roseabeth Moss. (1977). *Men and Women of the Corporation*. Basic Books, New York.

Levitan, Sar A., and Clifford M. Johnson. (1983). "Labor and Management: The Illusion of Cooperation." *Harvard Business Review*, pp. 8–16.

Maccoby, Michael. (1976). *The Gamesman: The New Corporate Leaders*. Simon and Schuster, New York.

Mannheim, Karl. (1936). *Ideology and Utopia*. Harcourt Brace, New York.

Marcuse, Herbert. (1964). *One-Dimensional Man*. Beacon Press, Boston.

Mills, C. Wright. (1956). *White Collar*. Oxford University Press, New York.

Moore, Wilbert E. (1962). *The Conduct of the Corporation*. Random House, New York.

Mulligan, Thomas M. (1987). "The Two Cultures in Business Education." *Academy of Management Review* 12, 4: 593–97.

Ouchi, William G. (1985). "Reflections on Management Education: Past, Present, and Future." *Selections*, Autumn, pp. 11–18.

Peters, Thomas J., and Robert H. Waterman. (1982). *In Search of Excellence: Lessons from America's Best-Run Companies*. Harper and Row, New York.

Presthus, Robert. (1962). *The Organizational Society*. Alfred A. Knopf and Random House, New York.

Schmotter, James W. (1984). "An Interview with Professor James E. Howell." *Selections*, Spring, pp. 9–14.

Schumpeter, Joseph A. (1942). *Capitalism, Socialism and Democracy*. Harper and Row, New York.

———. (1949). "Science and Ideology." *American Economic Review* 39: 345–59.

Scott, William G., and David K. Hart. (1973). "Administrative Crisis: The Neglect of Metaphysical Speculation." *Public Administration Review*, pp. 415–22.

Veblen, Thorstein. (1904). *The Theory of Business Enterprise*. Mentor Books, New York, 1958.

———. (1918). *The Higher Learning in America. A Memorandum on the Conduct of Universities by Business Men*. Sagamore Press, New York, 1957.

Walker, George Lee. (1985). *Chronicles of Doodah*. Houghton-Mifflin, Boston.

Weis, William L. (1990). "What's Going on in Business Schools?" *Management Accounting* 71: 49–52.

Whyte, William H., Jr. (1956). *The Organization Man*. Simon and Schuster, New York.

Zaleznik, Abraham. (1989). *The Managerial Mystique: Restoring Leadership in Business*. Harper and Row, New York.

Index